Lincoln Christian College

W9-BVH-043

The Acquisition of Phonology

THE ACQUISITION OF PHONOLOGY

A CASE STUDY

NEILSON V. SMITH

Reader in Linguistics
University College London

CAMBRIDGE

at the University Press · 1973

Published by the Syndics of the Cambridge University Press
Bentley House, 200 Euston Road, London NW1 2DB
American Branch: 32 East 57th Street, New York, N.Y.10022

© Cambridge University Press 1973

Library of Congress Catalogue Card Number: 72–95409

ISBN: 0 521 20154 3

Printed in Great Britain
at the University Printing House, Cambridge
(Brooke Crutchley, University Printer)

Contents

[v]

Abbreviations and notational conventions

Elements within /.../ represent phonemic sequences of adult English: English Standard Pronunciation (ESP).

Elements within |...| represent phonemic sequences of A's system.

Elements within [...] represent phonetic sequences.

The alphabet of the International Phonetic Association (IPA) is used. Any deviations from standard usage are noted in the text, though the following are listed here:

(1) A subscript ̩, e.g. [s̩], indicates a lamino-alveolar articulation.
(2) A comma , after a consonant, e.g. [ɹ,], indicates palatalisation.
(3) A superscript ', e.g. [ə'weː], indicates primary stress.
(4) A dot above or beneath a consonant, e.g. [g̣] or [ḅ], indicates a voiceless, lenis articulation.

In the statement of phonological rules and conditions the usual notational conventions of generative phonology as given in Chomsky and Halle, 1968 (*SPE*), are used:

[...] enclose distinctive features or bundles of distinctive features.
{...} enclose a disjunction of rules or features.
(...) enclose an optional sequence.
/ means 'in the environment of', that environment being specified by the position of the following dash ——
→ means 'is realised as' in realisation rules and phonetic rules; it means 'implies' in morpheme structure conditions.
→ followed by Ø means 'is deleted'.
# indicates a word-boundary.
⟨...⟩⟨...⟩ paired angle brackets indicate that of the sequences within the brackets both or neither must be chosen.
Greek letters, α, β..., are variables ranging over + and −.
(...)* indicates a recursive sequence. (Elsewhere * = a non-attested form.)

opt   optional
oblig   obligatory

Rules and conditions are abbreviated as follows:

R   realisation rule
MS   Morpheme structure condition
Ph   phonetic rule

The numbering of rules and conditions is exemplified as follows:

R1	realisation rule number 1.
R1′	a modification of R1.
R1″	a modification of R1′ (and so on).
R1A	a new rule interpolated between R1 and R2.
R1(i) R1(ii)	two rules which are reflexes of a former single rule, R1, which has split.
R1/2	a conflation of two formerly separate rules, R1 and R2, which have fallen together as the result of modifications to either one of them.

TO MY MOTHER AND FATHER –
FREDA AND VOYNE SMITH

Preface

This book has grown out of a paper of the same title which was circulated to a number of friends and colleagues in the early part of 1970, and which has served as the basis for seminar papers at various universities and meetings over the last two years.

It is aimed at three classes of reader: (i) psycholinguists working on problems of language and language acquisition, and cognitive development in general; (ii) general linguists, especially those working in the field of generative phonology; and (iii) speech therapists and all those connected medically with the observation and treatment of infant speech. Accordingly I have made a point of giving an informal treatment of all the observed phenomena in terms of traditional phonetic and phonemic categories, as well as a formalised analysis in terms of distinctive feature theory; so that the non-linguist can skip most of the formalism, while the linguist can skim through the traditional description with the minimum loss of time. It is suggested that chapter 3 (and especially 3.2) be skipped at a first reading by the non-linguist, and returned to subsequently for exemplification of the points made in later chapters.

I am deeply indebted to all those who have given me the benefit of their remarks either on the original paper or on oral presentations of different aspects of my findings. In particular I should like to express my gratitude to John Trim who first encouraged me to expand the earlier study into a monograph, and who has continued to give help and advice throughout the period of writing. Of the many who have contributed to this work by offering comment or criticism, I would especially thank Ed Allan, Bernard Comrie, Frank Heny, Dick Hudson, Ruth Kempson, Jay Keyser, Shil Meeussen, Terry Moore, John Ritter, Robin Smith and John Wells. Needless to say, responsibility for the description and discussion presented is mine alone. I am also particularly indebted to Ruth Kempson for taking on the chore of typing a large part of the final version for me.

Finally I would express my thanks to my wife, Saras, for her help and patience during the writing of the book; and most of all to my son whose enthusiasm and cooperation as an informant have made it all not only possible but a pleasure.

N. V. SMITH

Introduction

It is obviously true that the speech of young children differs radically from the speech of adults, but that children end up speaking essentially identically to their parents. It is equally, though perhaps less obviously, true that this deviation from the adult norm is non-random in character, and that the child's performance differs in regular and predictable ways from that of his putative models.

Given these facts and a child learning English, I decided to attempt a characterisation of the child's language in rigorous linguistic terms in order to establish the nature of these regularities. What I expected to find was a constantly developing and interacting competence and performance[1] unique to the child, moving steadily from a more idiosyncratic and simple system to one which was more complex and more closely isomorphic with the system of the adult language: a progression reflecting the supposed universal hierarchy sketched most clearly and succinctly in Jakobson's 'Les lois phoniques du langage enfantin' (Jakobson, 1949). However, although the child's performance was immediately accessible for observation, it was by no means self-evident what the nature of his phonological competence was. Accordingly the data were analysed simultaneously in two ways: one assuming that the child's competence was essentially idiosyncratic and roughly equivalent to his performance; one assuming that the child's competence was essentially equivalent to the input he was exposed to – i.e. the adult language.

It soon became apparent that there was a wider range of phenomena in the child's process of language acquisition to be explained than is indicated in the opening paragraph above. In addition to the mere fact of regularity, any theory of language acquisition must be able to account for at least the following classes of data observed in the acquisitional process:

(1) *Exceptions or the non-random nature of irregularities in the acquisition process.* After starting out by saying that the most striking fact of language acquisition is its regularity, it may seem paradoxical to continue

---

[1] In the sense of Chomsky, 1965; see esp. p. 4.

[1]

by emphasising irregularities. However, an example of each should make matters clear. If the child's phonological acquisition is regular, this means that once the correlations between the adult system and the child's performance have been worked out, one can correctly predict the child's output for any arbitrary word of the adult language. For instance, observing that a child said:

> [wiːt] for *feet*
> [wiŋə] for *finger*
> ⌊wæː] for *fire*

and so on, one could correctly predict his form for *fork* – namely [wɔːk] – with a [w] regularly substituting for /f/ in initial position.

However, there was a small class of exceptions to this generalisation, of which the clearest was *feather* which, instead of the expected *[wɛdə], became [tɛdə]. At first sight inexplicable, this item was later seen to fall naturally into a class of 'restructured' elements where /s/ and /f/ were frequently interchanged by the child; although, as adult /s/ was regularly realised as [t] at this stage, the appearance of [t] for /f/ was apparently random but actually easily explicable. The details of this rather complex process are not relevant at this stage of the exposition, and are taken up in detail in chapter 4. What is relevant is the general importance of exceptional features in the acquisition process; since, despite being exceptional, these are usually not random and frequently provide evidence for the nature of unexceptional forms. Indeed, the importance of exceptions and the need specifically to characterise the form of their exceptionality is one major reason for the massive documentation of rules and forms apparent in this monograph. If an argument hinges on the interpretation of an abnormality, the facts of normality must be established unambiguously first.

(2) *The many–many correspondence of segments in the child's system to those in the adult system.* The regularity mentioned above must not be interpreted as implying a one–one correspondence between terms in the child's system and those in the adult system. Thus adult /l/ was realised by the child:

> sometimes as [l]: e.g.   *lorry* → [lɔliː]
> sometimes as [d̪]: e.g.   *light* → [d̪ait]
> and sometimes as [ġ]: e.g. *like* → [ġaik]

Likewise, adult /s/ was differentially treated as:

Ø e.g.   *sun* → [ʌn]
[ġ] e.g.   *sock* → [ġɔk]
[t] e.g.   *mice* → [mait]
or [ḅ] e.g.   *whistle* → [wiḅu]

Whereas in different environments all of adult /t, d, s, z, ʃ, ʒ, θ, ð, tʃ, dʒ, r, l, j/ might be neutralised as [ḍ], as in:

teeth → [ḍiːḍ] or [ḍiːt]
door → [ḍɔː]
scissors → [ḍidə]
zoo → [ḍuː]
shirt → [ḍəːt]
garage → [ġæəḍ]
there → [ḍɛː]
chair → [ḍɛː]
John → [ḍɔn]
rain → [ḍeⁱn]
lady → [ḍeːdiː]
yes → [ḍɛt]

In all these cases the child's substitutions were regular, in the sense of being purely phonologically conditioned, and merely demonstrate the complexity of the relationship between adult and child forms. They were not exceptional in the way the substitution in *feather* was.

(3) *The across-the-board nature of changes in the child's developing phonology.* Regularity is characteristic of the child's phonological behaviour not only at one specified point in time, but also longitudinally through time. That is, changes in the child's output occur virtually simultaneously to phonologically defined classes of items and not piecemeal to individual lexical items. Thus when initial [f] was produced correctly, it was substituted at essentially the same time for all the words beginning with /f/ in the adult language, and for none of those beginning with /w/, even though /f/ and /w/ were neutralised as [w] in the child's early output. Accordingly the examples cited in (1) above became: [fiːt], [fiŋgə], [fæːr] and [fɔːk] at stage 15, while *window, wash,* and so on remained with an initial [w].

One caveat remains to be made to the above statement: namely, that a change from say [w] to [f] was in the nature of things rarely absolutely abrupt, and there was frequently a brief period when words with an adult /f/ were realised alternatively with [w] and [f]. Such free variation never occurred in words with an adult /w/.

(4) *The appearance of non-English sounds or sequences in the child's phonology.* In many cases the child produced quite regularly sounds or sound sequences which do not occur in the adult language. For instance, voiceless sonorants [ɬ, m̥, n̥] as in:

> *slug* → [ɬʌg]
> *Smith* → [m̥is]
> *sneeze* → [n̥i:d]

or an initial velar nasal, [ŋ], as in:

> *neck* → [ŋɛk]
> *snake* → [ŋe:k]

(5) *Puzzles.* The most interesting instance of the many–many correspondence cited above is provided by the phenomenon of 'puzzles'. That is, the child appears unable to produce a particular sound or sequence in the correct place, but is perfectly capable of producing it as his interpretation of something else. For instance, by completely regular rules *puddle* was pronounced [pʌgəl] whilst *puzzle* was pronounced [pʌdəl]. That is, we have the array:

> /pʌzəl/ → [pʌdəl]
> /pʌdəl/ → [pʌgəl]

(6) *Recidivism.* That is, the loss of a contrast which has already been established. For instance, at the stage where /s/ and /l/ both became [d̪] for the child, *side* and *light* fell together as [d̪ait]. Then as [l] was correctly reproduced for the adult /l/, a contrast developed resulting in the differentiation of these items as: *side* → [d̪ait] and *light* → [lait]. However, the next relevant change in the child's system was the substitution of [l] for the adult /s/, so that the two items fell together again as [lait]. That is, we have a progression from a stage where there is homonymy:

> $\left.\begin{array}{l} side \\ light \end{array}\right\} \to$ [d̪ait]

to a stage where the items are differentiated:

> *side* → [d̪ait]
> *light* → [lait]

and then a further stage where there is homonymy again:

$$\left.\begin{array}{l} side \\ light \end{array}\right\} \rightarrow [lait]$$

(7) *The child's ability to understand his own speech.* That is, the child can understand imitations or tape-recordings of his own speech, provided these are representative of the stage of development that he is at. For instance, if he hears [sɔːt], he will correctly identify this as *shirt*, *if* this is how he still pronounces it. There are further qualifications to this ability which need not be elaborated until the relevant section.

These various phenomena, among others, are accounted for at an observationally adequate level[1] by the two rule-based analyses which were mentioned earlier and descriptions of which are given in chapter 1. Both analyses are treated synchronically: that is, taking the first stage studied as a static system (chapter 2) and also diachronically or longitudinally: that is, tracing all the changes in this system over a period of some two years (chapter 3). Having thus juxtaposed and compared these two analyses, it is then demonstrated in chapter 4 that, contrary to what might be expected either *a priori* or on a superficial inspection of the classes of phenomena listed above as being in need of explanation, only the analysis which presupposes an adult competence for the child and which treats the child's phonology as a mapping from the adult's system attains descriptive adequacy. This is seen to be true in that all these phenomena can be explained in terms of such an analysis whereas only a fraction of them can be explained under the assumption that the child operates an autonomous system. More importantly, each part of the analysis is motivated independently and a set of putatively universal constraints on both the form and function of mapping rules between adult and child language is proposed.[2] The section ends with a suggested psychological model able to account satisfactorily for the phenomena described. The last chapter (chapter 5) is devoted to a discussion of various substantive problems in phonological theory on which it is suggested that phenomena of acquisition may cast light.

For reasons already touched on above, and as most accounts of language acquisition raise questions in the minds of the readers which never

[1] Cf. Chomsky, 1964, esp. pp. 925–7, for a discussion of levels of adequacy.
[2] If these constraints are indeed universal then the analysis has, at least in part, attained a level of explanatory adequacy; see Chomsky, 1964, pp. 925–7.

occurred to the writer, I have included, as Appendix C, a comprehensive diachronic lexicon of the items on which the present study is based. It is hoped that this material may both be of use to other researchers and also, of course, provide a detailed enough corpus for the validity of my own claims to be checked by those interested.

I *Background*

1.1 The child and his milieu

Although observations of other children speaking English and other languages have been made intermittently, this book is specifically a case study of one child learning to speak English Standard Pronunciation (ESP),[1] or at least something isomorphic to ESP. The following background details may indicate that the assumption that it is ESP being learnt is, strictly speaking, unrealistic, but it is justified in as much as there appear to be no features of the child's language which are crucially affected by differences from the standard language.

The child, Amahl ['æma:l][2] (hereinafter A), was born on 4 June 1967 in Boston, Massachusetts, of an English father and an Indian mother, and stayed in the U.S.A. until his first birthday, when he came to the U.K. Thus, although he did not speak until much later, A was exposed to a considerable amount of American English at a stage when he was gaining an at least latent knowledge of the language.

The father's (my) English is ESP with some minor deviations from what is normally considered the 'Received Pronunciation'. Specifically these are:

(1) The use of tense /i:/ in unstressed final position in words such as *city*: /siti:/ instead of RP /siti/.

(2) The occasional (random) use of pre-consonantal and final /r/.

(3) The occasional (random) use of pre-vocalic 'dark' /l/ ([ɫ]).

(4) The glottalisation of /d/ pre-consonantally and finally.

(5) The use of a flapped [ɾ] for post-consonantal /r/.

For A's mother, a medical doctor, English is the fourth language, following Hindi, Bengali and Marathi. She speaks 'Standard Indian English' which, although phonetically widely different from ESP, is structurally not dissimilar. The most important divergences are:

(1) The regular use of pre-consonantal and final (but not intrusive) /r/.

---

[1] See Trim, 1961.
[2] Frequently mispronounced outside the family as [æ'ma:l] or [ə'ma:l]. When embedded in a Hindi sentence, normally: [əməl].

(2) The neutralisation of the /v – w/ distinction (in favour of a bilabial, usually frictionless, continuant).

(3) The neutralisation in fast speech of the /ɔ – ɔː/, /əu – uː/ and /ei – ɛ/ distinctions.

The major phonetic differences are the usual ones:

(1) The monophthongisation (to [eː]) of /ei – ɛ/.
(2) The greater tenseness of all vowels.
(3) The retroflexion of /t, d/.
(4) The fuller voicing of voiced obstruents.
(5) The occasional confusion of /s – ʃ/ when both sounds occur in the same word.

For five months, from the age of 19 months to two years, A lived with his paternal aunt (my sister). Her dialect is ESP, as is that of her husband and two children; the latter aged two years older and two months younger than A. The onset of A's speech was late (around 20 months) and occurred within this period. Accordingly, data for the very early stages of acquisition are inadequate for fully explicit rules representing them to be formulated, and concentrated study did not start until the end of the twenty-fifth month. However, this lacuna is not serious as the earliest stages are those most adequately covered by earlier researchers, and are also phonologically the least complex.

From 26 months A, together with his parents, spent six weeks in India where he was exposed to considerable Hindi and Marathi. However, he has been brought up monolingual and, although he had a slight receptive knowledge of Hindi for some months, speaks none.[1] He has never had any knowledge of Bengali or Marathi.

From 30 months he has been attending day nurseries, play groups and nursery schools in Luton and Harpenden (Bedfordshire and Hertfordshire respectively), whence he has acquired some distinctly non-ESP diphthongs.

In general A is lively and intelligent[2] with a large vocabulary. He has no irregularities of the speech organs or hearing.

---

[1] His reaction to being enjoined to speak Hindi, or even being addressed in it, was usually anger. On the few occasions when he did say anything in Hindi, it was with an English accent. For instance, his response to [əməl lərka hai] ('Amahl is a boy') was [æməl nɔt ə lɔːkə, æməl ə boi] ('Amahl is not a "lurker", Amahl's a boy').

[2] In an IQ test (Stanford–Binet) administered at 4 years 4 months, he scored at the 6 year 6 month level. On Raven's Progressive Matrices he scored at the 6-year level.

1.2 The linguistic theory presupposed

The theoretical framework for the description is that of generative phonology as set forth in Chomsky and Halle (1968) and Stanley (1967). Familiarity with the notions and notations of these works is presupposed in the formalisation of the rules and in several places in the theoretical discussion of individual points of interest. Elsewhere, however, familiarity with elementary phonetics and phoneme theory should be sufficient to enable the reader to assimilate the core of the book. Where any inconsistency between the formal and informal descriptions arises (as the result of a difference in detail, for instance) the formalised version is to be taken as definitive.

1.3 The method and scope of study

1.3.1 Method. All the data analysed were taken down in phonetic transcription on index cards. A tape-recorder was used occasionally,[1] especially when testing A's response to his own speech, but most of the description is based on non-recorded material. In most cases the data were spontaneous utterances from the child, although on some occasions recourse was had to asking him to name things, e.g.:

NVS What's this? [pointing to the telephone]
A   [dɛwiːbuːn]

Where it was particularly desired to elicit a form which illustrated (or it was suspected would illustrate) a special phenomenon, I would ask him, all else having failed, to say a word:

NVS Say 'zinc' *or* Can you say 'zinc' for me?
A   [ġik] *or* [wɔt ġik dɛdiː] (What's 'zinc', Daddy?)

All such directly elicited examples are enclosed in parentheses in the text and in Appendix C; e.g. '(zinc – [ġik])'. In general A was a good and willing informant, and I do not think this elicitation is in any way misleading. Typically, a sound or contrast he was able to repeat after me, he would be able to produce spontaneously a few days or at most a few weeks later. The usual response, when he was asked to say something 'correctly' after he had already attempted to say it in his own way, is exemplified by the following dialogue, recorded when I was puzzled by

---

[1] I am grateful to Dr Adrian Fourcin for making a tape-recorder available to me for part of the study.

his ability to pronounce the nasal in *hand* ([ɛnd]) but not in *jump*:

NVS Say 'jump'

A   [d̪ʌp]

NVS No, 'jump'

A   [d̪ʌp]

NVS No, 'jummmp'

A   [uːli: d̪ɛdi: ġæn d̪eː d̪ʌp] ('Only Daddy can say "jump"')!

By contrast, on one or two occasions, he spontaneously came up to me and announced his ability to produce a new sound or sequence. Thus after rendering *quick* as [kip] quite regularly for a year or more, he suddenly said: 'Daddy, I can say [kwik]'; without, to my knowledge, having been in any way prompted.

Data were collected systematically from 2 years 2 months to age four; sometimes at intervals of a week, sometimes every day; depending partly on the (in)stability of his system, partly on the time available. If I detected any change at all in what he said, I always made a note of it, with the result that I am confident that only minor changes can have been missed over the period studied. The only lengthy gap occurred during the visit to India when, deliberately, only isolated jottings were made.

1.3.2 Scope. With the exception of a brief discussion of certain grammatical conditionings of the acquisition of phonology, this study is devoted exclusively to the sound system of the language.[1] Even within phonology emphasis has been placed very heavily on the consonant system, with details of intonation or the vowel system given only when they cast light on the consonants. The reasons for this are:

(1) The development of the consonant system was much more complex, and therefore gave rise to a greater number of theoretically interesting phenomena. As far as I know there were no classes of phenomena evidenced by the development of the vowel system which were not manifested more clearly by the consonant system.

(2) The impracticability of using a tape-recorder consistently in the early stages made the analysis of intonation extremely difficult.[2]

---

[1] I have excluded all details of the non-linguistic, cognitive, development of A for a number of reasons. First, as a linguist not a psychologist, I am not competent in this direction; second, I strongly suspect that the general cognitive development of the child is not relevant to his acquisition of phonology, even though it certainly is in his acquisition of syntax/semantics: third, the human life-span is finite.

[2] Elsewhere the use of a tape-recorder is not as helpful as might be expected. It is no use having a perfect recording of [ġʌk], if you do not know whether it corresponds to the adult *dog, duck, luck, truck* or *stuck.*

(3) A's mother's speech differs more from ESP in the vowel than in the consonant system (cf. p. 7 above).

(4) There was far more phonetic free variation in the vowel system than in the consonant system, which made the details of the analysis less clear-cut.

(5) There is far more dialectal and idiolectal phonetic variation in the vowel system than in the consonant system of English, and A was exposed to an unusually wide cross-section of dialects.

1.4 The method of analysis

As mentioned in the Introduction, A's phonology is analysed in two quite distinct ways: first as a function of or mapping from the adult language which the child is assumed to be learning (ESP); and second as a self-contained 'independent' system, in much the same way as one would analyse any unknown language.

1.4.1 The child's phonology as a function of the adult language.

This part of the analysis consists at each stage of a single set of ordered rules which have as their input the adult surface forms (cf. the father's English characterised above), i.e. those forms to which the child is exposed, and maps these into the forms of the child's system (cf. 1.4.2 below). The rules are couched in terms of distinctive features, but for the sake of clarity examples are given in phonemic transcription. Thus, to take the example of *zinc* quoted above, we start with the adult form /ziŋk/ and apply to it a set of rules which result in the child's form [ġik]. To oversimplify, this involves two rules:

(1) A rule deleting the nasal before a voiceless consonant.
(2) A rule converting /z/ to [ġ] when the /z/ begins a syllable which closes with a velar.

Although these rules seem *ad hoc* in isolation, it will be seen later that they are actually extremely general. It will also become apparent that at least one further rule must apply in the derivation of [ġik] from /ziŋk/: specifically, one which neutralises the voicing distinction between /k/ and /g/. Given that there is no phonemic distinction of voice in A's speech, the form [ġik] is representable phonemically as |gig|,[1] and the contrast between the initial and final segments is due to phonetic rules internal

---

[1] For the abbreviatory notations used here, see p. viii, above. Briefly, /×/ = adult phonemes; |×| = A's phonemes; [×] = phonetic representation.

to A's phonology. In other words, the rules mapping ESP onto A's system have as their input the adult phonemic form, and as their output the child's phonemic form prior to the application of the phonetic rules of his own system. The theoretical status of these rules is discussed in detail in chapter 4.

1.4.2 The child's phonology as an independent system. This part of the analysis is subdivided into three:

(1) A list of those segments which are phonemically distinctive for A's idiolect, characterised in terms of a matrix of distinctive features. Technically, this is a distinctive feature specification of the systematic phonemic elements of the language; traditionally, a phoneme inventory.[1]

(2) An unordered set of morpheme structure conditions (see Stanley, 1967) accounting for the restrictions; segmental, sequential and canonical, on the set of features displayed in (1). *Inter alia*, these conditions characterise the structure in terms of consonants and vowels of all the items in the child's vocabulary; state restrictions on the appearance of specific segments in certain positions, e.g. that *h* cannot occur finally; state redundancies in the matrix of (1) and provide indirectly an enumeration of the 'structural types' typical of Waterson's study (Waterson, 1971 *a*).

(3) A list of phonetic rules internal to the child's own idiolect. For instance, rules giving the distribution of voiced and voiceless plosives at a stage before these are distinct.

Both types of analysis, the mapping from the adult language and the independent, are treated diachronically as well as synchronically. That is, sets of rules for a particular stage of the child's acquisition are set up, and then changes in his phonological output are characterised in terms of changes to these sets of rules. In other words, the developmental changes are treated as changes of rules controlling the realisation of classes of items, not as changes of individual items.

---

[1] The distinction between a traditional phoneme inventory and a generative phonology's set of underlying segments (as exemplified in, e.g., Chomsky and Halle, 1968, pp. 176–7) is largely neutralised, as the child's highly restricted phonological system displays none of the alternations which chiefly motivate such a divergence. (For discussion, see pp. 180 f. below.)

2 The child's phonology at two years

The first stage of A's acquisition of speech for which data are virtually complete dates from 2.60[1] and I will take this as the *point de départ* for all the analysis presented.

2.1 A's phonology as a mapping from adult English

2.1.1 Informal exemplification of the realisation rules.
To express the regular relationships between A's phonology described as a self-contained system below and the phonology of the language which he was acquiring, I have formulated a set of REALISATION rules which take the adult surface form as input and give the child's form (prior to the application of phonetic rules) as output. These rules are strictly ordered, and any adult form will be subject to any rule which is applicable.[2] Discussion of and justification for the ordering will be given after the formal statement of the rules on pp. 22–30 below.

Aside from a few exceptions, dealt with in section 2.1.4, the following rules predict the treatment of any word of ESP by A:

(1) A nasal consonant is deleted before any voiceless consonant.

> stamp → ḍɛp[3] phonemically |dɛb|
> bump → ḅʌp phonemically |bʌb|
> drink → ġik phonemically |gig|
> tent → ḍɛt phonemically |dɛd|
> uncle → ʌgu phonemically |ʌgu|
> empty → ɛbi: phonemically |ɛbi:|
> thank you → ġɛgu: phonemically |gɛgu:|

---

[1] A's age is given in years and days to avoid the problem of dealing with fractions when changes occur within a month or even a few days of each other. See Appendix A.

[2] See the sample derivations in 2.1.3 below.

[3] In the exemplification the forms are given as if all rules had applied. Moreover, although the output of the realisation rules gives a phonemic representation (displayed only for rule R1), the words are actually cited in a phonetic transcription: i.e. assuming the application of the phonetic rules (see 2.2.4 below). Square brackets are omitted from tabulated examples.

(2) A voiced consonant is deleted after a nasal consonant.

window → winu:	angry → ɛɲi:
mend → mɛn	round → ḍaun
handle → ɛɲu	hand → ɛn
finger → wiɲə	band → ḅɛn

Taken together, rules R1 and R2 account for such (later recorded) minimal pairs as:

mend → mɛn
meant → mɛt

(3) The alveolar consonants /n/ and /t, d/ become velars, [ŋ] and [g] before a syllabic [l̩].

handle → ɛɲu	beetle → ḅi:gu
pedal → ḅɛgu	bottle → ḅɔgu

This is one of the most widespread rules found in children acquiring English as their first language. It is noteworthy that with A it applies only to the stop consonants; continuants (/s, z/ etc.) are not affected, cf. the example of *puzzle/puddle* discussed in the Introduction (p. 4), and the example:

whistle → wibu

and neither are the affricates /tʃ, dʒ/. At this stage there were no examples of affricates in this position, but later (stage 23), when the rule was still operative, words such as:

cudgel → kʌdᶻəl
satchel → sætˢəl

indicate that only stops are involved. It will be observed later that the conditioning environment is not only syllabic [l̩] (or [əl]) but any [l] after an alveolar stop:

antler → æŋklə (stage 28)

It is of interest that a comparable rule has been observed in children acquiring German as their first language. For instance, I have heard a two and a half year old German boy (C) regularly produce the following:

Dreck → glɛk
Andreas → æŋˈgle:əs etc.

where the uvular [R] has apparently imposed velarisation of the preceding alveolar, before itself becoming an alveolar lateral.

(4) Syllabic [ḷ] vocalises to [u]; e.g. the examples given for R3 above, and also:

apple → ɛbu   tickle → ġigu
nipple → mibu   uncle → ʌgu
table → ḅeⁱbu

The question whether this rule should be expressed in terms of syllabic [ḷ], [əl] or what, is discussed below, p. 24.

(5) In some cases a continuant consonant preceded by a nasal and a vowel, itself becomes a nasal.

noisy → nɔ:ni:
penis → ḅinin
smell → mɛn

This rule is somewhat marginal as there are just as many cases where it does not apply as where it does:

nice → nait
mice → mait
Smith → mit

(6) /l/ is deleted finally and preconsonantally.

ball → ḅɔ: bolt → ḅɔ:t
bell → ḅɛ   elbow → ɛbu:
trowel → ḍau   milk → mik
wheel → wi:

(7) /s/ is deleted preconsonantally.

biscuit → ḅigik   spoon → ḅu:n
escape → ġeip   scream → ġi:m
skin → ġin   swing → wiŋ
Smith → mit

This too is an extremely widespread rule, and is probably universal[1] although later development of the rule may give rise to a superficially contradictory set of examples (see p. 167 below). Although no examples occurred at this stage, it should be noted that /s/ was not deleted before /j/.

(8) In a word of the structure /CwCV/ the second consonant becomes bilabial. That is, whenever an initial consonant is immediately followed by /w/, the next consonant assimilates to [p], [m] or [f].

---

[1] Obviously restricted to those languages which have clusters of /s/ plus consonant.

Although this rule was completely regular for a prolonged period, all the clear examples come from later stages, e.g. from stage 9:

squat → ġɔp   twice → ḍaif
squeeze → ġi:ḅ   queen → ġi:m

The only evidence for this rule at stage 1 is the solitary example of:

bird → ḅi:bi:p

where what A was really attempting to say was 'tweet-tweet'. Note that rules R7 and R8 give very clear evidence of the need for ordering. That is, the sequences /sw/ and /Cw/ (where C is any consonant but /s/) behave quite differently. Thus:

sweetie → wi:di: (/s/ → ∅ by R7)

but: twice → ḍaif   (/t/ is retained, as [ḍ]; the /w/ causes the final consonant to become [f], and is itself later deleted by R16).

(9) In a word of the structure /sVC/ the /s/ is optionally deleted if the C is labial or alveolar.

soup → u:p   seat → i:t
soap → u:p   sun → ʌn

This rule is optional to account for:

sun → ḍʌn (in free variation with [ʌn])
scissors → ḍidə
soon → ḍu:n

The important point is that when the following consonant is a velar the rule can never apply:

sing → ġiŋ
sock → ġɔk

(10) In a word of the structure /ʃVC/ the /ʃ/ is optionally deleted if the C is labial or velar.

sharp → a:p
sugar → ugə

This rule is optional to account for:

shopping → wɔbin

Data are rather scarce for both this and the preceding rule, R9, but it is important to notice here that /ʃ/ was never deleted before alveolars:

shirt → ḍə:t
shine → ḍain
shoulder → ḍu:də

The diachronic development of these two rules is interesting (see p. 65 below).

(11) /z/ is deleted finally.

The most obvious effect of this rule is to eliminate the distinction between a large class of singulars and plurals:

eye/eyes → ai
shoe/shoes → ḍu:

Moreover, as A had no contrast anywhere between singular and plural, e.g. [wut] and [wi:t] were in free variation for both *foot* and *feet*, it is probably the case that other non-plural or *pluralia tantum* examples of this rule:

nose → nu: glasses → ġa:gi:
please → ḅi: scissors → ḍidə

had been analysed by him into a stem and a plural morpheme. That is, we have an indirect example of the grammatical conditioning of A's acquisition of phonology. (For further discussion, see pp. 67f. below.) It should be noted that /z/ was differently interpreted elsewhere:

zebra → wi:bə
lazy → ḍe:di:

and that /s/ in final position was not deleted:

kiss → ġik
mice → mait

(12) A nasal consonant following an unstressed vowel becomes alveolar: [n].

bottom → ḅɔdin   working → wə:gin
crying → ġaiin   taking → ġeⁱgin
driving → waibin

The only exceptions to this rule occur if the consonant immediately preceding the unstressed vowel is itself a velar nasal, in which case an ESP velar nasal is retained. Thus beside the examples above, we have:

> singing → ġiŋiŋ
>
> (and later) longing → lɔŋiŋ
>
> banging → bæŋiŋ etc.

Nearly all the examples of the operation of this rule involve the verbal suffix *-ing*, but there were some later examples which indicate that the conditioning environment was in fact phonological not syntactic:

ceiling → li:lin	something → wʌpin
pudding → budin	nothing → nʌtin etc.

(13) /h/ is deleted everywhere.

hair → ɛ	head → ɛt
hammer → ɛmə	hurt → ə:t
hand → ɛn	

(14) An initial or post-consonantal unstressed vowel is deleted.

away → we:	banana → ba:nə
escape → ġe:p	belong → bɔŋ

The perhaps unexpected inclusion of the last two examples here is obviously dependent on the operation of further rules (in fact, R16).

(15) /t/ and /d/ are optionally deleted before /r/.

> driving → waibin
>
> troddler → lɔlə (a kind of pedal-less bicycle)
>
> trolly → lɔli:

In fact this rule is very marginal: the three examples cited are the only ones affected, and it may well be better simply to treat these as exceptions (see the formalisation of this rule below, p. 28).

(16) Post-consonantal sonorants, /l, r, w, j/ are deleted.

angry → ɛŋi:	flower → wæwə
brush → bʌt	play → be:
crumb → ġʌm	new → nu:
cloth → ġɔk	bird → bi:bi:p (see above, p. 16)

This is another extremely widespread rule with claims to universality: at least as far as the deletion of /l/ and /r/ is concerned. Note that the term 'sonorants' covers the nasals as well as liquids and glides, thereby allowing R16 to produce, for instance:

> banana → ba:nə

via the intermediate stage – bna:nə – occasioned by rule R14.

(17) Non-nasal alveolar and palato-alveolar consonants harmonise to the point of articulation of a preceding velar.

cloth → ġɔk	good (night) → ġug (nait)
glasses → ġaːgiː	coach → ġoːk
kiss → ġik	kitchen → ġigən
biscuit → b̥igik	

The rule excludes nasals because of such examples as:

skin → ġin
corner → ġɔːnə

There was one exception to the rule:

greedy → ġiːdiː

It is probable that this rule should really be more general, applying in the environment of labials as well as velars:

cf. whistle → wibu

but the data are too fragmentary for a decision to be made with any confidence.

(18) /l, r, j/ are subject to the following treatment:

(a) They are neutralised as [l] where /l, r, j/ are the only consonants in the adult word, when the rule applies.
lorry → lɔliː
yellow → lɛluː
hello → ɛluː

(b) They become [w] or are deleted when intervocalic.
telephone → d̥ɛwiːbuːn
follow → wɔwoː
corridor → ġɔiːd̥ɔː

The data are insufficient to determine whether the different treatment of /l/ and /r/ is random or rule-governed.

(c) They behave like the other alveolar consonants elsewhere, i.e. are neutralised as [d̥].

light → d̥ait
write → d̥ait
yes → d̥ɛt

(19) Alveolar and palato-alveolar consonants harmonise to the point of articulation of a following consonant; obligatorily if that consonant is velar, optionally if it is labial.

Examples with a following velar:

dark → ġa:k   snake → ŋe:k
drink → ġik   stuck → ġʌk
leg → ġɛk   taxi → ġɛgi:
ring → ġiŋ   chocolate → ġɔgi: (from: 'chockie')
singing → ġiŋiŋ   motor-car → mu:ġəġa:

Note that the process is not limited to word-initial position, e.g. *motor-car*, and that it may give rise to words 'impossible' in English, e.g. *snake*.

Examples with a following labial:

knife → maip   room → wum
nipple → mibu   rubber → ḅʌbə
stop → ḅɔp   shopping → wɔbin
table → ḅe:bu   zebra → wi:bə

Note that the process applies differentially to stops (*table, stop*, etc.) and some continuants (*room, zebra, shopping*, etc.). The rule is optional before labials to allow for:[1]

stop → ḍɔp (in free variation with [ḅɔp])
stamp → ḍɛp
drum → ḍʌm

This form of consonant harmony was very typical of A's speech, and in fact some form of consonant harmony appears to be universal.

(20) /f, v/ become [w] prevocalically.

feet → wi:t   flower → wæwə
finger → wiŋə   caravan → ˈġæwəwæn
fire → wæ:

Once formulated in terms of distinctive features (see below, p. 30) this rule also applies to the output of rule R19, thereby accounting for the initial [w] in:

shopping → wɔbin   room → wum
zebra → wi:bə   driving → waibin

---

[1] It may be obligatory if the consonant is a nasal, but the number of examples is too small to be certain.

(21) Post-consonantal alveolar consonants are deleted.

    empty → ɛbi:
    taxi → ġɛgi:
    mixer → migə

There are not many words with consonant clusters left by this stage of the rules; but clusters of two obstruents have not been simplified as yet, and this rule performs this function.

(22) Alveolar consonants are optionally deleted in final position.

broken → ḅugu:	moon → mu:
carpet → ġa:bi:	open → ubu:
cupboard → ġʌbə	telephone → ḍɛwi:bu:

The rule is optional to allow for such examples as:

    moon → mu:n   (in free variation with [mu:])
    telephone → ḍɛwi:bu:n (in free variation with [ḍɛwi:bu:])
    head → ɛt   etc.

(23) All alveolar and palato-alveolar consonants fall together as alveolars. That is, /ʃ, ʒ,[1] tʃ, dʒ, j, r/ are neutralised as (ultimately) |d| – with allophones [t], [d], [ḍ].

brush → ḅʌt	yes → ḍɛt
church → ḍə:t	write → ḍait
John → ḍɔn	

(24) All non-sonorant consonants are non-continuant, non-strident, non-affricated and non-lateral. This neutralises the affricates /tʃ, dʒ/, the stridents /f, v, s, z, ʃ, ʒ, tʃ, dʒ/ and the non-sonorant continuants /f, v, θ, ð, s, z, ʃ, ʒ/ as |d| or, in the case of /f/ in non-initial position, as |b| – with allophones [p], [b], [ḅ].

bus → ḅʌt	John → ḍɔn
brush → ḅʌt	bath → ḅa:t
zoo → ḍu:	other → ʌdə
church → ḍə:t	knife → maip

(25) All consonants are voiced.

teddy → ḍɛdi:	kiss → ġik
Daddy → ḍɛdi:	sock → ġɔk
drink → ġik	lock → ġɔk

[1] No examples occurred at this stage, but cf. *garage*→ [ġæəḍ] from stage 9.

This rule gets rid of the adult voicing contrast, and every word which contains a voiceless consonant in ESP is affected. It should be noted that this rule refers to the child's system; it does NOT affect the phonetic rule which gives the allophonic differences between [d] and [ḍ] or [ġ] and [k] above, and which is discussed in 2.2.1 below.

(26) All non-vowels are true consonants.

This rule eliminates the difference between consonants and glides for A. In his system, as described below, there is no crucial difference between these two categories. The motivation for this rule becomes clearer when we see the consonantal behaviour of /w/ for A at later stages (see below, p. 107), but note already that [v] and [w] are in free variation for A, and that ESP /v/ usually corresponds to his |w|.

2.1.2 Formal statement of the realisation rules. The realisation rules listed and exemplified above can be formalised as follows. The same numbering is retained.

(1) $[+\text{nasal}]^1 \to \emptyset /$——$ [-\text{voiced}]$

R1 must precede R21 and R25.

R1 must precede R21 as the latter also acts to simplify consonant clusters, but deletes the second rather than the first. R1 deletes the nasal in, e.g., *tent* → [dɛt], whereas if R21 preceded, *tent* would become [dɛn].

R1 must precede R25 as the latter neutralises the voicing distinction essential to the correct statement of the environment of R1. Were R25 to precede R1 there would be no means of distinguishing *mend* and *meant* for instance.

(2) $[+\text{cons}] \to \emptyset /[+\text{nasal}] \overline{[+\text{voiced}]}$

R2 must precede R3 and R25.

The justification for making R2 precede R3 is slight. At this stage it means that R3 can be more simply formulated, i.e. it refers merely to one segment rather than a sequence. However, by the next stage R2 has been modified so that it no longer operates intervocalically, with the result that R3 has to be complicated anyway (cf. the development of R2 and R3 in 3.1 p. 54 below).

R2 must precede R25 for the same reason as must R1.

---

[1] See Appendix B for the matrix of distinctive features presupposed for the adult consonant system which is the input to these rules.

It would be possible to conflate R1 and R2 as:

$$[+\text{cons}] \rightarrow \emptyset / \left\{ \begin{array}{l} \overline{[+\text{nasal}]}\ [-\text{voiced}] \\ [+\text{nasal}]\ \overline{[+\text{voiced}]} \end{array} \right\}$$

but this still fails to capture adequately the generalisation that nasal clusters are simplified differentially according to the voicing of the non-nasal segment; and the saving of one $\emptyset$ is not particularly exciting.[1]

$$(3)\quad \begin{bmatrix} +\text{coronal} \\ -\text{del rel} \end{bmatrix} \rightarrow \begin{bmatrix} -\text{coronal} \\ -\text{anterior} \end{bmatrix} / \underline{\quad} \left(\begin{bmatrix} +\text{syllabic} \\ -\text{stress} \end{bmatrix} \right) [+\text{lateral}]$$

It is clear that R3, as formulated here, misses the generalisation that the 'velarisation' of coronals takes place before a velarised (dark) [ɫ]. There are various ways of expressing this, but none seems entirely satisfactory. For instance, if we use the redundant features [+high, +back] as an additional characterisation of the (usually syllabic) /l/, we can then express the change as:

$$\begin{bmatrix} +\text{cor} \\ -\text{d.r.} \end{bmatrix} \rightarrow \begin{bmatrix} +\text{high} \\ +\text{back} \end{bmatrix}$$

i.e. an assimilation rule, and then let marking conventions convert the coronals to velars (see Chomsky and Halle, 1968, p. 429, n. 15, for a comparable instance). The trouble with this alternative is that the rule needs a more complex environment and that even its structural change is no simpler, as we have to use the two features [high] and [back] in place of the two features [coronal] and [anterior], and still invoke a series of linking conventions. The position would be improved if our evaluation metric was somewhat more sophisticated such that a change of a feature to the same feature in its environment was less costly than a change to an unrelated feature,[2] i.e. if:

$$[+\text{cor}] \rightarrow \begin{bmatrix} +\text{high} \\ +\text{back} \end{bmatrix} / \underline{\quad} \begin{bmatrix} +\text{lateral} \\ +\text{high} \\ +\text{back} \end{bmatrix}$$

were less complex than:

$$[+\text{cor}] \rightarrow \begin{bmatrix} -\text{cor} \\ -\text{ant} \end{bmatrix} / \underline{\quad} \begin{bmatrix} +\text{lateral} \\ +\text{high} \\ +\text{back} \end{bmatrix}$$

[1] The merit of the conflation is that it does allow the collapsing of two rules which are part of a 'conspiracy' to reduce clusters. On the other hand it makes use of the suspect device of disjunctive brackets. For discussion of both these points, see 5.3.

[2] At present this is the case only if there are two such changes, such that the *a* notation can be used to abbreviate the possibilities. This is clearly not feasible here.

leaving aside the problem of the redundancy of the environmental features. An alternative convention, which in this case would have the same result, would be to evaluate as less costly a change involving features relatively low in a feature hierarchy, i.e. here [high] and [back] are presumably lower in the hierarchy and hence more likely to change than [coronal] and [anterior] (see Smith, 1969, p. 406, for comparable suggestions on evaluation).

A further difficulty is that, in general, it is not the case that the marking conventions link into A's realisation rules. (For a brief discussion of this, see 5.3.1 below.)

R3 must precede R6, R7, R19 and R24.

R3 must precede R6 as the latter removes /l/ in final position, a segment which is necessary for stating the environment of R3.

The justification for making R3 precede R7 came in fact at a much later stage but may be adduced now. With words such as *pistol* where there is a sequence /st/ rather than a single segment in the environment before /(ə)l/, the child's form turns up with an alveolar not a velar – [pitəl] – in other words, /st/ is treated like /s/ not /t/.[1] If the /s/ were deleted by R7 before the operation of R3 there would be no means of capturing this fact.

R3 must precede R19 as the assimilation exhibited in this latter rule may operate to a velar segment produced by R3. For instance, the word *noddle* turns up as [ŋɔgu], where the [g] has arisen as a result of R3, and the /n/ has become [ŋ] as a result of R19.

R3 must precede R24 as the latter rule neutralises the distinction between segments with delayed release and those with non-delayed release, a crucial part of the structural description of the rule.

(4) $[+\text{syllabic}] \rightarrow \begin{bmatrix} +\text{high} \\ +\text{back} \\ -\text{tense} \end{bmatrix} / [\overline{-\text{stress}}] \; [+\text{lateral}] \; \#$

Contrary to the informal description of this rule on p. 15, this formalisation turns a schwa to [u] before a final /l/. The justification for this is the manner of the disappearance of this rule, where the two segments were treated differently, e.g. *apple* was first [ɛbu], then [æbul] with [u] not [ə], and only later was it [æpəl] with [ə]. At this stage the earlier characterisation in terms of syllabic [l] would have been sufficient.

R4 must precede R6 and R18.

---

[1] This was generally the case with A; see below, p. 60.

R4 must precede R6 for the same reason as must R3.

R4 must precede R18, specifically part (c) of R18, as the latter neutralises the $/d - l/$ distinction in certain environments. (It should be observed that the need for R4 to precede R18 is marginal, as R6 would in any case remove all such occurrences of $/l/$ before R18 could apply.)

(5) $\begin{bmatrix} +\text{coronal} \\ +\text{continuant} \end{bmatrix} \underset{\text{opt}}{\rightarrow} [+\text{nasal}]/[+\text{nasal}] \ [+\text{syllabic}]\text{——}$

R5 must precede R6 and R24.

R5 must precede R6 as the coronal continuant which is turned optionally into a nasal, may begin as a lateral which would otherwise be removed by R6.

R5 must precede R24 because the latter neutralises the continuant/non-continuant distinction crucial to the statement of the former.

(6) $[+\text{lateral}] \rightarrow \emptyset/\text{——}\left\{ \begin{matrix} \# \\ [+\text{consonantal}] \end{matrix} \right\}$

R6 must precede R17, R18 and R24.

R6 must precede R17 as final $/l/$ is always deleted and does not harmonise with a preceding labial or velar in the way the other coronals do.

R6 must precede R18 and R24 as, together, these two latter rules eliminate the distinction between $/l/$ and the other coronals in favour of [d], which is non-sonorant and non-lateral.

(7) $\begin{bmatrix} +\text{coronal} \\ +\text{anterior} \\ +\text{continuant} \\ +\text{strident} \\ -\text{voiced} \end{bmatrix} \rightarrow \emptyset/\text{——}[-\text{syllabic}]$

The specifications [−voiced] and [+anterior] are probably redundant, as there were no examples of pre-consonantal $/z/$ or $/\int/$ in the data. The specification of the environment as [−syllabic] rather than [+consonantal] is made to include $/w/$ in the purview of the rule ($/j/$ became a problem later; see below, p. 58).

R7 must precede R8, R16, R21, R24 and possibly R23 and R25.

R7 must precede R8 because of the differential treatment of $/sw/$ and $/Cw/$ clusters (where C is any consonant other than $/s/$); see the remarks on p. 16 above.

R7 must precede R16 for an analogous reason; namely, the differential treatment of $/s/$ plus sonorant and $/C/$ plus sonorant clusters.

R7 must precede R21 for the same reason as must R1.

R7 must precede R24 because the latter neutralises the continuant/non-continuant and strident/non-strident distinctions crucial for stating the former.

If preconsonantal /z/ or /ʃ/ occurred in the adult forms that A reinterpreted, and if such forms were treated differently to preconsonantal /s/, then R7 would have to precede R23 and R25. There is no evidence.

$$(8) \quad [+\text{consonantal}] \rightarrow \begin{bmatrix} -\text{coronal} \\ +\text{anterior} \end{bmatrix} / [+\text{cons}] \begin{bmatrix} -\text{cons} \\ +\text{ant} \end{bmatrix} [+\text{syll}] \text{——}$$

R8 must precede R16 and R17.

R8 must precede R16 as the latter deletes, *inter alia*, post-consonantal /w/ which is the crucial part of the environment of R8.

R8 must precede R17 to account for the change of, e.g., *quite* to [kaip] rather than *[kaik].

$$(9) \quad \begin{bmatrix} +\text{coronal} \\ +\text{continuant} \\ +\text{strident} \\ +\text{anterior} \end{bmatrix} \underset{\text{opt}}{\rightarrow} \emptyset / \# \text{——} [+\text{syllabic}] \, [+\text{anterior}]$$

R9 must precede R19, R23 and R24.

R9 must precede R19 to prevent the harmonisation of the initial /s/ to [b̥] in examples such as *soup* (→ [u:p]).

R9 must precede R23 as the latter neutralises the distinction between anterior and non-anterior consonants, a distinction which is essential for the operation of this and the following rule.

R9 must precede R24 because the latter neutralises the continuant/non-continuant and strident/non-strident distinctions crucial to the statement of the former.

$$(10) \quad \begin{bmatrix} +\text{coronal} \\ +\text{continuant} \\ +\text{strident} \\ -\text{anterior} \end{bmatrix} \underset{\text{opt}}{\rightarrow} \emptyset / \# \text{——} [+\text{syllabic}] \, [-\text{coronal}]$$

R10 must precede the same rules, R19, R23 and R24, as must R9.

R10 must precede R19 to prevent the harmonisation of initial /ʃ/ to [b̥] or [ġ] in words such as *sharp* (→ [a:p]) and *sugar* (→ [ugə]).

R10 must precede R23 and R24 for the same reasons as must R9.

$$(11) \quad \begin{bmatrix} +\text{coronal} \\ +\text{continuant} \\ +\text{strident} \\ +\text{anterior} \\ +\text{voiced} \end{bmatrix} \rightarrow \emptyset / \underline{\quad\quad} \#$$

R11 must precede R17, R24 and R25.

R11 must precede R17 to prevent the final /z/ in forms such as *goes* from harmonising to the initial consonant.

R11 must precede R24 as the latter neutralises the continuant/non-continuant, strident/non-strident and delayed release/non-delayed release contrasts, and final /z/ is treated differently from final /d/, /ð/ and /dʒ/.

R11 must precede R25 as the latter neutralises the adult voicing contrast, and final /z/ and /s/ are treated differently.

$$(12) \quad [+\text{nasal}] \rightarrow \begin{bmatrix} +\text{coronal} \\ +\text{anterior} \end{bmatrix} / X \begin{bmatrix} +\text{syllabic} \\ -\text{stress} \end{bmatrix} \underline{\quad\quad}$$
$$\text{where } X \neq /\eta/$$

R12 must precede R19 as otherwise a stem final coronal consonant followed by an /iŋ/ suffix[1] would itself become velar, whereas it in fact retains its coronality.

$$(13) \quad \begin{bmatrix} -\text{syllabic} \\ -\text{consonantal} \\ -\text{sonorant} \end{bmatrix} \rightarrow \emptyset$$

R13 must precede R18, specifically part (a) of R18, as the presence of an initial /h/ in the adult form does not prevent the appearance of an [l] in the child's form: cf., e.g., *hello* → [ɛlu:], and note the remarks on MS2 below, p. 48. It would be possible to order R13 after R18 if we complicated the environment of the latter. This would then enable us to group all context-free realisation rules in a block; cf. the discussion in section 4.3.6.

$$(14) \quad [+\text{syllabic}] \rightarrow \emptyset / \# (C) \overline{[-\text{stress}]} \, C \begin{bmatrix} +\text{syllabic} \\ +\text{stress} \end{bmatrix}$$

R14 must precede R16 *or* R21.

R14 must precede R16 as the deletion of an unstressed interconsonantal vowel may give rise to a cluster which is then simplified by the latter rule, e.g. *banana* → [bạ:nə] discussed on p. 18 above. We should in

---

[1] In fact, as mentioned on p. 18, the /iŋ/ need not be a separate morpheme.

fact get the correct result even if R14 did not precede R16 as long as it preceded R21. I have made it precede R16 on the slender basis of my intuition that *belong* and *banana* ([bɔŋ] and [ba:nə]) are the result of the same process, and that *belong* loses its /l/ by the same rule which gives us [bu:] from *blue*. There is some evidence for the latter in that *belong* became [blɔŋ] as soon as other [Cl] clusters appeared. Unfortunately the treatment by A of words containing unstressed initial syllables was inconsistent; cf. the following examples taken from various stages:

tomato → ma:du:	behind → aind
potato → be:du:	without → aut
pyjamas → da:mə	etc.

The last two may be explicable in terms of their internal structure, but the pair *potato* and *pyjamas* seems to indicate that it is impossible to make a generally valid statement (see 4.3.4. below).

$$(15) \quad \begin{bmatrix} +\text{coronal} \\ +\text{anterior} \\ -\text{continuant} \end{bmatrix} \underset{\text{opt}}{\rightarrow} \emptyset/ \# \text{———} \begin{bmatrix} +\text{coronal} \\ +\text{continuant} \end{bmatrix}$$

The environment [+coronal, +continuant] in fact refers to /l, r, j, s, z, θ, ð, ʃ, ʒ/, but non-sonorants and /l/ do not occur in this position in English; and /j/ did not occur in the data.

R15 must precede R16, R21 and R24.

R15 must precede R16, as otherwise /dr/ clusters of this exceptional type would be reduced to [d] rather than [r]. As R15 is optional and R15 and R16 together cover all cases of consonant plus sonorant clusters, it would of course be possible to order R16 first and make it optional and R15 obligatory. The sequence given has been chosen because R16 expresses the regular situation, R15 the exceptional one.

R15 must precede R21 for the same reason as must R1.

R15 must precede R24 as the latter neutralises the distinction between continuant and non-continuant segments; a contrast needed to state the input to the former rule.

$$(16) \quad [+\text{sonorant}] \rightarrow \emptyset/[+\text{consonantal}]\text{———}$$

R16 must precede R18, specifically part (c) of R18, as the latter makes /l, r, j/, all of which may potentially occur postconsonantally, nonsonorant.

$$(17) \quad \begin{bmatrix} +\text{coronal} \\ -\text{nasal} \end{bmatrix} \rightarrow \begin{bmatrix} -\text{coronal} \\ -\text{anterior} \end{bmatrix} / \begin{bmatrix} -\text{coronal} \\ -\text{anterior} \end{bmatrix} [+\text{syllabic}]\text{———}$$

There is no evidence to indicate that R17 should precede any other rule.[1]

$$(18) \quad \begin{bmatrix} +\text{coronal} \\ +\text{continuant} \\ +\text{sonorant} \end{bmatrix} \rightarrow \left\{ \begin{array}{l} [+\text{lateral}] / \left\{ \begin{array}{l} \left(\begin{bmatrix} +\text{cor} \\ +\text{cont} \\ +\text{son} \end{bmatrix} \right) [+\text{syll}]\underline{\quad\quad}[+\text{syll}] \\ \underline{\quad\quad}[+\text{syll}] \begin{bmatrix} +\text{cor} \\ +\text{cont} \\ +\text{son} \end{bmatrix} [+\text{syll}] \end{array} \right\} \quad \text{(a)} \\[3em] \left\{ \begin{array}{l} \begin{bmatrix} -\text{cons} \\ -\text{cor} \\ +\text{ant} \end{bmatrix} \\ \emptyset \end{array} \right\} / [+\text{syll}]\underline{\quad\quad}[+\text{syll}] \quad\quad \text{(b)} \\[2em] [-\text{son}] \quad\quad\quad\quad\quad\quad\quad\quad\quad\quad\quad\quad\quad\quad \text{(c)} \end{array} \right.$$

The subparts of this rule are disjunctively ordered.

R18 must precede R19 and R24.

R18 must precede R19 so that the coronal /l/ in words such as *like* can be made non-sonorant before it is made non-coronal by R19.

R18 must precede R24 as the latter operates on the output of part (c). That is an /l, r, j/ which is not retained as [l], converted to [w], or deleted by R18(a, b), becomes non-sonorant by R18(c) and then becomes non-continuant and non-lateral (i.e. [d]) by R24 (see the examples on p. 19 above).

$$(19) \quad [+\text{coronal}] \rightarrow \begin{bmatrix} -\text{coronal} \\ \alpha\text{anterior} \end{bmatrix} / \underline{\quad\quad}[+\text{syllabic}] \begin{bmatrix} -\text{coronal} \\ \alpha\text{anterior} \end{bmatrix}$$

Originally this rule was probably more general, with the input simply specified as [+consonantal].[2] This is indicated by various 'remnant' forms such as:

Cooper → pu:pə
Grandpa → ḅʌbʌ

That the harmony was never quite complete is shown by the nonce early form [ḍɔk] for *sock* which, by stage 1, was invariably [g̈ɔk].

R19 must precede R20 so that the latter can convert to [w] not only the adult /f, v/, i.e. [−coronal, +anterior] segments, but also those segments, such as an original /z, ʃ, r/ which are made [+anterior] by the

---

[1] But cf. the discussion on rule ordering in 4.2.2.
[2] The fact that in the present system (i.e. Chomsky and Halle, 1968) it is *not* more simple is an anomaly I have indicated before; see p. 24 above.

operation of R19. (See the examples on p. 20 above, and the derivations in 2.1.3 below.)

$$
(20) \quad \begin{bmatrix} -\text{coronal} \\ +\text{anterior} \\ +\text{continuant} \\ -\text{lateral} \end{bmatrix} \rightarrow [+\text{sonorant}]/\underline{\hspace{1.5em}}[+\text{syllabic}]
$$

The somewhat unexpected feature [−lateral] is to exclude /l/ from the set of items which harmonise to [w] before labials. That is, we have:

> room → wum
> Robbie → wɔbi:
but: slipper → ḅibə   *wibə

There was, in fact, one exception: *rubber-band* → [ḅʌbəbæn] instead of the expected *[wʌbəbæn]. This was probably a remnant form from a period of more general consonant harmony, but data are too scarce to be sure.

The feature [+sonorant] is used rather than the more likely [−consonantal] because of the apparently consonantal status of [w] in A's own speech. (See below, p. 46, and R26.)

R20 must precede R24 as the latter neutralises the continuant/non-continuant distinction crucial for the former.

(21) $[+\text{coronal}] \rightarrow \emptyset/[+\text{consonantal}]\underline{\hspace{1.5em}}$

(22) $[+\text{coronal}] \underset{\text{opt}}{\rightarrow} \emptyset/\underline{\hspace{1.5em}}\#$

Were it not for the optionality of R22 these two rules could be conflated, though the saving effect would be minimal.

(23) $[+\text{coronal}] \rightarrow [+\text{anterior}]$

Note that this rule is equivalent to MS8 (see below, p. 50).

$$
(24) \quad [-\text{sonorant}] \rightarrow \begin{bmatrix} -\text{del rel} \\ -\text{strident} \\ -\text{continuant} \\ -\text{lateral} \end{bmatrix}
$$

We need the specification [−sonorant], rather than [−syllabic], so that those occurrences of /l, r, j/ which were made [−sonorant] by

R18(c) fall together with |d|, whereas those occurrences of /l/ and /w/ which survive, or are created by R20, retain their status.

(25) [+segment] → [+voiced]

(26) [−syllabic] → [+consonantal][1]

For a tabular display of all the ordering relations, see 4.2.2 below; and for a discussion of the implications of the formal differences between the last few rules and all the preceding ones, see 4.3.6.

2.1.3 Derivations exemplifying the realisation rules. Having enumerated the realisation rules above, I will now further illustrate their working by giving a number of derivations showing mappings from ESP to A's phonological system. It should be noted throughout that vowel changes and allophonic or free variation accounted for by A's phonetic rules (see 2.2.4 below) are left unexplained. The form of the derivations is given as follows. The first line has the relevant example in orthography, followed by a phonetic representation of A's pronunciation of it, and a phonemic representation of it in terms of his system. The next line starts with the word in ESP phonemic transcription and relates this by an arrow to an intermediate form, to the right of which occurs (in parentheses) the number of the realisation rule which effects the change. Succeeding lines take the right hand side of the preceding line as input, and show the effect of further rules upon it. The derivation continues until no more rules can apply; i.e. their structural description is not satisfied by the form in question, or we have reached the end of the rules. It should be observed that the stages intermediate between the adult phonemic representation in /.../ and the child's phonemic representation in |...| have no theoretical status. It may even be the case that the intermediate form can only be represented by means of an (unpronounceable) matrix of distinctive features (see (ii) below).

(i) *snake*	[ŋeːk]	|ŋeːg|
/sneik/	→ neik	(7)
neik	→ ŋeik	(19)
ŋeik	→ ŋeig	(25)[2]

---

[1] 'True consonants' (see p. 22) thus means: [−syllabic, +consonantal]. Note that this definition is not co-extensive with that in Chomsky and Halle, 1968.

[2] Rules which apply vacuously are not specified, e.g. R26 in each derivation.

(ii) *like*   [ġaik] |gaig|

$$/\text{laik}/ \quad \rightarrow \quad \begin{bmatrix} 1 \\ -\text{son} \end{bmatrix} \text{aik} \quad \text{(18c)}$$

$$\begin{bmatrix} 1 \\ -\text{son} \end{bmatrix} \text{aik} \quad \rightarrow \quad \begin{bmatrix} -\text{cor} \\ -\text{ant} \\ -\text{son} \\ \cdot \\ \cdot \end{bmatrix} \text{aik} \quad \text{(19)}$$

$$\begin{bmatrix} -\text{cor} \\ -\text{ant} \\ -\text{son} \\ \cdot \\ \cdot \end{bmatrix} \text{aik} \quad \rightarrow \quad \begin{bmatrix} -\text{cor} \\ -\text{ant} \\ -\text{son} \\ -\text{del rel} \\ -\text{cont} \\ -\text{lateral} \end{bmatrix} \text{aik} \quad \text{(24) i.e. gaik}$$

gaik   → gaig   (25)

(iii) *stamp*   [ḍɛp] |dɛb|

/stæmp/   → stæp   (1)
stæp   → tæp   (7)
tæp   → tæp   (19) fails to apply – note that
                                        it is optional if $\alpha = +$

tæp   → dæb   (25)

(iv) *knife*   [maip] |maib|

/naif/   → maif   (19)
maif   → maip   (24)[1]
maip   → maib   (25)

(v) *handle*   [ɛŋu] |ɛŋu|

/hændəl/   → hænəl   (2)
hænəl   → hæŋəl   (3)
hæŋəl   → hæŋul   (4)
hæŋul   → hæŋu   (6)
hæŋu   → æŋu   (13)

(vi) *driving*   [waibin] |waibin|

/draiviŋ/   → draivin   (12)
draivin   → raivin   (15)

---

[1] The change from a labio-dental to a bilabial articulation is assumed.

$$\text{raivin} \quad \rightarrow \begin{bmatrix} \text{r} \\ -\text{son} \end{bmatrix} \text{aivin} \quad (18)$$

$$\begin{bmatrix} \text{r} \\ -\text{son} \end{bmatrix} \text{aivin} \rightarrow \begin{bmatrix} -\text{son} \\ -\text{cor} \\ +\text{ant} \end{bmatrix} \text{aivin} \quad (19)$$

$$\begin{bmatrix} -\text{son} \\ -\text{cor} \\ +\text{ant} \end{bmatrix} \text{aivin} \rightarrow \begin{bmatrix} +\text{son} \\ -\text{cor} \\ +\text{ant} \end{bmatrix} \text{aivin} \quad (20) \text{ i.e. waivin}$$

$$\text{waivin} \quad \rightarrow \text{waibin} \quad (24)$$

Note that the rules as formulated make the counter-intuitive claim that /r/ goes from [+sonorant] to [−sonorant] to [+sonorant]. This is clearly farcical; even if there are precedents in the literature (cf. the treatment of the underlined vowel in *tabu̲lar*, [tæbjələ] in Chomsky and Halle, 1968, p. 197, which is inserted by rule as a lax *u*; is tensed and unrounded by a second rule, and is then made lax and reduced by a third rule!) and is probably an indication that the child is really operating in terms of segments of a phonemic nature rather than a featural nature, and that the rules are to that extent inadequate (see below, p. 189, for some discussion).

(vii)	*milk*		[mik]	|mig|
	/milk/	→	mik	(6)
	mik	→	mig	(25)

(viii)	*lorry*		[lɔli:]	|lɔli:|
	/lɔri:/	→	lɔli:	(18, 23)

(R18 makes /r/ lateral; R23 makes it anterior)

(ix)	*smell*		[mɛn]	|mɛn|
	/smɛl/	→	smɛn	(5)
	smɛn	→	mɛn	(7)

The change of the /n/ to [−lateral] is assumed. If it were required to capture this formally, it would necessitate adding [−continuant] to R5, deleting the feature [lateral] from R24 and having a final rule: [−continuant] → [−lateral].

2

(x)	*tweet*		[ḅiːp]	|biːb| (cf. p. 16 above)
	/twiːt/	→	twiːp	(8)
	twiːp	→	tiːp	(16)
	tiːp	→	piːp	(19)
	piːp	→	biːb	(25)

(xi)	*sun*		[ʌn]/[ḍʌn]	|ʌn/dʌn|
(a)	/sʌn/	→	ʌn	(9) If the option is chosen.
(b)	/sʌn/	→	sʌn	(9) If the option is not chosen.
	sʌn	→	tʌn	(24)
	tʌn	→	dʌn	(25)

(xii)	*sugar*		[ugə]	/ugə/
	/ʃugə/	→	ugə	(10) Assuming the option is taken.

(xiii)	*please*		[ḅiː]	|biː|
	/pliːz|	→	pliː	(11)
	pliː	→	piː	(16)
	piː	→	biː	(25)

(xiv)	*banana*		[ḅaːnə]	|baːnə|
	/bəˈnaːnə/	→	bnaːnə	(14)
	bnaːnə	→	baːnə	(16)

(xv)	*cloth*		[ġɔk]	|gɔg|
	/klɔθ/	→	kɔθ	(16)
	kɔθ	→	kɔx	(17)
	kɔx	→	kɔk	(24)
	kɔk	→	gɔg	(25)

(xvi)	*empty*[1]		[ɛbiː]	|ɛbiː|
	/ɛmptiː/	→	ɛptiː	(1)
	ɛptiː	→	ɛpiː	(21)
	ɛpiː	→	ɛbiː	(25)

(xvii)	*broken*		[ḅuguː]	|buguː|
	/brəukən/	→	bəukən	(16)
	bəukən	→	bəukə	(22)
	bəukə	→	bəugə	(25)

[1] With the meaning 'cup'.

The vowel pattern is the manifestation of a remnant vowel harmony rule.

(xviii) *slipper* [b̰ib̰ə] |bibə|

/slipə/ → lipə (7)

lipə → $\begin{bmatrix} l \\ -\text{son} \end{bmatrix} \text{ipə}$ (18)

$\begin{bmatrix} l \\ -\text{son} \end{bmatrix} \text{ipə} \rightarrow \begin{bmatrix} -\text{cor} \\ +\text{ant} \\ -\text{son} \\ +\text{lat} \end{bmatrix} \text{ipə}$ (19)

Because of the specification [+lateral], R20 cannot apply.

$\begin{bmatrix} -\text{cor} \\ +\text{ant} \\ -\text{son} \\ +\text{lat} \end{bmatrix} \text{ipə} \rightarrow \begin{bmatrix} -\text{cor} \\ +\text{ant} \\ -\text{son} \\ -\text{lat} \\ -\text{cont} \end{bmatrix} \text{ipə}$ (24) i.e. bipə

bipə → bibə (25)

2.1.4 Exceptions. The rules formulated and exemplified above account for about 97 per cent of A's vocabulary. There is, however, a small residue of irregular forms for which the rules make the wrong predictions. I list these here:

1 aeroplane → [ɛ:bəʔe:n]
2 brief-case → [b̰i:kkeit]
3 Granna → [læla:] (cf. Grandpa → [b̰ʌbʌ])
4 greedy → [ġi:di:]
5 lawn-mower → [mɔ:mə]
6 little → [d̰idi:]
7 lolly → [ɔli:]
8 telephone → [dɛwi:bu:]

I am not treating as exceptional for present purposes either: (a) words which are imitations of adult baby forms:

cat → ['mi:au]   dog → [wowo]
chocolate → [ġɔki:/ġɔgi:]   urinate → [wi:wi:]

or (b) are exceptional only in that they retain a canonical form exemplifying the vowel harmony of a yet earlier stage:

broken → [b̰ugu:] (see example (xvii) above)
open → [ubu:]

Examples 3 and 6 above come partially under this rubric but have other exceptional features as well. Example 3 appears to exemplify consonant harmony conditioned by the liquid of the adult form /ˈgrӕnaː/. To account for [lӕlaː] we should have to extend R15 to non-coronals, and assume that in a word containing all sonorants the liquids were favoured. The quality of the vowel is positionally determined; see *broken* etc. above. The form *Grandpa* → [b̥ʌbʌ] is analogous except that for reasons unknown the dominant consonant was the /p/, i.e. /grӕmpaː/ loses the /m/ by R1, the /r/ by R16, is voiced by R25 and merely requires an extension of R19 to non-coronals again to provide the child's form.[1] Example 5, *lawn-mower*, appears to be the converse of 3 with regard to the dominance or otherwise of the nasal. Example 6, *little*, is odd, and was exceptional throughout A's development (see Appendix C). Example 1, *aeroplane*, is perhaps partially regular, if we consider the metathesis rule which became productive at a later stage (see pp. 98 f. below) and which would transpose /r/ and /p/. We would thus have the derivation:

/ɛərəplein/ → ɛərəpein	(16)
ɛərəpein → ɛəpərein	(metathesis)
ɛəpərein → ɛəpəein	(18b)
ɛəpəein → ɛəbəein	(25)

leaving the only irregularity the glottal stop, which is not completely unexpected in such an environment.

Example 2, *brief-case*, seems to be merely a case of irregular but not surprising assimilation. Example 7, *lolly(pop)*, I have no explanation for unless it was a subconscious avoidance of homonymic clash: *lolly* should have become [lɔliː] which was also the form assumed by *lorry* and *trolley*. However, as massive homonymy never worried A at any other time this seems an unlikely reason. Example 8, *telephone*, is irregular in having [b] instead of [w]. In fact there are too few examples to tell whether this is really regular; i.e. that rule R20 should be constrained to initial position and that *caravan* → [ˈgӕwəwӕn], here described as regular, is really irregular; or whether they are both regular and we should have different rules in this one position for /f/ and /v/.

---

[1] One other pre-stage 1 example of a comparable nature occurred: *Cooper* → [puːpə]. The voicelessness appeared to be random.

2.2 A's phonology as a self-contained system

In the first part of this chapter I set up an ordered series of realisation rules mapping adult forms of English into the (phonemic) forms that the child actually produced. In this section I want to look at the formal properties of the system that the child appeared superficially to be utilising; i.e. his output, as opposed to the system he was exposed to. The discussion in chapter 4 will show that I agree largely with Stampe (1970, p. 4) that 'no evidence whatsoever has been advanced to support this assumption [that the child has a phonemic system of his own – NVS]'; but without attempting a detailed analysis of the putative system, and viewing its properties both synchronically and diachronically, it is impossible to judge whether or not it actually does have any psychological reality for the child.

2.2.1 Informal exemplification of A's system. Restricting ourselves to the consonant system for the moment, we can describe A's phonology by reference to only eight phonemes:

$$|b \quad d \quad g \quad m \quad n \quad ŋ \quad w \quad l|$$

That is, we have a voiced plosive series: bilabial, alveolar and velar (b, d, g); a nasal series with the same points of articulation (m, n, ŋ); and two continuants: one labio-velar semi-vowel (w) and a lateral liquid (l).

It should be emphasised that the child's phonetic output is not as simple as the reduced system above might lead one to believe. Although the eight phonemes cited were the only consistently distinctive segments, they had different realisations as the result of allophonic and free variation. Thus the plosives, represented here by |b, d, g|, each had three allophones:

voiceless, unaspirated, lenis in initial position	[b̥, d̥, g̊]
voiced, unaspirated, lenis in medial position	[b, d, g]
voiceless, fortis (aspirated or unaspirated) in final position	[p, t, k]

The nasals and continuants had no obvious allophonic variants, but the latter had a number of free variants. Thus |w| was realised usually as a voiced, labio-velar frictionless continuant, [w]; but often (especially intervocalically) as a voiced labio-dental fricative, [v]; and occasionally as a voiced bilabial fricative, [β]. The lateral liquid was most usually apico-alveolar, but occasionally a laminal variant was heard; and once or twice a lengthened, quasi-syllabic variant appeared.

Although the statement of allophonic variation for the plosives above reflects the commonest situation, it was not unusual to hear the 'wrong' allophones on occasions; for instance, an initial [p, t, *or* k] or a final [ḅ, ḍ *or* ġ]. This latter was particularly common if the relevant plosive was not utterance final; e.g. [ġug nait] for *goodnight*. It is, however, quite certain that there was no controlled contrast between voiced and voiceless, aspirated or unaspirated until a much later stage (see p. 112 below).

Examples of all the consonant phonemes, followed by an illustrative word in phonetic and phonemic transcription, together with their adult equivalent in ordinary orthography, are given below:

|b|	[ˈḅe:bu]	|be:bu|	table
	[ḅʌp]	|bʌb|	bump
|d|	[ˈḍɛdi:]	|dɛdi:|	Daddy, teddy
	[a:t]	|a:d|	hard
|g|	[ġʌk]	|gʌg|	truck
	[ġip]	|gib|	crib
	[ġə:gən]	|gʌgən|	curtain
|m|	[mɔ:]	|mɔ:|	more
	[ġi:m]	|gi:m|	cream
|n|	[nu:]	|nu:|	nose
	[ġɔ:nə]	|gɔ:nə|	corner
	[ġin]	|gin|	skin
|ŋ|	[ŋeⁱk]	|ŋe:g|	snake
	[ġiŋiŋ]	|giŋiŋ|	singing
|w|	[ˈwinu:]	|winu:|	window
	[ˈġæwəwæn]		
	[ˈġæwəvæn]	|gɛwəwɛn|	caravan
|l|	[ˈlɔli:]	|lɔli:|	lorry
	[ɛlu:]	|ɛlu:|	hello

The vowel system at this stage was both more fluid and more complex, in that A appeared to control a greater number of contrasts than he did in the consonant system, but with a much greater degree of alternation and free variation. The system was as follows:

$$|i:\quad i\quad e:\quad ɛ\quad æ:\quad a:\quad ə:\quad ʌ\quad ɔ\quad o:\quad u\quad u:|$$

That is, we have close front and back vowels, which have both tense (i:, u:) and lax (i, u) congeners; half-close front and back tense vowels (e:, o:); half-open lax vowels (ɛ, ɔ, ʌ); and two tense open vowels (æ:, a:). There was also a schwa (ə) occurring in unstressed syllables only;

and two diphthongs (ai, au) and a partially controlled tense central vowel (ə:).

The relationship of these vowels to adult ESP is fairly straightforward. An enumeration of the correspondences exemplifying each of A's vowels follows:

|i:| corresponds to adult /i:/   [wi:t] = feet
|i| corresponds to adult /i/   [ġiŋ]   = ring
|e:| corresponds to adult /ei/ [ḍe:n] = rain

There was frequently a diphthongal offglide to this segment, thus: [eⁱ]; but the onset was consistently closer than ESP.

|ɛ| corresponds to adult /e/   [b̦ɛn] = pen
             /æ/   [mɛn] = man (*and* 'men')
             /ɛə/ [ḍɛ]   = chair
|æ:| corresponds to adult /aiə/ [wæ:] = fire

In my speech /aiə/ is frequently monophthongal.

|a:| corresponds to adult /a:/ [a:t]   = hard
|ə:| corresponds to adult /ə:/ [wə:gin] = working

It is hard to be certain whether |ə:| was distinct from |a:| on the one hand and |ʌ| on the other. Phonetically all occurred, but there was probably only a two-way contrast phonemically.

|ʌ| corresponds to adult /ʌ/   [b̦ʌt] = brush
|ɔ| corresponds to adult /ɔ/   [ġɔk]   = cloth

This was only intermittently distinct from |ʌ|.

|o:| corresponds to adult /ɔ:/ [mo:]   = more
             /oi/ [no:ni:] = noisy
|u| corresponds to adult /u/   [wut]   = foot
             [ḷ]   [b̦ɔgu] = bottle
|u:| corresponds to adult /u:/ [ġu:]   = screw
             /əu/ [u:p]   = soap *and* soup
|ai| corresponds to adult /ai/ [ḍait] = light
|au| corresponds to adult /au/ [ḍaun] = down

On occasions |ai| and |au| lost the offglide and fell together with |æ:|. There was one occurrence of [ɔi]: *boy* → [b̦ɔi], although elsewhere /oi/ was treated as |o:|, and later as a sequence |o: i:|. No examples of /iə/ or

/uə/ were recorded at this stage, but they too were later treated as either sequences:

> beard → b̥iːaːt
> ear → iːə

or were reduced to the first element:

> poor → b̥u (/puə/ in my speech).

With the exception of isolated comments of relevance to the consonantal system, I will have little more to say about A's vowels.

2.2.2 Informal statement of morpheme structure conditions. In addition to an inventory of segments, it is obviously also necessary to state the restrictions on the co-occurrence of these segments. In other words we want to know that |giːm| (*cream*) is a possible morpheme for A, whilst *|gliːm| is not; that |ŋ| can occur initially in A's speech even though it cannot in ESP, but that it only occurs word finally if the final syllable of the word is stressed, and so on. The following conditions list all such restrictions for which there is sufficient evidence to make fairly rigorous statements.

(1) All morphemes[1] are of the form:

$$(C) \ V \ (V) \ (C(V(C(V(C)))))$$

where C is a consonant and V is a vowel, and parentheses indicate optionality. That is, every morpheme must contain a vowel which may be preceded by at most one consonant, and may be followed by another vowel or an alternating sequence of consonants and vowels up to a maximum of three syllables. Thus we have:

V	ε	(hair)	CVCV	b̥ɔgu	(bottle)
CV	b̥uː	(blow)	CVCVC	b̥ɔdin	(bottom)
CVC	b̥aːt	(bath)	CVCVCV	b̥ʌdəwai	(butterfly)
VC	æt	(ant)	CVCVCVC	d̥εwiːbuːn	(telephone)

The optional vowel (V) is inserted for the sake of a mere two or three examples of the type: CVVCV [g̊ɔiːdoː] (corridor) – which was trisyllabic – but this possibility was not really established until a little later. In other words, we can say essentially that A's vocabulary contains words built on a strictly alternating sequence of consonants and vowels.

---

[1] As the vast majority of A's words are monomorphemic at this stage, and even where polymorphemic fail to give rise to exceptions to this canonical form, we could use *word* just as well here.

(2) Within a word all consonants must be |l| or none must be |l|. That is, we have a form of consonant harmony which allows such possibilities as:

lɔli:	(lorry)	lɔlə	(troddler)
ɛlu:	(hello)	ɔli:	(lolly)
læla:	(Lalla – a name)		

where all the consonants are |l|; but which excludes such possibilities as ESP |lait| (→ [ḍait]), /laik/ (→ [ġaik]), /bɔːl/ (→ [ḅoː]), etc.

(3) |w| and |l| may not occur word finally. That is, whereas the plosives and nasals are relatively unrestricted in their privileges of occurrence, the two continuants are restricted to initial and medial position. In the case of |w| this is a restriction parallel to one for /w/ in the adult language;[1] in the case of |l| it is a peculiarity of A's own system.

(4) Within a word an alveolar consonant may not precede a velar consonant. Given that we have no consonant clusters, 'precede' here means 'precede with an intervening vowel'. In other words, in a morpheme of the structure: $|C_1VC_2VC_3\ldots|$ C_1 cannot be an alveolar, |d, l, n| if C_2 is a velar, |g, ŋ|; C_2 cannot be an alveolar if C_3 is a velar, and so on. That is, we have examples such as:

ġɔk	(cock)	mik	(milk)
ḅɛk	(back)	wɔːk	(walk)
ŋeⁱk	(snake)		

but nothing like ESP:

/laik/ → ġaik
/dʌk/ → ġʌk
/nɛk/ → ŋɛk etc.

Examples of this constraint operating between C_2 and C_3 are limited (the number of polysyllabic items in A's vocabulary was not great), but a typical one is:

mu:gəga: (motor-car)

In fact the converse of this condition also operated if we exclude nasals from the account. That is, within a word a non-nasal alveolar consonant may not follow a velar consonant. Clearly, as we have already excluded

---

[1] But note that |w| is A's reflex of several other ESP consonants (e.g. some occurrences of /f/), so it cannot be assumed that the constraints will necessarily be the same. Cf. p. 107 below, where the constraint is in fact lifted.

|l| from cooccurring with any other consonant, we are really saying that |d| may not follow a velar. Accordingly we have:

ġɔ:nə   (corner)
ġin   (skin)

but nothing comparable to the adult /gud/ (→ [ġug]), /kə:tən/ (→ [ġə:gən]) /kəutʃ/ (→ [ġo:k]), etc.

There was one exception to this condition, namely:

ġi:di: (greedy)

It should, perhaps, be mentioned that at an earlier stage, the condition was more general, and prohibited alveolars from occurring with labials as well. See, for example, the somewhat conservative form:

b̥e:bu   (table)

and the free variation between [b̥ɔp] and [d̥ɔp] for *stop*.

(5) Within a word an alveolar nasal |n| may precede only other alveolar consonants; alternatively, it may not precede labials or velars. That is, we have such examples as:

nait   (nice)
nɔ:ni: (noisy)

but there is nothing comparable to the adult /naif/(→ [maip]), /sneik/ (→ [ŋeik]), /nipəl/ (→ [mibu]) and so on.

The converse of this condition does not apply. We do find examples such as:

mu:n   (moon)
winu: (window) etc.

(6) The velar nasal |ŋ| may precede only another velar segment |ŋ, g|. Thus we have:

ŋeik   (snake)
ŋʌŋgə   (nanga[1])

but nothing like: *[ŋe:p] or *[ŋu:t].

(7) Of the nasal consonants |m, n, ŋ| only the alveolar nasal |n| can occur in an unstressed syllable. The only exception to this is that a velar

---

[1] This example is taken from the next stage, and is A's attempt at an anglicised version of the Hindi [nəŋgə] – *naked*. It is included merely to indicate that the gap of |ŋ – ŋ| is fortuitous in a way that the gap |ŋ – m| is not fortuitous: viz. A knew no adult word of ESP of the form /n – ŋ/.

nasal |ŋ| may occur in this position provided that the preceding consonant is itself |ŋ|. Thus we have:

ġigən (kitchen)
ġiŋiŋ (singing)

but nothing comparable to the adult /bɔtəm/ (→ [b̥ɔdin]), /rʌniŋ/ (→ [d̥ʌnin]), /teikiŋ/ (→ [ġeigin]) and so on.

There are probably other conditions statable; this is certainly the case as regards vowels, for instance, but those above give a reasonably complete statement of the restrictions on A's idiolect.

With eight consonants, and taking the most common canonical forms, |CVC| and |CVCV| (accounting for 146 out of 225 words recorded vocabulary at this stage; i.e. 65 per cent) one should expect 128 ($= 8^2 \times 2$) consonantal combinations in a totally unconstrained system; whereas in fact we only get 49; while 58 are excluded and we have 21 random gaps.[1] Of these 49 combinations many occur more than once, either as homophones: thus [ġʌk] ($= |gʌg|$) means all of *duck, stuck, jug, rug, luck, truck*, etc. or with different vowels; e.g. both [wæwə] – *flower* and [wɔwo:] – *follow* are examples of |wVwV|. Table 1 displays all the recorded occurrences.

The vertical axis C_1 shows the initial consonant in |CVC(V)| structures. The horizontal axis C_2 shows the second consonant in |CVC(V)| structures. Each square is potentially divided into two triangles: the top left representing a |CVC| form, the bottom right a |CVCV| form. A tick, ✓, indicates that the relevant form occurs and is exemplified below; a number, 2, 3, 4, 5 or 6, indicates that the form does not occur and is excluded by the MS condition numbered; a gap indicates that the relevant form does not occur, but is not excluded by any MS condition, and is accordingly viewed as random.

Thus if we take the top row where the initial consonant (C_1) is |b|, we see that the forms: |bVb, bVbV, bVd, bVdV, bVg, bVgV, bVn and bVnV| all occur; that |bVm, bVmV, bVŋ, and bVŋV| are all random

---

[1] A gap is deemed 'random' and therefore not to be accounted for by MS conditions if it satisfies the following two criteria:

   (i) There was no realisation rule precluding its occurrence.
   (ii) The gap was filled at a subsequent stage, and at a stage still otherwise characterised by the same MS conditions; e.g. |b – ŋ| does not occur at stage 1, but at stage 2 [b̥æŋ] – *bang* appeared.

If we took merely |CVC| forms the number of gaps would decrease to only five. It should be noted incidentally, that all these conditions generalise to other canonical forms as well. The two types |CVC| and |CVCV| have only been taken for exemplificatory purposes and because they constitute the majority of examples.

TABLE I. *All recorded instances of consonantal combinations at stage 1*

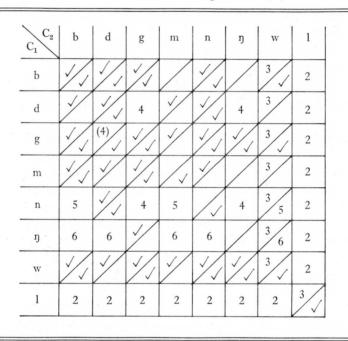

C₁ \ C₂	b	d	g	m	n	ŋ	w	l
b	✓ / ✓	✓ / ✓	✓ / ✓		✓ / ✓		3 / ✓	2
d	✓ /	✓ / ✓	4	✓ /	✓ / ✓	4	3 /	2
g	✓ / ✓	(4) / ✓	✓ / ✓	✓ / ✓	✓ / ✓	✓ / ✓	3 / ✓	2
m	✓ / ✓	✓ / ✓	✓ / ✓	✓ /	✓ /		3 /	2
n	5	✓ / ✓	4	5	✓ /	4	3 / 5	2
ŋ	6	6	✓ /	6	6		3 / 6	2
w	✓ / ✓	✓ / ✓	✓ / ✓	✓ / ✓	✓ / ✓	✓ / ✓	3 / ✓	2
l	2	2	2	2	2	2	2	3 / ✓

gaps; that |bVw| is excluded by MS3 whereas |bVwV| occurs, and that both |bVl| and |bVlV| are excluded by MS2.

Some possibilities: e.g. |ŋVl| would be excluded by several conditions (2, 3, 6), but only the most general is given. The parentheses around |gVd| and |gVdV| are to indicate that MS4 excludes both, but that |gVdV|, exceptionally, occurs.

All items occurring are exemplified below, working from left to right and top to bottom. The examples are given in phonetic transcription, so it must be remembered that the first item, for instance, while phonetically [bɔːp], is phonemically |bɔːb|. The list is exhaustive of the CVC(V) canonical forms found, but obviously not of the data as a whole. The totality of the data at stage 1 is reconstructible from Appendix C.

bɔːp	burp	bɛdə	better
beⁱbiː	baby	buk	book
baːt	bath	bugu:	broken

ḅə:n	burn	mait	mice
ḅa:nə	banana	mik	milk
(¹wi:bæwu:	wheel-barrow)¹	migə	mixer
ḍæp	stamp	mɔ:mə	lawn-mower
ḍə:t	shirt	mɛn	mend
ḍidə	scissors	nait	nice
ḍʌm	drum	nɔ:di:	naughty
ḍɔn	John	nɔ:ni:	noisy
(ḍʌnin	running)¹	ŋeⁱk	snake
ġip	crib	wɔp	shop
ġʌbə	cupboard	wi:bə	zebra
ġi:di:	greedy	wɔt	wash
ġɔk	cloth	wɔ:k	fork
ġa:gi:	glasses	(wə:gin	working)¹
ġi:m	cream	wum	room
ġi:n	clean	wʌn	one
ġɔ:nə	corner	winu:	window
ġʌŋ	tongue	wiŋ	swing
(ġiŋiŋ	singing)¹	wiŋə	finger
(¹ġæwəwæn	caravan)¹	wɔwu:	follow
maip	knife	lɔli:	lorry
mibu	nipple		

2.2.3 Formal statement of morpheme structure conditions. The foregoing characterisation of A's phonology at 2 years 60 days can be formalised along the following lines. The inventory of distinctive systematic phonemes, restricting ourselves to the consonants, can be expressed in the following matrix (table 2):[2]

TABLE 2. *Matrix of A's consonant phonemes at stage 1*

	b	d	g	m	n	ŋ	w	l
consonantal	+	+	+	+	+	+	+	+
syllabic	–	–	–	–	–	–	–	–
coronal	–	+	–	–	+	–	–	+
anterior	+	+	–	+	+	–	+	+
nasal	–	–	–	+	+	+	–	–
continuant	–	–	–	–	–	–	+	+

[1] Although CVCV items of the requisite shape did not occur at this stage, the examples given seem close enough to warrant their inclusion here.

[2] See Appendix B for a matrix characterisation of the adult consonant system.

Notes

(1) Following the suggestion in Chomsky and Halle, 1968 (p. 354), I use the major class features [consonantal] and [syllabic]; the feature [vocalic] is not used.[1] All consonants are $\begin{bmatrix} +\text{consonantal} \\ -\text{syllabic} \end{bmatrix}$; vowels are $\begin{bmatrix} -\text{consonantal} \\ +\text{syllabic} \end{bmatrix}$.

(2) Given the configuration $\begin{bmatrix} -\text{syllabic} \\ +\text{consonantal} \end{bmatrix}$, or even simply [−syllabic], it would of course be possible to characterise eight segments in terms of only three distinctive features. Four are used here to preserve congruity of specification with the adult system and a direct phonetic correlation of features at the phonemic and phonetic levels.

(3) |w| is characterised as [+consonantal] for three reasons:

(a) There is no evidence that A has more than a consonant/vowel distinction; and restricting his phoneme inventory to two classes simplifies the rules.

(b) |w| is in free variation and/or complementary distribution (see p. 37 above) with [v] and [β]. The choice of 'w' rather than 'v' as the relevant symbol was partly arbitrary, partly determined by the former's greater frequency of occurrence and the greater number of adult words with /w/ to which |w| corresponded. At a later stage (see p. 107 below) it will be seen further that [w] is in complementary distribution with [f], which is clearly [+consonantal].

(c) The realisation rules also require that |w| be [+consonantal] (see p. 59 below).

(4) |w| is characterised as [+anterior] (cf. Chomsky and Halle, 1968, p. 307) partly because it is here being used as a true consonant; partly because even when it is clearly a glide there is evidence from the realisation rules that /w/ must be characterised as [+anterior] (see R8, p. 26 above, and the treatment of *whistle* by, perhaps, R17, p. 19 above).

Although the vowel system is not the main focus of attention here (see 1.3.2 above), I provide in table 3 a characterisation of A's distinctive vowels at stage 1.

For comments on this system, see above, p. 39; and for the general problem of characterising vowel systems with more than three tongue heights in terms of binary features, see Smith, 1970–1.

[1] For some discussion of this usage, see 5.2.1.

TABLE 3. *Matrix of A's vowel phonemes at stage I*

	i:	i	e:	ε	æ:	a:	ə:	ʌ	ɔ	o:	u	u:
consonantal	−	−	−	−	−	−	−	−	−	−	−	−
syllabic	+	+	+	+	+	+	+	+	+	+	+	+
high	+	+	−	−	−	−	−	−	−	−	+	+
back	−	−	−	−	−	+	+	+	+	+	+	+
low	−	−	−	+	+	+	+	+	+	−	−	−
tense	+	−	+	−	+	+	+	−	−	+	−	+
round	−	−	−	−	−	−	+	−	+	+	+	+

The morpheme structure conditions given informally in 2.2.2 above are formalised here, preserving the same numbering as before; though it should be noted that these conditions are not themselves ordered. Conditions MS1 and MS2 are canonical or 'positive' conditions (see Stanley, 1967); MS3–MS7 are sequential; and conditions MS8–MS10, which have no equivalent above, are segmental; i.e. they merely specify redundancies in the matrix.

All morphemes must be of the form characterised by MS1 or MS2:

MS1   # ([−syllabic]) [+syllabic] ([+syllabic]) ([−syllabic]
                                   [+syllabic])* ([−syllabic]) #

or, equivalently,   # (C) V (V) (CV)* (C) #

where $C = \begin{bmatrix} -\text{syllabic} \\ +\text{consonantal} \end{bmatrix}$ and $V = \begin{bmatrix} +\text{syllabic} \\ -\text{consonantal} \end{bmatrix}$.

Note that these abbreviations differ from those in general use: specifically, C does not represent a disjunction. The star notation[1] – (CV)* – is used instead of the multiple parentheses of p. 40 above, as the former captures the notion 'indefinitely long sequence of alternating consonants and vowels' without having to specify the length of the longest word. In other words when A learns his first quadrisyllabic word the parentheses of p. 40 would have to be extended, whereas the star notation claims there is no change (beyond the addition of one item to the lexicon). The latter seems intuitively correct.

$$\text{MS2} \quad \# \left(\begin{bmatrix} +\text{consonantal} \\ \alpha\text{coronal} \\ \beta\text{continuant} \end{bmatrix} \right) V \begin{bmatrix} +\text{consonantal} \\ \gamma\text{coronal} \\ \delta\text{continuant} \end{bmatrix} V \ldots \#$$

where either: $\alpha = \beta = \gamma = \delta$
        or: $(\alpha \neq \beta)$ *and* $(\gamma \neq \delta)$

[1] See Chomsky and Halle, 1968, p. 344.

This condition says that either all the Greek variables must agree, or that the specification for both the initial and medial consonants must be different for these features. This is clearly a highly inelegant formulation, but if we abide by Stanley's well-motivated requirement that 'in the theory of MS conditions we *require* that positive conditions be used in stating restrictions on syllable structure' (1967, p. 432); if, in other words, we do not have recourse to the use of directionality in the statement of the conditioning of this harmony, then there is no immediately obvious alternative. Even if we reverted to the former characterisation of '1' as $\begin{bmatrix} +\text{vocalic} \\ +\text{consonantal} \end{bmatrix}$, there is still the problem that a natural class $\begin{bmatrix} \alpha\text{vocalic} \\ \alpha\text{consonantal} \end{bmatrix}$ would incorrectly predict that glides should behave the same way. In fact the problem will arise whenever we have a constraint on a single element (here '1'), where this element is specified by two or more features, so we cannot solve the problem by keeping |w| as [−consonantal], as we should still need to specify the segment as [+sonorant] or [−nasal] as well.

There are two ways round the impasse. One is to treat this kind of consonant harmony as Lightner (1965) suggests, by means of a lexical feature (his 'abstract morpheme marker') [LIQUID] for instance, and then have a rule:

$$[+\text{consonantal}] \rightarrow \begin{bmatrix} +\text{coronal} \\ +\text{continuant} \end{bmatrix} / [\overline{+\text{LIQUID}}]$$

But, in addition to the unfortunate fact that Lightner's convention would associate [LIQUID] with vowels as well as consonants, we still need a further disjunctive sub-part to the rule:

$$[+\text{consonantal}] \rightarrow \left\{ \begin{matrix} [-\text{coronal}] \\ [-\text{continuant}] \end{matrix} \right\} / [\overline{-\text{LIQUID}}]$$

which seems quite wrong.[1] The other, preferred, alternative is to lift the restriction that MS conditions must be stated in terms of those features which are systematically utilised in lexical representations, and use *phonetic* features.[2] Thus in the present case, we could use the phonetic

---

[1] This would be equivalent to the older: $[+\text{segment}] \rightarrow \left\{ \begin{matrix} [-\text{vocalic}] \\ [-\text{consonantal}] \end{matrix} \right\}$ i.e. specifying the unnatural class of consonants, glides and vowels; and just as suspect as the disjunction usually abbreviated as 'C'.

[2] As far as I know, this constraint has not been made explicitly in the literature. However, it seems well-motivated on general grounds, and appears to correspond to accepted practice.

feature [lateral], which is totally redundant at the systematic phonemic level, but must be specified somewhere to provide the correct phonetic output,[1] and then reformulate MS2 as:

MS2′ $\#\left(\begin{bmatrix}+\text{consonantal}\\ \alpha\text{lateral}\end{bmatrix}\right)\text{V}\begin{bmatrix}+\text{consonantal}\\ \alpha\text{lateral}\end{bmatrix}\text{V}...\#$

MS3 $\text{C}\rightarrow[-\text{continuant}]/\underline{\quad}\#$

MS4 $\text{C}\rightarrow[-\text{coronal}]/\underline{\quad}\text{V}\begin{bmatrix}-\text{coronal}\\ -\text{anterior}\end{bmatrix}$

MS4a $\text{C}\rightarrow[-\text{coronal}]/\begin{bmatrix}-\text{coronal}\\ -\text{anterior}\end{bmatrix}\text{V}\overline{[-\text{nasal}]}$

(See the discussion of MS4 on pp. 41–2 above)

MS5 $\text{C}\rightarrow[-\text{coronal}]/\overline{[+\text{nasal}]}\text{V}[-\text{coronal}]$

MS6 $\text{C}\rightarrow[+\text{anterior}]/\overline{[+\text{nasal}]}\text{V}[+\text{anterior}]$

Note that these last two conditions, both of which clearly describe different manifestations of consonant harmony involving nasal consonants, and which are superficially very similar, are not collapsible beyond the trivial generalisation captured by:

$$\begin{bmatrix}+\text{consonantal}\\ +\text{nasal}\end{bmatrix}\rightarrow\begin{Bmatrix}[-\text{coronal}]/\underline{\quad}[-\text{coronal}]\\ [+\text{anterior}]/\underline{\quad}[+\text{anterior}]\end{Bmatrix}$$

MS7 $[+\text{nasal}]\rightarrow\begin{bmatrix}+\text{coronal}\\ +\text{anterior}\end{bmatrix}/\text{X}\begin{bmatrix}+\text{syllabic}\\ -\text{stress}\end{bmatrix}\underline{\quad}$

Where $\text{X}\neq|\eta|$.

If we wished to avoid the verbal condition X could be characterised by the triple disjunction:

$$\begin{Bmatrix}[-\text{nasal}]\\ [+\text{coronal}]\\ [+\text{anterior}]\end{Bmatrix}$$

---

[1] If A is really operating the adult system (see chapter 4, *passim*), this objection would disappear; but in this section I am assuming that the child is operating an independent system.

It is worth noting that while the presence of the phonetic feature [lateral] allows us to sidestep the problem of formalising the sentence 'within a word all consonants must be |l| or none must'; if the consonant harmony had operated on a segment which did not have such a simple, unitary phonetic specification we should still have faced the same problem. Presumably it is no more likely that a grammar should contain MS2 than that it should contain the same condition with 'r' substituted for 'l'. In this case, short of making up some *ad hoc* phonetic (or diacritic) feature characterising 'r', there is no satisfactory way of stating the restriction.

It should be noted that all of MS 2, 4, 5, 6, 7 impose harmonic constraints of some kind or other on A's language. For some discussion of consonant harmony in general, see 4.3.1.

MS8 [+ coronal] → [+ anterior]
MS9 [+ nasal] → [− continuant]
MS10 [+ continuant] → [+ anterior]

These last three segmental conditions exclude the eight non-occurring but logically possible combinations of the four features [coronal, anterior, nasal, continuant] used to specify A's systematic phonemic segments. MS9 should perhaps be excluded as it obtains by definition (see Chomsky and Halle, 1968, p. 317) and is therefore universal; but the other two, MS8 and MS10, represent specific constraints on A's system. Accordingly, we shall see that MS8 and MS10 change through time, whilst MS9 does not.[1]

2.2.4 Phonetic rules of A's system. Finally, we need to specify the phonetic output of A's phonology by means of a set of phonetic rules, which operate on the phonemic representations generated by the MS conditions or, equivalently, by the realisation rules. It is not intended to give a 'conventional' (but as yet unexemplified!) set of *n*-ary specifications of the features used; rather, a finer phonetic specification in terms of other features will be added to the segments defined phonologically.[2] Moreover, even these rules are intended to be illustrative rather than exhaustive.

$$\text{Ph}_1 \left\{ \begin{array}{l} [+\text{continuant}] \\ [+\text{nasal}] \end{array} \right\} \rightarrow [+\text{voiced}]$$

That is, sonorants are always voiced in all positions.

---

[1] Except, that is, that features may be added to the right-hand side of MS9. See p. 113 below, where MS9′ is:

$$[+\text{nasal}] \rightarrow \begin{bmatrix} -\text{continuant} \\ +\text{voice} \end{bmatrix}.$$

[2] The real problem at issue, as in the difficulty with formulating MS2 above, is the relationship between the set of phonological features and the set of phonetic features; and within this problem, the further one of which set of features the MS conditions should range over. At first sight it might seem obvious that all features relevant, phonologically or phonetically, should be included in the 'segment structure' rules of the language being described; but this would have the unfortunate result – to take a very simple example – of rules having the exactly opposite effect of each other. Thus phonologically all segments in A's system are [+ voiced], but some of them are phonetically [− voiced], i.e. we have one condition [+ segment] → [+ voiced], and a later rule [+ segment$_i$] → [− voiced].... This is avoided if [voiced] is not specified at all until we reach the phonetic rules.

$$\text{Ph2} \begin{bmatrix} -\text{continuant} \\ -\text{nasal} \end{bmatrix} \rightarrow \begin{Bmatrix} \begin{bmatrix} -\text{voiced} \\ +\text{HSP}^1 \end{bmatrix} /\underline{\quad}\# \\ \begin{bmatrix} -\text{voiced} \\ -\text{HSP} \end{bmatrix} /\#\underline{\quad} \\ \begin{bmatrix} +\text{voiced} \\ -\text{HSP} \end{bmatrix} \end{Bmatrix}$$

This accounts for the plosive allophones discussed on p. 37.

$$\text{Ph3} \begin{bmatrix} +\text{continuant} \\ +\text{coronal} \end{bmatrix} \rightarrow [+\text{lateral}]$$

$$\text{Ph4} \begin{bmatrix} +\text{continuant} \\ -\text{coronal} \end{bmatrix} \rightarrow \begin{Bmatrix} [-\text{consonantal}] \\ \begin{bmatrix} +\text{delayed release} \\ -\text{distributed} \\ -\text{sonorant} \end{bmatrix} \end{Bmatrix}$$

This accounts for the allophones of |w| discussed on p. 37.

---

[1] Heightened sub-glottal pressure.

3 *Longitudinal analysis of A's phonology*

After the initial analysis of A's speech at 2 years, as presented in chapter 2, further data were collected and analysed regularly until the child was 4. These data were then analysed as changes in the sets of rules characterised above: the conditions and rules of his own system becoming, in general, more complex; the set of realisation rules becoming in general more simple. The development was cut up into a sequence of some 29 stages, delimited – somewhat arbitrarily – on the basis of whether there was any interesting change between two times. Thus, when A's phonological development was in a state of flux a 'stage' might correspond to a few days or even less; when he was relatively stable a 'stage' might correspond to a few months (this was especially the case near the end of his acquisition). A table of stage/age correlations is given as Appendix A, p. 208. Although it is probably impossible to record every change in a child's developing speech, I think it is safe to say that I have missed no major changes in the period under review, within the limitations of the study as set out on pp. 10–11 above.

As it would be extremely repetitive to present the totality of all rules for all stages, the majority of rules being stable between any two successive stages, in the case of the realisation rules (3.1) I have dealt with the changes piecemeal taking one rule at a time and tracing its development until either it disappeared or stabilised in the adult form. However, as this gives an undesirably atomistic impression of the child's development, I have made cross-references to other rules or conditions with which the one under discussion interacted, and occasionally two or more rules have been discussed simultaneously. Most importantly I have included table 4 (p. 102) presenting all changes at all stages, so that the total set of rules for any particular stage can be reconstructed quickly and easily by the reader. In the case of the development of the child's phonology as a self-contained system (3.2), I have proceeded by stages, listing the changes at each stage and periodically recapitulating the total set of Morpheme Structure Conditions for a given stage. A second chart of changes is given as table 11 (p. 131).

3.1 Longitudinal analysis of A's phonology as a mapping from ESP

Rule R1 deleting nasals before voiceless consonants (pp. 13, 22) persisted unchanged until stage 11 when it became optional.[1] At this time some words (the minority) retained the nasal:

bent → b̭ɛnt

mantelpiece → mæŋkəlb̭i:t

the majority still lost the nasal:

pencil → b̭ɛtəl

think → ġik

and a few occurred with or without the nasal:

something → wʌpin *or* wʌmpin

panther → b̭ædə *or* b̭ændə etc.

The rule remained optional until stage 13 when it disappeared, i.e. all adult nasals were retained correctly.

The loss of rule R1 had no effect on the other realisation rules, as the only one which would have been 'fed' by the disappearance of R1 had itself been lost earlier (see rule R21 below). One effect of the loss of rule R1 was to *simplify* the morpheme structure conditions. Specifically, when a voicing contrast first appeared in A's speech (at stage 7; see below pp. 112f.) a constraint had to be added to his grammar that nasal plus consonant clusters were always voiced throughout. With the appearance of nasals before voiceless consonants, this constraint was now dropped (see MS13, p. 116).

Rule R2, deleting voiced consonants after nasals (pp. 14, 22), was complicated to apply only in final position at stage 2:

$$2' \quad [+\text{cons}] \rightarrow \emptyset/[+\text{nasal}] \; \overline{[+\text{voice}]} \; \#$$

so that we had:

angry → æŋgi:

number → nʌmdə (*sic*; see below and p. 106) etc.

but orange → ɔin

band → b̭æn

---

[1] At this stage the rule is characterised as (1′):

$$[+\text{nasal}] \overset{\text{opt}}{\rightarrow} \emptyset/ \text{——} [-\text{voice}]$$

See the abbreviatory devices on p. viii, and table 4, p. 102.

Within the period of stage 2, R2′ itself became optional, giving free variants of the kind:

 friend → wɛn/wɛnd

and by stage 3 rule R2 had disappeared.

 The change in rule R2 at stage 2 led to complications in the statement of R3 at the same stage (for discussion, see rule R3 below) and the addition of a further rule (R27) at the end of the realisation rules (below). The immediate major effect of rule R2's optionality, and subsequent disappearance, was to make more complex MS1 (p. 104) to enable it to account for consonant clusters. In other words this was the cause of the first deviation in A's speech from a completely regular CVCV... format.

 Once nasal plus consonant clusters had appeared, of course, it was also necessary to state restrictions on them in the morpheme structure conditions (see p. 106, MS 11, 12, 13), of which the last, representing a divergence from ESP, parallels the new realisation rule R27:

$$[+\text{cons}] \rightarrow [+\text{coronal}] / \begin{bmatrix} +\text{anterior} \\ +\text{nasal} \end{bmatrix} \underline{\quad}$$

accounting for the unexpected cluster |md| in addition to |nd| and |ŋg| (for discussion, see pp. 106–7).

Rule R3, velarising alveolar stops before /l/ (pp. 14, 23), persisted in some form or other for the duration of the study, still being optional at age 4. The first change, at stage 2, was necessitated entirely by the optionality of rule R2.[1] Once R2 has become optional or disappeared, the input to R3 must be extended to include nasal clusters. That is, where before we had:

 pedal → b̩ɛgu
 handle → ɛŋu

we now have:

 handle → æŋgu

If R3 were left unchanged it would only produce [æŋgu] and we would need another rule to effect the natural homorganicity of [ŋg].[2]

---

 [1] I.e. the change in R3 is an artifact of the rule system being used; but I see no way of avoiding the problem.

 [2] That homorganicity is not always natural for A, and that therefore we cannot use marking conventions here, is shown by R27 and MS13 (see below, p. 106, and on marking conventions, p. 199).

Rather than insert an *ad hoc* assimilation rule, I accordingly complicate R3 to become the transformational rule:

$$3' \left(\begin{bmatrix} +\text{cor} \\ +\text{nas} \end{bmatrix}\right) \begin{bmatrix} +\text{cor} \\ -\text{del rel} \end{bmatrix} \rightarrow \left(\begin{bmatrix} -\text{cor} \\ -\text{ant} \end{bmatrix}\right) \begin{bmatrix} -\text{cor} \\ -\text{ant} \end{bmatrix} / \underline{\hspace{1cm}} \left(\begin{bmatrix} +\text{syll} \\ -\text{stress} \end{bmatrix}\right) [+\text{lat}]$$
$$\hspace{2cm} \text{\small I} \hspace{1.5cm} \text{\small 2} \hspace{2cm} \text{\small I} \hspace{1.5cm} \text{\small 2}$$

R3' remained constant until stage 14 when it underwent what was probably not an actual change, but a modification necessitated by new data. The crucial example was *pistol* which did not exhibit velarisation but regularly became [pitəl] (contrast *spittle* → [pikəl]). That is, although /sC/ clusters were reduced to |C| in general, in this environment they functioned like /s/ and not like /t/. (This was, in fact, generally the case with /st/ clusters – see the discussion on the development of |s| below, p. 60.) Accordingly rule R3 must be further complicated as follows:

$$3'' \left(\begin{bmatrix} +\text{cor} \\ +\text{nas} \end{bmatrix}\right) \begin{bmatrix} +\text{cor} \\ -\text{del rel} \end{bmatrix} \rightarrow \left(\begin{bmatrix} -\text{cor} \\ -\text{ant} \end{bmatrix}\right) \begin{bmatrix} -\text{cor} \\ -\text{ant} \end{bmatrix} / X \underline{\hspace{1cm}} \left(\begin{bmatrix} +\text{syll} \\ -\text{stress} \end{bmatrix}\right) [+\text{lat}]$$
$$\hspace{2cm} \text{\small I} \hspace{1.5cm} \text{\small 2} \hspace{2cm} \text{\small I} \hspace{1.5cm} \text{\small 2}$$

Condition: X ≠ /s/

This clearly misses the observation that clusters containing a continuant segment function like a continuant but there is no *non ad hoc* way of characterising this statement in the present theory.

The only other change in R3 was that it became optional at stage 29, giving us:

bottle → bɔkəl/bɔtəl

and disappeared shortly thereafter.[1]

It is noteworthy that the presence or absence of R3 made no difference to the Morpheme Structure Conditions in the early stages, as although /d, t, n/ before /l/ were velarised to |g, k, ŋ|,[2] ESP /s, z/ etc. were all neutralised as |(t) d| in all positions; thus while:

puddle → pʌgəl
puzzle → pʌdəl

It was only later, when /s, z/ were established as distinctive for A's own system (stage 21) that a real gap appeared – viz. *puddle* still became [pʌgəl]; *puzzle* now became [pʌzəl] and no adult form could appear as [pʌdəl], a sound sequence A was then apparently unable to produce! (On 'puzzles' of this kind, see chapter 4, p. 149.)

[1] I.e. soon after A's fourth birthday, the arbitrary end-point of this study.
[2] To |g, ŋ| only, before the voicing contrast was established.

Rule R4, converting /ə/ to |u| before a (dark) /l/ (pp. 24–5), gave forms such as:

   handle → æŋgu[1]

At stage 10 this rule became optional giving such pairs as

   circle → ġə:ġə *or* ġə:ġu

before disappearing by stage 12.

   (There was one exceptional occurrence of an item at stage 5, where rule R4 appears to be optional:

   pencil → bɛḍu *or* bɛtəl)

Rule R5, nasalising a continuant consonant after a nasal in the same syllable (pp. 15, 25), had apparently disappeared by stage 2, but as it was of such marginal status originally (see p. 15) it is hard to be sure if the forms occurring at stage 1 were not just remnants.

Rule 6, deleting /l/ finally and pre-consonantally (pp. 15, 25), underwent a variety of changes. At stage 3, /l/ vocalised to |u| after front vowels, optionally before consonants, obligatorily finally, and was deleted elsewhere:

   bell → bɛu
   elbow → ɛbo *or* ɛubo

but *ball* was still [bɔ:]. To account for this, R6 is split into two parts:

$$\text{R6(i)} \quad [+\text{lat}] \xrightarrow{<\text{opt}>} \text{u}/ \begin{bmatrix} -\text{back} \\ +\text{syll} \end{bmatrix} ---- \begin{Bmatrix} \# \\ \langle[+\text{cons}]\rangle \end{Bmatrix}$$

$$\text{R6(ii)} \quad [+\text{lat}] ---\to \emptyset/ ---- \begin{Bmatrix} \# \\ [+\text{cons}] \end{Bmatrix}$$

The division into two parts is necessitated by the optionality of (i) as opposed to the obligatoriness of (ii); and by the fact that the environment of (ii) is not simply 'elsewhere' but a sub-part of the environment of (i). However, the separation of R6(i) and R6(ii) is cast in doubt by their later development. At stage 5, R6(ii) in turn becomes optional, giving us:

   all → ɔ:l *but* ball → bɔ:
   hold → u:d *but* shoulder → ḍu:ldə

That R6(i) remains as it was is demonstrated by:

   spill → bɪu *beside* Gilbert → ġi:bət

---

[1] The |l| has been deleted by rule R6.

The further development of rule R6 is obscured by the appearance from around stage 6 of a rule of metathesis,[1] serving to eliminate clusters of /l/ followed by a labial (the rule was later generalised to all non-coronals). This rule will be formalised below (p. 101); for the moment it is sufficient to draw attention to the possibility that examples such as:

    shelf → wɛp
    silver → wivə

and the contrast

    wheel → wi:u
    wheelbarrow → wi:bæu

may be due at least in part to the *quality* of the consonant following the /l/ and not merely to the fact that it is a consonant. Moreover, there was the further difficulty at stage 6 that R6(ii) reverted to being obligatory, i.e. final l's disappeared again.

e.g. girl → gol at stage 5
but girl → gəu at stage 6 and 7.

It was not until stage 8 that |l| again appeared with any frequency and then at stage 9 rule R6 disappeared. Even then it should be noted that although |l| appears regularly in final and preconsonantal position, there were no occurrences before labials:

    hole → o:l
    hold → o:ld
    felt → wɛlt

but: self → lɛf
    elf → ɛf
    bulb → ḅʌbl (monosyllabic – taken from stage 17) etc.

It is important to note that R6 disappeared *before* rule R4 became optional. Hence for *handle*, for instance, we had forms such as:

    æŋgu (R4 and R6 operate)
    æŋgul (R4 operates – R6 does not)
    æŋgəl (neither R4 nor R6 operates – after stage 10)

but we never find *[æŋgə] which would have necessitated R6 operating without R4.

The changes in R6 also affected the Morpheme Structure Conditions

[1] The crucial data were so few, and there were so many alternative possibilities that it was not until stage 10 that the metathesis rule could be unambiguously stated; by which time rule R6 had disappeared (see below, pp. 98 ff.).

of A's own system – specifically MS3, accounting for the possibilities of final continuants (p. 111).

Rule R7, deleting /s/ preconsonantally (pp. 15, 25), interacted closely with several other rules. At stage 13, after a number of changes, rule R25 (p. 31 above and p. 96 below) finally disappeared, with the result that there was now a voicing contrast in initial position – e.g. *pin* and *bin*, hitherto both [b̥in], were now differentiated as in the adult language. Moreover, those plosives which in A's speech were in initial position by virtue of the operation of rule R7 were also realised as voiceless. That is, for A not only had *pin* and *bin* been neutralised as [b̥in] but so had *spin*; and now that a voicing distinction was made the post-/s/ plosive was equated with the voiceless rather than the voiced member of the pair [p, b]. This necessitates the insertion of a new realisation rule before rule 7, making plosives voiceless after adult /s/. Thus the new rule R6A would be:

$$6A \quad \begin{bmatrix} C \\ -son \end{bmatrix} \rightarrow [-voiced]/\#/s/\text{------}$$

Then *spin* becomes [sp^{h}in] by rule 6A and [p^{h}in] by rule 7,[1] giving us the mapping:

$$\begin{matrix} /pin/ \\ /spin/ \end{matrix} \Big\rangle |pin|$$

$$/bin/\text{------}\rightarrow|bin|$$

At stage 15 the new rule 6A itself changed. At first sight this appeared to be a generalisation to all consonants, giving rise to a series of voiceless sonorants |ɬ, m̥, n̥, w̥|, but adult /j/ was still excluded from the rule. That is, we have:[2]

sleep → ɬi:p	slug → ɬʌg
slide → ɬaɪd	Smith → m̥ɪt

---

[1] I am using a superscript ^{h} to indicate – *ad hoc* – that the [p] is voiceless. It might be argued that the second segment in *spin* is already voiceless and that therefore R6A is redundant. However, it would appear that in the adult language post-/s/ consonants are not specified for voicing (as there is no contrast; see the discussion of Twaddell, 1935, about whether *spin* was to be analysed as /sp/ or /sb/). Moreover, the formulation of R6A here is justified by its subsequent development – see below.

[2] The appearance of such 'voiceless sonorant' segments appears to be very common in children's speech. I have noted it both in various English children, and comparable examples in a German child C (aged 2½):

> e.g. schlafen → ɬa:fən
> cf. lachen → la:kən
> and Schmetterling → m̥ɛtəlɪŋ *or* mɛtəlɪ̥ŋ

the last presumably by metathesis.

snail → n̥eɪl   sweeping → w̥iːpin
sneeze → n̥iːd   sweet → w̥iːt etc., etc.
smoke → m̥oːk

but suit → tʰuːt not *[juːt] or *[ɹuːt]

(initial /j/ was replaced by either |j| or |r| at this stage, e.g. *yet* → jɛt/ɹɛt).
Accordingly R6A is replaced by R6A′ with the unpleasant disjunction:

$$
6A' \quad \left\{ \begin{array}{l} [+\text{cons}] \\[2pt] \begin{bmatrix} -\text{cons} \\ -\text{syll} \\ -\text{cor} \end{bmatrix} \end{array} \right\} \rightarrow [-\text{voiced}]/\#/s/\text{\textemdash}
$$

For a few hours only, there appeared to be a three-way contrast for A
among [w w̥ and f]:

with → wid
switch → w̥it
fish → fit

but almost immediately |w̥| fell together with |f| giving

switch
fish ⟩ fit

It is difficult to state precisely which contrasts were controlled and which
were not at this point, as the contrast |f/w| itself was still unstable within
A's system, and giving rise to considerable free variation:

find → faɪnd/waɪnd/ɣaɪnd
foot → fut/ɸut
fork → fɔːk/wɔːk[1]

It may in fact be the case that the |f/w| contrast, which began very ten-
tatively at stage 13, was itself the slightly delayed result of the loss of
rule 25 – i.e. the rule which gave an initial voicing contrast (see above)
to the other segments. It should be noted that apart from one or two
absolute exceptions (see p. 151) there is no |v/w| contrast initially for A
either.

   To account for the falling together of |f| and |w̥| and still exclude /j/
from the domain of the rule we can split R6A′ into two parts: R6A(i)
and R6A(ii). The first part makes /w/ consonantal after /s/ but leaves /j/
unaffected; the second then captures the basic generalisation that all
[+cons] segments are devoiced.

---

[1] /w/ was always realised as |w| – never as |f|.

6A(i) $\begin{bmatrix} -\text{syll} \\ -\text{cons} \\ -\text{cor} \end{bmatrix} \rightarrow [+\text{cons}]/\#/\text{s}/\text{——}$

6A(ii) $[+\text{cons}] \rightarrow [-\text{voiced}]/\#/\text{s}/\text{——}$

It may well be that R6A(i) should be generalised to prevocalic position, thus accounting for the lack of contrast between /v/ and /w/; and that we only need to exclude /j/.

The next change to affect rule R7 is a change to rule R24, or at least one associated with rule R24 – i.e. the rule which neutralises distinctions between adult stridents and non-stridents, affricates and non-affricates (see above, pp. 21, 30, and below, pp. 92 ff.). Sporadically at stage 19, and consistently at stage 20, there appeared affricates |tˢ| and |dᶻ| in A's system, as the reflexes of the adult segments /s, θ, ʃ, tʃ/ and /dʒ/ respectively,[1] and also as the reflex of the adult sequence /st/ (see the discussion of R3 on p. 24 above).

chain → tˢeɪn   jammed → dᶻæmd
chalk → tˢɔ:k   gently → dᶻɛŋkli:
say → tˢeɪ
same → tˢeɪm
shake → tˢeɪk
shut → tˢʌt
thing → tˢiŋ
thumb → tˢʌm

and also: start → tˢa:t
sticky → tˢiki:
study → tˢʌdi: etc.[2]

---

[1] /j, z, r/ → |r| initially; /ð/ → |d| initially – see below, p. 79.

[2] In fact, all of these were at first in free variation with |t| or |d| but, as all adult segments behaved alike, this is irrelevant. (For further details see the vocabulary in Appendix C.) This treatment of adult /s/ is not completely idiosyncratic to A. For instance his cousin, R, who realised /s/ as [θ]:

see-saw → θi:θɔ :
slide → θlaɪd
spider → θpaɪdə

but had /t/ correctly as [t]:

tea → ti:
it's → itθ

realised /st/ as [θ]:

stick → θik
stink → θiŋk
stones → θəunð etc. (data recorded at 3 years 2 months

cf.   spanner → pʰænə
            scrape → kɹeɪp
            smack → m̥æk etc.

We could account (albeit *ad-hocly*) for this behaviour of /st/ clusters if we complicated rule R7 to R7′ as follows:

$$7' \quad /s/ \rightarrow \emptyset/\text{——}\left\{\begin{matrix}[-\text{cor}]\\ [+\text{son}]\end{matrix}\right\}$$

i.e. /s/ is deleted before non-coronals – e.g. /p, k/ – and before sonorants – e.g. /n, l/ – but is retained elsewhere – i.e. before /t/. Rule R24 would then convert the sequence /st/ to |tˢt| and a further rule necessary anyway, would delete the |t|. Alternatively we could simply insert a rule deleting /t/ after /s/ and order it before R7. This would be further motivated at stage 21 by the treatment of /str/ and /θr/ clusters which lost the /r/, as opposed to /tr/ clusters which retain it; i.e. the rule subsequently deleting /r/ will then be simpler.

strawberry → tˢɔːbəɹiː: three → siː:
stroller → səulə   throw → səu
strong → s̥oŋ   etc.[1]

but tree → tɹiː:
     trousers → tˡɑuzə   etc.

Accordingly, let us retain R7 unchanged and insert R6B before it:

$$6B \quad \begin{bmatrix} +\text{cor} \\ +\text{ant} \\ -\text{cont} \\ -\text{nasal} \end{bmatrix} \rightarrow \emptyset/\#/s/\text{——} \quad \text{(i.e. /t/ is deleted after /s/)}$$

At stage 23 appear the first |s| plus consonant clusters derivative from an underlying /s/,[2] specifically |sl| in free variation with |ɬ|:

---

[1] By stage 21, |tˢ| has been largely replaced by |s| – see below p. 124.

[2] At stage 22 there appeared the first clusters consisting of |s| plus |r|, but these were not reflexes of an adult /s/ but rather either /ʃ/ or /θ/. Thus we have:

           thread → srɛd
           shreddies → srɛdiz

The appearance of |sr| clusters in the child's speech is a clear counter-instance to Fry's claim that: 'While the child will often use analogy in forming grammatical sequences that are not permitted in the adult language, he will not form phoneme sequences that go against the prohibitions of the system and then later have to discard them; he simply does not utter such sequences' (1966, pp. 196–7).

slicer → ɬaisə *or* slaisə
slipper → ɬipə *or* slipə
slowly → ɬəuli: *or* sləuli: etc.[1]

This can be accounted for by changing both R6A(ii) and R7 as follows:

6A(ii)′ $[+\text{cons}] \xrightarrow[<\text{opt}>]{} [-\text{voiced}]//s/\langle\overline{[+\text{lat}]}\rangle$

7′ $/s/ \rightarrow \emptyset/\!\!-\!\!-\!\!\begin{bmatrix} +\text{cons} \\ -\text{voiced} \end{bmatrix}$

that is, /l/ is devoiced optionally after /s/, and if it is devoiced the /s/ must be deleted: if it is not devoiced then /s/ is not deleted. Note that R6B is unchanged and still ordered before R7.

At stage 24 the free variation between |sl| and |ɬ| has been replaced by the exclusive appearance of |sl|. That is, R6A(ii)′ has been changed to:

6A(ii)″ $[+\text{cons}] \rightarrow [-\text{voiced}]/\#/s/\overline{[-\text{lat}]}$

(Incidentally we now also have |sr| clusters from adult /str/ as well as adult /ʃr/ and /θr/ as the result of changes in R6B; see below p. 63.) At stage 25 further |s| plus consonant clusters appeared in the following order:

(1) |sn| e.g. snail → sneɪl *cf. earlier* n̥eɪl
            snap → snæp *cf. earlier* n̥æp

(2) |sw| e.g. sweep → fi:p *and then* swi:p
            sweet → fi:t *and then* swi:t[2]

(3) |sm| e.g. smell → m̥ɛl *and then* smɛl
            Smith → m̥is *and then* smis

(4) |sp| and |sk(r)| e.g. spill → pil *and then* spil
            skipping rope → kipin — *and then* skipin ɹəup *etc.*

Eventually, it seems that we have the operation of two processes: first, the extension of |s| plus consonant clusters to all the sonorants – conflating (1), (2), (3) above – i.e. we have reverted to the original form of

[1] When asked to attempt other s+C clusters, A's response was to produce [s:] followed by his usual form, e.g.:
NVS Say 'smoke'
A [s: – m̥əuk].
[2] *Swimming-pool* occurred in the two forms [sfimin pu:l] and [swimin pu:l] – the first being a kind of intermediate stage between [fimin] and [swimin]. This was not general.

R6A (p. 58 above), and R6B and R7′ are unchanged: viz. halfway through this stage we have:

6A $\begin{bmatrix} +\text{cons} \\ -\text{son} \end{bmatrix} \rightarrow [-\text{voiced}]/\#/s/\text{——}$

6B $/t/ \rightarrow \emptyset//s/\text{——}$

7′ $/s/ \rightarrow \emptyset/\text{——}[-\text{voiced}]$

and second, we have the elimination of R7′ but with R6A and R6B still present:

6A $\begin{bmatrix} +\text{cons} \\ -\text{son} \end{bmatrix} \rightarrow [-\text{voiced}]/\#/s/\text{——}$ (unchanged)

6B $/t/ \rightarrow \emptyset//s/\text{——}$ (unchanged)

7 GONE

Then at stage 26 R6B is eliminated and we have |st(r)| clusters as well:

strawberry → stɹɔːbɹiː etc.

The continued existence of R6A is moot: it no longer serves any purpose, and is presumably made redundant by modifications to A's Morpheme Structure Conditions.

The only /s/ cluster still not occurring in A's speech was /sj/ which was realised as |s| – i.e. in common with all /Cj/ clusters, the /j/ simply disappeared until stage 29:

suit → suːt

cf. new → nuː etc.

This is simply accounted for, as R7 deleted /s/ preconsonantally – and /j/ is not a consonant (unlike /w/ which becomes consonantal by 6A(i)) – so we should not expect /sj/ to become anything but |s|, by rule 16 (below p. 73). The only complication is that /t+j/ clusters also get realised as |s| for a while – i.e. once again a cluster containing a continuant is treated like a continuant (cf. /st/, p. 60 above):

tune → suːn (*or* tuːn)

In summary then, the treatment of /s + C/ clusters was as follows:

(1) All preconsonantal /s/'s disappeared

(2) All preconsonantal /s/'s disappeared and post-/s/ plosives were voiceless

(3) All preconsonantal /s/'s disappeared and all post-/s/ consonants were voiceless, giving rise to a series of 'voiceless sonorants'

(4) All preconsonantal /s/'s disappeared, except that /st/ clusters were treated like simple /s/'s (like most coronal fricatives) – viz. were first affricated to [tˢ] and then simply became [s]

(5) sr clusters appear, but |s| does not come from /s/

(6) sl clusters appear ⎫ first in free variation with voiceless
(7) s+sonorant clusters appear ⎬ sonorants, then exclusively (for or-
                              ⎭ dering see p. 62)

(8) s+plosive clusters appear, where the plosive is |p| or |k|

(9) s+t clusters appear

(10) s+j clusters appear (when other Cj clusters appeared at stage 29)

All of these changes (1)–(10) involved some change or other in the Morpheme Structure Conditions for the relevant stage, except for changes (2) and (4) (see below, pp. 112–30).

Rule R8, labialising C_2 in a C_1w V C_2 syllable (pp. 15, 26), persisted unchanged until stage 11, when the structural description was complicated to include [−lateral]:

$$8' \quad \begin{bmatrix} +\text{cons} \\ -\text{lat} \end{bmatrix} \rightarrow \begin{bmatrix} -\text{coronal} \\ +\text{anterior} \end{bmatrix} / \text{Cw V} \underline{\quad\quad}$$

as a result of such words as (*twill* → ḍil) and (*dwell* → ḍɛl) beside:

quick → ġip
quite → kaɪp
twice → ḍaɪp etc.

In fact there were no previous examples where /l/ was labialised, and what we have is probably merely new data, rather than a change in the rule, i.e. R8 should always have been R8'. Similar doubt obtains with respect to /r/, for which only one example was found (at stage 14), viz. *quarry*, which gave the irregular and therefore uninterpretable output of [kʰɔfəri:]. Clearly rule 8 is trying to apply, but the details are obscure.

At various stages – 11 and 16 – the rule failed to operate when C_2 was a velar, i.e. we have:

quick → ġip *or* ġik   (11)
squeak → kʰi:k   (16)

but this tendency was never stabilised. There was also some variation with regard to the feature [continuant] in the structural change of the rule, as we have:

twice → ḍaɪf *or* ḍaɪp

but squeeze → ġi:b *never* *ġi:v etc.

But in both these cases the data are too few to be sure.

The rule abruptly disappeared at stage 25, in conjunction with a change in rule R16. The manner of R8's disappearance was remarkable. One evening A came up to me quite spontaneously and said 'Daddy, I can say [kwik]'[1] having said [kip] for about two years. It is puzzling that he should have this degree of awareness. For some discussion of the psychological status of the phonological representation and rules imputed to A, see below, pp. 136ff.

The loss of R8 had no effect on A's morpheme structure conditions, beside the linked effect of the modification to R16 (p. 72).

Rules R9 and R10, respectively deleting /s/ and /ʃ/ initially (pp. 16, 26), will be taken together because of their mutual interaction.

At stage 1, these rules accounted for the asymmetrical data:

sun → ʌn

soap → u:p

but sock → ġɔk

and sharp → a:p

sugar → ugə

but shine → ḍaɪn

At stage 3, R9 and R10 fell together as a result of the environment of R10 changing from [−coronal] to [−anterior]. Whereas before, /ʃ/ was deleted before labials and velars, now it is only deleted before velars, i.e. *sharp* has now become [wa:p],[2] but *sugar* is still [ugə] and *shine* is still [ḍaɪn]. As R9 remains unchanged we have:

$$
9 \quad
\begin{bmatrix}
+\text{cor} \\
+\text{cont} \\
+\text{strid} \\
+\text{ant}
\end{bmatrix}
\overset{\text{opt}}{\to} \emptyset / \# \text{———} [+\text{syll}]\ [+\text{ant}]\ \text{(unchanged)}
$$

$$
10' \quad
\begin{bmatrix}
+\text{cor} \\
+\text{cont} \\
+\text{strid} \\
-\text{ant}
\end{bmatrix}
\overset{\text{opt}}{\to} \emptyset / \# \text{———} [+\text{syll}]\ [-\text{ant}]
$$

[1] And was immediately able to produce correctly all the other relevant examples – *queen, twice,* etc. – which had hitherto all proved impossible for him.

[2] Assuming the operation of rules R19 and 20.

S T A

which clearly must be collapsed into:

$$
9/10 \quad \begin{bmatrix} +\text{cor} \\ +\text{cont} \\ +\text{strid} \\ \alpha\text{ant} \end{bmatrix} \overset{\text{opt}}{\rightarrow} \emptyset / \# \text{———} [+\text{syll}] \begin{bmatrix} \alpha\text{ant} \\ -\text{cont} \end{bmatrix}
$$

It is necessary to add [−cont] to the environment of R9/10 to account for the behaviour of *soft* → [wɔpt]. This has no effect on their conflatability.

In the meantime, at stage 2, a new rule (R10A) applying to /j/ has appeared.[1] This rule deletes /j/ before a velar consonant preceded by a round vowel:

yoghourt → u:gə
yolk → u:k

cf.   (yacht → ḍɔt)
yak → ġæk
(yucca → ġʌġə)
young → ġʌŋ

i.e. 10A $\begin{bmatrix} +\text{cor} \\ -\text{cons} \end{bmatrix} \rightarrow \emptyset / \text{———} \begin{bmatrix} +\text{round} \\ +\text{syll} \end{bmatrix} \begin{bmatrix} -\text{cor} \\ -\text{ant} \end{bmatrix}$

Then at stage 4 the conflated R9/10 itself changes to take account of the quality – rounded or unrounded – of the vowel preceding the environmental consonant, i.e. we have:

$$
9/10' \quad \begin{bmatrix} +\text{cor} \\ +\text{cont} \\ +\text{strid} \\ \alpha\text{ant} \end{bmatrix} \overset{\text{opt}}{\rightarrow} \emptyset / \# \text{———} \begin{bmatrix} +\text{round} \\ +\text{syll} \end{bmatrix} \begin{bmatrix} -\text{cont} \\ -\text{cor} \\ \alpha\text{ant} \end{bmatrix}
$$

As can be seen there is also a further restriction as to the following consonant which effects deletion – now only non-coronals do.[2] Thus /s/ is deleted only before labials after a rounded vowel – contrast:

soap → u:p
with   sip → wip

and /ʃ/ is deleted only before velars and after rounded vowels – contrast:

sugar → ugə
with   shack → γæk

---

[1] It would be more accurate, perhaps, to say: a rule for which no evidence had hitherto been available.

[2] That is, the environment of the original R9 has been complicated to include [−coronal] which, of course, was in the specification of the original R10.

Clearly if we simplify 9/10' by the omission of the feature [strident], and 10A by the omission of the feature [consonantal] we can conflate the two as:

$$\text{10A}' \quad \begin{bmatrix} +\text{cor} \\ +\text{cont} \\ \alpha\text{ant} \end{bmatrix} \overset{\text{opt}}{\to} \emptyset / \underline{\hspace{1cm}} \begin{bmatrix} +\text{round} \\ +\text{syll} \end{bmatrix} \begin{bmatrix} -\text{cont} \\ -\text{cor} \\ \alpha\text{ant} \end{bmatrix}$$

but this structural description includes /l, r/ which, without a feature [vocalic] it is hard to exclude. (It also includes /θ, ð/ but no examples with these occur.) The easiest way round this difficulty is achieved by complicating the structural description by adding a disjunction:

$$\left\{ \begin{matrix} [-\text{sonorant}] \\ [-\text{consonantal}] \end{matrix} \right\}$$

i.e. the other specification [+coronal, +continuant, αanterior] must be satisfied and either [−son] or [−cons] must also be part of the segment concerned. So we have:

$$\text{10A}' \text{ (revised)} \quad \begin{bmatrix} +\text{cor} \\ +\text{cont} \\ \alpha\text{ant} \\ \left\{ \begin{matrix} [-\text{son}] \\ [-\text{cons}] \end{matrix} \right\} \end{bmatrix} \overset{\text{opt}}{\to} \emptyset / \# \underline{\hspace{1cm}} \begin{bmatrix} +\text{round} \\ +\text{syll} \end{bmatrix} \begin{bmatrix} -\text{cont} \\ -\text{cor} \\ \alpha\text{ant} \end{bmatrix}$$

which, given its complexity, its optionality, and the paucity of examples with which to corroborate it, is probably not worth formulating. In other words, we could account virtually as economically for the same facts by assuming that a certain set of words has been restructured in the lexicon (see below, p. 143, for a discussion of the notion restructuring) but the data are at worst highly suggestive. This rule, whether validly formulated or not, disappeared at stage 6; although *yoghourt* and *yolk* continued to vacillate for some time between retaining and deleting the initial consonant (see the lexicon in Appendix C).

Rule R11, deleting /z/ finally (pp. 17, 27), is interestingly complicated in its development by the morphological status of the /z/. This may be either simply the last segment of a monomorphemic word – e.g. *cheese* – or one of four different morphemes: plural, as in *eyes*; the third person singular suffix, as in *says*; the reduced form of *is*, as in *Amahl's going*; or the possessive, as in *Amahl's one* or *it's Amahl's* (where the two different phonological environments of the possessive are treated differently). The first change in this rule occurred tentatively at stage 7 when the pre-final possessive {z} was realised as |d| provided it was preceded by a vowel, but none of the others were. So we have:

> nose → nu:
> eyes → aɪ
> Daddy's going → ḍædi: ġoin[1]
> Daddy's one → ḍædi: wʌn
> it's Daddy's → it ḍædiḍ

cf.
> it's Amahl's → it æməl
> Daddy says... → ḍædi: ḍeɪ

By stage 9 monomorphemic items are still produced without final /z/:

> nose → nu:
> cheese → ḍi:[2]
> always → ɔ:lwe:

but plurals are now normally realised correctly,[3] where the preceding segment is a suppletive vowel (*these, those*), or the anaptyctic vowel inserted after stridents.

> those → ḍo:ḍ   these → ḍi:ḍ
> pages → ḅe:diḍ
> slices → laɪḍit
> horses → ɔ:ḍiḍ

It is worth noting that even now the appearance of the plural and present tense morphemes is only partially conditioned by phonological processes:

contrast six → ġikt
          box → ḅok(t)
with   cheeks → ġi:k
          takes → ġeɪk
or   lift → lipt
with   lips → lip

where a sequence which is pronounceable for A is not realised because of its position in a grammatical system.

At stage 10 the tendency first noted at stage 9 for monomorphemic

---

[1] In this and later examples, the syntactic conditioning is obvious in that A had no copula or form of *be* except in contrastive stress: e.g.
    I'm cutting → aɪ kʌtin

[2] *cheese* and *please* are beginning to have free variants [ḍi:d] and [ḅi:ḍ] at this stage.

[3] Phonologically correctly. His semantic/syntactic use of plurals was still largely haphazard.

items to be given a reflex of their final -z (p. 68, n. 2) is continued: definitively in the case of verbs:

seize → ḍi:ḍ   was → wɔḍ
lose → lu:ḍ   freeze → wi:d etc.

less markedly in the case of non-verbs, which remained z-less for a much longer period:

nose → nu: until stage 16 (or later)
scissors → ḍidə until stage 16 etc.

At stage 14 words ending in a vowel are correctly pluralised:

pea → pʰi:
peas → pʰi:d
but   ball → bɔːl
balls → bɔːl (cf. hold → oːld)
pen → pʰɛn
pens → pʰɛn (cf. find → waɪnd)
dog → dɔg
dogs → dɔg

At stage 17 the possessive marker in sentence-final position is extended to post-sonorants generally, so we have:

it's Amahl's → it æməld
it's the wall's → it ə wɔːld
(*a* and *the* are neutralised as [ə])

but we still have:

it's Amahl's one → it æməl wʌn
two walls → tu: wɔːl

By stage 18 the plural marker has been generally adopted,[1] and we have:

[1] Except where A's form of the plural marker t/d is the same as the final consonant of the stem: e.g. cat/cats → [kæt]. But note that with a word like *cloth* → [klɔt] A does have a different plural form: [klɔtid], presumably because his internalised form of the word has /θ/ and not /t/, even though [t] occurs in the surface. Comparable data occur a little later (e.g. stage 23) where we have the singular/plural pairs:

bath → baːs
baths → baːsiz
Smith → smis
(the) Smiths → smisiz etc.
cf.   spot → spɔt
spots → spɔts

It would seem that the -iz plural allomorph has been generalised to all [− cor, − del rel] segments – not to [− strid] segments – but this does not affect the claim that *cloth* and *cat* have different final segments for A even at a stage when they turn up as [klɔt] and [kæt] for him. (See the discussion of plurals on p. 148 below.)

> sleeves → ɬiːvd   tunes → tʰuːnd
> apples → æpəld   worms → wəːmd

cf.   lips → lipt etc.

It was not until stage 21, by which time /z, s/ were being realised as [z, s] or [dz, ts], that the use of {z} as possessive before a word was correctly implemented:

> Amahl's Daddy → æməlz dædiː

and not until stage 23 that its use as a reduced verb appeared:

> Amahl's going → æməlz goin

These last of course were not peculiar to /z/, but included the other allomorphs as well, e.g.:

> Saras is going → sʌɹəs iz goin

Rule R12, making a nasal in an unstressed syllable alveolar (pp. 17–18), was restricted at stage 2 to apply only to velar nasals; that is, while we still have an |n| in:

> going → g̊oin
> squatting → g̊ɔpin etc.

we now have an |m| in:

> bottom → b̥ɔd̥əm

The exceptional retention of |iŋ| when preceded by a stem ending in a velar nasal was constant.[1] So we have:

$$
12' \quad \begin{bmatrix} +\text{nasal} \\ -\text{anterior} \end{bmatrix} \rightarrow \begin{bmatrix} +\text{coronal} \\ +\text{anterior} \end{bmatrix} / X \begin{bmatrix} +\text{syllabic} \\ -\text{stress} \end{bmatrix} ___
$$

Condition: where X ≠ /ŋ/

This rule was still completely operative at age 4 years 4 months.

Rule R13, deleting /h/ (pp. 18, 27), became optional at stage 14 when A had free variants such as:

> hat → æt/hæt
> huge → uːd/huːd etc., as well as,

e.g.   hand → hænd (always)

and had disappeared by stage 16.

---

[1] At stage 8 there were one or two examples of |ŋ| finally, e.g.:

> morning → mɔːnin *or* mɔːniŋ
> doing → duːin *or* duːiŋ

But this soon disappeared again.

Rule R14, deleting unstressed initial syllables (pp. 18, 27), had already become optional by stage 2, when A had:

away → weː *or* əˡweː
enough → nʌp *or* ɪˡnʌp etc.

and disappeared soon afterwards. This, however, cannot be interpreted as meaning that all unstressed syllables were correctly produced after this. Rather, their treatment was so diverse that they didn't lend themselves to any strictly formalised characterisation (cf. the discussion of some other words with unstressed initial syllables and their different treatment below, pp. 172–3).

Rule R15, optionally deleting /t/ and /d/ before /r/ (pp. 18, 28), was so peripheral as scarcely to merit inclusion (p. 18). The only other attested example resulting from it was:

draught → waːft/waːpt

at stage 3; and by stage 4, rule R15 had disappeared.

Rule R16, deleting post-consonantal sonorants (pp. 18, 28), first changed at stage 9 with the appearance of post-consonantal |l| as the reflex of both adult /l/ and /r/. At first this |l| was restricted to occurring after non-coronals and non-continuants, and was only optionally present even there. That is, we have [b̪æk] or [blæk] for *black*, [ġʌm] or [glʌm] for *crumb* etc.; but *frog* is still [woġ], *floor* is still [wɔː], and *drawer* is still [dɔː], *trunk* is [ġʌk] etc. /w/ and /j/ are still deleted after all consonants:

new → nuː
quite → kaɪp etc.

This change necessitates splitting R16 into three parts: one to delete /w/ and /j/ as before, one to account for the neutralisation of /l/ and /r/ as |l|, and finally one to account for the selective appearance of this |l|. Thus we have:

16(i)　$\begin{bmatrix} -\text{cons} \\ -\text{syll} \end{bmatrix} \to \emptyset/[+\text{cons}]\underline{\quad}$

16(ii)　$\begin{bmatrix} +\text{cons} \\ +\text{son} \end{bmatrix} \to [+\text{lat}]/[+\text{cons}]\underline{\quad}$

16(iii)　$\begin{bmatrix} +\text{cons} \\ +\text{son} \end{bmatrix} \xrightarrow{\langle\text{oblig}\rangle} \emptyset / \left[\left\langle \left\{ \begin{matrix} +\text{cons} \\ +\text{cor} \\ +\text{cont} \end{matrix} \right\} \right\rangle \right] \underline{\quad}$

R16(ii) would apply to post-consonantal nasals as well as /l, r/ but these only occur after /s/ which has already been deleted by rule R7 (cf. p. 25). This formulation in fact conceals considerable phonetic complexity. Thus there was free variation not only between the presence and absence of post-consonantal |l|, but this |l| was either syllabic or non-syllabic; there was an occasional anaptyctic [ə]; the |l| was occasionally pronounced inter-labially; there were one or two random occurrences of [ɹ], and of [kx] for |kl| etc.:

e.g.   grater → gleɪtə or gḷeɪtə

green → kliːn or kxiːn

bread → bə'ɹɛd or blɛd etc.

At stage 10, the word *truck* appeared as [ġlʌk] providing strong evidence that R16, or at least R16(iii), should now *follow* rule R19, although we have seen (p. 28 above) that R16 must precede R18 and that R18 must precede R19. The only way of preserving the original ordering would be by making R16(iii) generally optional, but this would then predict that |l| should sometimes be preserved after /t, d/ even when this /t/ or /d/ was not later velarised, and no such examples occurred. Accordingly an assumption of rule re-ordering appears to be the only tenable one, which is of interest given that there is no other example of rule re-ordering throughout the period of acquisition. There was also some over-generalisation of the appearance of |l| such that a post-consonantal |l| appeared displaced to the right of either a preceding or following consonant, or after a following vowel, or both, or neither:

chocolate → ġɔkit or glɔklit

glue → glu: or guːl

Gilbert → gilbət or gilblət etc.

To account for this, we need a further (transformational) rule R16(iv) of the form:

16(iv)   C...C l V...C...

1   2 3 4   5   ⇒ 1 (3) 2 (3) 4 (3) 5 (3)[1]

Clearly R16(iii) and R16(iv) have a profound effect on the morpheme structure conditions of A's language, though 16(iv) might be better viewed as a new morpheme structure condition interfering with the

---

[1] This rule appears to belie the 'across-the-board' nature of changes (see below, p. 138) but note that it only applies to adult forms containing a post-consonantal /l/ or /r/ – not at random. I suspect that this is really a performance limitation rather than a part of A's competence.

regularity of the realisation rules (see note 1 on p. 72 and MS1 on p. 115 below).

Rule R16(i) was reasonably stable until stage 25 except for the sporadic replacement of post-consonantal /j/ by |r|[1] from stage 19 on:

> onion → ʌnɹən
> stew → tɹuː
> beautiful → bɹuːtəfəl etc.

beside the more usual:

> tulip → tuːlip
> cube → kuːb
> few → fuː etc.

Then, at stage 25, post-consonantal |w| appeared and forms such as:

> quick → kwik
> queen → kwiːn
> twice → twaɪs

were produced correctly;[2] though post-consonantal /j/ was still deleted:

> new → nuː   cute → kuːt
> few → fuː   piano → pænəu etc.

We have then:

$$16(i)' \qquad \begin{bmatrix} -\text{cons} \\ -\text{syll} \\ +\text{cor} \end{bmatrix} \rightarrow \emptyset / C\text{———}$$

which remained until stage 29 when it finally became optional and then disappeared.[3]

At stage 10 the restriction on R16(iii) that allowed post-consonantal |l| only after non-continuants began to be lifted, and simultaneously the neutralisation of /l/r/ in this position (effected by 16(ii)) began very tentatively to disappear. That is, we had:

> froth → wɹɔf *or* wɔt *or* wɔf
> brown → b̥aun *or* blaun *or* bɹaun etc.

although, e.g., ground → g̊aund *or* glaund only.

---

[1] Note that |r| was the regular reflex of adult /j/ for A in initial position.

[2] Note that the change in this rule coincided with the disappearance of rule R8 (see above, p. 65, especially the remarks on the nature of R8's disappearance).

[3] It is worth noting that it was only slightly before this (stage 24) that A has even some control of /j/ in initial position.

There were still no occurrences of post-consonantal |l/r| after coronals:

> drawer → dͻ: etc.

although, as mentioned above, adult forms with /tr/ may become |gl| – i.e. the post-consonantal liquid is retained as long as the point of articulation of the consonant is also made non-coronal:

> truck → glʌk
> troddler → glͻglə

and cf.   drink → ġɹiŋk (stage 12).

Thus we have:

16(ii)′ $\begin{bmatrix} +\text{cons} \\ +\text{son} \end{bmatrix} \overset{\text{opt}}{\to} [+\text{lat}]/[+\text{cons}]\text{——}$

i.e. R16(ii) is now optional; and R16(iii) is restructured as:

16(iii)′ $\begin{bmatrix} +\text{son} \\ +\text{cons} \end{bmatrix} \overset{\langle \text{oblig}\rangle}{\longrightarrow} \emptyset / \begin{bmatrix} +\text{cons} \\ \langle +\text{cor}\rangle \end{bmatrix}\text{——}$

At stage 12 post-consonantal |r| begins to appear after coronals as well, so we have

> drive → daɪv

but   driving → dɹaɪvin
> through → du:

but   three → tɹi:
> trolley → dͻli:

but   tray → tɹeɪ etc.

That is, R16(iii)′ has become generally optional, losing the specification of the feature [+coronal]:

16(iii)″ $\begin{bmatrix} +\text{son} \\ +\text{cons} \end{bmatrix} \overset{\text{opt}}{\to} \emptyset / \text{C——}$

R16(iii) had disappeared by stage 13, R16(ii) by stage 14. Rule R16(iv) underwent no structural changes but merely became less and less frequent as A gradually mastered the complexities of clusters. It had disappeared by stage 12.

Rule R17, harmonising a post-vocalic non-nasal coronal consonant to a preceding velar (pp. 19, 28), was restricted at stage 2 to apply only to continuants. Thus at stage 1 we had:

> glasses → ġa:gi: coach → ġo:k
> kiss → ġik   curtain → ġə:gən etc.

but at stage 2, *glasses* etc. have the same harmonised form, but *curtain* is now [ġɔːdən]: viz. R17 has become R17′:

17′ $\begin{bmatrix} +\text{cor} \\ -\text{nas} \end{bmatrix} \rightarrow \begin{bmatrix} -\text{cor} \\ -\text{ant} \end{bmatrix} / \begin{bmatrix} -\text{cor} \\ -\text{ant} \end{bmatrix} [+\text{syll}] \overline{[+\text{cont}]}$

The rule had disappeared by stage 4 when:

cloth → ġɔt
kitchen → ġidən

etc.

(*Glasses* appeared to be restructured (see p. 143 below) and resisted change until stage 11.)

Rule R18, accounting for the various behaviour of /l, r, j/ (pp. 19, 29), was subject to a variety of changes. Let us take R18A first, converting /r/ and /j/ to |l| before or after another liquid. (In fact only three of the four logical possibilities occurs, as /j/ does not occur intervocalically except as the result of a low-level phonetic glide rule,[1] or after some kind of morphological boundary – e.g. *beyond*.) That is, we have:

really → liːli: r → l/——V l V
lorry → lɔli: r → l/l V——V
yellow → lɛləu   j → l/——V l V

This rule persisted until stage 28, when we have:

Larry → læli:
yelling → lɛlin etc.

and when A is conscious of his own inability to say these words. The only member of this class apparently mastered was the rVlV type – e.g. *realise, really, ruler* etc., which were correct intermittently from stage 15.

Rule R18B, either labialising or deleting /r, l/ intervocalically, was simplified at stage 4 so that only the latter possibility was left: intervocalic /l, r/ were deleted, not labialised – e.g. we have:[2]

collar → kɔə   very → vɛi:
telephone → dɛiːbuːn   forehead → wɔːiḍ etc.
Sellotape → dɛiːteːp

---

[1] The only exception to this for A was *radio* which he produced as [leːdiːdo:] where an adult form /reɪdiːjəu/ is presumably the input (stage 4 onwards).

[2] It should be noted that this rule is too powerful as it stands as the deletion rule did not apply to examples such as *silly* and *sorry*. This is accounted for in the changes to the rule discussed on pp. 80–1 below.

Thus we have:

18B′ $\begin{bmatrix} +\text{cor} \\ +\text{cont} \\ +\text{son} \end{bmatrix} \rightarrow \emptyset/\text{V}\underline{\quad\quad}\text{V}$

By stage 11 the scope of the rule was restricted to /r/ so that we have:

garage → gæit
mirror → miːə etc.
but   pillow → b̥ilo
television → dɛliːwidən etc.

viz: $\begin{bmatrix} +\text{cor} \\ +\text{cont} \\ +\text{son} \end{bmatrix} \rightarrow \emptyset/\text{V}\ \overline{[-\text{lat}]}\ \text{V}$

After this, the rule disappeared somewhat spasmodically. Most inter-vocalic /r/'s were retained from stage 12 onwards but a few examples persisted until much later.

Rule R18C, which neutralises /l, r, j/ with the other coronals (ulti-mately as |d|) if they haven't been retained or deleted by R18A, B, becomes optional at stage 2, with the result that we have free variation between |l| and |d| and |r| and |d|:

lady → leːdiː/deːdiː
rat → ɹæt/d̥æt
ray → ɹeː/d̥eː[1]

This free variation occurs only before a vowel followed by a coronal consonant or word boundary. The only two examples with /j/ both had |d| as their realisation. The data are insufficient to determine whether this is due to a change in the structural description of the rule, or merely a fortuitous gap. The words concerned were:

yawn → d̥ɔːn
(yacht → d̥ɔt)

There was a tendency – from stage 4 – for /j/ to be realised as [j] or [ɣ]:

young → g̊ʌŋ/ɣʌŋ/jʌŋ

but |j| was not established for A until stage 24, and it was still later before its articulation presented him with no difficulty. At the same

---

[1] In fact [ɪ] was not systematically distinctive for A until stage 8 or even later (see MS rules, p. 114).

stage (4) there was a parallel tendency for /r/ to become a lateral:

radio → leːdiːdoː
red → lɛd *or* ɹɛd
ribena → laɪbiːnə *or* ɹaɪbiːnə *or* ḍaɪbiːnə
round → ɹaun *or* laund
row → loː

This can be formalised by complicating the structural change of R18C from [−sonorant] to the disjunction $\left\{ \begin{matrix} [+\text{lat}] \\ [-\text{son}] \end{matrix} \right\}$ and complicating the environment to exclude /j/, viz:

$$18\text{C}' \qquad \begin{bmatrix} +\text{cor} \\ +\text{cont} \\ +\text{son} \end{bmatrix} \rightarrow \left\{ \begin{matrix} [+\text{lat}]/\overline{[+\text{cons}]} & \text{(a)} \\ [-\text{son}] & \text{(b)} \end{matrix} \right.$$

Where (a) is optional.

That is, /l, r/ optionally become lateral – i.e. are neutralised as |l|, or failing that, /l, r, j/ are all made non-sonorant.

By stage 6, the optionality of (a) has been virtually dropped; i.e. /l/r/ are consistently neutralised as |l| and never become |r| or |d|[1] and /j/ regularly becomes |d|,[2] i.e. R18C″ is equivalent to 18C′ less the condition.

At stage 8 a significant number of /r/'s appeared in free variation with |l| in words with an adult /r/:[3]

rain → leːn
raining → leːnin *or* ɹeːnin *or* ḍeːnin
red → ɹɛḍ *or* lɛd *or* ḍɛḍ
right → ɹaɪt *or* laɪt *or* jaɪt[4]
(*write* always → [laɪt])

There was also at this stage the first occurrence of [l] for /j/:

yesterday → lɛdədeɪ

To formalise the now optional conversion of /r/ to |l| we need to place a new condition of optionality on R18C, but this time referring to the structural change rather than the environment. This implies that R18C′

---

[1] With one or two remnant exceptions for |d| (see examples at stage 8), and random exceptions for |r| (see Appendix C).

[2] Except in words such as yellow → lɛlo covered by R18A. The tendency for /j/ to become |j| was not maintained (see above, p. 76).

[3] And only these, i.e. never for adult words with initial /l/. See the discussion on p. 135 below.

[4] It is interesting that the *only* words containing [ɪ] were also the *only* words in free variation with the otherwise disappeared |d|, and the unestablished [j].

should have been stated not with a verbal condition but with the angled bracket notation as follows:

$$
18C' \quad \begin{bmatrix} +\text{cor} \\ +\text{cont} \\ +\text{son} \end{bmatrix} \xrightarrow{\langle\text{opt}\rangle} \left\{ \begin{matrix} [+\text{lat}]/[\overline{\langle+\text{cons}\rangle}] \\ [-\text{son}] \end{matrix} \right\}
$$

Then R18C″ would merely lose the optional condition, and the new R18C‴ would reinstate it as:

$$
18C''' \quad \begin{bmatrix} +\text{cor} \\ +\text{cont} \\ +\text{son} \end{bmatrix} \xrightarrow{\langle\text{opt}\rangle} \left\{ \begin{matrix} [\langle+\text{lat}\rangle]/\overline{[+\text{cons}]} \\ [-\text{son}] \end{matrix} \right\}
$$

At stage 10 |r| was firmly established, but /j/ was now more frequently (although still with massive free variation) becoming |l| – i.e. we have:

$$
18C'''' \quad \begin{bmatrix} +\text{cor} \\ +\text{cont} \\ +\text{son} \end{bmatrix} \rightarrow \left\{ \begin{matrix} [+\text{lat}]/[\overline{-\text{cons}}] \\ [-\text{son}] \end{matrix} \right\}
$$

where the whole rule is optional, so that adult /j/ surfaces as |l| or |d| or |j|, e.g.:

> unicorn → du:nikɔ:n/ju:nikɔ:n
> yolk → lo:k/jo:k etc.

By stage 12, this tendency was more firmly established and besides other free variants /j/ is now also regularly replaced by [ɹ] initially. Thus we have:

unicorn → lu:nikɔ:n	yoghourt → lɔgət
use (V) → lu:d *or* du:d	yolk → lo:k *or* ɹo:k
using → du:din *or* ju:din	you → ɹu:
yacht → ɹɔt	young → lʌŋ *or* ɹʌŋ
yes → ɟɛt *or* dɛt	your → dɔ:
yet → dɛt	yoyo → loɹo *or* ɹoɹo

At the same time rule R18C seems to have extended its domain as well. Marginally from stage 11, and more consistently from stage 12, initial /z/ was also interpreted as [ɹ] or even [l]. That is, we have:

> zebra (previousy [wi:bə]) now → li:bɹə or ɹi:bɹə
> zip (previously [wip] then [dip]) now → ɹip or dip etc.

Ignoring /z/ we can modify R18c to account for the alternation of |r| and |l| for /j/ by making the structural change [+cons], this being the only feature distinguishing /j/ from /r/, (and then [±ant] to include [l]). To include /z/ as well gives rise to two problems: first we need to specify a natural class /j, z/ (which must exclude [ð] e.g.:

    that → d̥æt

    there → d̥ɛ etc.)

and second we need to specify the natural class /l, r/.[1] As both of these are very cumbersome there seems little point in complicating R18C yet further, so I leave the rule unformulated. (Note that it might be thought that /j/ and /z/ should just be treated separately but this would involve the double statement of a rather strange pattern of free variation. Moreover, the position of the two rules in the ordering is quite close – we know the ordering of R18C for /j/ already, and the rule changing /z/ must at least precede R24.)

The pattern of free variation for the reflexes of /j/ continued much as indicated above from stage 12 until stage 16.[2] By stage 17 /j/ was consistently |r|:

    use → ɹuːd   yet → ɹɛt

    yes → ɹɛt   yoghourt → ɹogət etc.

    yesterday → ɹɛtədeɪ

and /z/ is far more consistent than heretofore, except that [ɹ] is now in free variation with a lamino-alveolar frictionless continuant (symbolised ⊕ here) as well as with [d]:

    zebra → ⊕iːbɹe *or* diːbɹə

    zip → ⊕ip *or* dip *or* ɹip

    zoo → ⊕uː *or* ɹu:

    zoos → ɹuːd (homophonous with *rude*)

    zoom → ɹuːm

By stage 18 |r| was stable for both /j/ and /z/. At stage 21, /z/ began to be realised as [z]:

    zoo → zuː

    zip → ɹip *or* zip

a process complete by stage 23. At the same time (stage 21) sporadic occurrences of [j] reappeared and were in free variation with both [ɹ] and [ɟ]:

    yes → ɹɛs *or* ɟɛs

    yet → ɹɛt *or* jɛt

    you → ɹuː *or* ɟuː *or* juː etc. (stage 24)

[1] See the discussion of ʋocalicɟ below p. 193. There is also the problem of specifying the optionality. This seems to be an occasion where A is operating in terms of some kind of phonemic unit, rather than in distinctive features (see below, p. 188).

[2] The evidence for /z/ is too scanty to be very revealing. Depressingly few common words begin with /z/ in English.

and [j] was not fully stabilised until stage 29 when R18C finally disappeared.

Further complications of rule R18, giving rise to |l|'s in A's speech which were not the reflex of /l/, appeared at stage 4. These had the effect of changing /s/[1] to |l| if /s/ was initial and the only other consonant in the word was |l| or |r| – thus:

> silly → lili: (*or* ḍili:)
> sorry → lɔli:

At stage 5 this process was generalised so that both /s/ and /ʃ/ became |l|, and not only before /l/ or /r/ but before any coronal consonant or no consonant:

> see → li:
> shade → le:t
> shadow → lædo *or* ḍædo *or* ɟædo
> Sona → lu:nə *or* ḍu:nə *or* u:nə
> sorry → lɔli:
> sun → lʌn *or* dʌn *or* ʌn

(There were some exceptions:

> sausage → ḍɔdiḍ
> shoulder → ḍu:ldə

although note that *sausage* appeared subsequently (stage 6) as [lɔdiḍ].) This process reached a peak at stage 6, began to die away again at stage 8 and had virtually disappeared by stage 10.

Clearly this rule is closely related to the processes reflected in R18A and R18C. Moreover, R18B, deleting intervocalic /l/r/, must not apply to items like *silly* and *sorry* in which the /s/ has been liquidised, and if we include this liquidisation in rule R18, then the customary disjunctive ordering will take account of this. Accordingly at stage 4, the structural description of R18 is simplified from

$$\begin{bmatrix} +\text{cor} \\ +\text{cont} \\ +\text{son} \end{bmatrix} \text{ to simply } \begin{bmatrix} +\text{cor} \\ +\text{cont} \end{bmatrix}$$

to include /s/ and /ʃ/ (there were no occurrences of the other coronal continuants, /z, ʒ, θ, ð/ in the relevant environments); and to exclude the

---

[1] Note that the changes involving /s/ are quite unrelated to those involving /z/.

possibility of deleting intervocalic coronal continuants, the environment of R18B is complicated by the addition of [+ sonorant]. Thus:

$$
18 \quad
\begin{bmatrix} +\mathrm{cor} \\ +\mathrm{cont} \\ +\mathrm{son} \end{bmatrix} \rightarrow
\left\{
\begin{array}{ll}
[+\mathrm{lat}] \Big/ \left\{
\begin{array}{l}
\left(\begin{bmatrix} +\mathrm{cor} \\ +\mathrm{cont} \\ +\mathrm{son} \end{bmatrix} \right) [+\mathrm{syll}]\!\!-\!\!-[+\mathrm{syll}] \\[4pt]
-\!\!-[+\mathrm{syll}] \begin{bmatrix} +\mathrm{cor} \\ +\mathrm{cont} \\ +\mathrm{son} \end{bmatrix} [+\mathrm{syll}]
\end{array}
\right\} & \text{(a)} \\[24pt]
\emptyset / \mathrm{V}\!\!-\!\!-\mathrm{V} & \text{(b)} \\[6pt]
\left\{ \begin{array}{l} [+\mathrm{lat}]/\overline{[+\mathrm{cons}]} \\ [-\mathrm{son}] \end{array} \right\} & \text{(c)}
\end{array}
\right.
$$

becomes:

$$
18' \quad
\begin{bmatrix} +\mathrm{cor} \\ +\mathrm{cont} \end{bmatrix} \rightarrow
\left\{
\begin{array}{ll}
[+\mathrm{lat}] \Big/ \left\{
\begin{array}{l}
\left(\begin{bmatrix} +\mathrm{cor} \\ +\mathrm{cont} \\ +\mathrm{son} \end{bmatrix} \right) [+\mathrm{syll}]\!\!-\!\!-[+\mathrm{syll}] \\[4pt]
-\!\!-[+\mathrm{syll}] \begin{bmatrix} +\mathrm{cor} \\ +\mathrm{cont} \\ +\mathrm{son} \end{bmatrix} [+\mathrm{syll}]
\end{array}
\right\} & \text{(a)} \\[24pt]
\emptyset / \mathrm{V}\ \overline{[+\mathrm{son}]}\ \mathrm{V} & \text{(b)} \\[6pt]
\left\{ \begin{array}{l} [+\mathrm{lat}]/\begin{bmatrix} +\mathrm{son} \\ +\mathrm{cons} \end{bmatrix} \\ [-\mathrm{son}] \end{array} \right\} & \text{(c)}
\end{array}
\right.
$$

In fact, as will be seen, the environment of R18C is similarly complicated, as it is only at the next stage that /s, ʃ/ are themselves liquidised in environments other than (a). Thus at stage 5, R18' will lose the [− sonorant] from part (c). Note that the loss of optionality at stage 6 of R18C (above, p. 77) coincides with the peak (almost complete) liquidisation of /s, ʃ/ as well. Stage 10, when /s/ reverts to |d|, coincides with the restriction of R18'''' to deal only with /j/ and not /l, r/ at all (p. 78).

Rule R19, harmonising coronal consonants to a following velar and labial (pp. 20, 29), originally (stage 1) had the condition that it was optional if α = +, i.e. the rule always worked before velars, but only operated part of the time before labials. By stage 3, this fissive tendency had become more apparent and R19 split into two parts: R19(i) and R19(ii):

$$
19(\mathrm{i}) \quad [+\mathrm{coronal}] \rightarrow \begin{bmatrix} -\mathrm{coronal} \\ -\mathrm{anterior} \end{bmatrix} \Big/ \!\!-\!\!-[+\mathrm{syll}] \begin{bmatrix} -\mathrm{cor} \\ -\mathrm{ant} \end{bmatrix}
$$

$$
19(\mathrm{ii}) \quad [+\mathrm{coronal}] \rightarrow \begin{bmatrix} -\mathrm{coronal} \\ +\mathrm{anterior} \end{bmatrix} \left\{ \begin{array}{l} \overline{[+\mathrm{nasal}]} \\ [+\mathrm{cont}] \end{array} \right\} [+\mathrm{syll}] \begin{bmatrix} -\mathrm{cor} \\ +\mathrm{ant} \end{bmatrix}
$$

R19(i) fulfils precisely the same function as R19 when a was equal to $-$: i.e. there has been no change. R19(ii) is also the same in essentials, but the environment has been complicated so that it only applies to nasals and continuants:

> knife → maɪp (there was one occurrence of [naɪp])
> nipple → mibu
> sharp → wa:p ⎱
> soft → wɔpt   ⎰ where R20 (q.v.) has also applied

but: table → ḍe:bu
> stamp → ḍɛp

At stage 4, R19(i) first becomes optional if the coronal consonant concerned is /j/. So we have:

> yolk → ġo:k *or* jo:k
> young → ġʌŋ *or* ɣʌŋ *or* jʌŋ

and almost immediately afterwards it becomes optional if the coronal is a liquid – so we have:

> long → ġɔŋ *or* lɔŋ[1]
but lick → ġik
> like → ġaɪk *or* ɣaɪk
> record → ġɛgɔ:ḍ etc.

The first change can be formalised by making R19(i) optional if the coronal is [−consonantal]:

$$\text{(Stage 4) 19(i)}' \; [+\text{cor}] \xrightarrow{\langle \text{opt} \rangle} \begin{bmatrix} -\text{cor} \\ -\text{ant} \end{bmatrix} / \langle \overline{[-\text{cons}]} \rangle \; [+\text{syll}] \begin{bmatrix} -\text{cor} \\ -\text{ant} \end{bmatrix}$$

It would be logically possible to analyse this change as being the result of /j/ changing from [+coronal] to [−coronal] for A. This position, however, is untenable, because /j/ still becomes |d| elsewhere (and later alternates with |l| and |r|). In fact I would suggest a general constraint that the categorisation of segments in terms of the universal set of distinctive features is *not* open to re-analysis by the child, and that only *rules* can be modified. The second change can be formalised by

---

[1] *long* was the only example at stage 4. By stage 5, free variation of l/g was complete:
> lego → lɛgo/ġɛgo
> like → laɪk/ġaɪk
> look → luk/ġuk

changing R19(i)′ so that the relevant coronal is [+sonorant] not
[−consonantal]:[1]

$$(\text{Stage } 4\text{–}5) \ 19(i)'' \ +[\text{cor}] \xrightarrow{\langle\text{opt}\rangle} \begin{bmatrix} -\text{cor} \\ -\text{ant} \end{bmatrix} / \overline{\langle[+\text{son}]\rangle} \ [+\text{syll}] \begin{bmatrix} -\text{cor} \\ -\text{ant} \end{bmatrix}$$

A little further evidence that [sonorant] is the relevant feature is provided by the nasal coronal /n/, which also assimilates optionally:

> neck → nɛk
> next → ŋɛkt

R19(ii) is unchanged at this stage, though in fact it applies to /θ/ for
the first time:

> thumb → wʌm

This was the only relevant example of /θ/ or /ð/ before a labial in A's
vocabulary. Hitherto he had always refused to say *thumb*, insisting it was
a *finger* ([wiŋgə]). This was presumably due to a semantic rather than a
phonological inhibition.

It should perhaps also be noted that this rule, like all others, applies
only within a word, and not across word boundaries.[2] The existence of
apparent exceptions to this generalisation, e.g.:

> motor car → muːgəgaː

is presumably the result of A's analysing 'motor car' as a single morpheme. This is supported by the existence of [muːgəgaːbaɪk] for *motor
bike* – i.e. 'motor-car-bike' – although further examples such as:

> tea-cup → ɖiːgəp
> tea-bag → ɖiːgəbbæɡ̇

cf.   tika → ɡ̇iːɡ̇ə (the so-called 'caste-mark')

make his basis for assigning items word-status appear singularly
arbitrary.

At stage 6 R19(ii) becomes optional if the coronal is a nasal or /l/:

> knob → mob̥ *or* nob̥
> lift → wipt

but: lifting → lip(t)in
cf.   slip → lip *or* wip (stage 7)

[1] With the traditional feature system characterising liquids and glides in terms of
[cons] and [voc] this progression is easily captured by successive additions to the environment (of [+cons] and then [−voc]). No such gradation in complexity suggests
itself with the current features.
[2] I.e. these rules are more akin to morpheme structure conditions than to phonological rules proper.

but remains obligatory with /r/:

room → wum

This would seem to indicate that the relevant variables for A are continuant *versus* non-continuant (and where /l/ is [−continuant] as opposed to /r/ which is [+continuant]; see Wells, 1971), and sonorant versus non-sonorant, rather than simply the [nasal] implied by rule R19(ii). Thus we have:

$$19\text{(ii)}' \quad [+\text{coronal}] \xrightarrow{\langle\text{opt}\rangle} \begin{bmatrix} -\text{cor} \\ +\text{ant} \end{bmatrix} \Bigg/ \left\{ \Bigg\langle \begin{bmatrix} +\text{son} \\ -\text{cont} \end{bmatrix} \Bigg\rangle \atop [+\text{cont}] \right\} [+\text{syll}] \begin{bmatrix} -\text{cor} \\ +\text{ant} \end{bmatrix}$$

By stage 9 R19(i) has consolidated so as to apply only to true consonants, i.e. /l/, /j/ and /r/ never harmonise,[1] but all the other consonants do. As these other consonants include /n/, the rule is rather hard to state without the feature [vocalic] (see p. 83, n. 1) as we can no longer economically characterise the class of 'true consonants' *or* the class of 'liquids'. Accordingly we have to have recourse to the disjunction:

$$\left\{ \begin{array}{l} [+\text{nasal}] \\ [-\text{sonorant}] \end{array} \right\}$$

viz. $19\text{(i)}''' \quad [+\text{coronal}] \rightarrow \begin{bmatrix} -\text{cor} \\ -\text{ant} \end{bmatrix} \Bigg/ \left\{ \begin{array}{l} [+\text{nas}] \\ [-\text{son}] \end{array} \right\} [+\text{syll}] \begin{bmatrix} -\text{cor} \\ -\text{ant} \end{bmatrix}$

At the same stage R19(ii) is further complicated, such that /l/ is never affected:

lip → lip (*wip)
loaf → lu:f (*wu:f)
lift → lipt (*wipt) etc.

/ʃ/ and /θ/ are always affected:

sharp → wa:p   shepherd → wɛpəd
shaving → we:vin   thumb → wʌm

/s/, /r/ and /n/ are optionally affected:

same → we:m *or* ḍeɪm *or* le:m
some → wʌm
roof → ɹu:p *or* wu:p
knife → naɪf *or* maɪf

No examples of /ʒ/, /ð/ or /j/ in the relevant environment occurred. As

---

[1] There was one exception to this statement: rake → leɪk /ʁeɪk/ɣeɪk .

the classes apparent here seem quite unnatural, I leave the rule un-formalised (see the discussion on features versus phonemes, below, pp. 185ff.).

At stage 10 R19(i) has to be complicated to allow for the presence of the recently acquired post-consonantal |l|; i.e. we now have:

> truck → ġlʌk
> troddler → glɔglə

and cf. later (stage 12):

> drink → gɹiŋk etc.

i.e. we have:

$$19(\mathrm{i})'''' \quad [+\text{coronal}] \rightarrow \begin{bmatrix} -\text{cor} \\ -\text{ant} \end{bmatrix} \Big/ \left\{ \begin{matrix} [+\text{nas}] \\ [-\text{son}] \end{matrix} \right\} ([+\text{lat}]) \ [+\text{syll}] \begin{bmatrix} -\text{cor} \\ -\text{ant} \end{bmatrix}$$

By this stage (10), R19(ii) is fast disappearing – only /ʃ/ is regularly realised as |w| and this is in free variation with |d|:[1]

> shave → deiv/weiv
> sharp → da:p/wa:p
> shampoo → dæpu etc.

and has gone by stage 11. Also at stage 11 occurred the first isolated exception to R19(i),[2] viz.:

> doctor → gɔktə *or* dɔktə

The rule became optional at stage 13:

> deck → dɛk *or* gɛk
> dog → dɔġ *or* gɔġ
> sock → kʰɔk *or* tʰɔk etc.

and finally disappeared at stage 14.[3]

Rule R20, converting labial continuants[4] to |w| (pp. 28–30), under-went a putative simplification at stage 2 which generalised the process to /l/ as well. Thus, while we have:

> slipper → þibə (*wibə)

[1] For the special case of 'some' and its compounds, see p. 145 below. There was one occurrence of /r/ → |w|: room → |wum| at stage 11.

[2] First except for one or two occurrences of /n/, e.g.:
> necklace → nɛkit
at stage 5.

[3] For the case of *take* which remained [keɪk] until stage 22, see 'Restructuring', p. 143 below.

[4] Whether these are underlying adult /f, v/, or coronal continuants which have been labialised by R19.

at stage 1, we have:

> sleep → wiːp (*biːp)

at stage 2. In fact, the data are too limited at this early period for one to be confident that this reflects accurately what is going on. It seems probable that stage 1 *slipper* and *rubber-band* (→ [bʌbəbæn]) are remnants of a 'proto-stage' before the appearance of |w| at all; and accordingly that *slipper* should be characterised as a restructured exception, and rule 20 have the form it has at stage 2 (20′) *ab initio*:

20′
$$\begin{bmatrix} -\text{coronal} \\ +\text{anterior} \\ +\text{continuant} \end{bmatrix} \rightarrow [+\text{sonorant}]/\!\!-\!\!-\!\![+\text{syllabic}]$$

At stage 8 there was a faint tendency for R20′ to become optional. Thus we have:

> find → waɪnd/faɪnd/βaɪnd
> fan → wæn/βæn etc.

As expected, the only words in which this free variation occurred were those which had an /f/ or /v/ in the adult form. That is, there were no cases of original coronal consonants surfacing with anything other than [w].

e.g.   room → wum (*fum...)
        shelf → wɛp (*βɛp...) etc.

This indicates that the process was a phonological not a phonetic one, even though earlier there had been a degree of phonetic free variation between [v], [β] and [w] (though never [f]) (see Ph4 on p. 51 above, and also the discussion on p. 135 below). By stage 11 even this tentative introduction of |f| had disappeared again and we were eventually back to the form of the rule at stage 2 (i.e. R20′). However, by this time, post-consonantal |l/r| had begun to appear (see above, pp. 73f.) and in these cases the underlying /f/ was usually left as a non-sonorant although it was mostly voiced,[1] i.e. we have:

> flag → γlæġ ⎫
> fly → γlaɪ/vlaɪ/ʋlaɪ etc.⎰ stage 9
> frog → flɔg/βɹɔg ⎫
> fruit → γluːt/wuːt⎰ stage 11

---

[1] That is, we have the interesting situation where a sound (labio-dental fricative) is produced in a complex environment earlier than in a simple environment.

but: fish → wit
        foot → wut
        (vexed → wɛkt) etc.

There were one or two examples of a [wl] or [wɹ] sequence, but these were never stabilised:

        frog → wlɔg (see above)
        frost → fɹɔt *or* wɹɔt
        floor → wɔ: *or* wlɔ:

Note that R20′ as formulated accounts for the different behaviour of /f/ before liquids and vowels as the environment of the rule is only satisfied by the latter case. (I have not accounted for the sporadic cases of |wl/wr| in the rule at all.)

At stage 14, rule R20′ again became optional so that we have free variation of the kind:

        finger → wiŋgə/fiŋgə
        Foster → wɔtə/fɔtə
        funny → wʌni:/γʌni: etc.[1]

As would be expected, only those items with an underlying /f/ or /v/ were affected in this way, not those with underlying /w/; i.e. A never produced a form such as [*fɔ:tə] for *water*. Rule 20 had disappeared by stage 16, when all words with an initial /f/ had an initial |f| for A with the exception of some interesting restructurings, for which see below, p. 143.

Rule R21, deleting post-consonantal alveolar consonants (pp. 21, 30), must be complicated at stage 2 as the result of a change in rule R2 such that the latter no longer deletes all post-nasal voiced consonants (see p. 53 above). That is, R21′ must be restricted to apply after non-nasal consonants:

21′ $[+\text{coronal}] \rightarrow \emptyset / \begin{bmatrix} +\text{cons} \\ -\text{nasal} \end{bmatrix}$ ——

and in fact, even after non-nasals the rule is now optional:

        doctor → ġɔġə *or* ġɔktə
        camera → ġæmdə etc.

There was some tenuous evidence that at stages 3 and 4 R21 was further

---

[1] Note that the loss of R19(ii) between stages 10 and 11 (see above, p. 85) had already removed underlying coronals (/ʃ/, r/ etc.) from the domain of R20.

modified to apply only after [−anterior] consonants (i.e. velars) as there were still some examples of deletion after velars, but none elsewhere:[1]

       taxi → ġægi:

       box → bɔk

       mixer → mɪgə

but cf.   doctor → gɔktə (and never *ġɔġə now)

       picture → b̜iktə

and   soft → wɔpt

       left → wɛpt etc.

But restructuring and free variation may account for this. At any rate, R21 had gone by stage 5.

Rule R22, optionally deleting final coronal consonants (pp. 21, 30), survived marginally until stage 2:

       bad → b̜æ:

       yoghourt → o:gə

but had gone by stage 3. (In fact *yoghourt* appeared sporadically without a final consonant until stage 16, but there were no other examples.)

Rule R23, neutralising the distinction between anterior and non-anterior coronals (pp. 21, 30), appeared at stage 2 to become optional in the event that the coronal concerned was /r/.[2] That is, from stage 2 on we have free variation between [ɹ] and [d]:

       rat → d̜æt *or* ɹæt

       ray → d̜e: *or* ɹe:

Moreover, from stage 4 on there are sporadic occurrences of [j] as a reflex of adult /j/:

       young → ġʌŋ *or* jʌŋ

and even though neither of these sounds [ɹ, j] was stabilised as a member of A's system until much later (stages 8 and 24 respectively) and from the viewpoint of A's internal system could be viewed as phonetic variants of |l| and |g|:[3]

cf.   red → ɹɛd̜ *or* lɛd̜ *or* d̜ɛd̜ etc.

it is necessary to modify R23 at both stages 2 and 4 to account for these

---

[1] With the single exception of *lifting* → |lipin| as late as stage 9.

[2] /r/ of course, is specified as [+coronal, −anterior].

[3] Although this would still obscure the fact that even though [ɹ] and [l], say, were in free variation in some words (and [j] and [g] in others), these words were exclusively those with an /r/ in the adult form. Thus *rat* was [d̜æt] or [ɹæt], *red* was [ɹɛd̜] or [d̜ɛd̜] or [lɛd̜] etc; but *lady* would be [de:di:] or [le:di:] and *never* [ɹe:di:]. See p. 135 below.

sporadic and infrequent but *not* random manifestations of [r] and [j]. Thus at stage 2 we have:

$$23'\qquad [+\text{coronal}] \xrightarrow{\langle\text{opt}\rangle} [+\text{anterior}]/\left[\left\langle\overline{\begin{matrix}+\text{son}\\+\text{cons}\end{matrix}}\right\rangle\right]$$

accounting for the occurrences of [ɹ]; and at stage 4 this is simplified to:

$$23''\qquad [+\text{coronal}] \xrightarrow{\langle\text{opt}\rangle} [+\text{anterior}]/[\langle\overline{+\text{son}}\rangle]$$

accounting for both [ɹ] and [j].

At stage 8 when |r| is established for A, R23 has to be complicated to exclude /r/ but still (optionally) include /j/:

$$23'''\qquad [+\text{coronal}] \xrightarrow{\langle\text{opt}\rangle} [+\text{anterior}]/\left\{\begin{matrix}\overline{[-\text{son}]}\\ [\langle-\text{cons}\rangle]\end{matrix}\right\}$$

This form persisted until stage 17 from which time /j/ was always realised as [−anterior], even though the reflex of the adult form was [ɹ] not [j] for some time:

> yet → ɹɛt etc.

This represented a simplification of R23''' to:

$$23''''\qquad [+\text{coronal}] \to [+\text{anterior}]/[\overline{-\text{son}}]$$

This version of the rule persisted until stage 29 (2 April 1971 onwards) when the affricates |ts| and |dz|, which had appeared distinctively from stage 20, acquired the correct adult palato-alveolar [tʃ, dʒ], rather than alveolar, form. Then we had:

$$23'''''\qquad [\text{coronal}] \to [+\text{anterior}]/\left[\begin{matrix}-\text{son}\\+\text{cont}\end{matrix}\right]$$

the form the rule had when A was four years old (i.e. he still had no [ʃ] and [ʒ] though he did have [tʃ] and [dʒ]).

The development of Rule R24, making non-sonorants also non-strident, non-continuant, non-affricated and non-lateral (see pp. 21, 30), was first complicated by the appearance of [ɸ] and [f] at stages 2 and 3:

> cough → ġɔɸ
> draught → (waːft) *or* waːpt
> stiff → ḍɪf

These sounds were not contrastive for A and in his 'idiolect' can be treated as allophones of |w| (see below, p. 107). However, as they occur only as reflexes of adult /f/ and never of adult /w/ or /p/ for instance, the realisation rules should take account of them. Thus at stage 2 we split R24 into two parts:

$$24(\text{i}) \quad [-\text{sonorant}] \xrightarrow{\langle\text{opt}\rangle} \begin{bmatrix} -\text{del rel} \\ +\text{cont} \end{bmatrix} \Big/ \left[\left\langle \overline{\begin{matrix} +\text{cont} \\ -\text{cor} \\ +\text{ant} \end{matrix}} \right\rangle \right]^1$$

24(ii) $[+\text{segment}] \rightarrow [-\text{strident}]^2$

where the linked (angle) brackets indicate that the rule is optional if the segment is /f/, obligatory otherwise. (Note that initial /f/ and /v/ will already have been converted to |w| by R20 (see p. 30 above) and so will not be affected.) It should be noted that after the first (elicited) success with the [ft] cluster in [wa:ft] (= *draught*) A quickly reverted to [pt] for this and all similar examples. That is, [f] (or [ɸ]) still occurred finally, but only [p] occurred pre-consonantally. This suggests the insertion of another rule before R24(ii) in the ordering which makes clusters non-continuant throughout. That this is more general than simply /ft/ → [pt] is indicated by such examples as:

> envelope → εmbəʔo:p (stage 9)
> anvil → æmbil (stage 27)

as well as left → wεpt (stage 3 onwards) etc.
This rule persisted until stage 19 (see below, p. 121) though exceptions began to appear from stage 17.

At stage 4, R24(i) is simplified by the omission of [−anterior] as voiced velar continuants appear sporadically as the reflex of coronal continuants which have been velarised by rule R19:

> shack → ɣæk
> look → ɣuk *or* guk
> young → ɣʌŋ *or* gʌŋ etc.

Thus we have:

$$24(\text{i})' \quad [-\text{sonorant}] \xrightarrow{\langle\text{opt}\rangle} \begin{bmatrix} -\text{del rel} \\ -\text{cont} \end{bmatrix} \Big/ \left[\left\langle \overline{\begin{matrix} +\text{cont} \\ -\text{cor} \end{matrix}} \right\rangle \right]$$

At stage 6 there were no examples of [ɣ] and the 'hypothesis' appeared to have been rejected, but at stage 7 there were several more cases:

> thinking → ɣikin
> ring → ɣiŋ *or* liŋ *or* ʁiŋ
> look → ɣuk *or* luk *or* lˠuk

---

[1] I have omitted the specification [−lateral] (see p. 30) for the sake of clarity. Nothing depends on this.

[2] I am assuming that /f, v/ are [−strident]: nothing depends on this (but see Woolley, 1968).

as putative structural pressure, in the form of both a symmetrical system for A (see below, p. 109) and a simpler realisation rule, favoured occurrences of [ɣ]. The sound persisted through stage 9. By this time sporadic appearances of [f] were occurring initially as well, as rule R20 became marginally optional (see p. 86 above) and while R24(ii) remains unchanged, R24(i) was modified again to:

$$\text{(Stage 9) 24(i)}'' \quad [-\text{son}] \rightarrow \begin{bmatrix} -\text{del rel} \\ -\text{cont} \end{bmatrix} / \left\{ \begin{matrix} \overline{[+\text{coronal}]} \\ [-\text{anterior}] \end{matrix} \right\}$$

As there are no [+continuant] velars in ESP, the presence of [−anterior] in this rule, necessitating the disjunction, might seem superfluous. However it is necessary in order to make those occurrences of, e.g., /s, ʃ, tʃ, dʒ/ which have been velarised by R19 become [g], not [ɣ]. This accretion could only be omitted at stage 13 when rule 19 became optional. We then had:

$$\text{(Stage 13) 24 (i)}''' \quad [-\text{son}] \rightarrow \begin{bmatrix} -\text{del rel} \\ -\text{cont} \end{bmatrix} / \overline{[+\text{coronal}]}^1$$

At stage 14, there was a faint tendency to insert a rule before R24 (see p. 167) converting /tʃ, dʒ/ either to [ṭ, ḍ], i.e. a palatalised alveolar plosive, or to [tɹ, dɹ], i.e. a cluster of the alveolar plosive plus [ɹ]:

$$\left. \begin{matrix} \text{jig} \rightarrow \text{ḍig} \\ \text{join} \rightarrow \text{dɹɔin} \end{matrix} \right\} \text{stage 14}$$

$$\left. \begin{matrix} \text{Jack} \rightarrow \text{dɹæk } or \text{ dæk} \\ \text{Jill} \rightarrow \text{ḍil } or \text{ dil} \end{matrix} \right\} \text{stage 15}$$

$$\left. \begin{matrix} \text{chalk} \rightarrow \text{tɹɔːk } or \text{ tʰɔːk} \\ \text{Jill} \rightarrow \text{dɹil } or \text{ dil} \end{matrix} \right\} \text{stage 16} \qquad \text{etc.}$$

This tendency never became completely regular or general[2] but per-

---

[1] Phonetically, A began to acquire affricates at stage 13:

$$\text{cupboard} \rightarrow \text{kʰʌbəd/kˣʌbəd}$$
$$\text{see} \rightarrow \text{tʰiː/tˢiː}$$

but these were mere phonetic free variants of aspiration, as A finally completed his voicing contrasts at this stage (see below re R25, pp. 95–6) and did not correlate at all with ESP affricates.

[2] Except in positions where consonant harmony conditioned it:

child → tˢaɪld *vs* children → tɹildɹən (stage 26)
chest → tˢɛst *vs* chest of drawers → tɹɛst əv dɹɔːz (stage 28)
jelly → dᶻɛliː (stage 27)
Trugel → tɹuːdɹɛl (stage 29)

Cf. the discussion of consonant harmony below (pp. 162–5). It is of interest that the reverse tendency also occurs in many children (e.g. A's cousin R):

drive → dʒaɪv
trees/cheese → tʃiːz

sisted sporadically until stage 20. I have not formalised a rule to account for it.

At stage 15, there appeared a voiceless alveolar lateral and voiceless nasals (see p. 58 above), which might seem to complicate R24(i). However, I am assuming that /ɬ/ and /n̥/ retain their sonorant status for the purposes of these rules, and will not therefore be affected by rule R24(i) which specifies $\begin{bmatrix} -\text{sonorant} \\ +\text{coronal} \end{bmatrix}$ only. Nothing depends on this assumption. The first major change in R24(ii) occurred at stage 20 when strident affricates [tˢ] and [dᶻ] appeared (in free variation with their plosive congeners) as the reflexes of /s, θ, ʃ, tʃ/ and /dʒ/ (for examples, see p. 60 above). As A treated alike the strident /s/ and non-strident /θ/ I assume that R24(i) has altered, to make ESP continuants and affricates optionally delayed-release or non-delayed-release, and that R24(ii) then makes coronal affricates strident.

$$24(\text{i})'''' \quad [-\text{sonorant}] \rightarrow \begin{bmatrix} -\text{continuant} \\ \pm\text{del rel} \end{bmatrix} \Big/ \begin{bmatrix} \overline{+\text{coronal}} \\ +\text{del rel} \end{bmatrix}^1$$

$$24(\text{ii})' \quad \begin{bmatrix} +\text{coronal} \\ +\text{del rel} \end{bmatrix} \rightarrow [+\text{strident}]$$

Thus we have: say → tˢeɪ *or* teɪ
thought → tɔːt
thumb → tˢʌm etc.

Initial /z/ which is not affected by this rule:

zoo → ɹuː
zed → ɹɛd

will already have been converted to |r| by rule R18C (see p. 78 above), but initial /ð/ which is also unaffected:

this → dit
those → dəudᶻ

---

[1] The notation [±Fᵢ] – e.g. here [±del rel] – is to be interpreted in the obvious way as saying that any segment which meets the structural description of the rule may end up as either [+Fᵢ] or [−Fᵢ]. This is equivalent here to having angle brackets as a specification of optionality:

$$[-\text{son}] \xrightarrow{\langle\text{opt}\rangle} \begin{bmatrix} -\text{cont} \\ \langle-\text{del rel}\rangle \end{bmatrix} \Big/ \begin{bmatrix} \overline{+\text{cor}} \\ +\text{del rel} \end{bmatrix}$$

but if the structural description of the rule does not itself include [αFᵢ] then the notations are not equivalent: see, e.g. R24(i)''''', on p. 93, where segments may or may not change from continuant to non-continuant and vice versa.

must be catered for by an additional interpolated rule, call it R23A, which converts /ð/ to |d|:

23A
$$\begin{bmatrix} -\text{sonorant} \\ +\text{coronal} \\ +\text{continuant} \\ -\text{strident} \\ +\text{voice} \end{bmatrix} \rightarrow [-\text{continuant}]/\#\text{———}$$

At stage 21, the previous free variation between [t]/[ts] and [d]/[dz] changes to free variation between [ts]/[s] and [dz]/[z]:[1]

cards → ka:dz *or* ka:z		softer → sɔftə	
cars → ka:dz *or* ka:z		star → sa: *or* tˢa:	
chair → tˢɛ³ *or* sɛə		say → tˢeɪ	
say → tˢeɪ *or* seɪ		stay → tˢeɪ	
shall → ʂæl		thing → sɪŋ *or* tˢɪŋ	
shut → tˢʌt		sing → sɪŋ *or* tˢɪŋ	
soft → tsɔft			

In other words, R24(i) has changed to:

$$[-\text{sonorant}] \rightarrow \begin{bmatrix} \pm\text{cont} \\ +\text{del rel} \end{bmatrix} / \begin{bmatrix} +\text{cor} \\ +\text{del rel} \end{bmatrix}$$

which is equivalent to:

24(i)′′′′′
$$\begin{bmatrix} +\text{coronal} \\ +\text{del rel} \end{bmatrix} \rightarrow [\pm\text{continuant}]$$

while R24(ii) has remained unchanged. The two halves of R24 can now be conflated again because of the identical treatment given to all [delayed release] segments, with the exception of /z/ and /ð/ already mentioned.

24′
$$\begin{bmatrix} +\text{coronal} \\ +\text{del rel} \end{bmatrix} \rightarrow \begin{bmatrix} \pm\text{continuant} \\ -\text{strident} \end{bmatrix}$$

By stage 22, the transition of the affricates to a pure continuant is almost complete. There are only two or three affricates left;[2] otherwise

---

[1] It is noteworthy that the affricate [tˢ] changed phonetically gradually during the transition from [t] to [s]. First there was a very slight offglide (in free variation with greater aspiration – see p. 91, n. 1); then a true affricate [tˢ]; then the same with a more prominent release [ts]; then a continuant with a slight initial closure [ᵗs]; and then finally a real fricative [s], where at first this [s] was usually lamino-alveolar rather than apico-alveolar. This gradualism was unexpected. See discussion, pp. 140ff.

[2] It is probable that /dʒ/ should be excluded from this generalisation. Whereas /tʃ/ consistently ended up as |s|, /dʒ/ usually ended up as |dz|:

jam → dzæm
jar → dza:

I have not accounted for this in the rules.

all the segments concerned, including /st/ clusters, are |s| or |z|:

chair → sɛ:	shut → sʌt
cheese → si:z	stamp → sæmp
scissors → sizəz	station → seɪsən
scratch → kɹæs	think → siŋk etc.

i.e. we have:

$$24''\qquad \begin{bmatrix} +\,\text{coronal} \\ +\,\text{del rel} \end{bmatrix} \rightarrow \begin{bmatrix} +\,\text{continuant} \\ +\,\text{strident} \end{bmatrix}$$

At stage 26, affricates began gradually to be reinstated this time selectively for the ESP affricates, instead of across the board for all ESP delayed release coronals, i.e. we have:

cheese → si:z *or* tˢi:z
chocolate → sɔklit *or* tsɔklit

but only: shut → sʌt (*tsʌt)

think → siŋk (*tˢiŋk) etc.

and by stage 27 this process was virtually complete. This change can be formalised simply by omitting the feature [−continuant] from the structural change of R24:

$$24'''\qquad \begin{bmatrix} +\,\text{coronal} \\ +\,\text{del rel} \end{bmatrix} \rightarrow +\,[\text{strident}]$$

This rule, together with rule R23 (p. 88), correctly characterises this part of A's system at age four – namely: the neutralisation of /s/ and /θ/ and /ʃ/ as [s], and in non-initial position, of /z/ and /ð/ and /ʒ/ as [z]:

breathe → bɹi:z (Jacques → zæk)
breeze → bɹi:z
(sin → sin)
thin → sin
shin → sin

but the distinction of /tʃ/ and /dʒ/ from the rest of these, as [ts] and [dz] up to stage 28, and as [tʃ] and [dʒ] at stage 29. Note that even after[tʃ] and [dʒ] were correctly realised as palato-alveolars, A was still quite un-able to produce [ʃ] or [ʒ].[1]

Rule R23A (changing /ð/ to |d| initially) was still operative at the close of the study.

---

[1] This was still true until the age of 4 years 6 months when /ʃ/ and /ʒ/ were finally mastered.

Rule R25, voicing all segments (pp. 21–31), and thereby accounting for the neutralisation of the voicing contrast in A's speech, persisted unchanged until stage 10. However, at stage 7, the first reflex of the adult voicing distinction, namely a difference of vowel length, appeared in A's speech:

card → ġa::ḍ[1]	used → ḍu::t
cart → ga:ḍ	pink → ḅik
juice → ḍu:t	pig → ḅi:k

Although A now had contrasts corresponding to voicing contrasts in the adult system, phonetically he still had no contrast in the *consonants*; and rule R25 was unchanged. The difference is characterised by an interpolated rule lengthening vowels before final voiced consonants before the voicing contrast is neutralised:

24A $[+\text{syllabic}] \overset{\text{opt}}{\rightarrow} [+\text{long}]/\underline{\hspace{1em}} \begin{bmatrix} +\text{cons} \\ +\text{voice} \end{bmatrix} \#$

(For a discussion of the perception of distinctive features and the position of [length] as opposed to [voice], see below, pp. 134–5.)

Rule R25 itself changed at stage 10 when it was complicated to allow final consonants not to be voiced:

25′ $[+\text{segment}] \overset{\langle\text{opt}\rangle}{\longrightarrow} [+\text{voiced}]/\underline{\hspace{1em}}\langle[-\text{segment}]\rangle$

i.e. before a boundary ([−segment]) the voicing rule is now optional; it is obligatory elsewhere. That is, *cart* and *card* are now distinguished by voicing *and* length:

cart → ġa:t
card → ġa::ḍ

At stage 11, the vowel lengthening before voiced consonants is generalised to all positions (not merely finally); and at the same time rule R25 itself generalises to post-vocalic position in general, not merely final position:

24A′ $[+\text{syll}] \overset{\text{opt}}{\rightarrow} [+\text{long}]/\underline{\hspace{1em}} \begin{bmatrix} +\text{cons} \\ +\text{voiced} \end{bmatrix}$

25″ $[+\text{cons}] \overset{\langle\text{opt}\rangle}{\longrightarrow} [+\text{voiced}]/\langle[+\text{syll}]\rangle\underline{\hspace{1em}}$

[1] Two colons indicate extra long vowel. N.B. [ḍ] and [t] were still in free variation in final position. The length contrast was much clearer after long vowels than after short vowels (i.e. the last pair was only marginally distinct).

We now have contrasts of the kind exemplified by:

muscle → mʌtu	probably → b̰lɔbli:
muzzle → mʌdu	pudding → b̰uḍin
properly → b̰lɔpli:	putting → b̰utin

However, all these contrasts are 'optional' or to be more precise not stable in A's speech. At stage 12 R24A loses its optionality as the voicing contrast is established both finally and intervocalically; and at the same time rule R25 is restricted to occurring in initial position, as the first initial contrasts appear:

choke → ko:k
joke → g̈o:k

25‴ $[+\text{cons}] \overset{\text{opt}}{\to} [+\text{voiced}]/ \# \text{---}$

By stage 13 both rules have gone as A's voicing distinctions match those of the adult language. To be precise, perhaps we should say that R25 has gone, as no further mapping from ESP to A's speech is required, but that R24A has merely become a phonetic rule of A's own phonology, rather than the realisation rule it was.

Rule R26, making all non-vowels consonants (pp. 22, 31), is strictly speaking not essential, having its main justification in the increased simplicity it brings to the statement of A's own system: viz. all segments are either $\begin{bmatrix} +\text{cons} \\ -\text{syll} \end{bmatrix}$ or $\begin{bmatrix} -\text{cons} \\ +\text{syll} \end{bmatrix}$; and we could if desired make do with only the feature [syllabic]. Moreover, when [f] first appears in A's speech it is as an 'allophone' of |w| and then later [w] and [f] form a voiced/voiceless pair beside p/b, t/d, k/g; and it would accordingly be odd to have them in different major categories. Again, the /v/w/ contrast of ESP was consistently neutralised (usually to |w|) by A, the distinction still not being stable at the end of the study. Lastly /w/ behaved like the other consonants for A with respect to its behaviour after /s/ (→ [f] – see p. 62) whereas /j/ did not. Accordingly, rule R26 is retained until the appearance of /j/ at stage 24 necessitates a change to:

26′ $\begin{bmatrix} -\text{syllabic} \\ -\text{coronal} \end{bmatrix} \to [+\text{consonantal}]$

i.e. |w/v| are still not distinct but |j| is now established. The rule began to waver at stage 29 when |v| and |w| were just beginning to be consistently operated.

Rule R27, the rule interpolated at stage 2 to account for the non-homorganicity of nasal clusters (p. 54 above), persisted, with some vacillation, until about stage 9, when the normal clusters appeared.

There remain to be discussed those interpolated rules which did not interact with any of the others cited above, but appeared independently at some stage or other in the development of A's speech.[1]

At stage 4, A began to insert homorganic consonants after nasal consonants, as a generalisation of his new-found ability to produce nasal plus consonant clusters from stage 2 (see p. 53 above). Thus beside:

> friend → wɛnd
> hand → ænd

we have: broken → ḅuːkənd[2]

> neck → ŋgɛk *or* ŋɛk
> ironing board → aɪndin ḅɔːḍ
> brown → ḅaund later bɹaund
> singing → ġiŋgiŋ (earlier ġiɲiŋ)

We can formalise this as rule R28:

$$28 \qquad \emptyset \overset{\text{opt}}{\to} \begin{bmatrix} +\text{cons} \\ -\text{cont} \\ -\text{nasal} \\ \alpha\text{cor} \\ \beta\text{ant} \end{bmatrix} \Bigg/ \begin{bmatrix} +\text{nasal} \\ \alpha\text{coronal} \\ \beta\text{anterior} \end{bmatrix} \text{———}$$

i.e. a consonant is inserted after a nasal, agreeing with that nasal in all other features but nasality. This rule persisted very haphazardly till about stage 15.

At stage 12, post-vocalic pre-final |r|'s appeared. Thus:

driver → dɹaɪvəɹ	Lucinda → luːˈtindəɹ
ear → iəɹ	remember → mɛmbəɹ
finger → wiŋgəɹ *or* wiŋgə	slipper → lipəɹ etc.
jar → daːɹ	

It is almost certain that this represents a generalisation of the linking [r] found in ESP to (sentence) final position. Although A's mother uses post-vocalic [ɹ] this is not thought to be the cause of A's using it: first because his mother has [ɹ] preconsonantally within a word, and there was *never* an example of this in A's speech; second [ɹ] occurred in words

---

[1] I am ignoring the need for a rule that reduces geminate clusters arising from the operation of other rules, and probably other, but I hope self-evident, minor rules.

[2] This was a year or so before he began this kind of addition as a morphological process – i.e. this was certainly a phonological process.

where no linking, or even intrusive [ɹ], occurs in ESP – e.g. *raw* as in:

    raw egg → ɹɔːɹɛg

and even in Hindi loan words, heard only from his mother, where no [ɹ] could ever have been heard:

    [aːṭaː] (flour) → aːtəɹ

Accordingly I postulate a rule R29:

$$29 \qquad \emptyset \overset{\text{opt}}{\to} [\text{ɹ}] / \begin{bmatrix} +\text{syll} \\ +\text{low} \end{bmatrix} \underline{\qquad} \#$$

This rule persisted until stage 19, after which final |r| only occurred in one or two random occurrences of *car* – [kaː(ɹ)], and *more* – [mɔː(ɹ)].

    Finally, at stage 10, there became apparent the operation of a regular rule of metathesis, which had perhaps been present for some time (see, e.g., p. 36 for a suggestion that it may have operated from the start). Before formulating any rule I will list the examples *in toto* with the stages at which they occurred indicated on the right. I have divided the examples into three sections: A, B, C, the reason for which will become apparent immediately:

A	ask	aːkt	14
	asp	æpt	14
	bulb	bʌbl	18
	(delve	dɛvl	20)
	desk	⎰ dɛkt	18
		⎱ dɛks	21
	film	flim	19
	helping	ɛplin	13
	husband	ʌptəmb	14
	milk	mlik	10
	risk	rikt	14
		⎧ lɛf	10
	self	⎨ ɬɛf	16
		⎩ slɛf	23
	selfish	lɛfit	11
		⎧ lɛf	10
	shelf	⎨ ɬɛf	16
		⎪ ɬɛf/tlɛf	18
		⎩ slɛf	23
		⎧ livlə	11
	silver	⎨ ɬivlə	18
		⎩ sivlə	23

	whisk	wiktə	16
	whisker	wiktə	14
	wolf	wufl	18
B	alligator	æɡəleɪtə	22
	animal	æmələn	25
	bicycle	baɪkəsəl	22
	Bosworthick	bɔtwəːkit	19
	delicate	dɛkələt	15
	difficult	ʃgipətul	13
		ˌgifətəlt	20
	elephant	ɛfələnt	18
	galloping	ɡæpəlin	19
	icicle	aɪkitəl	16
	miserable	mizbəɹəl	23
	plastic	plækit	19
	testicle	tɛkətəl	19
C	aeroplane	ɛːbəʔeɪn	1
	blancmange	bɔˈtɔm	11
	Copydex	dɔpiːɡɛk	10
	Christmas	ġiptit	9
	chutney	ḍaːtin	8
	elephant	ɛpininin	2
	finish	ˌwitiː	4
		witin	7
		fintiː	15
	giraffe	riːˈdzæf	27
	Greco	ɡɛkəl	10
	magnet	mæŋgit	10
	mendable	mɛlbədən	24
	music	muːɡiː	2
	penis	pitin	4
	rhinoceros	haɪnɔɹətət	19
	saliva	ləvlaɪvə	15
	slippers	dipələ	11
	(solvent	tɔləmpt	15)
	supposed	əspəuzd	28
	trafficator	kætiweiːtə/	8
		kæwitiːleːtə	
	violet	læːwit	15

4-2

All the examples in A have in common the fact that an adult consonant cluster consisting of a coronal consonant followed by a non-coronal consonant is rearranged so that either the cluster occurs in the reverse sequence: that is $C_1C_2 \rightarrow C_2C_1$, e.g. the first five examples; or the first consonant (the coronal one) is transposed with the preceding vowel, e.g. *film, milk, self, shelf* etc.[1] Various points need to be made:

(1) [bʌbl] is monosyllabic, in contrast with [bʌbḷ] (*bubble*).

(2) The analysis of *self* and *shelf* was at first completely opaque, particularly as at stage 10 there were still isolated examples of /s/ being realised as |l| (see p. 80 above), but their subsequent development makes any alternative analysis of the data unlikely.

(3) Many of the examples cited also occurred in alternative forms, though most of them persisted for some time in the shape shown here. For further details the reader is referred to Appendix C.

The examples in B are comparable to those in A, in that again a pair of consonants occurring in the sequence coronal non-coronal has its sequence reversed. In this case, however, there is intervening material, either a vowel or a sequence of vowel consonant vowel, between the metathesising consonants.

In the case of both A and B there is clear adherence to the principle of metathesis first propounded for diachronic studies by C.-J. Bailey (1970) namely, that metathesis always works to shift a coronal consonant to the right of a non-coronal consonant.

The examples in C are either (1) exceptions to this principle, viz. *Copydex, magnet* and *violet*; or (2) too far removed from the adult form for the analysis to be clear, e.g. *blancmange, mendable, solvent*; or (3) involve only coronal consonants, e.g. *giraffe, penis*; or (4) only one consonant and a vowel, e.g. *chutney, supposed*.

Magnet appears to be representative of a class of true exceptions to Bailey's principle – namely those clusters consisting of C + N will metathesise to N + C[2] irrespective of the point of articulation of the consonants. There were no other examples in A's speech, but [siŋgəl] for /signəl/ is a common example in children's speech.[3] *Difficult* is *sui generis* in that the first and third consonants switch, except for the retention of the original voicing; *violet* was an apparently random mistake – it did not recur.

---

[1] A third means of dealing with undesirable (marked) clusters was simply to delete the first consonant, e.g. *helping* → [ɛplin] or [ɛpin].

[2] If they metathesise at all, that is.

[3] I am grateful to John Wells for pointing this out to me.

Of the others, some may lend slight further support to Bailey's principle: for *aeroplane*, see above, p. 36; and *elephant* – [εpinin] probably represents a derivation of the kind:

> εlifənt → εfilint (metathesis and vowel harmony)
> εfilint → εfinint (nasal assimilation; see R5, p. 25)
> εfinint → εpinint (see R24, p. 30)
> εpinint → εpinin (see R22, p. 30)

All the stages are independently motivated – only the combination and ordering is wrong. In general, words of more than two syllables caused severe problems for A at the very early stages, but it seems that there is nonetheless some kind of principle behind the deformations he subjects them to. Whatever tortuous analysis is made, words like *elephant* will remain exceptions, but even exceptions are not entirely random.

Because of the sporadic nature of the metathesis rule or rules, and because of the problem of restructuring (see below, p. 143) it is difficult to know when it appeared and disappeared in A's phonology. As a rough approximation, and limiting ourselves to the regular examples in A and B, we can say that it appeared at stage 10, and disappeared about stage 25. A rough formalisation of the rule is:

30

$$X \ V \ [+\text{coronal}] \ [-\text{coronal}] \ Y$$

$$1 \quad 2 \qquad 3 \qquad\qquad 4 \qquad 5 \Rightarrow \begin{Bmatrix} 1\ 2\ 3\ 4\ 5 \\ 1\ 3\ 2\ 4\ 5 \end{Bmatrix}$$

Rule R30 must precede rule R7.

Rule R30 must precede rule R7 as examples like /a:sk/ metathesise the /s/ and /k/ rather than deleting the /s/. The /s/ later becomes [t] by rule R24. Words such as *icicle* and *testicle* also seem to indicate that metathesis must follow rule R3 which velarises coronals to velars (e.g. /bɔtəl/ → |bɔkəl|) as we have [aıkitəl] and [tɛkətəl], where [təl] is not otherwise normal for A. However, as the underlying form contains /s/ or /st/, this is inconclusive, as only stops are affected by R3 (see p. 14 above). If *difficult* → [gipətul] is regular, this would tend to confirm the ordering of metathesis between R3 and R7, but here there is the problem that the underlying form ends in /əlt/, not simply /əl/. I leave it numbered as R30.

To conclude this section, I present table 4, a chart of all the rules and their changes for all stages of A's phonology from 1 to 29. This serves both to give a bird's eye view of the changes *in toto*, and also to allow the reconstruction of the entire set of rules characterising any given stage.

Lincoln Christian College

TABLE 4. *Changes in the realisation rules for all stages*

Rule	1	2	3	4	5	6	7	8	9	10	11	12	13	14	15	16	17	18	19	20	21	22	23	24	25	26	27	28	29
1	o	o	o	o	o	o	o	o	o	o	o	*	o	∅															
2	o	*	∅																										
3	o	*	o	o	o	o	o	o	o	o	o	o	o	o	o	*	o	o	o	o	o	o	o	o	o	o	o	o	*
4	o	o	o	o	o	o	o	o	o	o	*	o	∅																
5	o	∅																											
6 i	o	o	< o	o	o	o	o	o	∅																				
6 ii			o	o	*	o	o	o	o	∅																			
6A i													*	o	< o	o	o	o	o	o	o	o	o	o	>*	∅			
6A ii															o	o	o	o	o	o	o	*	*						
6B																*	o	o	o	o	o	∅							
7	o	o	o	o	o	o	o	o	o	o	o	o	o	o	o	o	o	o	o	o	o	o	*	o	∅				
8	o	o	o	o	o	o	o	o	o	o	o	*	o	o	o	o	o	o	o	o	o	o	o	o	∅				
9	o	o	>*																										
10	o	o	>*	o	o	∅																							
10A	—	*	o	>*	o	∅																							
11	o	o	o	o	o	o	o	o	o	o	o	o	o	o	o	*	o	o	*	*	o	o	*	o	∅				
12	o	*	o	o	o	o	o	o	o	o	o	o	o	o	o	o	o	o	o	o	o	o	o	o	o	o	o	o	o
13	o	o	o	o	o	o	o	o	o	o	o	o	o	*	o	∅													
14	o	*	o	∅																									
15	o	o	o	∅																									
16 i	o	o	o	o	o	o	o	o	< o	o	o	o	o	o	o	o	o	o	o	o	o	o	o	o	*	o	o	o	∅
16 ii										*	o	*	o	∅															
16 iii										*	o	*	∅																
16 iv										o	o	∅																	
17	o	*	o	∅																									
18A	o	o	o	o	o	o	o	o	o	o	o	o	o	o	o	o	o	o	o	o	o	o	o	o	o	o	o	o	∅
18B	o	o	o	*	o	o	o	o	o	o	*	∅																	
18C	o	*	o	o	*	*	*	o	*	o	*	o	*	o	o	o	*	o	*	o	o	*	o	*	o	o	o	o	o
19 i	o	o	< *	*	o	o	o	*	*	o	o	*	∅																
19 ii			o	o	*	o	o	o	*	*	∅																		
20	o	*	o	o	o	o	o	*	o	o	*	o	o	*	o	∅													
21	o	*	o	o	∅																								
22	o	*	∅																										
23	o	*	o	*	o	o	o	*	o	o	o	o	o	o	o	o	o	*	o	o	o	o	o	o	o	o	o	o	*
23A																			*	o	o	o	o	o	o	o	o	o	o
24 i	o	*	o	o	o	o	o	*	o	o	o	*	o	o	o	o	o	o	*	>*	o	o	o	*	o	o	*		
24 ii	o	o	o	o	o	o	o	o	o	o	o	o	o	o	o	o	o	*											
24A							*	o	o	o	*	*	∅																
25	o	o	o	o	o	o	o	o	o	*	*	*	∅																
26	o	o	o	o	o	o	o	o	o	o	o	o	o	o	o	o	o	o	o	o	o	o	o	o	*	o	o	o	∅
27	—	*	o	o	o	o	o	o	∅																				
28				*	o	o	o	o	o	o	o	o	o	o	∅														
29													*	o	o	o	o	o	o	∅									
30													*	o	o	o	o	o	o	o	o	o	o	o	o	o	o	∅	

Key

o no change from previous stage (or = stage 1)

* change in rule, or point of onset of new rule

> collapse of rules

< separation of rules (with the number of the rules inserted)

∅ stage of disappearance of rule

→ rule continues in operation beyond the end of the study

— rule not yet appeared

By presenting the diachronic development of the rules atomistically the status of the individual stages has been obscured. However, by referring to table 4 and cross-referring to the development of the individual rules one can quickly build up a complete picture of any desired stage of development.

3.2 Longitudinal analysis of A's phonology as a self-contained system

The changes in A's phonology taken as a self-contained system will be described in stages, rather than piecemeal by rule; and will furthermore be treated largely as a function of the already described changes in the realisation rules. In other words, although the developing system *can* be viewed as independent, the changes taking place in it will be explicitly related to – in one way explained by – the changes in the realisation rules as the child approximates more closely to the adult form. We shall see in chapter 4 that his system should probably *only* be viewed as a function of the adult language, and has no valid status apart from this at all.

In view of this claim it might seem redundant to present the longitudinal analysis of A's phonology as a self-contained system in such detail. I have done so as this claim is likely to be controversial, and rests not only on the positive evidence of the explanatory power of the realisation rules, but also on the negative evidence of the lack of explanatory power of the changes in the MS conditions characterising A's own system. Since I have presented this latter analysis in depth, the reader who wishes to challenge my conclusions will find his path facilitated. A second justification lies in the fact that the formalisation of the MS conditions permits a clear and explicit overview of the effects of the realisation rules at any stage as implementing the universal tendencies elaborated in chapter 4, and allows one to evaluate the 'conspiratorial' nature of these rules in a simple fashion.

For the sake of convenience I repeat here the set of morpheme structure conditions set up at stage 1 (see pp. 47–50 above) as a *point de départ* for the longitudinal study of A's system. All changes will be treated in terms of additions to, deletions from and complications of these conditions, although periodically a revised distinctive feature matrix will be given for a particular stage as a clear indication of the number of 'phonemic' segments operating in A's speech.

MS1 $\quad$ #(C)V(V)(CV)*(C)#

MS2 $\quad$ # $\left(\begin{bmatrix} +\text{consonantal} \\ \alpha\text{coronal} \\ \beta\text{continuant} \end{bmatrix}\right)$ V $\begin{bmatrix} +\text{consonantal} \\ \gamma\text{coronal} \\ \delta\text{continuant} \end{bmatrix}$ V...#

where: either $\alpha = \beta = \gamma = \delta$
or $(\alpha \neq \beta)$ *and* $(\gamma \neq \delta)$

MS3 $\quad$ C → [−continuant]/——#

MS4 $\quad$ C → [−coronal]/——V $\begin{bmatrix} -\text{coronal} \\ -\text{anterior} \end{bmatrix}$

MS4A $\quad$ C → [−coronal]/ $\begin{bmatrix} -\text{coronal} \\ -\text{anterior} \end{bmatrix}$ V [$\overline{-\text{nasal}}$]

MS5 $\quad$ C → [−coronal]/[$\overline{+\text{nasal}}$] V [−coronal]

MS6 $\quad$ C → [+anterior]/[$\overline{+\text{nasal}}$] V [+anterior]

MS7 $\quad$ [+nasal] → $\begin{bmatrix} +\text{coronal} \\ +\text{anterior} \end{bmatrix}$/X $\begin{bmatrix} V \\ -\text{stress} \end{bmatrix}$—— where X ≠ |ŋ|

MS8 $\quad$ [+coronal] → [+anterior]

MS9 $\quad$ [+nasal] → [−continuant]

MS10 $\quad$ [+continuant] → [+anterior]

In general, exemplification will be kept to a minimum, as in nearly all cases examples can be found by cross-referring to the relevant realisation rule.

Stage 2. The most obvious change in A's system from stage 1 was the appearance of consonant clusters and the corresponding modification to MS1. The first change was caused by R2 (deleting post-nasal voiced consonants) becoming optional and leading to the complication of MS1 as follows:

MS1' $\quad$ #(C)V $\left(\left\{\begin{matrix} V \\ \begin{bmatrix} +\text{cons} \\ +\text{nasal} \end{bmatrix} \end{matrix}\right\}\right)$ (CV)* (C)#

i.e. the third segment may now be a vowel or a nasal consonant. Whereas previously there had been the possibiilty only of vowel sequences, e.g.:

corridor → ġɔi:dɔ:

now there are also nasal plus consonant sequences, e.g.:

angry → æŋgi:

Within this stage MS1′ was simplified to MS1″ by the omission of [+nasal], viz.:

$$\text{MS1}'' \quad \#(C)V \left(\left\{ \begin{array}{c} V \\ [+cons] \end{array} \right\} \right) (CV)^* (C) \#^1$$

that is, we also have non-nasal consonant clusters, e.g.:

      doctor → ġɔktə

as a result of R21 (deleting post-consonantal coronals) becoming optional.

Secondly, as a result of the optionality of R18C (above, p. 76), MS2 stating that all or none of the consonants in a word must be |l|, is relaxed to allow the second consonant to be any kind of coronal, i.e. we have:

      lady → leːdi: (or ḍeːdi:)

but: like→ ġaɪk (*laɪk)

As there are no comparable cases where |l| is medial and a coronal consonant initial, this allows us to simplify MS2 by making it directional (see the discussion on p. 48 above), viz.:

$$\text{MS2}' \quad C \rightarrow [+coronal] / \left[\begin{array}{c} +coronal \\ +continuant \end{array} \right] V \text{——} V$$

MS4, 6, 8, and 9 remained unchanged but MS4A and MS5 had both disappeared by stage 2. The former, excluding sequences such as [gud] (above, p. 42) disappeared as the result of R17 (velarising final coronals) being restricted to ESP continuants (above, p. 74); the latter, restricting occurrences of |n| to cases where the following consonant was also alveolar (above, p. 42), went as the result of the optionality of R19. Strictly speaking, the loss of MS5 is not directly dependent on any change in R19 as R19 is already optional when α = + (above p. 81). The absence of any items where |n| preceded a labial at stage 1, and their appearance at stage 2 – e.g. *number* → [nʌmdə] – is probably fortuitous.

MS7, limiting nasals in unstressed syllables to |n|, is simplified by losing the specification [+coronal] as a direct result of the comparable complication of R12 (above, p. 70).

The changes in rules R3, R20 and R22 had no effect on A's 'internal' system. The one problem remaining is that concerning MS10 and the effect on it of the apparent optionality of R23 (see the discussion on

---

¹ Alternatively: $\#(C)V \left(\left\{ \begin{array}{c} C \\ V \end{array} \right\} \right) (CV)^* (C)\#$

where the third term could be represented most simply as [+seg], i.e. we can have: CVV, CVC, CVVC, CVCC, but not CVVCC. Contrast stage 4 below.

p. 88 above, especially n. 3) whereby sporadic occurrences of [ɹ] appeared. Although these occurrences were clearly not random, it is equally clear that A had not stabilised [ɹ], and accordingly I leave his phonology unchanged in that regard. The lack of change in MS8, 9, 10 indicates that A was still operating with the same number of 'underlying' segments.

As a result of the changes to MS1 it is necessary to add three more conditions to A's phonology:

$$\text{MS}11 \quad [\ ] \rightarrow [+\text{syllabic}] / \begin{bmatrix} -\text{nasal} \\ +\text{cons} \end{bmatrix} [+\text{cons}]\underline{\quad\quad}$$

i.e. non-nasal clusters appear only medially, whereas nasal clusters appear medially and finally.[1]

$$\text{MS}12 \quad X \begin{bmatrix} C \\ -\text{nasal} \end{bmatrix} [C]\ Y \rightarrow X \begin{bmatrix} -\text{anterior} \\ -\text{coronal} \end{bmatrix} [+\text{coronal}]\ Y$$

i.e. non-nasal clusters are |gd| (phonetically [kt]).

$$\text{MS}13 \quad C \rightarrow \begin{bmatrix} \alpha\text{coronal} \\ \alpha\text{anterior} \end{bmatrix} / \begin{bmatrix} \alpha\text{anterior} \\ +\text{nasal} \end{bmatrix}\underline{\quad\quad}$$

Once nasal clusters appeared it was, of course, necessary to specify the point of articulation of the component elements (cf. MS12). The first cluster to appear was |ŋg|:

> angry → ɛŋgi:
> handle → ɛŋgu etc.

closely followed by |nd|:

> inside → indaɪd
> hand → ɛnd etc.

However, the next nasal plus consonant cluster to appear was not the expected |mb| but rather |md|:

> number → nʌmdə[2]
> camera → ġɛmdə

This implies that it is not possible to have a rule assigning the features of the following consonant to the nasal, viz. [+nasal] → [αF_iβF_j] but

---

[1] This may well be a fortuitous gap.
[2] There was no hesitation or vacillation at all on A's part. Even when asked to repeat an exaggeratedly stressed 'num*b*er', he consistently said [nʌmdə].

rather that we need a rule or rules assigning features of the nasal to the consonant. In this case we have:

$$C \rightarrow \begin{bmatrix} + \text{coronal} \\ + \text{anterior} \end{bmatrix} \Big/ \begin{bmatrix} + \text{anterior} \\ + \text{nasal} \end{bmatrix} \underline{\quad}$$

and: $\quad C \rightarrow \begin{bmatrix} - \text{coronal} \\ - \text{anterior} \end{bmatrix} \Big/ \begin{bmatrix} - \text{anterior} \\ + \text{nasal} \end{bmatrix} \underline{\quad}$

which collapse to the form MS13 above. Note that this conflation is simpler than the 'usual' (ESP) rule of nasal assimilation which would require a further feature and variable to be specified:

$$\text{viz. } C \rightarrow \begin{bmatrix} \alpha \text{coronal} \\ \beta \text{anterior} \end{bmatrix} \Big/ \begin{bmatrix} + \text{nasal} \\ \alpha \text{coronal} \\ \beta \text{anterior} \end{bmatrix} \underline{\quad}$$

It is interesting that a normally unexpected sequence, and one which would be deemed highly marked, can be formulated more simply than the expected unmarked sequence. What I had hitherto considered a defect of the theory seems on this evidence to be after all an advantage.

The final modification from stage 1 to stage 2 concerns both MS3 and a phonetic realisation rule. At stage 1 all continuants were always voiced (see Ph1, p. 50) whereas plosives were subject to considerable allophonic variation (see Ph2, p. 51). At stage 2, |w| is subject to the same rules as the plosives, with the result that there is now a voiceless labial in final position, be this [ɸ] or [f]:

cough → ġɔɸ
stiff → dif

This means that the distribution of the allophones of plosives is at least partially paralleled by those of |w|. That is, MS3 must be complicated to MS3′:

MS3′ $\quad C \rightarrow [-\text{continuant}]/[\overline{+\text{coronal}}] \; \#$

to allow |w| to occur finally, while still excluding |l| from this position, and Ph1 and 2 must be modified to cover [f, ɸ] as well.[1] If it seems counter-intuitive to treat [f] (/[ɸ]) as a variant of |w| note that apart from the fact that [f] and [w] are in complementary distribution (and phonetically 'similar'), /f/ regularly becomes |w| initially, e.g. *foot* → [wut], and later adult /w/ became |f| after an /s/, e.g. *sweet* → [fi:t] (see above,

---

[1] This is another occasion where it would be advantageous to have a classification which separated out liquids and glides in terms of [voc] and [cons] instead of the system used here. See discussion below, p. 193.

p. 62). That this is the simplest way to characterise A's system *qua* A's system is accordingly uncontroversial.

Stage 3. Changes in the morpheme structure conditions from stage 2 to stage 3 were minimal, despite a number of changes in the realisation rules for the corresponding period. In fact the only notable changes: the disappearance of MS11 which had been introduced at stage 2 to account for the asymmetrical distribution of non-nasal consonant clusters (see above, p. 54), and the simplification of MS12 to allow [pt] as well as [kt] clusters, viz.:

$$\text{MS12}' \quad X \begin{bmatrix} C \\ -\text{nasal} \end{bmatrix} [C] \; Y \rightarrow X \; [-\text{coronal}] \; [+\text{coronal}] \; Y$$

were not directly related to any realisation rule, but rather resulted from the filling of (probably random) gaps already allowed for by optional rules.

The disappearance of R2 and R22 had no effect on the morpheme structure conditions, as both had been optional before; and similarly the conflation of R9 and R10 and the division of R19 merely led to certain canonical forms being more or less common, without giving rise to any new ones. The only other change was the division of R6 into two parts (above, p. 56), which in fact gave rise to the possibility of new vowel sequences such as |ɛu| in *bell* → [b̥ɛu], but this degree of delicacy in the vowel system is not accounted for in the morpheme structure conditions given. We probably also need a further phonetic rule to account for the free variation between [f] and [p] in *draught* → [waːpt] or [waːft]. However, as this example is unique (all clusters normally being non-continuant throughout for some time yet), I leave this unformalised.[1]

Stage 4. As the result of changes in R19 (above, p. 82) there begin to appear now occurrences of [ɣ] (or [j]) corresponding to ESP continuants, especially /l/ and /j/, which have been velarised by consonant harmony. Thus we have:

like → ġaɪk, ɣaɪk, ɟaɪk
look → ġuk, ɣuk
shack → ɣæk
young → ġʌŋ, ɣʌŋ, ɟʌŋ etc.

[1] However, by stage 4 this free variation has been replaced by a stable situation where clusters are regularly non-continuant throughout. Accordingly, at stage 4, MS12 is complicated to state this.

Although these occurrences of [ɣ] were always in free variation with [g] and A never therefore developed a stable contrast between [g] and [ɣ], it is significant that [ɣ] only appeared as the reflex of an underlying continuant. In other words, [ɣ] was always in free variation with [g], but [g] was not always in free variation with [ɣ]. Accordingly it seems necessary to postulate a further systematic phonemic segment for A at this stage. That is, we now have the matrix shown in table 5:

TABLE 5. *Matrix of A's consonant phonemes at stage 4*

	b	d	g	m	n	ŋ	w	l	ɣ
coronal	−	+	−	−	+	−	−	+	−
anterior	+	+	−	+	+	−	+	+	−
continuant	−	−	−	−	−	−	+	+	+
nasal	−	−	−	+	+	+	−	−	−

where the addition of |ɣ| (see p. 45 for the earlier situation) has led to a more symmetrical system, and in fact to the loss of MS10. Conversely, the limitations in the occurrence of |ɣ| necessitate complicating MS3 to exclude it from final position.

The other major change at this stage was the further modification of MS2 and MS4, also a consequence of changes in the scope of applicability of R19. That is, in addition to the examples given above, we have the first occurrence of |l| before a velar in the same syllable, although there was still no occurrence of |l| before a labial.

e.g.   long → ġɔŋ *or* lɔŋ
but: label ← webu

As striking as the changes in the morpheme structure conditions at this stage was the amount of phonetic free variation in the articulation of individual sounds. In addition to the regular (largely allophonic) alternation among voiced, voiceless lenis and voiceless fortis plosives (above, p. 37) and the free variation among [g ɣ ɟ j ʎ l] for ESP /l/ and /j/ – see the examples above and also:

lego → ġɛgo/jɛgo/ʎɛgo/ɣɛgo
yolk → ġoːk/ɟoːk etc.

A appeared to be 'experimenting' with the feature [distributed], so that we had alternations between apico-alveolar and lamino-alveolar, and between bilabial and labio-dental consonants:[1]

>light → laɪt *or* l̯aɪt
>nose → nu: *or* n̯u:
>have → æɣ̥ *or* æβ

This stage also saw the first occurrence of a phonetic length contrast, dependent on the deletion of intervocalic /r/ by R18:

>tie → d̯ʌi:
>diary → d̯ʌ:i:

However, as this was the only example for several weeks and as there were already established diphthongs in A's system, it is simplest to treat this as a contrast between a CV structure (*tie*) and where V is a diphthong, and a CVV structure (*diary*) where each of the V's is a monophthong.

The morpheme structure conditions for stage 4 then are:

MS1‴ $\#$ (C)V(V)(C)(CV)*(C) $\#$ [2]

MS2″ $C \rightarrow \left\{ \begin{array}{l} [+\text{coronal}] \\ [-\text{anterior}] \end{array} \right\} \bigg/ \left[\begin{array}{l} +\text{coronal} \\ +\text{continuant} \end{array} \right]$ V——V

MS3″ $C \rightarrow [-\text{continuant}] \bigg/ \left\{ \begin{array}{l} [+\text{coronal}] \\ [-\text{anterior}] \end{array} \right\} \#$ [3]

MS4′ $C \rightarrow [-\text{coronal}]/[\overline{-\text{continuant}}]$ V $\left[\begin{array}{l} -\text{coronal} \\ -\text{anterior} \end{array} \right]$

MS6 $C \rightarrow [+\text{anterior}]/[\overline{+\text{nasal}}]$ V $[+\text{anterior}]$

MS7′ $[+\text{nasal}] \rightarrow [+\text{anterior}]/X \left[\begin{array}{l} \text{V} \\ -\text{stress} \end{array} \right]$ —— where X $\neq$ |ŋ|

MS8 $[+\text{coronal}] \rightarrow [+\text{anterior}]$

MS9 $[+\text{nasal}] \rightarrow [-\text{continuant}]$

---

[1] [ɣ] and [ɹ] differ with respect to the feature [distributed] as well as other features.

[2] The earlier disjunction of term 3 has been separated out to (V) (C) to allow for the possibility of VVCC sequences, e.g. *orange* → [ɔind]. The need for this modification is doubtful; there was so much free variation in the vowels that it is hard to be certain if [ɔi] (VV) was really distinct from the diphthong [oi] (V) as in *boy* → [b̥oi].

[3] The need for a feature [labial] is clearly apparent (see discussion on p. 197). It would be possible to rephrase MS3 as:

$$C \rightarrow \left[\begin{array}{l} -\text{cor} \\ +\text{ant} \end{array} \right] / [\overline{+\text{cont}}] \#$$

but this loses continuity with the preceding stage and, more importantly, predicts the value of two features high in the hierarchy by reference to one relatively low in the hierarchy, a reversal of the usual practice.

MS12′ $X \begin{bmatrix} C \\ -\text{nasal} \end{bmatrix} [C] \, Y \rightarrow X \begin{bmatrix} -\text{coronal} \\ -\text{continuant} \end{bmatrix} \begin{bmatrix} +\text{coronal} \\ -\text{continuant} \end{bmatrix} Y$

(cf. fn. 1, p. 127)

MS13 $C \rightarrow \begin{bmatrix} \alpha\text{coronal} \\ \alpha\text{anterior} \end{bmatrix} \Big/ \begin{bmatrix} \alpha\text{anterior} \\ +\text{nasal} \end{bmatrix} \underline{\hspace{2em}}$

Stage 5 shows a regression to the period before stage 4 in that the symmetrical system which arose as a result of the addition of $|\gamma|$ becomes asymmetrical again, as [ɣ] disappears. That is, the matrix of features is once again as at stage 1, and MS10 has reappeared (above, p. 104).

MS1 and MS2 remain unchanged, but as the result of R6(ii) becoming optional (see p. 56) there are now occurrences of final [l] and so MS3 disappears. Apart from these modifications the morpheme structure conditions are the same as at stage 4, ignoring a couple of isolated exceptions to MS12′:

> Ganesh[1] → ġəˈneːt *or* ġeˈneːʃt
> shoulder → ḍuːldə

and a single elicited and unrepeated exception to MS13:

> jumping → ḍʌmpin

in place of the expected, and subsequently attested [ḍʌɓin].

One other class of examples should be mentioned at this point, specifically that where ESP /l/ is preceded by a high front vowel (usually a diphthong):

> boiler → bɔijə
> crocodile → ġɔgudæjə
> pilot → ɓaɪjət

in which the child's reflex regularly contains a [j] glide. As this [j] was not stable anywhere else, and was in complementary distribution with [l], I have treated it as an allophonic variant of the latter, rather than setting up a further phonemic segment.[2]

Stage 6 showed few significant changes in the morpheme structure conditions. The loss of R9/10/10A (above, p. 67) made no difference to the set of possible morphemes for A and the change in R18 to make part (C) obligatory (above, p. 77) merely removed the inconvenient sporadic occurrences of [ɹ] in favour of a generalisation of [l]. The only effective

---

[1] The Hindu elephant-headed God. [ʃ] didn't reappear for over two years! [ld] clusters were normal from stage 9 (see p. 57 above).

[2] It would be equally possible to insert [j] in the relevant environment as a predictable phonetic glide.

rule change was the change in R19(ii) which became optional at this point (above, p. 83). This meant that ESP words with an [l] followed by a labial are finally produced by A in the same way. That is, beside the earlier:

> lift → wipt

we now have:

> lifting → lip(t)in etc.

Accordingly MS2 finally disappears.[1]

Stage 7. The appearance of R24A at this stage, lengthening vowels before voiced consonants, before R25 neutralises the voicing distinction (above, p. 95) involved a radical change in A's set of underlying segments, and several additions to the morpheme structure conditions. Although the original phonetic distinction was purely one of vowel length (above, p. 95) I have treated the new contrasts involved as being representatives of a voicing distinction. This is justified partly because of the reflex of this contrast in the underlying (adult) forms, and partly because of the subsequent development of this contrast within A's own system. Moreover, it has the advantage that, in an analysis largely devoted to the consonant system, the changes effected are immediately apparent.

The matrix of systematic phonemic segments for this stage will then add the feature [voice], and have the form shown in table 6.

The data are really insufficient to be certain whether the voicing contrast applies to plosives (|b d g|) or to non-sonorants (|b d g w|).[2] As [f] had already been analysed as a positional variant of |w| (above, p. 107) and there were several occurrences of an incipient |f/v| contrast in final position:

> cough → ġɔɸ *or* kɔf
>
> have → æβ *or* æv

(it will be remembered that [w/v/β/ʋ] are in free variation:

> clever → ġɛvə *or* gɛʋə
>
> driver → ḍaɪβə)

it has been assumed that the introduction of a voicing contrast started more, rather than less, generally, i.e. to include |w/f|.

---

[1] The fact that /r/ still invariably becomes |w| before labials (i.e. the change in R18 applies only to /l/) makes no difference to the disappearance of MS2.

[2] Assuming quite arbitrarily for the moment that [w] is non-sonorant. Note that this is another example of where we need [vocalic] – i.e. |b, d, g, w| is the class $\begin{bmatrix} -\text{voc} \\ -\text{nas} \end{bmatrix}$.

The addition of a voicing contrast through the appearance of R24A involved complications to MS9, 10 and 13 and the addition of two more conditions MS14 and MS15. MS9 must specify that nasals are not only non-continuant, but also that they are voiced; MS10 must specify that continuants are anterior – as before – and furthermore that if coronal then also voiced; MS13 extends the constraints on nasal clusters to ensure that they are voiced throughout. The new segmental condition, MS14, restricts the scope of the voicing contrast; and finally MS15 restricts the voicing contrast to final position.

TABLE 6. *Matrix of A's consonant phonemes at stage 7*

	b	d	g	p	t	k	m	n	ŋ	w	f	l
coronal	−	+	−	−	+	−	−	+	−	−	−	+
anterior	+	+	−	+	+	−	+	+	−	+	+	+
continuant	−	−	−	−	−	−	−	−	−	+	+	+
nasal	−	−	−	−	−	−	+	+	+	−	−	−
voiced	+	+	+	−	−	−	+	+	+	+	−	+

The set of morpheme structure conditions at stage 7 then is as follows:

MS1‴   # (C)V(V)(C)(CV)*(C) #

MS4′ $C \rightarrow [-\text{coronal}]/[\overline{-\text{cont}}] \ V \begin{bmatrix} -\text{coronal} \\ -\text{anterior} \end{bmatrix}^1$

MS6 $C \rightarrow [+\text{anterior}]/[\overline{+\text{nasal}}] \ V \ [+\text{anterior}]$

MS7′ $C \rightarrow [+\text{anterior}]/X \begin{bmatrix} V \\ -\text{stress} \end{bmatrix} [\overline{+\text{nasal}}]$ where X $\neq |ŋ|$

MS8 $[+\text{coronal}] \rightarrow [+\text{anterior}]$

MS9′ $[+\text{nasal}] \rightarrow \begin{bmatrix} -\text{cont} \\ +\text{voice} \end{bmatrix}$

MS10′ $\begin{bmatrix} +\text{continuant} \\ \langle +\text{coronal} \rangle \end{bmatrix} \rightarrow \begin{bmatrix} +\text{anterior} \\ \langle +\text{voice} \rangle \end{bmatrix}$

MS12′ $X \begin{bmatrix} C \\ -\text{nasal} \end{bmatrix} [C] \ Y \rightarrow X \begin{bmatrix} C \\ -\text{cor} \\ -\text{cont} \end{bmatrix} \begin{bmatrix} C \\ +\text{cor} \\ -\text{cont} \end{bmatrix} Y^2$

---

[1] There was one example: *needle* → [niːgu], which suggests that the environment should be [+son] rather than [−cont] (assuming still that [w] is non-sonorant).

[2] Interestingly, there was one exception to this condition: *whisker* → [witkə], but by stage 14 this had regularised itself to the metathesised form [wiktə]. Stage 14 was the next stage at which this word was attested at all – it should have become regular by stage 10 (see pp. 98ff.).

$$\text{MS13}' \quad C \rightarrow \begin{bmatrix} \alpha coronal \\ \alpha anterior \\ + voice \end{bmatrix} \bigg/ \begin{bmatrix} \alpha anterior \\ + nasal \end{bmatrix} \underline{\quad\quad}$$

MS14 $[+sonorant] \rightarrow [+voiced]$

MS15 $[-syllabic] \rightarrow [+voiced]/\underline{\quad}[+syllabic]$[1]

In addition, of course, there will have to be a phonetic rule corresponding exactly to R24A – namely one lengthening vowels before a voiced consonant – and another phonetic rule stating that plosive clusters are typically voiceless, even intervocalically, e.g.:

> afternoon → a:ptənu:n
> whiskers → witkə etc.

The important point, of course, is that there is no contrast.

Stage 8 saw the first consistent, though still infrequent, use of [ɹ] for the adult /r/, e.g. *red* → [ɹɛd/lɛd̪/dɛd̪] etc. (see p. 77 above) as the result of a further change in R18C. This entails a further addition to the set of systematic phonemic segments, an addition to the segmental morpheme structure conditions (MS16) – as [ɹ] only occurs before alveolars at first;[2] cf. the parallel development of |l| (p. 105, above) – and a fairly drastic restructuring of the segmental conditions (MS8 and MS10 restructured; MS14 disappears). Accordingly, we have the results shown in table 7.

The change in R20 whereby [f] appeared sporadically in initial position (above, p. 86) was too inconclusive to warrant any change in A's system,[3] and the only other noteworthy innovation (not formalised here) was a contrast between [ɛ] and [æ], hitherto in free variation.

Stage 9's most characteristic innovation was the appearance of clusters consisting of a (non-coronal) consonant followed by [l], corresponding to the splitting up of R16 into its four sub-parts. This involved the complication of MS1 to include |l| after non-final consonants, and the addition of a condition (MS17) on the nature of possible consonants ap-

---

[1] This seems a cack-handed way of expressing the constraint, but given the present abbreviatory conventions, it seems to be the simplest as well!

[2] This patterned repetition of an acquisitional process was typical of A. It would be interesting to know how general this is. For some brief discussion, see below, p. 142.

[3] In general, I have used hindsight to justify such decisions. There were as many initial [f]'s as [ɹ]'s at this stage, but whereas [ɹ] increased regularly and steadily over the next couple of stages until its distribution approximated that of ESP, [f] disappeared again for several stages (see table 11, p. 131, and discussion, p. 152).

pearing before |l|. At the same time, |l| also appeared pre-consonantally, e.g.:

    felt → wɛlt
    called → ġɔːld

as the result of the loss of R6, necessitating a change in MS12′, which had previously excluded clusters of coronal consonants.[1] Other minor changes were: the normalisation of homorganicity in nasal clusters as a result of the loss of R27 (hence the modification to MS13 below); and

TABLE 7. *Matrix of A's consonant phonemes at stage 8*

	b	d	g	p	t	k	m	n	ŋ	w	f	l	r
coronal	−	+	−	−	+	−	−	+	−	−	−	+	+
anterior	+	+	−	+	+	−	+	+	−	+	+	+	−
continuant	−	−	−	−	−	−	−	−	−	+	+	+	+
nasal	−	−	−	−	−	−	+	+	+	−	−	−	−
voiced	+	+	+	−	−	−	+	+	+	+	−	+	+

where, presumably, |l| and |r| are further distinguished by the phonetic feature [lateral] (cf. p. 51, Ph3).

the gradual loss of the restriction on consonants co-occurring with |r| – i.e. the desuetude of MS16. MS16A still operated unchanged. Thus we have:

MS1′′′′   # (C(l)) V (V) (C) (C(l)V)* (C) #[2]

MS4′ $C \rightarrow [-\text{cor}]/[\overline{-\text{cont}}] \, V \begin{bmatrix} -\text{cor} \\ -\text{ant} \end{bmatrix}$

MS6 $C \rightarrow [+\text{ant}]/[\overline{+\text{nasal}}] \, V \, [+\text{ant}]$

MS7′ $C \rightarrow [+\text{ant}]/X \begin{bmatrix} V \\ -\text{stress} \end{bmatrix} [\overline{+\text{nasal}}] \text{ where } X \neq |\eta|$

MS8′ $\begin{bmatrix} \alpha\text{cor} \\ -\text{ant} \end{bmatrix} \rightarrow [\alpha\text{cont}]$

MS9′ $[+\text{nasal}] \rightarrow \begin{bmatrix} -\text{cont} \\ +\text{voice} \end{bmatrix}$

MS10′′ $\begin{bmatrix} +\text{cor} \\ +\text{cont} \end{bmatrix} \rightarrow [+\text{voiced}]$

MS12′′ $X \begin{bmatrix} C \\ -\text{son} \end{bmatrix} [C] \, Y \rightarrow X \begin{bmatrix} C \\ -\text{cor} \\ -\text{cont} \end{bmatrix} \begin{bmatrix} C \\ +\text{cor} \\ -\text{cont} \end{bmatrix} Y$

[1] Though it might well be that MS12 is at least partially equivalent to the rule of metathesis (above, p. 101), which ensured that clusters ended in a coronal consonant, and became established around stage 10.

[2] The repetition of the |l| is an indication that we need a syllable structure condition rather than a morpheme structure condition (below, p. 191).

MS13′ $C \rightarrow \begin{bmatrix} \alpha cor \\ \beta ant \\ +voice \end{bmatrix} / \begin{bmatrix} \alpha cor \\ \beta ant \\ +nasal \end{bmatrix}$————

MS15 $[-syll] \rightarrow [+voiced]/$————$[+syll]$

MS16A $\begin{bmatrix} +coronal \\ +continuant \end{bmatrix} \rightarrow [+anterior]/[+segment]$————

MS17 $C \rightarrow \begin{bmatrix} -cont \\ -cor \\ -nasal \end{bmatrix} /$————$|l|$

Stage 10 is largely equivalent to stage 9, except that the newly introduced possibility of having post-consonantal |l| is incipiently extended to |r|, and at the same time there is an even more tentative move towards simplifying MS17 to allow clusters with a continuant. Both phenomena can be exemplified by the example:

froth → wɹɔt

See the remarks to R16(iii) on p. 27 above. The changes involved are:

MS1′′′′′ $\# \left(C \left(\begin{bmatrix} +cor \\ +cont \end{bmatrix} \right) \right) V (V) (C) \left(C \left(\begin{bmatrix} +cor \\ +cont \end{bmatrix} \right) V \right)^{*} (C) \#$

MS17′ $C \rightarrow \begin{bmatrix} -coronal \\ -nasal \end{bmatrix} /$————$\begin{bmatrix} +cor \\ +cont \end{bmatrix}$

All the other conditions remain unchanged.[1]

Stage 11 was largely characterised by two related changes involving voicing. First, R1 deleting nasals before voiceless consonants (above, p. 53) became optional, and so allowed the simplification of MS13 by the omission of [voice]; and secondly changes in R24A and R25 led to the appearance of a voicing contrast not only in final position but medially too. Accordingly MS15 can be simplified to operate only in initial position. The changes were:

MS13″ $C \rightarrow \begin{bmatrix} \alpha cor \\ \beta ant \end{bmatrix} / \begin{bmatrix} \alpha cor \\ \beta ant \\ +nas \end{bmatrix}$————

MS15′ $[-syll] \rightarrow [+voiced]/\#$————[2]

with all other conditions as at stage 10.

[1] The metathesis rule (above, p. 101) does not have any effect, as there were always enough exceptions to it to make the setting up of a morpheme structure condition futile. See Appendix C for the extensive free variation in the items discussed on p. 99.

[2] It would be interesting to know if there is any (adult) language which has such a condition. I know of none.

Stage 12. The set of systematic segments remains unchanged at this stage, and the only developments worth noting are again those involving the liquids |l| and |r|. As a result of a change in R16(iii) (above, p. 74), MS17 is further simplified to allow clusters of a *coronal* consonant plus |r|, but must simultaneously be complicated to reflect the incipient adult restriction against coronals plus |l|.

With the disappearance of R18B (deleting intervocalic /r/) MS16A must be relaxed to allow |r| in medial as well as initial position. At first sight it would appear that once again the adult restriction had been approximated – viz. |r| can only occur pre-vocalically. However, at this same stage R29 appears, generating |r|'s in final position after low vowels (above, p. 98). Accordingly we have a simpler restriction for the time being for A – namely that |r| occurs freely except pre-consonantally. The conditions obtaining at this stage[1] were:

$$\text{MS1}''''' \quad \# \left(C \left(\begin{bmatrix} +\text{cor} \\ +\text{cont} \end{bmatrix} \right) \right) V\ (V)\ (C) \left(C \left(\begin{bmatrix} +\text{cor} \\ +\text{cont} \end{bmatrix} \right) V \right)^* (C)\ \#$$

$$\text{MS4}' \quad C \rightarrow [-\text{cor}]/\overline{[-\text{cont}]}\ V \begin{bmatrix} -\text{cor} \\ -\text{ant} \end{bmatrix}$$

$$\text{MS6} \quad C \rightarrow [+\text{ant}]/\overline{[+\text{nasal}]}\ V\ [+\text{ant}]$$

$$\text{MS7}' \quad C \rightarrow [+\text{ant}]/X \begin{bmatrix} V \\ -\text{stress} \end{bmatrix} \overline{[+\text{nasal}]}\ \text{where } X \neq |\eta|$$

$$\text{MS8}' \quad \begin{bmatrix} \alpha\text{cor} \\ -\text{ant} \end{bmatrix} \rightarrow [\alpha\text{cont}]$$

$$\text{MS9} \quad [+\text{nasal}] \rightarrow \begin{bmatrix} -\text{cont} \\ +\text{voice} \end{bmatrix}$$

$$\text{MS10}'' \quad \begin{bmatrix} +\text{cor} \\ +\text{cont} \end{bmatrix} \rightarrow [+\text{voiced}]$$

$$\text{MS12}'' \quad X \begin{bmatrix} C \\ -\text{son} \end{bmatrix} [C]\ Y \rightarrow X \begin{bmatrix} C \\ -\text{cor} \\ -\text{cont} \end{bmatrix} \begin{bmatrix} C \\ +\text{cor} \\ -\text{cont} \end{bmatrix} Y$$

$$\text{MS13}'' \quad C \rightarrow \begin{bmatrix} \alpha\text{cor} \\ \beta\text{ant} \end{bmatrix} \Bigg/ \begin{bmatrix} \alpha\text{cor} \\ \beta\text{ant} \\ +\text{nas} \end{bmatrix} \underline{\qquad}$$

$$\text{MS15}' \quad [-\text{syll}] \rightarrow [+\text{voiced}]/ \#\underline{\qquad}$$

$$\text{MS16A}' \quad [+\text{seg}] \rightarrow \begin{Bmatrix} [-\text{cor}] \\ [+\text{ant}] \end{Bmatrix} / \underline{\qquad} C$$

[1] Matrix as at stage 8, see p. 115, above.

$$\text{MS}17'' \quad C \to \begin{bmatrix} -\text{nasal} \\ \langle -\text{cor} \rangle \end{bmatrix} / \text{\_\_\_\_} \begin{bmatrix} +\text{cor} \\ +\text{cont} \\ \langle +\text{lat} \rangle \end{bmatrix}$$

Stage 13 was marked most notably by a process of simplification which eliminated some of the complexities by which A's speech deviated from ESP. The most notable of these was the result of the optionality of R19(i) (above, p. 85) which by relaxing the velar consonant harmony constraint removed MS4 completely and simplified MS6 to the form it has in ESP,[1] i.e. simply excluding |ŋ| from initial position:

MS6'   [+nasal] → [+anterior]/ #——

Second the disappearance of R24A and R25 (above, p. 96) led eventually to the elimination of MS15, which had previously neutralised the adult voicing contrast in initial position.[2] In fact this change was obscured until stage 14 because it was only then that |f| as well as the other voiceless consonants began to appear in initial position. Thus for stage 13, MS15 is complicated to:

$$[-\text{syll}] \to [+\text{voiced}]/ \# \begin{bmatrix} +\text{cont} \\ -\text{cor} \\ +\text{ant} \end{bmatrix}$$

The other main development now was also partially a function of the completion of the acquisition of voicing contrasts. At this stage A (usually) had the correct allophones of the voiced and voiceless segments; for instance, voiceless plosives were aspirated initially, etc. However, in a number of cases this aspiration was replaced by affrication, most notably with |t|, less so with |k|, not at all with |p|:

see → tʰiː or tˢiː
say → tˢeɪ
cupboard → kʰʌbəd *or* kˣʌbəd
peel → pʰiːl (never *pɸiːl) etc.

It is important to note that these affricates were non-contrastive and did not correlate with ESP affricates (see p. 122, n. 2).

Stage 14 was noteworthy almost exclusively for the appearance of |h| when R13 became optional. This added one segment to the set of syste-

---

[1] I am ignoring the extremely well-motivated derivation of adult /ŋ/ from /Ng/ in ESP, as there is no evidence (except perhaps R28, p. 97) that A had anything other than /ŋ/ as his underlying form. See discussion on p. 180.

[2] The phonetic rule corresponding to R24A (p. 95, above) will, of course, remain (though it should probably be revised to read [+son] rather than [+syll]) to allow for the phonetic lengthening of nasals and |l| before voiced consonants.

matic phonemes, and saw the first use of the combination of features [−consonantal, −syllabic] in A's system. This addition necessitated two further morpheme structure conditions: a segmental one, MS18, filling in the values of the features other than [consonantal] and [syllabic] for |h|:

$$\text{MS18} \quad \begin{bmatrix} -\text{cons} \\ -\text{syll} \end{bmatrix} \rightarrow [-\text{cor}, -\text{ant}, +\text{cont}, -\text{nas}, -\text{voice}]$$

and a sequential one, MS19, limiting |h| to prevocalic position:

$$\text{MS19} \quad [+\text{seg}] \rightarrow [+\text{syll}]/\begin{bmatrix} -\text{syll} \\ -\text{cons} \end{bmatrix}\underline{\quad}^1$$

The only other change was the final disappearance of MS15 (above, p. 113) (for words with ESP /f/); i.e. even the voiceless congener of |w| now occurs initially. It should be noted that /f/ occurs as [f] everywhere by this stage; /w/ occurs as [w] initially and as [v] medially and finally. The validity of this analysis is only put in question by the occurrence of *one* consistently irregular item:

> very → vɛ(ɹ)i:

which invariably and uniquely had initial [v]. For some discussion of absolute exceptions, see below, p. 151. For the rationale behind treating |w/f| as a voiced/voiceless pair, see above p. 107. The differentiation of |f/w| also entails the addition of a further morpheme structure condition excluding clusters involving |w| while permitting those with |f|. Although it could be included under MS17, the double set of angle brackets entailed makes it easier to add a rule:

$$\text{MS17A} \quad C \rightarrow [-\text{voice}]/\overline{[+\text{cont}]}\begin{bmatrix} +\text{cor} \\ +\text{cont} \end{bmatrix}$$

Finally, there is also some evidence in favour of syllable structure rather than morpheme structure conditions at this stage, namely the item:

> twenty → tɛmti:

whose sequence |mt| contravenes MS13, but is quite regular in terms of the realisation rules. For further discussion, see below, p. 191.

Stage 15. Although the appearance of R6A at stage 13 had had no effect on A's own system, merely increasing the number of morphemes beginning with voiceless as opposed to voiced consonants, the generalisation

---

[1] Strictly speaking, the left-hand side of MS8 should also add [+cons] to exclude /h/. Though presumably this would really have been necessary *ab initio* to prevent all vowels becoming non-continuant!

of this rule at stage 15 to all consonants (more precisely its splitting into two sub-parts 6A(i) and 6A(ii); see p. 59, above) led to drastic changes, both in the number of systematic phonemic segments available to A, and in the conditions governing their distribution. The changes were particularly striking in that they gave rise to a set of phonemically distinct voiceless sonorants [m̥, ṇ, ɬ] which had no unitary equivalent in the underlying ESP system at all. Presupposing that all segments are [+consonantal, −syllabic] except |h| which is [−consonantal, −syllabic] we have the results shown in table 8.

TABLE 8. *Matrix of A's consonant phonemes at stage 15*

	b	d	g	p	t	k	m	n	ŋ	m̥	ṇ	w	f	l	ɬ	r	h
coronal	−	+	−	−	+	−	−	+	−	−	+	−	−	+	+	+	−
anterior	+	+	−	+	+	−	+	+	−	−	+	+	+	+	+	−	−
continuant	−	−	−	−	−	−	−	−	−	−	−	−	+	+	+	+	+
nasal	−	−	−	−	−	−	+	+	+	+	+	−	−	−	−	−	−
voiced	+	+	+	−	−	−	+	+	+	−	−	+	−	+	−	+	−

The effect of this expanded set of segments was to necessitate modifications to morpheme structure conditions 1, 9 and 10, and add a second case to MS19 to account for the restriction of voiceless sonorants – like |h| – to prevocalic position. The total conditions at this stage then were:

$$\text{MS1}''''' \quad \# \left(C \left(\begin{bmatrix} +\text{cor} \\ +\text{cont} \\ +\text{voice} \end{bmatrix} \right) \right) V (V) (C) \left(C \left(\begin{bmatrix} +\text{cor} \\ +\text{cont} \\ +\text{voice} \end{bmatrix} \right) V \right)^{*} (C) \#$$

MS6′ $[+\text{nasal}] \rightarrow [+\text{anterior}]/\#\ \underline{\quad\quad}$

MS7′ $C \rightarrow [+\text{anterior}]/X \begin{bmatrix} V \\ -\text{stress} \end{bmatrix} \overline{[+\text{nasal}]}$ where $X \neq |\eta|$

MS8′ $\begin{bmatrix} \alpha\text{cor} \\ -\text{ant} \\ +\text{cons} \end{bmatrix} \rightarrow [\alpha\text{continuant}]$

MS9′ $[+\text{nasal}] \rightarrow [-\text{continuant}]$[1]

MS10′′′ $\begin{bmatrix} +\text{cor} \\ -\text{ant} \end{bmatrix} \rightarrow [+\text{voiced}]$[2]

[1] Note that we have reverted to the condition before the introduction of the feature [voiced] (p. 113, above). More interestingly the universal (definitional) part of the condition has never changed.

[2] Were it not for |r| MS10 could have been abolished altogether. In fact if we made |h| the voiceless congener of |r|, this would still be possible. Phonetically this would make good sense, but is not justified phonologically.

$$\text{MS12}'' \quad X \begin{bmatrix} C \\ -son \end{bmatrix} [C] \; Y \to X \begin{bmatrix} C \\ -cor \\ -cont \end{bmatrix} \begin{bmatrix} C \\ +cor \\ -cont \end{bmatrix} Y$$

$$\text{MS13}'' \quad C \to \begin{bmatrix} \alpha coronal \\ \beta anterior \end{bmatrix} / \begin{bmatrix} \alpha coronal \\ \beta anterior \\ +nasal \end{bmatrix} \text{——}$$

$$\text{MS16A}' \quad [+seg] \to \left\{ \begin{matrix} [-coronal] \\ [+anterior] \end{matrix} \right\} / \text{——} C$$

$$\text{MS17}'' \quad C \to \begin{bmatrix} -nasal \\ \langle -cor \rangle \end{bmatrix} / \text{——} \begin{bmatrix} +coronal \\ +continuant \\ \langle +lateral \rangle \end{bmatrix}$$

$$\text{MS17A} \quad C \to [-voice] / \overline{[+cont]} \begin{bmatrix} +coronal \\ +continuant \end{bmatrix}$$

$$\text{MS18} \quad \begin{bmatrix} -cons \\ -syll \end{bmatrix} \to \begin{bmatrix} -coronal \\ -anterior \\ +continuant \\ -nasal \\ -voice \end{bmatrix}$$

$$\text{MS19}' \quad [+seg] \to [+syll] / \left\{ \begin{matrix} \begin{bmatrix} -syll \\ -cons \end{bmatrix} \\ \begin{bmatrix} +son \\ -voice \end{bmatrix} \end{matrix} \right\} \text{——}$$

Stage 16 represented merely a period of consolidation during which the new segments introduced at the previous stage became more frequent and more firmly established. The changes in the realisation rules – the loss of the rule (R13) optionally deleting /h/, a minor change in R18C (above, p. 79) and the loss of R20 optionally converting /f/ to |w| – made no difference whatever to the morpheme structure conditions, only to the weighting of the various canonical forms of the lexicon.

Stage 17 again showed no significant change. The modification to R11 represented grammatical rather than phonological development (above, p. 69) and the consolidation of |r| for /j/ indicated by the change in R23 had no effect internally to A's system.

Stage 18. Exactly the same remarks apply here as at stage 17. No significant change.

Stage 19 showed one or two slight modifications to the preceding system. First the rule converting /f/ to |p| before consonants (unformalised, p. 90, above) disappeared, i.e. we now have:

left → lɛft (earlier: lɛpt)

with a corresponding simplification of MS12. Second, R29 accounting for final |r| in A's speech (above, p. 98) disappeared, leading to the complication of MS16A to its adult form, i.e. excluding [ɹ] from final as well as preconsonantal position.

There were also one or two sporadic occurrences of slightly affricated plosives [tˢ] and [dᶻ], but these were insufficient to warrant change in A's system until the next stage.

Stage 20. After the prolonged period[1] of consolidation following the innovations of stage 15, stage 20 again showed a number of changes. Most important is the appearance of alveolar affricates [tˢ] and [dᶻ] in contrast[2] with their plosive congeners, as a result of changes in R24 (above, p. 92). This gives us the matrix shown in table 9.

TABLE 9. *Matrix of A's consonant phonemes at stage 20*

	b	d	g	dz	p	t	k	ts	m	n	ŋ	m̥	n̥	l	ɫ	w	f	r	h
coronal	−	+	−	+	−	+	−	+	−	+	−	−	+	+	+	−	−	+	−
anterior	+	+	−	+	+	+	−	+	+	+	−	+	+	+	+	+	+	−	−
continuant	−	−	−	−	−	−	−	−	−	−	−	−	−	+	+	+	+	+	+
nasal	−	−	−	−	−	−	−	−	+	+	+	+	+	−	−	−	−	−	−
voice	+	+	+	+	−	−	−	−	+	+	+	−	−	+	−	+	−	+	−
strident	−	−	−	+	−	−	−	+	−	−	−	−	−	−	−	−	−	−	−

The use of the feature [strident] rather than, say, [delayed release] to characterise the affricates is largely arbitrary. The addition of the affricates led to the addition of a further segmental morpheme structure condition (MS20) and the complication of MS17 to exclude |tˢ| and |dᶻ| from occurring in clusters. There were no other significant changes, so we have:

$$\text{MS1}''''' \neq \left(C \left(\begin{bmatrix} +\text{cor} \\ +\text{cont} \\ +\text{voice} \end{bmatrix} \right) \right) \text{V (V) (C)} \left(C \left(\begin{bmatrix} +\text{cor} \\ +\text{cont} \\ +\text{voice} \end{bmatrix} \right) \text{V} \right)^{*} \text{(C)} \#$$

MS6' [+nas] → [+ant]/#——

---

[1] Nearly three months; see Appendix A, p. 208.

[2] On p. 92 [t] and [tˢ] for instance are said to be in free variation. This is in fact the case; they are described as being in contrast because different sets of items allow [tˢ] or [t] in free variation (roughly those with underlying ESP stridents), other items allow only [t] (roughly those with ESP non-strident); below, p. 135 *et passim*.

MS7′ $\quad$ C → [+ant]/X $\begin{bmatrix} V \\ -\text{stress} \end{bmatrix}$ $\overline{[+\text{nasal}]}$ where X ≠ ŋ

MS8′ $\quad$ $\begin{bmatrix} \alpha\text{cor} \\ -\text{ant} \\ +\text{cons} \end{bmatrix}$ → [αcont]

MS9′ $\quad$ [+nas] → [−cont]

MS10‴ $\quad$ $\begin{bmatrix} +\text{cor} \\ -\text{ant} \end{bmatrix}$ → [+voiced]

MS12‴ $\quad$ X $\begin{bmatrix} C \\ -\text{son} \end{bmatrix}$ [C] Y → X $\begin{bmatrix} C \\ -\text{cor} \end{bmatrix}$ $\begin{bmatrix} C \\ +\text{cor} \\ -\text{cont} \end{bmatrix}$ Y

MS13′ $\quad$ C → $\begin{bmatrix} \alpha\text{cor} \\ \beta\text{ant} \end{bmatrix}$ / $\begin{bmatrix} \alpha\text{cor} \\ \beta\text{ant} \\ +\text{nas} \end{bmatrix}$ ——

MS16A″ $\quad$ [+seg] → $\left\{\begin{matrix} [-\text{cor}] \\ [+\text{ant}] \end{matrix}\right\}$ / —— $\left\{\begin{matrix} C \\ \# \end{matrix}\right\}$

MS17‴ $\quad$ C → $\begin{bmatrix} -\text{strid} \\ -\text{nas} \\ \langle-\text{cor}\rangle \end{bmatrix}$ / —— $\begin{bmatrix} +\text{cor} \\ +\text{cont} \\ \langle+\text{lat}\rangle \end{bmatrix}$

MS17A $\quad$ C → [−voice]/$\overline{[+\text{cont}]}$ $\begin{bmatrix} +\text{cor} \\ +\text{cont} \end{bmatrix}$

MS18′ $\quad$ $\begin{bmatrix} -\text{cons} \\ -\text{syll} \end{bmatrix}$ → [−cor, −ant, +cont, −nas, −voice, −strid]

MS19′ $\quad$ [+seg] → [+syll] / $\left\{\begin{matrix} \begin{bmatrix} -\text{syll} \\ -\text{cons} \end{bmatrix} \\ \begin{bmatrix} +\text{son} \\ -\text{voice} \end{bmatrix} \end{matrix}\right\}$ ——

MS20 $\quad$ [+strid] → [+cor, −cont, −nas]

It should be mentioned that, phonetically, there were one or two occurrences of [tʃ] and [dʒ] for |tˢ| and |dᶻ|; and also one or two occurrences of pure continuants – [s].[1] In fact with the last example there was even one exception to the additional part of rule MS19 – viz. *three* → [s̺ɹiː] where a strident is followed by a liquid. This phenomenon was not normal until stage 22.

---

[1] There are also modifications to other phonetic rules as a result of the appearance of affricates; e.g. the rule stating the distribution of voiceless aspirated consonants must be complicated. These minor readjustments are ignored.

Stage 21 is virtually identical to stage 20, except that, corresponding to further changes in R24, the affricates [tˢ] and [dᶻ] have now been normally replaced by [s] and [z].[1] The only change this necessitates in table 9 is the replacement of [− continuant] by [+ continuant] for these particular segments. Unfortunately this also entails changes in the morpheme structure conditions, to wit: the post-consonantal liquids specified in MS1 must be more precisely characterised to exclude |z|, i.e. in place of

$$\begin{bmatrix} +\text{cor} \\ +\text{cont} \\ +\text{voice} \end{bmatrix}$$

we need:

$$\begin{bmatrix} +\text{cor} \\ +\text{cont} \\ +\text{son} \\ +\text{voice} \end{bmatrix}^2$$

and the new condition MS20 changes [− continuant] to [+ continuant]. On the credit side, the phonetic rule mentioned on p. 123, n. 1, will be simplified again. The other realisation rule changes had no effect on A's own system.

Stage 22 showed only minor change from stage 21. MS17, complicated earlier to exclude stridents from clustering, must be simplified again as we now have |sr| clusters (corresponding to ESP /θr/ or /ʃr/):

thread → sɹɛd
shreddies → sɹɛdiz etc.[3]

Stage 23. The only important innovation, corresponding to changes in R6A(ii) and R7 (above, p. 62) was the appearance of |sl| clusters, which now occur in free variation with |ɫ|:

slipper → ɫipə *or* slipə

To avoid a confusing multiplicity of angle brackets, it is easiest to account for the constraints on clusters by restructuring MS17 and 17A as the three rules:

MS17(i)   C → [− nasal]/——$\begin{bmatrix} +\text{coronal} \\ +\text{continuant} \end{bmatrix}$

---

[1] It is of interest that the early occurrences of [s] were frequently laminal rather than apical; cf. the onset of |l, n| etc. above, p. 109.

[2] The use of distinctive features here seems counter-productive; a phonemic analysis would be simpler (simpler, at least, than a distinctive feature analysis omitting [vocalic]; see below, p. 188).

[3] |zr| clusters are excluded by MS17A, equivalent to MS17(ii) below.

MS17(ii) $C \rightarrow [-\text{voice}]/\overline{[+\text{cont}]} \begin{bmatrix} +\text{coronal} \\ +\text{continuant} \end{bmatrix}$

MS17(iii) $C \rightarrow [+\text{continuant}]/\overline{[+\text{coronal}]} \begin{bmatrix} +\text{cor} \\ +\text{cont} \\ +\text{lat} \end{bmatrix}$

There was also an interesting new phonetic rule at this stage – namely, one which allowed |t| to alternate freely with [ʔ] intervocalically and finally.[1]

e.g.   little → liʔəl

that → dæʔ

Stage 24 saw the expected disappearance of |ɬ| in favour of |sl| clusters, though |m̥| and |n̥| were still quite stable. The only further change entailed by this reduction was an optional one whereby MS19 could be characterised as excluding voiceless nasals rather than all voiceless sonorants from non-initial position.

A more problematic change was the appearance with some reasonable consistency of |j|. This sound had occurred spasmodically since stage 4, but it was only now that it occurred at all regularly as anything more than a phonetic link (above, p. 111) or a random variant of [ɣ] (above, p. 108). Accordingly, we have one further term in the matrix for this stage, and a slight modification to MS18. The morpheme structure conditions *in toto* now are:

$$\text{MS1}''''' \quad \# \left(C \left(\begin{bmatrix} +\text{cor} \\ +\text{cont} \\ +\text{son} \\ +\text{voice} \end{bmatrix} \right) \right) V \ (V) \ (C) \left(C \left(\begin{bmatrix} +\text{cor} \\ +\text{cont} \\ +\text{son} \\ +\text{voice} \end{bmatrix} \right) \right)^{*} (C) \ \#$$

MS6' $[+\text{nas}] \rightarrow [+\text{ant}]/\#\text{——}$

MS7' $C \rightarrow [+\text{ant}]/X \begin{bmatrix} V \\ -\text{stress} \end{bmatrix} \overline{[+\text{nasal}]}$ where $X \neq |\eta|$

MS8' $\begin{bmatrix} \alpha\text{cor} \\ -\text{ant} \\ +\text{cons} \end{bmatrix} \rightarrow [\alpha\text{cont}]$

[1] Glottalisation appears to be a common feature in children's speech, even where there is, presumably, no adult model. Thus I have often observed a glottal stop or creak as a secondary articulation with fricatives:

e.g. A's cousin R   bath → baːʔθ

half → haːʔf   etc.

This phenomenon only occurred much later with A and only when a nasal was followed by a fricative:

e.g.   spoonful → spuːnʔfəl

MS9′ $[+\text{nas}] \rightarrow [-\text{cont}]$

MS10‴ $\begin{bmatrix} +\text{cor} \\ -\text{ant} \end{bmatrix} \rightarrow [+\text{voiced}]$

MS12‴ $X \begin{bmatrix} C \\ -\text{son} \end{bmatrix} [C] \, Y \rightarrow X \begin{bmatrix} C \\ -\text{cor} \end{bmatrix} \begin{bmatrix} C \\ +\text{cor} \\ -\text{cont} \end{bmatrix} Y$

MS13′ $C \rightarrow \begin{bmatrix} \alpha\text{cor} \\ \beta\text{ant} \end{bmatrix} / \begin{bmatrix} \alpha\text{cor} \\ \beta\text{ant} \\ +\text{nas} \end{bmatrix} \underline{\quad}$

MS16A″ $[+\text{seg}] \rightarrow \left\{ \begin{matrix} [-\text{cor}] \\ [+\text{ant}] \end{matrix} \right\} / \underline{\quad} \left\{ \begin{matrix} C \\ \# \end{matrix} \right\}$

MS17(i) $C \rightarrow [-\text{nas}] / \underline{\quad} \begin{bmatrix} +\text{cor} \\ +\text{cont} \end{bmatrix}$

MS17(ii) $C \rightarrow [-\text{voice}] / \overline{[+\text{cont}]} \begin{bmatrix} +\text{cor} \\ +\text{cont} \end{bmatrix}$

MS17(iii) $C \rightarrow [+\text{cont}] / \overline{[+\text{cor}]} \begin{bmatrix} +\text{cor} \\ +\text{cont} \\ +\text{lat} \end{bmatrix}$

MS18″ $\begin{bmatrix} -\text{cons} \\ -\text{syll} \end{bmatrix} \rightarrow [\alpha\text{cor}, \, \alpha\text{voice}, \, -\text{ant}, \, -\text{nas}, \, +\text{cont}]^1$

MS19‴ $[+\text{seg}] \rightarrow [+\text{syll}] / \left\{ \begin{matrix} \begin{bmatrix} -\text{syll} \\ -\text{cons} \end{bmatrix} \\ \begin{bmatrix} +\text{nas} \\ -\text{voice} \end{bmatrix} \end{matrix} \right\} \underline{\quad}$

MS20 $[+\text{strid}] \rightarrow [+\text{cor}, \, +\text{cont}, \, -\text{nas}]$

Stage 25. Following the disappearance of the voiceless lateral [ɬ] at stage 24, stage 25 saw the gradual disappearance of the voiceless nasals |m̥| and |n̥| in favour of the correct clusters |sm| and |sn|. At the same time,[2] clusters consisting of |sw| and then |sp| and |sk| also appeared. As these changes coincided with the loss of R8 and a change in R16 which together gave rise to the other consonant plus |w| clusters (above, pp. 65 and 73) the innovations can be treated simultaneously though, even then they necessitate some restructuring of the morpheme struc-ture conditions. The matrix is now as shown in table 10.

[1] |j| is assumed to be $\begin{bmatrix} -\text{cons} \\ -\text{syll} \end{bmatrix}$ (unlike |w|). It is also assumed to be [+coronal] both because of its ESP equivalent's behaviour in the realisation rules (see, e.g.,p.76) and because of its phonetic properties. For a full matrix, see Table 10 below.

[2] For a stricter chronology than is suggested here, see p. 62 above.

The major restructuring of the morpheme structure conditions resided in the splitting of MS12 to MS12(i) and MS12(ii) to account for the wider range of final consonant clusters,[1] and in the addition of MS21 accounting for the absence of |st| clusters but the occurrence of |sp| and |sk| clusters, and of MS22 accounting for the restrictions on what consonant can precede |w|.

TABLE 10. *Matrix of A's consonant phonemes at stage 25*

	b	d	g	z	p	t	k	s	m	n	ŋ	w	f	l	r	h	j
consonantal	+	+	+	+	+	+	+	+	+	+	+	+	+	+	+	−	−
syllabic	−	−	−	−	−	−	−	−	−	−	−	−	−	−	−	−	−
coronal	−	+	−	+	−	+	−	+	−	+	−	−	−	+	+	−	+
anterior	+	+	−	+	+	+	−	+	+	+	−	+	+	+	−	−	−
continuant	−	−	−	+	−	−	−	+	−	−	−	+	+	+	+	+	+
nasal	−	−	−	−	−	−	−	−	+	+	+	−	−	−	−	−	−
voice	+	+	+	+	−	−	−	−	−	+	+	+	+	−	+	+	−	+
strident	−	−	−	+	−	−	−	+	−	−	−	−	−	−	−	−	−

The increased complexity of consonant clusters both medially and finally suggests that, in place of morpheme structure conditions exclusively, we should have a combination of morpheme structure conditions and syllable structure conditions. However, to preserve homogeneity of presentation I will continue to give rough morpheme structure conditions, and discuss the putative advantages of incorporating the notion syllable in the discussion below (see p. 191).

Accordingly, we now have:

$$\text{MS1} \quad \# \left((s)\, C \left(\begin{bmatrix} +\text{cons} \\ +\text{voice} \\ +\text{cont} \\ -\text{strid} \end{bmatrix} \right) \right) V \,(V)\,(C) \left(C \left(\begin{bmatrix} +\text{cons} \\ +\text{voice} \\ +\text{cont} \\ -\text{strid} \end{bmatrix} \right) V \right)^{*} (C) \#$$

MS6′ $[+\text{nas}] \rightarrow [+\text{ant}]/\# \underline{\qquad}$

MS7′ $C \rightarrow [+\text{ant}]/X \begin{bmatrix} V \\ -\text{stress} \end{bmatrix} \overline{[+\text{nasal}]}$ where $X \neq |\eta|$

MS8′ $\begin{bmatrix} \alpha\text{cor} \\ -\text{ant} \\ +\text{cons} \end{bmatrix} \rightarrow [\alpha\text{cont}]$

MS9′ $[+\text{nas}] \rightarrow [-\text{cont}]$

MS10‴ $\begin{bmatrix} +\text{cor} \\ -\text{ant} \end{bmatrix} \rightarrow [+\text{voiced}]$

---

[1] MS12 should probably have been modified somewhat earlier.

$$\text{MS12(i)} \quad \begin{bmatrix} C \\ -\text{nas} \end{bmatrix} \rightarrow \left\{ \begin{matrix} [+\text{cont}] \\ [-\text{cor}] \end{matrix} \right\} / \text{——} [+\text{cor}] \#$$

$$\text{MS12(ii)} \quad \begin{bmatrix} C \\ -\text{nas} \end{bmatrix} \rightarrow \begin{bmatrix} +\text{cor} \\ +\text{cont} \end{bmatrix} / \text{——} [-\text{cor}] \#$$

$$\text{MS13}' \quad C \rightarrow \begin{bmatrix} \alpha\text{cor} \\ \beta\text{ant} \end{bmatrix} / \begin{bmatrix} \alpha\text{cor} \\ \beta\text{ant} \\ -\text{nas} \end{bmatrix} \text{——}$$

$$\text{MS16A}'' \quad [+\text{seg}] \rightarrow \left\{ \begin{matrix} [-\text{cor}] \\ [+\text{ant}] \end{matrix} \right\} / \text{——} \left\{ \begin{matrix} C \\ \# \end{matrix} \right\}$$

$$\text{MS17(i)} \quad C \rightarrow [-\text{nas}] / \# \text{——} \begin{bmatrix} +\text{cor} \\ +\text{cont} \end{bmatrix}$$

$$\text{MS17(ii)} \quad C \rightarrow [-\text{voice}] / \overline{[+\text{cont}]} \begin{bmatrix} +\text{cor} \\ +\text{cont} \end{bmatrix}$$

$$\text{MS17(iii)} \quad C \rightarrow [+\text{cont}] / \overline{[+\text{cor}]} \begin{bmatrix} +\text{cor} \\ +\text{cont} \\ +\text{lat} \end{bmatrix}$$

$$\text{MS18}'' \quad \begin{bmatrix} -\text{cons} \\ -\text{syll} \end{bmatrix} \rightarrow [\alpha\text{cor}, \alpha\text{voice}, -\text{ant}, -\text{nas}, +\text{cont}]$$

$$\text{MS19}''' \quad [+\text{seg}] \rightarrow [+\text{syll}] / \begin{bmatrix} -\text{syll} \\ -\text{cons} \end{bmatrix} \text{——}$$

$$\text{MS20} \quad [+\text{strid}] \rightarrow [+\text{cor}, +\text{cont}, -\text{nas}]$$

$$\text{MS21} \quad C \rightarrow \begin{bmatrix} -\text{cont} \\ -\text{cor} \\ -\text{voice} \end{bmatrix} / |\text{s}| \text{——} \quad \text{i.e. only } |\text{sp}|, |\text{sk}|$$

$$\text{MS22} \quad C \rightarrow |\text{t, k, s}| / \text{——} |\text{w}|^{1}$$

Stage 26 saw two innovations: the development of affricates systematically different from their plosive and fricative congeners – viz. we now have a three-way contrast |t, s, ts| and |d, z, dz|; and the appearance of |st(r)| clusters. These changes correspond to the loss of rules R6A and R6B (above, p. 63) and a modification to R24 (above, p. 94) respectively. (For examples, see the pages cited above and Appendix C.) To account for them within A's system we need to make the following

¹ More formally:

$$C \rightarrow \begin{bmatrix} -\text{voice} \\ \left\{ \begin{matrix} [+\text{cor}] \\ [-\text{ant}] \end{matrix} \right\} \end{bmatrix} / \# \, (\text{s}) \text{——} \begin{bmatrix} -\text{cor} \\ +\text{ant} \end{bmatrix}$$

another case where we need the feature [labial].

changes: (a) simplify MS21 by the omission of [−coronal]; but simultaneously complicate it by adding [−delayed release] to exclude the new affricates:

$$C \rightarrow \begin{bmatrix} -\text{cont} \\ -\text{voice} \\ -\text{del rel} \end{bmatrix} / |s| \underline{\quad}$$

(b) simplify MS20 by the omission of [+continuant]:

$$[+\text{strid}] \rightarrow \begin{bmatrix} +\text{coronal} \\ -\text{nasal} \end{bmatrix}$$

It should be noted that at this stage the affricates are alveolar [ts, dz] *not* palato-alveolar, and there is accordingly no need to modify MS8 as yet.

Stages 27 and 28 merely saw the gradual consolidation of the changes effected in the preceding two stages, together with the loss of rule R18A (above, p. 75) – that is, the last of the consonant (liquid) harmony constraints.[1]

Stage 29, the final stage of the analysis, was marked by a number of further changes:

(i) R3 (velarising coronals before syllabic [ḷ]) became optional (cf. p. 55)
(ii) R16(i) (deleting post-consonantal [j]) disappeared (cf. p. 73)
(iii) R18C (effectively replacing /j/ by |r|) disappeared (cf. p. 80)
(iv) R23 (making all non-sonorant coronals [−anterior]) was relaxed to produce |tʃ, dʒ| (cf. p. 89)
(v) R26 (neutralising the /v/w/ contrast) finally began to waver (cf. p. 96)

Of these, (i) and (iii) had little effect on A's system as there had been absolute exceptions to R3 from the beginning (see p. 151 below), and /j/ had been sporadically present since stage 24 (see p. 125); (iv) merely changed the phonetic realisation of segments already established for A – i.e. he now has palato-alveolar affricates like the adult ones rather than simply alveolar – but this necessitates changes in MS10. However (ii) and (v) effected real changes: (ii) generalised the possible post-consonantal segments to all non-nasal sonorants – i.e. to the adult system's

---

[1] This is in fact an over-simplification: 'lorry', for instance, was not correct until 4 years 48 days; see the discussion on the child's awareness of his deformations below, p. 137; and there was still sporadic harmony with items such as:
Trugel → [tɹudɹɛl] etc.

STA

/r, l, w, j/; and (v) finally established a |v/w| contrast, characterised in this case by the introduction of a further distinctive segment |v|.[1]

Thus by this time A's system is substantially the same as ESP. The only divergences are as follows:

(1) He has no /ʃ, ʒ, θ, ð/

(2) He accordingly lacks clusters involving these items, but does have one cluster, |sr|, not found in ESP:

thrush → sɹʌs
shreddies → sɹɛdiz etc.

(3) He has |−in| for /−iŋ/ in unstressed syllables.

In addition, there are a number of unsystematic differences:

(4) He has a number of restructured or still unstable representations for various items:

bottle → bɔkəl *or* bɔtəl

(5) Unstressed initial syllables are frequently replaced by |ri:|:[2]

estate → ɹi:ˈsteɪt
thermometer → ɹi:ˈmɔmitə etc. (see p. 172)

(6) Some vowels are divergent:

square → skweɪjə
there → deɪjə
but   chair → tˢɛ:

(7) Clusters of nasal followed by continuant become nasal plus stop:

something → sʌmpin
anvil → æmbil etc.[3]

The total set of changes, which led (diachronically) to the situation characterised here, can be displayed diagrammatically (table 11) in the same way that the changes in the realisation rules were displayed (table 4, p. 102 above).

---

[1] The same remarks as obtained with respect to item (i) also apply to the position of (v). Although there was no established contrast earlier, some items (specifically *very*) had *always* appeared with [v] *ab initio*, whereas others (most) (e.g. *vest*) had always been [w] ([wɛt]) or had alternated freely among several possibilities.

[2] There is a host of other morphological (and syntactic) divergences – e.g. plurals which require voicing in ESP do not for A:

houses → [hausiz]   etc.

But these are ignored here.

[3] This should perhaps have been included in a realisation rule (presumably R24), but examples are rather infrequent in ESP; see the entries for *envelope* and *canvas* in Appendix C.

TABLE II. *Changes in the morpheme structure conditions for all stages*

MS																Stage													
	1	2	3	4	5	6	7	8	9	10	11	12	13	14	15	16	17	18	19	20	21	22	23	24	25	26	27	28	29
1	o	*	o	o	o	o	o	o	*	*	o	o	o	o	o	*	o	o	o	o	o	o	*	o	o	o	*	o	o
2	o	*	o	*	o	∅																							
3	o	*	o	*	∅																								
4	o	o	o	*	o	o	o	o	o	o	o	o	o	o	∅														
4A	o	∅																											
5	o	∅																											
6	o	o	o	o	o	o	o	o	o	o	o	o	o	o	∅														
7	o	*	o	o	o	o	o	o	o	o	o	o	o	o	o	o	o	o	o	o	o	o	o	o	o	o	o	o	o
8	o	o	o	o	o	o	o	*	o	o	o	o	o	o	o	o	o	o	o	o	o	o	o	o	o	o	o	o	*
9	o	o	o	o	o	o	o	*	o	o	o	o	o	o	o	*	o	o	o	o	o	o	o	o	o	o	o	o	o
10	o	o	o	∅ᵃ	*	o	*	*	o	o	o	o	o	o	o	*	o	o	o	o	o	o	o	o	o	o	o	o	*
11	—	*	∅																										
12	—	*	*	*	o	o	o	o	*	o	o	o	o	o	o	o	o	o	o	*	o	o	o	o	o i / o ii	o	o	o	o
13	—	*	o	o	o	o	*	o	*	o	*	o	o	o	o	o	o	o	o	o	o	o	o	o	o	o	o	o	o
14	—	—	—	—	—	—	*	∅																					
15	—	—	—	—	—	—	*	o	o	o	*	o	*	∅															
16	—	—	—	—	—	—	*	∅																					
16A	—	—	—	—	—	—	—	*	o	o	*	o	o	o	o	o	o	*	o	o	o	o	o	o	o	o	o	o	*
17	—	—	—	—	—	—	—	—	*	*	o	*	o	o	o	o	o	o	o	*	o	o	* i / ii / iii	o	o	o	o	o	*
17A	—	—	—	—	—	—	—	—	—	—	—	—	—	*	o	o	o	o	o	o	o	o	o	o i / ii / iii	o	o	o	o	o
18	—	—	—	—	—	—	—	—	—	—	—	—	—	*	o	o	o	o	o	o	o	o	o	*	o	o	o	o	*
19	—	—	—	—	—	—	—	—	—	—	—	—	—	*	*	o	o	o	o	o	o	o	*	*	o	o	o	o	o
20	—	—	—	—	—	—	—	—	—	—	—	—	—	—	—	—	—	—	—	*	*	o	o	o	o	*	o	o	*
21	—	—	—	—	—	—	—	—	—	—	—	—	—	—	—	—	—	—	—	—	—	—	—	*	*	o	o	*
22	—	—	—	—	—	—	—	—	—	—	—	—	—	—	—	—	—	—	—	—	—	—	—	*	o	o	o

ᵃ *Sic.*

Key

o   no change from previous stage (or = stage 1)
*   change in rule, or point of onset of new rule
<   separation of rules (with the number of the rules inserted)
∅   stage of disappearance of rule
—   rule not yet appeared

4 The nature of the acquisition of phonology

In the Introduction two alternative methods for the analysis of a developing phonology were proposed, and various classes of data which they would have to account for were listed. Subsequently both methods were pursued to their logical conclusion, assuming without argument that the child's speech could be validly described from either point of view: as a mapping from the adult system on the one hand, and as a self-contained system with its own independent properties on the other.

In the light of these analyses and the phenomena they characterise I wish, in this chapter, to argue that the former analysis is the correct one, and that there is no useful sense in which the child can be said to have his own system.

Given that the realisation rules state the regularities between the surface (phonemic) system of the adult language and the phonemic output of the child, ignoring minor allophonic and free variation within the latter, it is trivially true that these rules can always achieve observational adequacy (Chomsky, 1964, pp. 925f.) as new rules can be created *ad hoc* for any conceivable form the child may produce. I suggest, however, that they achieve descriptive adequacy if it can be shown that all aspects of these rules have independent justification. The argument will accordingly proceed as follows.

First, I will present five kinds of evidence to show that the input to the realisation rules, the adult surface phonemic forms, is in fact a direct representation of the child's own competence (4.1.1), and three further pieces of evidence to show that the child's divergences from the adult forms cannot, at least in some cases, be due to his motor inability to produce particular sounds or sound sequences (4.1.2). Second, I will argue that the realisation rules are inherently plausible, on the basis of their formal linguistic properties as reflected in diachronic rule simplification and in rule ordering (4.2). Third, I will propose a set of putatively universal constraints on possible realisation rules, which, by explicitly characterising the general tendencies displayed by children in the acquisition of their phonology, will also serve as an explanation for the complexity of the relation between the adult's and the child's forms (4.3). Fourth, having argued the case for realisation rules, I will indicate briefly that there is very little evidence for the claim that the child has a system of his own (4.4.1) and none at all for any other, more abstract, system (4.4.2); and finally, I will attempt to show that the various phenomena described in the preceding sections can be largely accounted for psychologically in terms of an extension of Morton's 'logogen' model (4.5).

4.1 The child's competence

4.1.1 The nature of the child's lexical representation. It is of fundamental importance to know whether the adult surface forms represent the competence of the child in any real sense, or whether the child's output mirrors his perception of the adult system, and the realisation rules are thus merely an artifact; or whether some position intermediate to these extremes must be taken. Kornfeld presents the two positions clearly: '(i) The child perceives speech in terms of *adult* phonological distinctions, but has motor problems in producing a phonetic copy of adult speech. This would mean that he perceives as the adult, but produces imperfectly – there is a mismatch between perception and production. (ii) The child perceives and produces in his *own* system. His phonological distinctions may not be the same as those of the adult' (Kornfeld, 1971, p. 218). For the reasons given immediately below, it seems clear that the first position is correct: namely, the child's competence[1] is a close reflection of the adult form he hears and that his deviant output is the result of the operation of a set of psychologically valid realisation rules.[2] It is *not* the case, however, that the phonetic divergence from the adult form is due solely to 'motor problems' as Kornfeld suggests. The reasons for this will become apparent in section 4.1.2 below.[3]

[1] At least in so far as the lexical representation of items is concerned. I am not claiming that the child shares all the adult phonological rules as well.

[2] P. Seuren (personal communication) has suggested the name of 'incompetence' rules for the realisation rules (see Smith, 1970, 1971) as they constitute a kind of filtering device of the child's competence, and have gradually to be unlearned as the child approximates more and more closely to the adult language. I have used the term 'realisation rules' as it has fewer undesirable implications. These rules, whatever their name, clearly have much in common with the general constraints suggested in Stampe's paper (Stampe, 1970).

[3] These reasons were already given in part in Smith (1970) which Kornfeld (mis)quotes.

There are five kinds of evidence supporting this position:
  (i) Perceptual factors (4.1.1.1)
  (ii) The use of distinctive features in the realisation rules (4.1.1.2)
  (iii) The 'across-the-board' nature of the acquisition process (4.1.1.3)
  (iv) The phenomenon of restructuring (4.1.1.4)
  (v) The form of plural formation (4.1.1.5)
I will deal with each of these in turn.

4.1.1.1 Perceptual factors. It has been commonly assumed that, because a child reproduces two distinct adult words in the same way, he cannot perceive the difference between them (see, e.g., Fry, 1966, p. 198; Waterson, 1971*b*, pp. 82–3 *et passim*; the discussion in Menyuk, 1971, pp. 72ff.; and p. 150, n. 2). This conclusion seems unwarranted. It is a commonplace that children – everyone, in fact – have a passive knowledge of language in advance of their active knowledge. All children respond appropriately to elementary verbal instructions from their parents before they can reproduce any of the words utilised in these instructions. Moreover, even in a de-contextualised situation, A was consistently able to discriminate such minimal pairs as *mouth* and *mouse* before he was able to speak at all. I tested for this by having pictures of, *inter alia*, a mouth and a mouse on flash cards, and asking A to 'bring me the picture of the mouth' or 'bring me the picture of the mouse' from the next room. He always responded correctly, even though at the time of writing (December 1971) he is still unable to produce the contrast between [s] and [θ]. Similar success was shown in games where A had to point out the correct picture or toy from a group; for instance: *a card* and *a cart* (both [ġaːt]); *a jug* and *a duck* (both [ġʌk]) etc.[1] The child's ability to discriminate [s] and [θ] for instance does not, of course, imply that he is doing it by reference to the same parameters as the adult (or the linguist). However, there is some evidence that the basis of differentiation is the same in the two cases even when superficially it might appear not to be. Let us look at the phonological feature [voice] and the associated phonetic feature of [length]. At stage 1 A had no voicing contrast himself (see p. 22 above) but there were cases where adult voiced/voiceless pairs were realised differently – for instance after nasal consonants, e.g. *mend* → [mɛn] and *meant* → [mɛt] as the result of rules 1 and 2 (p. 14 above). Now, given that the nasal consonant itself is

---

[1] I would hypothesise that the child doesn't begin to speak until he has learnt to perceive at least the majority of the contrasts present in the adult language. It should not be difficult to devise experiments to test this.

similarly voiced in both environments, the greatest phonetic difference is one of length. Before a voiced consonant a nasal, like all sonorants, is long, before a voiceless one short. The natural assumption that *length* not *voice* was the perceptually relevant feature for the child was apparently corroborated by the acquisition of the voicing contrast itself. At stage 7 a rule was interpolated in the ordering to lengthen vowels before final voiced consonants (see p. 95, above), giving a contrast of length in such pairs as *card* and *cart* and no discernible difference of articulation in the final consonant itself, and it was only from stage 10 that voicing as well as length was a distinguishing feature.[1] However, that voicing was at least one of the perceptually relevant features for A was shown by his correct identification of deformed adult words. When I said *bat* with a very long [æ:] and a voiceless final [tʰ] and *bad* with a very short [æ] (shorter than in *bat*) and a voiced [d], A identified them correctly and each time spontaneously repeated them with the *usual* length difference and identical sounding plosives at the end.

This would indicate that the child's phonological representations are reasonably close to, if not identical with, the adult surface forms.

This hypothesis would then also account for the frequently observed fact (see, e.g., p. 88, n. 3) that A had (completely) free variation between, e.g., [l] and [r] for adult words beginning with /r/, whereas he invariably had [l] for adult words beginning with /l/. That is, if we view A's language as a self-contained system, we have an example of the traditional problem of 'overlapping phonemes' (Bloch, 1941) where there is no apparent rhyme or reason for the fact that one class of items containing [l] has this sound in free variation with [r], whereas another class of items containing [l] has this sound invariably. If we assume that the child's forms really contain [r] in the former case – i.e. the adult form – this problem does not arise. Moreover, it immediately enables us to account for the correct development of particular items through time; i.e. given that *light* and *right* are both [lait] at stage i, only *right* and never *light* is pronounced with an *r* or an *l* at stage i + 1. If the child stored items in his brain the way he pronounced them, we would expect mistakes to occur when he progressed, such that for a time at least, *light* should also vacillate between *l* and *r*. Such mistakes never occurred (see also 4.1.1.3 below).

There is also some evidence that the rules relating the adult and child

---

[1] Furthermore at a stage well before the emergence of the voicing contrast A had a length difference arising from the deletion of intervocalic /r/, such that *tie* and *diary* were distinguished as [dʌi:] and [dʌ:i:] respectively (see above, p. 110).

forms must have some kind of psychological reality; namely the child's reaction to his own deformations. When A's 'mispronunciations' were repeated back to him – either by me or by a tape-recording of himself – he was able correctly to identify them, subject to two conditions. These were first, that he still have that particular deformation in his speech, and second, that the deformation not correspond directly to another non-deformed adult word. Thus when exposed to a recording of himself saying [ġi:b] (with or without contextualisation) A was able to identify it as *squeeze* by performing the relevant action with a piece of cloth, at a time when he still regularly pronounced *squeeze* in this way. However, when exposed to the same recording at a later stage when he no longer made this transformation he was totally unable to identify what [ġi:b] meant – even when relevant context was supplied. This was more striking with the example *start*, produced by A (at stage 22) as [sa:t]. At this time he immediately recognised what is in fact a fairly minor deviation correctly; but at stage 26, by which time he could say [sta:t] himself, he was totally baffled by hearing his own voice saying: 'Can I *sart* the tape-recorder Daddy?' and similar utterances; asking me repeatedly what he was asking to do with the tape-recorder, etc. Clearly, he not only has a representation of the adult surface form stored in his brain, but he also has stored the means of relating his own form to it as well, either by an arbitrary pairing (an extremely unlikely hypothesis[1]) or by having available in some form the set of realisational rules charac-terising the inter-relationships between the adult form and his form. The added complexity afforded by the existence of adult forms corres-ponding to his deformations of other adult forms is best illustrated by A's reaction to my pronunciation of /ʃ/ according to his rules in, *inter alia*, *ship*, *shirt* and *shoe*:

NVS   What's a [sə:t]?
A   [immediately points to his shirt]
NVS   What's a [su:]?
A   [immediately points to a shoe]
NVS   What's a [sip]?
A   When you drink [imitates]
NVS   What else does [sip] mean?
A   [puzzled, then doubtfully suggests *zip*, though pronouncing it quite correctly]

[1] Because one would expect far less consistency on the child's part in such a case.

NVS   No: it goes in the water.

A   A boat.

NVS   Say it.

A   No. I can only say [sip].

One further example of the same phenomenon is worth citing as it involves one of the pairs known earliest to be discriminated by A – namely *mouth/mouse*.

NVS   What does [maus] mean?

A   Like a cat.

NVS   Yes: what else?

A   Nothing else.

NVS   It's part of you.

A   [disbelief]

NVS   It's part of your head.

A   [fascinated]

NVS   [touching A's mouth] What's this?

A   [maus]

Only after a few more seconds did it dawn on him that they were the same.

This seems to imply that the adult form is not only available to the child as his phonological representation of the word, but also that the adult form has priority in some way. That is, the strategy of going through his realisation rules is only open to him if the adult form has no immediate correlate in his own word-store (see Morton and Smith, 1972, for further discussion; and below, p. 183).

Further evidence for the psychological reality of the adult forms for A not only subconsciously but even consciously comes from the way he learned items such as *quick* (see above, p. 65) where he quite spontaneously came up and announced his ability to produce a new word correctly, in contrast to his earlier deformation.

The same awareness was shown also on later occasions with the transition from [lɛlo] to [jɛlo] for *yellow* and [lɔli:] to [lɔri:] for *lorry* – when A went around recounting how when he was a baby (the same morning!) he had said [lɔli:], but now he was big he could say [lɔri:].

4.1.1.2 The use of distinctive features in the realisation rules.

It is undeniable that the realisation rules characterise the regular relationship between the adult surface forms and the child's forms, whether they do so remotely in the way the child's brain effects the relationship or not. Given these regularities, however, and the data presented in the previous chapters and in Appendix C should suffice to demonstrate their existence, it is necessary to use in their statement not merely the set of distinctive features which characterise the phonology of A's language as an independent system, but also *all* those features which characterise the phonology of the adult system.[1] Thus the set of features used for A's own consonant system at stage 1 was (see p. 45 above):

[coronal, anterior, nasal, continuant]

whereas the set for ESP (see Appendix A) was given as:

[coronal, anterior, nasal, continuant, voiced, delayed release, lateral, strident, sonorant]

which is precisely the same set as is necessary correctly to formulate the realisation rules. For instance:

[voiced] is needed in rules (1), (2), (11) and (25)
[del rel] is needed in rules (3) and (24)
[lateral] is needed in rules (3), (4), (6), (18) and (20)
[strident] is needed in rules (7), (9), (10), (11) and (24)
[sonorant] is needed in rules (13), (16), (18), (20) and (24)

That this use of all the adult distinctive features is not a logical necessity resulting from the need to map all the adult segments into segments in A's system, is obvious if we look at the realisation rules carefully. Thus an extremely simple set of rules – and one which one might have expected *a priori* – would have been the set limited to the last half dozen rules, i.e. the set which characterises the grosser simplifications of A's system, such as: all coronals end up as |d|, all labials end up as |b|, all consonants are voiced, etc. But the interesting point is that this gross strategy is only applicable after about twenty other rules have effected some quite subtle differentiations on the adult forms; differentiations which presuppose that the child's competence includes precisely those features which are low in the hierarchy and which he is actively unable yet to manipulate in his own speech. (For further discussion see 4.3, p. 161 below.)

4.1.1.3 The 'across-the-board' nature of the acquisition process.
It has frequently been observed that when a child learns to pronounce a

---

[1] *Mutatis mutandis* the same statement would apply irrespective of the phonetic parameters used: phonemic, prosodic or featural.

new sound or combination of sounds he immediately utilises it correctly in all the relevant words, rather than adding it piecemeal to each word as he re-hears it after his new-found ability.[1]

To exemplify from A's development: once he had learnt to produce clusters of a consonant plus [l] (stage 9, p. 114) for both of adult /Cl/ and /Cr/, this cluster appeared immediately and correctly in words which it is quite certain he had not heard since before the critical day:

> ground → glaund (previously [ġaund])
> footprint → wutplit etc.

quite spontaneously. Similarly once |ɬ| appeared for /sl/ it appeared in all words containing initial /sl/ at nearly the same time:

> slug → ɬʌg
> slipper → ɬipə etc.

In fact, this generalisation applies to all the changes in A's phonology and a virtually unlimited number of examples can be inferred by a careful study of the chronological sequence of change itemised in Appendix C.

The interest of this phenomenon is that not only can the child recognise and discriminate the items of the adult language which he is himself still unable to reproduce – something we have seen already in the immediately preceding pages – but that these sounds and sound sequences must have been stored in the brain 'correctly' in order for their appearance to be so consistently right. In other words the logical possibility that each word is stored in the brain in terms of, say, a numerical subscript (or with the phonetic shape plus other arbitrary features) is patently untenable; and it is clear that words are stored in essentially the form in which they are represented by the linguist, i.e. the adult form. Furthermore, the fact that the changes occur in precisely the correct set of words is further evidence that it must be the adult forms that the child has internalised. We have already seen examples of this with regard to the differentiation of /l/ and /r/ (p. 135) and the correct development of, e.g., [f] (pp. 86f.), but one more example is probably in order. Thus before consonant + |l| clusters appeared at all, there was neutralisation of such adult examples as *bed* and *bread* as [b̪ɛd]. Once clusters appeared these were differentiated as [b̪ɛd] and [blɛd] respectively, and likewise for many comparable examples. Again the lack of mistakes – i.e. the fact that *bed* and such items *never* appeared as [blɛd] – is a clear indication

---

[1] This is, in fact, something of an oversimplification; see the Excursus, p. 140 below.

that the child's internalised form is the adult one. It should be pointed out at this stage that the appearance of rule (R16(iv)) (p. 72 above) does *not* constitute a counter-example to this claim, as the child only inserted *extra* *l*'s in words which already had an /l/ or /r/ in the adult form. In other words, if the other realisation rules are 'incompetence' rules, R16(iv) is a 'mal-performance' rule.[1]

Lastly, the consistency of the child's development is a clear indication, if such is needed, that the process of the acquisition of phonology is *rule-governed* rather than atomistic in nature.

Excursus on the phonetic progression of acquisition; and on repeated trends in the acquisition process

Here and elsewhere the 'across-the-board' nature of the acquisition process has been remarked on. However, this should not be taken to imply complete simultaneity in the realisation of a particular phonetic change. Usually any change was spread over a period of several days or, rarely, weeks, with free variation between the old and new forms occurring first in a few words, then in a majority, and then again in just a few stragglers. Let us look for example at the (very typical) disappearance of rule 19(i) – the rule which accounts for the realisation of *duck* as [ɡʌk] etc. From stage 9 this rule applied only to true consonants, and apart from some ambiguity with regard to the nasal /n/ (above, p. 85) was a hundred per cent regular. At stage 11 there appeared a single isolated exception in free variation with a regular form:

doctor → ɡɔktə *or* dɔktə

Then at stage 12 there was one other single exception, also in free variation with a regular form:

choke (N) → koːk *or* tʰoːk

while *doctor* occurred only in the form [ɡɔktə] again. The rule became genuinely optional at stage 13, with the distribution of data shown in table 12. At stage 14, when the rule was said (above, p. 85) to have disappeared, the distribution was as shown in table 13. By the next stage there was only the single (restructured, see p. 144) exception of *take*. (It is interesting in this regard that *take* occurred in the correct form [tʰeɪk] as early as stage 13.) Thus there was a period of nearly six weeks between the first isolated exception to the rule and its complete disappearance.

This kind of gradualism can be easily explained in terms of rule optionality, or, equivalently, in terms of coexistent systems controlled simultaneously by the child:[2] i.e. at stage *n* the child controls system A containing rules 1, 2, 3, 4...*m*, then at stage *n*+1 he controls this system *plus* system B, which is identical to system A except that it does not contain rule i (or does contain

---

[1] I am indebted to Professor C. E. Bazell for drawing my attention to the potential difference between incompetence and mal-performance rules.

[2] I know of no evidence to decide between these very similar positions.

rule *m*+1). When a rule ceases to be optional – i.e. has disappeared – this presumably indicates loss of control of system A and control of only system B, C, etc.

The interaction is a little more complicated when the gradualism expresses itself in the phonetic exponents of the segments concerned, rather than or as

TABLE 12. *Incidence of velar consonant harmony at stage 13*

Harmonised only		Either			Not harmonised at all	
anything	ɛniːkiŋ	desk	dɛk	*or* gɛk	dagger	dægə[a]
cheek	kʰiːk	dog	dɔg	*or* gɔg	drinking	dɹiŋkin
cheque	kɛk	drink	diŋk	*or* gliŋk etc.	drunk	dɹiɲt
choke	kʰoːk	duck	dʌk	*or* gʌk	strong	tɹɔŋ
doctor	ġɔktə	sock	tʰɔk	*or* kʰɔk	tongue	tʌŋ
flapjack	læpgæk	sugar	tʰugə	*or* kugə		
joke	ġoːk	take	tʰeɪk	*or* kʰeɪk		
stroke	ġɹoːk	think	tʰiŋk	*or* kiŋk		
thing	ġiŋ/kiŋ					
tickle	kikəl					

[a] It was typical that the first word to occur with no harmonised variation at all was one which was almost certainly entirely new to his vocabulary. However, the spread of examples given here indicates that the differences can *not* in general be explained on the basis of frequency and consequent greater 'reinforcement'. Cf. the parallel but *not* simultaneous development of the two presumably equally common items *sit* and *say*, below.

TABLE 13. *Incidence of velar consonant harmony at stage 14*

Harmonised only		Either		Not harmonised at all			
chocolate	kʰɔklit	tickle	tʰikəl/kʰikəl	chalk	tʰɔːk	jug	dʌg
take	kʰeɪk			choke	tʰoːk	sick	tʰik
				circle	tʰəːkəl	singing	tʰiɲiŋ
				dark	daːk	sink	tʰiŋk
				desk	dɛk	sock	tʰɔk
				dig	dig	stick	tʰik
				doctor	dɔktə	strong	tʰɹɔŋ
				dog	dɔg	sugar	tʰugə
				duck	dʌk	thank you	tʰæŋkuː
				flapjack	læpdæk	think	tiŋk
				jig	d,ig	tuck	tʰʌk

well as in the words containing these segments. Thus, while the transition from, say, [ġʌk] to [dʌk] is perforce abrupt,[1] this is not necessarily the case – and in fact was not the case in the transition from [t] to [s]. Let us exemplify both types of gradualism with the examples *say* and *sit* taken over the period from stages 19 to 23. I have idealised the parallelism of the two examples for

[1] Dismissing the possibility of [g͡dʌk] as an intermediate stage, arbitrarily but apparently realistically!

the sake of exegesis. If a large enough number of words were taken, however, this development would be seen to be genuine:

	say	*sit*
Stage 19	tʰeɪ	tʰit
	tʰeɪ/tˢeɪ	tʰit
	tˢeɪ/tseɪ	tʰit/tˢit
	tseɪ/ᵗseɪ	tˢit/tsit
	ᵗseɪ/ṣeɪ	tsit/ᵗsit
	ṣeɪ/seɪ	ᵗsit/ṣit
	seɪ	ṣit/sit
Stage 23	seɪ	sit

(See p. 93, n. 1 for the phonetic correlates of these symbols. [ṣ] indicates a laminal fricative, [s] an apical one.)

Presumably we have here the gradual mastering of a complex articulation proceeding *pari passu* with the mastery of a new phonological rule. It is not at all obvious, however, why the processes should develop in such parallel fashion, and seems to indicate a close integration of the brain mechanisms responsible for the two phenomena; perhaps along the lines suggested on p. 182 below.

Whereas the form of acquisition discussed immediately above is presumably general, there were several points of detail which were presumably peculiar to A – though without a widespread survey it is hard to distinguish the general from the particular. It will suffice to mention four of these:

(i) On several occasions A progressed to the normal (i.e. unmarked) adult articulation of an apical consonant *via* a stage when he used a laminal consonant, e.g.:

(a) The development of [l]/[n] *via* [ḷ] [ṇ] etc. (see above, p. 109).[1]
(b) The development of [s] *via* [ṣ] (see above, p. 93).
(c) The development of [dʒ] *via* [d̥] – a palatalised and somewhat laminal alveolar plosive (see above, p. 91).
(d) When asked to say /ʃ/ (still replaced with [s] by A at 4 years 4 months) he concentrates hard and produces a laminal [ṣ] in place of his usual apico-alveolar one. This is never generalised to spontaneous speech situations.

(ii) The end of the word appeared to be of more significance in most cases for A than the beginning, e.g.:

(a) Harmony rules (R18, R19) were conditioned by the final rather than the initial consonant.
(b) Voicing contrast began at the end of the word and worked backwards (see above, p. 95).

---

[1] Where it is suggested that this may be 'experimentation' with the feature [distributed] – i.e. a more general process than simply apical/laminal alternation.

(c) Unstressed initial syllables generally disappeared, but unstressed final syllables rarely did. Similarly rules deleting initial consonants (e.g. R9 and R10) subsisted longer than those deleting final consonants (e.g. R22).

(iii) The feature [coronal] seems of special relevance to A in that it is the one perhaps most explicitly perceived by him (see the discussion of distinctive features below, p. 195), and has to be specified in no fewer than twenty of the thirty or so rules set up. This may, of course, be no more than the reflection of the fact that English has a very large number of coronal consonants, but it would be interesting to have comparative data from other children. To take a single, but suggestive, example – A's cousin R also had a rule of consonant harmony which was conditioned by the presence of a final velar: but whereas for A the set of consonants which harmonised with this velar was simply the natural class [+cor] (see p. 29), for R it was not.[1] Thus we have:

	A		R
sock → ġɔk (harmony)		sock → dɔk (no harmony)	
fork → wɔːk (no harmony)[2]		fork → ġɔːk (harmony)	

(iv) The environment for the development of a particular contrast was frequently repeated. The clearest example is the treatment of /l/, /s/ and /r/ by A. At first |l| only occurred before another |l| in the same word (see p. 41). Then at stage 2 |l| began to occur before any other *coronal* consonant, not just before |l| (see p. 105) and finally at stage 4 /l/ began to appear elsewhere as well (see p. 109). Likewise, at stage 4 /s/ was optionally realised as |l| before another /l/, and from stage 5 before any other coronal consonant (see p. 80) (and even very tentatively in other positions a little later – see p. 153). In other words we have an exact replication – slightly later – of the conditioning environments needed earlier. Lastly, at stage 8 when |r| appeared consistently, it did so only before coronal consonants,[3] spreading to other positions later.

Without many further studies in depth, it would be futile to speculate on the possible implications of these tendencies. Those interested can work out many more on the basis of the data in Appendix C, for the sake of comparative study.

4.1.1.4 Restructuring. Perhaps the strongest evidence for the claim that the child internalises the adult surface forms of lexical items, even when these are but little like what he produces, comes from the phenomenon of restructuring.

In general when a rule changes, all the items subject to it change at

---

[1] I have insufficient data to be sure of the precise range of the harmonisation in R's case.

[2] All /f/'s become |w| for A at this stage.

[3] It should be noted that this may merely be the result of the operation of R19 (harmonising coronals to velars and labials) for by stage 9, when this rule only applied to true consonants (p. 84), we see the gradual appearance of /r/ before labials and velars.

much the same time as described in 4.1.1.3 above (p. 138). For instance when the rule harmonising a coronal consonant to a following velar (rule 19, p. 81) became optional and then disappeared (stage 14) we had the changes exemplified in detail on p. 141 above, all completed within a couple of stages. But there was one exception to this regular progression: *take*, which had appeared perfectly 'regularly' as [ġeɪk][1] up until now, did *not* assume a form with an initial |t|[2] – rather it remained in a harmonised form, [kʰeɪk], until stage 23. What had happened was that A had restructured[3] the item /teɪk/ as /keɪk/. As long as rule R19 is operative /teɪk/ and /keɪk/ would anyway be neutralised as [keɪk], but as soon as R19 disappears they should be separated – as, in all other cases, comparable examples were separated. That this was an instance of restructuring and not some phonological difficulty is shown by the presence of items such as *talk* which correctly changed to [tɔːk] – and more strikingly by the fact that the derived forms *taking* and *taken* also retained an initial velar:

taking → keɪkin
taken → kukən

This last was A's 'regular' strong form for *taken*, and was replaced by [tukən] at stage 23 when [keɪk] was finally replaced by [teɪk].

Before examining more complex and more interesting examples of restructuring, it should perhaps be noted at this point that it is not always obvious whether we are dealing with restructuring or rule optionality.[4] In the case of *take* (and rule 19) where we have maybe a hundred or more examples which are regular and only one exception, it is clear that restructuring has taken place. Conversely, when a rule first wavers before disappearing – e.g. rule 19 again at stage 13 – and we have roughly half the examples appearing in one form and half in the other (with a significant number of words in free variation between the two) and where, moreover, all the items have changed to the new form within a stage or two (see above, p. 141), it is equally clear that we have coexistent systems – with and without the rule in question – such that it is simplest to deal in terms of rule optionality. The only difficulty arises when the number of examples is small and is represented almost ex-

---

[1] The inconsistency in the voicing of the initial segment is due to separate changes.
[2] Except for two isolated occurrences: see Appendix C and p. 140.
[3] 'Relexicalised' might be a better term; see King, 1969, esp. p. 48.
[4] Or even phonetic malperformance; see e.g. the problems A had with words such as *frog* at stage 11 (→[flɔg/wɔg/wlɔg/βrɔg]) where several factors are at work simultaneously.

clusively by well-established items – e.g. the examples of /s/ and /ʃ/ being deleted in initial position (rules R9 and R10).[1] If some words (especially those new to the child's vocabulary) appear in both new and old forms, this is, of course, direct evidence of optionality – e.g. the four-way variation of *sun* as [ʌn/dʌn/lʌn/rʌn] at stage 9 – although even here it seems probable that [ʌn] is the result of a restructured item co-existing with three other alternants whose diversity is due to rule optionality. However, wherever there is any doubt as to the status of a particular item a clear test for restructuring is to make up words of like phonological form to that of the suspect item and see if the child can say them. Thus, for example, A quite happily accepted that a picture I drew was of 'a take' and repeated it correctly, even though no amount of correction and repetition would make him stop saying [keɪk] for the homophonous verb. I assume then that at least in some clear cases the notion of restructuring is well-defined.

One such clear case of restructuring, and one of particular relevance to the present discussion, was provided by the development of a group of words beginning with /s/ – namely *some* and its compounds *somebody*, *something*, *sometimes*, *somewhere*. In the earliest stages /s/ (and other coronal continuants) preceding a vowel plus labial became |w| – by rules R19 and R20, thus falling together with /f/ which in initial position was always converted to |w| by rule 20 alone. Thus for A /w/ may have three different sources:

(1) adult /w/, e.g. one → wʌn
　　　　　　　　 wet → wɛt
(2) adult /f/, e.g. fish → wit
　　　　　　　　 foot → wut
(3) adult coronal continuants, e.g. same → we:m
　　　　　　　　　　　　　　　　 some → wʌm
　　　　　　　　　　　　　　　　 sip → wip

When rule 19 – in fact 19(ii) – disappeared through stages 10 and 11 (see above, p. 85) all the relevant words changed:

　　　　　same → ḍeɪm (stage 10 onwards)
　　　　　sip → ḍip (stage 10 onwards) etc.
　　　　　some → (ḍʌm)/wʌm[2] (stage 11)

[1] At the time these rules were operative, I hadn't appreciated the conditioning factors for the deletion and therefore had omitted to elicit other crucial data. Words like *soup* and *soap* (→ [u:p]) may well have been restructured.

[2] [ḍʌm] occurred once or twice on elicitation.

except for all the *some* compounds which retained their initial |w|:

somebody → wʌmbɔdi: (stages 11, 12, 13)
something → wʌ(m)pin (stages 11, 12, 13, 14, 15, 16)
sometimes → wʌmḍaɪm (stage 11)
somewhere → wʌmwɛ (stage 13)

and by stage 14 *some* itself had reverted completely to [wʌm]; items with initial /f/ or /w/ remained unchanged:

fish → wit
one → wʌn

This state of affairs remained constant until stage 15–16 when rule 20 (converting /f/ etc. to |w|) was lost. Thus:

       fish → fit (stage 16)
       foot → fut (stage 15 onwards) etc.
but   one → wʌn
and cf: same → tʰeɪm (stage 16 onwards)
       Simon → tʰaɪmən (stage 17 onwards) etc.

At this point, *some* and its compounds all adopted an initial [f]:

some → fʌm (stage 16 onwards)
somebody → fʌmbɔdi: (stage 22 onwards)
something → fʌmpin (stage 16 onwards)
sometimes → fʌmtaɪmd (stage 20 onwards)
somewhere → fʌmwɛ (stage 16 onwards)

Thus it would appear that the restructuring which had taken place was not simply to initial |w| – the surface form for A – but to initial |f| – an underlying (i.e. adult) form which at that time had the same surface realisation as /w/, but was phonologically kept distinct. The possible suggestion that the retention of [w] in *some* and its compounds is due to the greater complexity of the latter is untenable, in view of the fact that items like *summer*, *symbol*, etc. behaved regularly; and *some* itself conformed to the pattern of its cognates.

    Indirect corroboration of this analysis of /s/ being restructured as 'underlying' /f/ was given by the reverse process – i.e. an adult /f/ being restructured as an underlying /s/,[1] again, however, with a different surface manifestation.

    In general, words with an initial consonant + sonorant cluster reduced the cluster to the consonant alone (see rule 16, p. 71), unless the con-

---
[1] This [s/f] confusion is, of course, phonetically quite plausible.

sonant was /s/, in which case only the sonorant was retained (see rule 7, p. 58):

cf.　　brush → b̥ʌt
　　　　clean → g̊iːn
　　　　friend → wɛnd
　　　　swing → wiŋ etc.

However, two words beginning with /fl/ dropped the /f/ rather than the expected /l/:

　　　　flower → læwə (stage 9)
　　　　flapjack → læpgæk (stage 10)
cf.　　flag → wæg̊ (later ɣlæg)
　　　　floor → wɔː (later ɣlɔː)
　　　　fly → waɪ etc.

At first blush it would seem that the above description in terms of 'dropping /f/ rather than /l/' is all one can say. But at stages 15–16 when adult clusters consisting of /sl/ changed their realisation in A's speech from |l| to |ɬ| (see pp. 58–62 above), e.g.:

　　　sleep was [liːp] at stage 14 but [ɬiːp] at stage 15
　　　slide was [laɪd] at stage 14 but [ɬaɪd] at stage 15

these two words also changed their initial segment to [ɬ], viz.

　　　　flower → ɬæwə
　　　　flapjack → ɬæpdæk

so that the simplest explanation of the irregularities is in terms of /f/ being restructured as /s/ rather than in terms of an extension of the environment causing sonorant devoicing from just /s/, to /s/ and some examples of /f/.

One last comparable example is worth mentioning: namely A's treatment of *feather*. At a stage (19) when [f] normally presented no difficulty to A whatsoever (but when [s] was still not present) he consistently pronounced *feather* as [tɛdə].[1] This seemingly bizarre substitution was explained at stage 20 when A developed alveolar affricates |tˢ/dᶻ| as reflexes of ESP /s, θ, ʃ, tʃ, dʒ/ (see pp. 60 and 92), as *feather* appeared with the variant forms [tɛdə] and [tˢɛdə] exactly as other items beginning with /s/ did – but unlike *any* item beginning with /t/:

　　　　sing → tˢiŋ/tiŋ
　　　　soft → tsɔft etc.

---

[1] This had also been the pronunciation before [f] was mastered but I failed to record the precise date – probably stage 12.

but   tie → taɪ

           torch → tɔ:tˢ etc.

Once more we have to hypothesise that an item has been restructured in terms of a segment present in the adult system but superficially not present in the child's system, unless, of course, we give up all attempt at explanation at all – further evidence that the adult surface forms and not his own surface manifestations are the entities with which the child deals.

4.1.1.5 Plural formation. Finally in this section, we have the different forms of plural formation used by A for items which were superficially similar. Thus on p. 69, n. 1 above we saw that at a time when /θ/ and /t/ were neutralised as [t] in final position for A:

           cloth → klɔt

           cat → kæt

the former was pluralised by the addition of the ending normal for words ending in coronal continuants, whereas the latter had no overt plural marker at all:

           cloths → klɔtid (Note *not* clothes)

           cats → kæt

presumably the latter is really:

           kæts → kætt → kæt

while the former is really

           klɔθiz → klɔtid

It is important to note that, although the plural form of *cloth* etc. represents a generalisation of the pattern found with, e.g., *horse*:

cf.   horse → ɔ:t

           horses → ɔ:tid

at the same stage for A, his form [klɔtid] could *not* be an imitation of what he heard, in the way [ɔ:tid] could be.

4.1.2 Evidence that the child's performance is not a clear reflection of his competence. The validity of postulating the adult system as the child's underlying representational system, and the psychological reality of the realisation rules has been established in 4.1.1, but it may still not be obvious that the characterisation of these mappings as being part of the child's competence rather than of his performance is correct.

There are three areas where it appears that, despite his undoubted ability to produce sounds or sound sequences identical to those of the adult language, the child in fact does not – as a result presumably of the structural pressure of the realisation rules themselves. These three areas are:

(1) Puzzles (4.1.2.1)
(2) Metathesis and absolute exceptions (4.1.2.2)
(3) Recidivism (4.1.2.3)

4.1.2.1 Puzzles. The first of these is the *puzzle* phenomenon mentioned on p. 55 above, a phenomenon which appears on the basis of my investigation to be extremely widespread, but one which has not been widely reported.[1] Let us look at two examples. Rule R3 (above, p. 23) velarising non-delayed-release coronals (/t, d, n/) to |k, g, ŋ| accounts for such examples as:

> pedal → ḅɛgu (stage 1)
> bottle → bɔkəl (stage 10)
> kennel → kɛŋəl (stage 27) etc.

in contrast with items containing delayed-release coronals /s, z, tʃ, dʒ/ etc., such as:

> whistle → wibu (stage 1)
> whistle → witəl (stage 13)
> pistol → pitəl (stage 14)
> satchel → sætˢəl (stage 23) etc.

Further, by rule 24 (above, p. 30) non-final /z/ was regularly neutralised with the other coronals as /d/, e.g.:

> zoo → ḍu:
> lazy → ḍe:di: etc.

But this means that while:

> puddle → pʌgəl

by the regular application of rule 3:

> puzzle → pʌdəl

by the equally regular application of rule 24.[2]

---

[1] But see p. 150, n. 3, below.
[2] It is worth mentioning that exactly the same results have been obtained when trying the same examples on many other children.

Similarly:

> noddle → nɔgəl (or ŋɔgəl earlier)
>
> but   nozzle → nɔdəl

At first sight it appears simply as if the child is incapable of producing a particular sequence.[1] /t/ and /d/ are perhaps 'misheard' as the velars /k, g/ in the environment of a following velarised /l/. But this clearly is false: the child can produce the sequence correctly, but only as the reflex of the wrong input; and can easily identify such pairs as *riddle* and *wriggle* correctly.[2] That this is not an isolated case can be seen from a comparable example provided by my nephew R. In general he replaces[3] ESP /s/, /z/ by [θ], [ð] – so he has:

saddle → θægəl	yes → jɛθ
nose → nəuð	stick → θik
spider → θpaɪdə *or* paɪdə	sick → θik etc.

But at the same time ESP /θ/ is replaced by [f] – so he has:

thing → fiŋ	thick → fik etc.

In other words he is fully able to say [θik] but only as the equivalent of adult [stik] or [sik]. When he attempts to say adult [θik] it comes out as [fik]. Again there was no perceptual confusion of the adult forms *thick*, *sick* etc.

Clearly the realisation rules are acting as some kind of constraining filter in these cases – imposing an interpretation of the adult items in conformity with the formal properties of the rules. In the first case here, the scope of the rule effecting velarisation is hypothesised by the child to cover only stops (/t, d, n/) and nothing else – and so the rule is applied in this way irrespective of his actual motor abilities. The reason for the application of the rule at all will become apparent when we look at the general properties of realisation rules in 4.3 and see that rule 3 is an example of consonant harmony. The child's actual motor ability only becomes apparent when we look at the total set of data he is manipulating.

---

[1] In the same way that he certainly is incapable under any circumstances of producing a correct [z] at this stage.

[2] It is worth noting that this phenomenon is incompatible with a theory of phonological acquisition such as Olmsted's which 'predicts learning, measured by correct pronunciation of phones, as a function of ease of perception' (Olmsted, 1966, p. 531).

[3] Data recorded at age 3 years 2 months. See also Leopold, 1939–49, vol. 2, para. 500 (esp. p. 274, n. 37), for a comparable, though less clear-cut, example; and a somewhat inconclusive discussion of the possible cause of such substitutions.

4.1.2.2 Metathesis and absolute exceptions. Second, we have two other situations in which the child produces spontaneously sequences which he is unable deliberately to imitate. These occur in cases of metathesis and in absolute exceptions, both of which can be illustrated with material similar to that relevant for *puzzles*.

Metathesis. Among the examples of metathesis listed on p. 99 above were three which resulted in a sequence of [t] followed by [əl] or a syllabic [l]:

> icicle → aɪkitəl
> testicle → tɛkətəl
> difficult → gipətul

surface forms which would normally be disallowed by the other incompetence rules; and which A was unable to imitate correctly when I produced his version. That is, if I said: 'say [aɪkitəl]' he would come back with '[aɪkikəl]' and ask what it meant, and likewise with the other examples; but if asked to say *icicle*, he regularly produced [aɪkitəl] with no difficulty at all. Again we clearly have to rule out any kind of motor inability as the underlying cause of velarisation.

Absolute exceptions. By 'absolute exceptions' I mean those items in A's vocabulary which not only failed to undergo some realisation rule, but by so failing appeared with a surface form otherwise disallowed by the conventions putatively internal to his system. Thus the appearance of *distance* as [ditən] at stage 7 is exceptional in that rule R1 would predict the form [ditət],[1] but the form [ditən] is a perfectly normal morpheme from every other point of view for A at this stage. By contrast, the word *very* appeared consistently with an initial [v] from its recorded use at stage 4 – whereas virtually all other ESP words beginning with /v/ had this converted to |w|, either exclusively or in free variation with [v, ʋ, β]. As this pronunciation of *very* occurred long before any other examples of [v] were consistently used, we had an absolute exception containing a sound not otherwise in the idiolect. The word *little* was consistently an exception in two different ways. For the first ten stages it appeared alternatively in the two forms [ɖiɖi:] and [lidi:] – forms which retained vowel harmony long after it had been given up elsewhere and which were also exceptions to the rule velarising alveolar stops before [əl] (R3). Then from stage 11 [lidi:] appeared in free variation with [litəl] – the latter form taking over completely from stage 14 on. That is,

---

[1] The voiceless intervocalic [t] was apparently random.

we no longer have vowel harmony, but the word is still an exception to (R3), and as a result appears with a surface form which should be excluded. (It may be worth noting that A could correctly imitate *little* even when it was not being used as an adjective. Thus I made up a game in which three abstract pictures (of the same size) were called [lɔtəl] [pitəl] and [litəl] respectively. When asked to name each of them in turn (as I hid the others for instance) he pronounced them quite consistently as: [lɔkəl], [pikəl] and [litəl]. Similarly if further pictures were added – called [lɔkəl], [pikəl] and [likəl], giving six possibilities for me – he distinguished only four of them verbally: [lɔkəl, pikəl, likəl and litəl], even though he had no difficulty pointing correctly to [lɔtəl] as opposed to [lɔkəl] and [pitəl] as opposed to [pikəl] when I said them.)[1]

Once more we have a clear demonstration of A's motor ability consistently to produce certain sounds or sequences but his total inability to use this motor skill appropriately in the mass of 'regular' cases. Again, hypothesising the psychological validity of the realisation rules, and the corresponding structural pressure these exert, will give a satisfactory explanation for these apparently anomalous discrepancies.

4.1.2.3 Recidivism.
Third and last we have the phenomenon of *recidivism* – by which I mean the loss of a systematic contrast or correct form after this has once been established by the child. Let us take two examples: first the early treatment of adult /s/ and /l/ and second the development of /tʃ/. At stage 1 /s/ and /l/ were normally neutralised as |d|, together with all the other coronal consonants, unless the /l/ occurred in a word containing only /l/'s or other coronal sonorants (see R18 and R24, pp. 29 and 30 above):

light → daɪt
soon → duːn
lorry → lɔliː

Sporadically from stage 2 – and generally from stage 4 – [l] began to appear in A's speech before any coronal consonant, and not merely before another /l/ – i.e. we have *lady* realised either as [deːdiː] or [leːdiː]. Also at stage 4 began a process whereby /s/ was realised either as |d| or as |l| in front of another /l/.

e.g.   silly → diliː *or* liliː

---

[1] Note that this appears to be inconsistent with the metathesised examples. I have no explanation for this, unless it be that the game reported in this paragraph was played at a later age than the metathesis tests.

Then at stage 5 /s/ (and shortly thereafter /ʃ/) became |l| before any coronal consonant (replicating the development of /l/), although it was still velarised to |g| before velars and labialised to |w| before labials[1] (see p. 80 above):

see → li:	sock → ġɔk
Sona → lo:nə *or* ḍo:nə	lego → lɛgo: *or* ġɛgo:
sausage → lɔdiḍ	like → laɪk *or* ġaɪk
shade → le:t	lift → wipt etc.
same → we:m	

Now originally two words such as *side* and *light* were both [ḍaɪt], but after the appearance of /l/ before any coronal consonant they became distinct as [ḍaɪt] and [laɪt] respectively. However, once /s/ was 'liquid-ised' the two words fell together again – perfectly regularly – as [laɪt]. Similarly *lunch* and *shut* were originally homophonous as [dʌt], were distinguished as [lʌt] and [dʌt] respectively, and then fell together again as [lʌt]. What appears to be happening is that the child is confronted with a number of perceptually discrete but for him unpronounceable sounds and proceeds to formulate hypotheses as to their nature in terms of the distinctive features already available to him. Having mastered the sonorant continuant [l] he presumably hypothesised that [continuant] rather than [fricative] was the crucial feature characteristic of /s/ and /ʃ/ as well as of /l/, and proceeded to realise any segment containing the features $\begin{bmatrix} + \text{cor} \\ + \text{cont} \end{bmatrix}$ as the only coronal continuant he could produce – namely an [l]. In fact, there was a very slight tendency to generalise beyond the examples given here, and extend the rule to /θ/ – *thank you* appeared briefly as [lɛŋku:] – and to all occurrences of /s/ irrespective of environment – viz. the isolated occurrences of:

sock → ɫɔk
som[2] → lo:m

but this trend was never adopted. Presumably the justification for this kind of strategy is that it always results in the distinction of more homophonous pairs than it produces. That is, although *side* and *light* were pronounced as new homophones, *side* would now be distinct (for the first time) from, e.g., *tight*, *died*, etc.

---

[1] At the same time /l/ was gradually being retained even before velars – though not yet before labials.

[2] A Hindi word (*som papri*) for a kind of biscuit.

The development of [tʃ] provides an example of a slightly different kind. Apart from minor differences /tʃ/ and /dʒ/ had been neutralised as |t| and |d|, with the other coronal obstruents up to stage 19. At stage 20 appeared the first affricate [tˢ] and [dᶻ] as reflexes of adult /s, θ, ʃ, tʃ and dʒ/ (see above, p. 93) in free variation with [t] and [d]. At stage 21 this free variation had been replaced by free variation between [ts] and [s] and [dz] and [z]; and by stage 22 the affricates had been entirely replaced by fricatives [s] and [z]. This state of affairs obtained until stage 26, when the same affricates reappeared, but this time only as the reflexes of the adult affricates – and again in free variation with fricatives. By stage 27 the affricates alone occurred without free variation and by stage 29 they had acquired the correct phonetic form [tʃ] and [dʒ], rather than [ts] and [dz]. Schematically we had the following progression:

	toe	*chair*	*say*[1]
Stage 19	tʰəu	tʰɛ	tʰeɪ
20	tʰəu	tʰɛ/tˢɛ	tʰeɪ/tˢeɪ
21	tʰəu	tˢɛ/ˢɛ	tˢeɪ/seɪ
22	tʰəu	sɛ	seɪ
26	tʰəu	sɛ/tˢɛ	seɪ
27	tʰəu	tˢɛ	seɪ
29	tʰəu	tʃɛ	seɪ

That is we have the appearance of an affricate in A's speech for an affricate in the adult system, and its disappearance again shortly thereafter, as it is replaced by a sound less close to the model than the earlier one. It is only when the child's affricate corresponds uniquely to an adult affricate that the sound is really established.[2] Here too, rather than make the odd claim that the child really has lost again some articulatory ability after he has once mastered it (e.g. the ability to produce affricates), we can invoke the psychological validity of the realisation rules and the structural pressure of their longitudinal development in terms of hypotheses based on the distinctive features available to the child, as an explanation for otherwise puzzling data.[3]

[1] This arrangement represents a slight idealisation of the data. The progression would be perfectly accurate for [tʃ] and [s] as abstractions; but no words actually developed precisely as *chair* is shown here. Full details can be inferred from Appendix C.

[2] Note that this example displays clearly the need for continual documentation throughout the acquisition process. The status of [tˢ] is quite different for A at stages 21 and 26. See also the remarks on the universality of preconsonantal /s/ deletion (below, p. 167).

[3] For a further example see the discussion of *puddle* on p. 55 above.

4.2 Formal evidence for the validity of the realisation rules

In the preceding section various kinds of evidence were presented to establish the validity of the earlier assumption that the input to the realisation rules was not only what the child was exposed to, but what he actually internalised. Having justified the psychologically real status of the input to the realisation rules, I wish now to give some independent support for the rules themselves in terms of their formal linguistic properties. I will take evidence of two types: first that of rule simplification from stage to stage; second that of rule ordering.

4.2.1 Rule simplification. Before giving examples of what is meant by rule simplification in the present context, it should be pointed out that only a minority of examples could ever be expected to display the relevant formal properties. The reasons for this are that sadly, but inevitably, the realisation rules are in some cases somewhat *ad hoc*; but chiefly that while the set of realisation rules as a whole can be expected to get simpler through time, this is effected mainly through the gradual disappearance of rules rather than merely by their individual simplification. Indeed, as the child's system becomes more complex and he makes finer distinctions in his own output, the rules can be expected to become more rather than less complicated. To take a hypothetical example, a progression from stage *n*, where 'all adult nasals become |n|', to a stage *n* + 1 where 'adult /n and ŋ/ become |n| but /m/ becomes |m|' would be an expected development, but one which represents a complication of the relevant realisation rule(s).

Accordingly, I will take three examples where the child's changing phonology progressed in ways which were to some extent surprising or *un*expected, and show how in each case the changes can be accounted for quite simply in terms of *expected* changes in the realisation rules.

The first example involves the development of rules R9 and R10 – i.e. those rules which delete /s/ and /ʃ/ selectively in various environments. The essential details of this rule have already been given (above, p. 66) and it will be sufficient here to reiterate the point that an otherwise opaque change in R10 from:

10
$$\begin{bmatrix} +\text{cor} \\ +\text{cont} \\ +\text{strid} \\ -\text{ant} \end{bmatrix} \rightarrow \emptyset / \# \text{———} [+\text{syll}] \ [-\text{cor}]$$

(i.e. /ʃ/ is deleted before labials and velars) to:

$$
10' \quad \begin{bmatrix} +\text{cor} \\ +\text{cont} \\ +\text{strid} \\ -\text{ant} \end{bmatrix} \rightarrow \emptyset/\#\!\!\!-\!\!\!-\!\!\!-[+\text{syll}]\ [-\text{ant}]
$$

(i.e. /ʃ/ is deleted only before velars)
allowed it to fall together with rule R9:

$$
9 \quad \begin{bmatrix} +\text{cor} \\ +\text{cont} \\ +\text{strid} \\ +\text{ant} \end{bmatrix} \rightarrow \emptyset/\#\!\!\!-\!\!\!-\!\!\!-[+\text{syll}]\ [+\text{ant}]
$$

(i.e. /s/ is deleted before labials and alveolars)
by means of the α notation (a variable ranging over $+$ and $-$) as:

$$
9/10 \quad \begin{bmatrix} +\text{cor} \\ +\text{cont} \\ +\text{strid} \\ \alpha\text{ant} \end{bmatrix} \rightarrow \emptyset/\#\!\!\!-\!\!\!-\!\!\!-[+\text{syll}]\ [\alpha\text{ant}]
$$

That is, the apparently arbitrary change in the environment of R10 can be explained as the result of structural pressure from the adjacent rule R9 inducing the conflation, and hence simplification, of the two rules.

The second example concerns the appearance of the voiceless sonorants [m̥ n̥ and ɬ] in A's system. In the early stages of his acquisition of phonology A had no systemic voicing contrast in his speech (R25) so that items such as *pit* and *bit* were neutralised as [b̥it]. Moreover, as the result of rule R7, deleting preconsonantal /s/, there was further neutralisation with regard to items beginning with /s/ plus consonant: e.g. *spit* was also realised as [b̥it]. At the time when A acquired a voicing contrast (stage 13) such that *pit* and *bit* were correctly differentiated as [pit] and [bit] the rule deleting preconsonantal /s/ was still operative, and *spit* now fell together with *pit* rather than *bit*, i.e. the consonant following the /s/ was always treated as voiceless. To make this explicit a new rule R6A was introduced (see p. 58 above) before R7 making post-/s/ plosives voiceless:[1]

$$
6A \quad \begin{bmatrix} +\text{cons} \\ -\text{son} \end{bmatrix} \rightarrow [-\text{voice}]/\#\ /s/\!\!\!-\!\!\!-\!\!\!-
$$

The next relevant stage in the child's progress was the appearance of

---

[1] Given that there is no contrast between voiced and voiceless consonants in this position, this rule is not as supererogatory as might at first appear (see p. 58, n. 1).

the 'non-English'[1] voiceless sonorants [ɬ m̥ n̥] as reflexes of the adult clusters /sl/, /sm/ and /sn/. This apparently anomalous development of a set of sounds (phonemically distinctive for his system) which he could never have heard is, in fact, immediately explicable in terms of a generalisation of the rule R6A. That is, whereas the structural description of R6A was initially $\begin{bmatrix} + \text{cons} \\ - \text{son} \end{bmatrix}$ this has now been simplified to just [+cons] – it has become:

6A' $[+\text{cons}] \rightarrow [-\text{voice}]/ \# /\text{s}/\text{———}$

which naturally effects the devoicing of not only the plosives but also the sonorants /l/, /m/ and /n/.[2] Again, an unexpected innovation seems perfectly natural in terms of the formal properties of the rules.

The third example involves the development of fricatives and affricates as accounted for by R24 (above, p. 92f.). At stage 20, rule R24 consisted of two parts, one, R24(i), making all adult fricatives and affricates (which are also coronal) either delayed-release or non-delayed-release, and the other, R24(ii), making all items which remained or became [+del rel] strident, i.e. we have:

(i) $\begin{bmatrix} + \text{del rel} \\ + \text{cor} \end{bmatrix} \rightarrow \begin{bmatrix} - \text{cont} \\ \pm \text{del rel} \end{bmatrix}$

(i.e. adult /s, tʃ/ etc. have free variants [t] and [ts] for A) and :

(ii) $\begin{bmatrix} + \text{del rel} \\ + \text{cor} \end{bmatrix} \rightarrow [+\text{strid}]$

(i.e. [ts] is strident)
where these two rules are crucially conjunctively ordered.

Then at stage 21 part (i) was simplified to:

(i) $\begin{bmatrix} + \text{del rel} \\ + \text{cor} \end{bmatrix} \rightarrow [\pm \text{cont}]$

(i.e. adult /s, tʃ/etc. have free variants [ts] and [s] for A) while

[1] See the Introduction, where the appearance of such sounds was given as one of the phenomena needing explanation. In fact it is arguable that *all* the child's output is non-English in that the set of systemic contrasts and the phonetic realisations of the segments he has command of are quite different from those of the adult language. However, it seems reasonably clear that items such as [b̥] are in some sense closer to the adult model ([p or b]) than [m̥] is to [sm] and that an initial [ŋ] (as in [ŋɛk] for *neck*) is 'further' from the adult language than the child's initial [n] (as in [nuː] for *new*) even though the articulation of the [n] is itself clearly not identical to an adult articulation. I am indebted to Professor A. C. Gimson for bringing this point to my attention.

[2] And in fact /w/; see above, p. 59.

part (ii) remained unchanged. The two parts can now be conflated, effecting further simplification, as:

$$24 \quad \begin{bmatrix} +\text{del rel} \\ +\text{cor} \end{bmatrix} \rightarrow \begin{bmatrix} \pm\text{cont} \\ +\text{strid} \end{bmatrix}^1$$

Once more the internal properties of the rules seem to cast light on the rather unobvious progression of phonetic change in A's speech.

Examples such as the foregoing could be multiplied considerably (see, e.g., the detailed discussion of the feature [coronal] and its definition in chapter 5, p. 195 below) but for present purposes it is sufficient to have demonstrated that the realisation rules are independently motivated on linguistic and perhaps psychological grounds, and are not merely an artifact of the method of description.

4.2.2 Rule ordering. In his article 'Some general properties of phonological rules' (*Language*, 1967) Chomsky suggested (p. 105) that 'the rules of the grammar must be partially ordered', going on to claim that the principle of rule ordering was an *a priori* part of the basis which made language acquisition possible (Chomsky, 1967, pp. 127–8). To the extent that one can establish the psychological validity of the realisation rules and to the extent that the ordering relations established among these rules are necessary, so is Chomsky's claim substantiated. The force of this is particularly clear in the very early stages when the child is controlling a set of mappings which necessitate some twenty-six ordered rules to characterise them. The details of this (partial) rule ordering were given for stage 1 in the initial formalisation of the realisation rules on pp. 21–31 above and can be represented in tabular form as below. Parentheses round a particular number indicate that it is ordered with respect to the relevant rule only on the assumption of transitivity of rule ordering.[2] Non-parenthesised numbers indicate a direct ordering relationship.

R1   must precede: 21, 25
2   must precede: 3, (6), (7), (18), (24), 25
3   must precede: 6, 7, (8), (16), (17), 18, (19), (21), 24

---

[1] For the $\pm$ notation see above, p. 92, n. 1. In fact the next change in this rule was a further simplification to:

$$\begin{bmatrix} +\text{del rel} \\ +\text{cor} \end{bmatrix} \rightarrow \begin{bmatrix} +\text{cont} \\ +\text{strid} \end{bmatrix}$$

i.e. the reduction of a complex specification on the feature [cont] to a simple one.

[2] See Anderson, 1970, for the suggestion that rule transitivity is not always necessary.

4	must precede:	6, (17), 19, (24)
5	must precede:	6, (17), (19), 24
6	must precede:	17, 19, 24
7	must precede:	8, 16, (17), (19), 21, 23, 24, 25
8	must precede:	16, 17, (19)
9	must precede:	18, (19), (20), 23, 24
10	must precede:	18, (19), (20), 23, 24
11	must precede:	17, 24, 25
12	must precede:	18, (19), (20), (24)
13	must precede:	19, (24)
14	must precede:	16, (19), 21, (24)
15	must precede:	16, (19), 21, 24
16	must precede:	19, (24)
17	need not precede any other rule	
18	must precede:	19, 20, (24)
19	must precede:	24
20	must precede:	24
21–26	need not precede any other rule	

To effect the mapping from ESP to A's output using unordered rules would necessitate the inclusion of a vast amount of repetitive and redundant data in the environment of virtually all these rules. (The sceptical reader may prove this for himself by trying to avoid such repetition without using ordered rules.) However, more interesting than the simple fact of this partial ordering is that the rules appeared to be ordered by the child even before it was superficially necessary for them to be so, and presumably they were, not partially, but totally ordered.[1]

This claim can best be illustrated by reference to rules R3 and R7. Rule 3 (above, p. 23) accounts for the velarisation of alveolars in such words as:

> bottle → bɔkəl
> muddle → mʌgəl etc.

and the absence of this velarisation where the alveolar has the feature [+del rel]:

> puzzle → pʌdəl
> muscle → mʌtəl etc.

---

[1] It is not claimed, of course, that the ordering given here is the correct total ordering – only that total ordering (including the partial ordering displayed above) is the most likely hypothesis.

Rule 7 (above, p. 25) accounts for the deletion of /s/ preconsonantally:

Smith → mit
skin → kin
biscuit → b̞igik etc.

In the early stages there was no evidence at all as to whether R3 preceded R7 or vice versa. (Although R3 had to precede R6 for independent reasons (see above, p. 24), there was no ordering between R6 and R7, and so the same output would arise if we had the ordering R3, R6, R7 as if we had R7, R3, R6.) However, at around stage 14 there appeared examples which made it clear that A had the rules ordered R3 > R7 as here, rather than the other way round. The first crucial word was *pistol*. With the ordering R3–R7 we should have the derivation:

pistəl → pistəl – i.e. R3 does not apply.
pistəl → pitəl – by R7.

With the ordering R7–R3 we should have the derivation:

pistəl → pitəl – by R7.
pitəl → pikəl – by R3.

As [pitəl] was in fact the form A produced, the ordering R3–R7 is the only correct one. It might be suggested that there was no ordering relation between R3 and R7 until A came across examples for which ordering was crucial. This, however, seems unlikely for various reasons. First, if this were the case, we should expect to find vacillation or hesitation among different possibilities for different words until the ordering had settled down, but this never occurred – A was never in any doubt at all. Second, both R3 and R7 had to be ordered with respect to other rules from stage 1 and the simplest hypothesis is that they were also ordered with respect to each other from the beginning, thereby imposing an unambiguous treatment of words such as *pistol* and *postal*, even though there was no means of predicting which form would actually occur. Third, in the whole diachronic development of A's phonology there was only one apparent case of rule reordering (see above, p. 72). To be more precise there was only one occasion on which it was not simpler to postulate a change in a realisation rule or various rules than to reorder two realisation rules. If A had been continually reordering rules (or ordering them for the first time) on the basis of new data, one would have predicted that reordering would have featured as a general mechanism of phonological change – but it did not.

A second, less clear-cut, example is provided by rules R14 and R16. Rule R14 (above, p. 18) accounts for the deletion of initial and post-consonantal unstressed vowels:

> away → we:
> escape → ġe:p etc.

Rule R16 (above, p. 18) accounts for the deletion of post-consonantal sonorants in such words as:

> angry → ɛɲi:
> play → ḅe:
> new → nu: etc.

The interesting example in this case was *belong* which appeared from about stage 7 as [bɔŋ]. Now, if we have the ordering R14 > R16 we get the derivation:

> belong → blɔŋ (R14)
> blɔŋ → bɔŋ (R16)

but with the reverse ordering we should have:

> belong → belong (R16 is inapplicable)
> belong → lɔŋ (by R14)

which should become [gɔŋ] by R18. Unfortunately this example is somewhat suspect for two reasons. First, if as is suggested on p. 28 above, *belong* and *banana* (→ [ḅa:nə]) are the result of the same process, then there was evidence for the ordering R14–R16 available from stage 1. Second, the status of rule R14 is somewhat questionable in view of the frequently inconsistent treatment of unstressed initial syllables (see pp. 27–28 above and Appendix C). Other examples could also be adduced, but all of them suffer from some degree of ambiguity. However, the evidence given seems sufficient to warrant the tentative conclusion of total ordering of rules by the child, at least until some alternative hypothesis can be supported. For a discussion of ordering as a reflection of the hierarchy in the 'universal tendencies' which govern realisation rules, see below, p. 177.

4.3 The function of realisation rules

On the basis of the above evidence the psychological and linguistic validity of the realisation rules and their input seem to be well established. It is still not clear though *why* there should be so many rules and why they should often be so complex. On p. 138 it was pointed out that we might logically expect there to be a mere half dozen or so extremely simple realisation rules resulting only in fairly massive neutralisation, e.g. the mapping represented in the following table, which results in the same set of segments as occurred distinctively in A's speech at stage 1

$$\frac{/\,p\,b\,f\,v \quad t\,d\,s\,z\,\int\,3\,\theta\,\eth\,t\!\int\,d\!3 \quad k\ g\,m\,n\,\eta\ w\,j\,r\,l\,h\,/}{|\quad b \qquad\qquad d \qquad\qquad\quad g\quad m\,n\,\eta\ w\quad l\ \emptyset\,|}$$

In this section I wish to enumerate what appear to be the general tendencies underlying the realisation rules – the tendencies which in some sense motivate this apparently superfluous complexity. It will then be seen that the kind of simplification exhibited in the mythical mapping above represents only *one* out of four functions that realisation rules can perform.

The tendencies which appear to be operating in the determination of the precise form of the child's acquisition of phonology are:

(1) A tendency towards *vowel* and *consonant harmony*.
(2) *Cluster reduction*, leading to a general canonical form CVCV...
(3) *Systemic simplification* of the type illustrated hypothetically at the beginning of this section.
(4) *Grammatical simplification*.

I shall examine each of these in turn and then see if it is necessary to postulate any further tendencies in explanation of the 'deformations' characterised by the realisation rules.

4.3.1 Vowel and consonant harmony. The first general function of realisation rules is to implement a tendency towards vowel and consonant harmony, and accounts for a large proportion of the changes imposed on the adult system by the child. Although it is clearly most productively operative within the word, and accordingly most apparent in polysyllables (for vowel harmony) and words with a CVC structure (for consonant harmony) it has also been reported for monosyllabic open-syllable languages to a limited extent (see Apronti, 1971) and I suspect that it is universal.[1]

[1] For Chinese, see Chao, 1951, e.g., p. 129, Kan.ta → Tan.ta; for French, see Grégoire, 1937, vol. I, pp. 229ff., and cf. vol. II, pp. 369ff.; for Hebrew, see Bar-Adon, 1971, e.g., p. 438, esp. n. 23a, and p. 441, n. 37. Compare also: Leopold, 1947, vol. II, esp. paras. 430ff.; Lewis, 1936, e.g., p. 183.

The two forms of harmony – vowel and consonant – may be inter-dependent – see, e.g., Fudge (1969, p. 262), 'bilabial consonants occurred only with back rounded vowels, e.g. [bo] "ball" or "book", [bɔm] "beating a drum"...; alveolar consonants occurred sometimes with back vowels, e.g. [dɔn] "down", but much more frequently with front vowels, [ti] "drink", [den] "again". The place of articulation of the final consonant (usually a nasal) was always the same as that of the initial.' This situation appears to obtain at the earliest stages, but they may operate individually. In A's case the only examples of vowel harmony were remnants of a stage prior to stage 1, e.g.:

little → ḍidi:
broken → ḅugu: etc.

(cf. pp. 35–6 above), but examples of consonant harmony are frequent, and exemplify most of the logical possibilities. Thus consonant harmony may operate in terms either of point or manner of articulation, from right to left or left to right; in terms of all the features constituting a segment or just one, etc. Let us look at the various cases found in A's speech. The most obvious and plentiful examples are those of point of articulation harmony; thus rule R19 gives us:

dark → ġa:k
knife → maɪp etc. (cf. p. 20 above)

where only point but not manner of articulation is affected and the dominant consonant (i.e. the one conditioning the harmony) is to the right. The same phenomenon with the dominant consonant to the left is provided by R17 (p. 19 above) giving:

cloth → ġɔk
kiss → ġik etc.[1]

Examples of manner of articulation harmony independent of point of articulation are less common,[2] but R5 (p. 15 above) seems to be an

[1] That in both cases it is a velar imposing harmony on an alveolar or palato-alveolar represents some kind of generalisation (not formalised here), but one apparently idiosyncratic to A. See, e.g., Velten, 1943, p. 282, where *duck* → [dat], and the example of A's cousin R cited on p. 143 above, where *fork* → [ġɔ:k].

[2] The possibility of voicing harmony is of course excluded until a stage (7) when there is a voicing contrast. Theoretically it might be possible to speak of the voicing neutralisation as the result of a harmony rule, rather than a system simplification rule, but as there were no examples of voicing harmony after stage 7 – except for R6A (p. 58 above) which imposes voicing harmony on s+consonant clusters, whereas other forms of harmony persisted – I keep it as the latter.

example, where a nasal consonant effects nasal harmony in any following continuant:

> noisy → nɔːniː
> smell → mɛn etc.

Harmony involving all the features of a segment (see below, pp. 165 and 176, for reduplication) as opposed to one or two (i.e. a combination of point and manner of articulation) is, as expected, characteristic of very early speech (e.g. helicopter → [ægəgəgə]) and gives rise to less complex correspondences between the adult and child's forms than partial harmony. Two rather more interesting cases of partial harmony are provided by R8 and R12. Rule R8 (p. 15 above) accounts for such forms as:

> squat → ġɔp
> twice → ḍaɪf
> queen → ġiːm etc.

At first it might appear as if this was not even remotely describable as an instance of consonant harmony: in the case of *twice* particularly it seems as if we have discord rather than anything else; in that the adult word has two alveolars /t/ and /s/ whereas the child has one alveolar [d] and one labio-dental [f]. However, the conditioning environment for this process is a post-consonantal /w/, which is partially characterised by the specification $\begin{bmatrix} -\text{coronal} \\ +\text{anterior} \end{bmatrix}$. What happens is that these features[1] of the /w/ impose harmony on the following consonant – e.g. /t/ in *squat* → $\begin{bmatrix} -\text{coronal} \\ +\text{ant} \end{bmatrix}$ – which effectively converts it to [p] and the /w/ itself is subsequently deleted by a general cluster reduction rule (R16). This is perhaps a further indication of the validity of taking the adult form as the representation internalised by the child. His own surface manifestations – e.g. [ḍaɪf] etc. – are quite arbitrary and idiosyncratic; but come very simply under the rubric of harmonisation rules viewed in the light of their underlying form.

Rule R12 (p. 17 above) is interesting because we have a form of consonant harmony involving point of articulation which only operates if a

---

[1] Note that in the formulation of this rule on p. 26 above the specification [−cor] for the /w/ is not given, as it is predictable given the specification [−cons, +ant]. This is probably an indication that phonological rules should apply in a non-abbreviated form, and only evaluation measures should be based on minimally specified feature sets (Kisseberth, 1971).

condition of manner of articulation is also fulfilled. Again, this is not immediately obvious, as the rule itself appears to produce both harmonic and non-harmonic sequences. Thus /ŋ/ in unstressed syllables is neutralised to |n| unless the segment preceding it is also /ŋ/. That is we have:

running → dʌnin
ceiling → liːlin etc.

and also: singing → ġiŋiŋ
banging → bæŋiŋ etc.

where consonant harmony appears to be operative quite simply on the basis of point of articulation. But when we have examples such as:

working → wɔːgin
taking → ġeːgin etc.

we see that /ŋ/ still becomes |n|, even after a velar, because the process is only blocked when there is total harmony in the adult form – i.e. /ŋiŋ/. In this case the consonant harmony is partially pre-existent in the adult system rather than imposed by the child, but only one extreme type of this harmony survives the child's filter.

Of the realisation rules discussed in chapters 2 and 3, the following all have consonant (or vowel and consonant) harmony as their motivation:

R3   velarising alveolars before dark [l][1]
R5   nasalising continuants after a nasal
R6A devoicing consonants after [s]
R8   labialising consonants after a /w/
R12 neutralising n/ŋ in some unstressed syllables
R17 velarising coronal continuants after a velar
R18A retaining /l/ only in words containing another liquid
R19 velarising or labialising coronals before a velar or a labial

It should be noted that 'reduplication' is merely a special case of consonant and vowel harmony (see p. 176 below).

4.3.2 Cluster reduction. The second general function of realisation rules is to reduce clusters of consonants or vowels. Again, we have a tendency which appears to be universal[2] (in those languages which have

---

[1] See p. 23 above for a brief discussion of the difficulty of formalising this rule so that its true nature is revealed.
[2] Frequent examples occur in the literature: e.g. Chao, 1951, esp. p. 128; Leopold, 1939–49, e.g., vol. II, paras. 313ff. *et passim*; Lewis, 1936, e.g., pp. 174ff.; Albright and Albright, 1956; *passim*; Grégoire, 1937, 1947, e.g., vol. I, pp. 206f. *et passim*, and cf. vol. II, pp. 369ff.; Bar-Adon, 1971, e.g., p. 462.

clusters of course – i.e. the overwhelming majority); and again we have a range of possible rule-types within the general tendency, and a situation where these possibilities appear to be ranged in some form of hierarchical order. The most clear-cut tendency is where one member of the cluster is a stop and the other is not, in which case the cluster is almost invariably reduced to the stop alone. This seems to obtain whether the stop is the first or second element concerned.

> stop → ḍɔp (R7, p. 15)
> play → ḅeɪ ⎫
> tree → ḍi: ⎪
> piano → pænəu ⎬ (R16, p. 18)
> clean → ġi:n ⎪
> queen → ki:m ⎭
> milk → mik (R6, p. 15)

If both elements are stops then the second usually[1] goes:

> taxi → ġɛgi: ⎫
> empty → ɛbi: ⎭ (R21, p. 21)

With nasal clusters the choice for reduction with A seemed to depend on the voicing of the non-nasal element, but these and the following examples are not claimed to be general.

> meant → mɛt (R1, p. 13)
> mend → mɛn (R2, p. 14)

Where both members of the cluster are continuants the retained element seems to be a fricative rather than a sonorant:

> floor → wɔ: (not [lɔ:]) (R16, p. 18)

(|w| is the usual reflex of adult /f/.) That is, the scope of the sonorant deletion rule is extended to fricatives as well as stops. The one regular exception to this in English[2] is where the fricative is /s/. In such cases /s/ always seems to disappear rather than the other element, despite its inherent prominence.

> slip → lip
> switch → wit etc.

cf.   twice → daɪf

---

[1] Data are too few to afford a valid basis of generalisation. It may well be that it is the coronal consonant which disappears in these cases.

[2] And in some other languages – e.g. German where /ʃl/ is regularly replaced by [l] and later [ɬ]:

e.g.   *schlafen* → [la:fən] and later [ɬa:fən]

There are two exceptions to the generalisation that mixed clusters reduce in favour of a stop. They are illustrated by:

driving → waɪbin (R15, p. 18)
stop → sɔp (R6B, p. 61)[1]

and I would suggest that both are only apparent counter-examples to the generalisation. The number of examples where a /d/ or /t/ was deleted before a following /r/ was extremely small (see p. 28 above) and I suspect that in these cases the cluster has been reinterpreted as a single element akin to /tʃ/ and /dʒ/. There is some evidence for this – namely where clusters had been mastered, but /tʃ/ had not been – there was a tendency for /tʃ/ and /dʒ/ to be realised as |tr| or |dr| (see p. 91 above):

chalk → tɹɔ:k
join → dɹɔin

It is also worth noting that even when /tʃ/ and /tr/ etc. were successfully and correctly distinguished by A, he still imposed consonant harmony on a sequence of them. Thus at stage 29 he had:

chest → tʃɛst
drawer → dɹɔ:
chest of drawers → tɹɛst əv dɹɔ:z
child → tsaɪld/tʃaɪld
children → tɹɪldɹən etc.

The second example – *stop* → [sɔp] – can only be explained if we take a number of stages into account. Up until stage 19 *stop* and all other similar items had simply dropped the initial /s/. However, at stage 20, when affricates [tˢ/dᶻ] begin to appear as reflexes of adult /s, θ, ʃ, tʃ, dʒ/, [tˢ] also appeared as the reflex of /st/ (see p. 60 above). This [tˢ] affricate then developed gradually into a pure fricative [s] in exactly the same way, irrespective of whether it was a reflex of a unit or a cluster in the adult language. Again we appear to have a reinterpretation by the child of a sequence of segments as a unit (further corroboration of this is seen in the effect of /st/ clusters on R3 – see the discussion about *pistol* on pp. 24 and 160) but the formalisation of R6B conceals this. If it were really the case that /t/ was being deleted after /s/ in these examples, we would also expect to find examples of /p/ and /k/ being so deleted. There are no such examples.

[1] There is one further unique exception: *lifting* → [lipin]; see p. 88, n. 1, above.

Cluster reduction leads to an 'ideal' canonical form of alternating consonants and vowels; but it does not necessarily give rise to forms consisting only of open syllables, as words may still end in a single consonant. Accordingly under the present rubric we also include rules which delete a consonant in final position: R6 and R22[1] (see examples on pp. 15 and 21) as these two go to ensuring that the child's language is characterised almost exclusively by a structure CVCV...

Of the realisation rules discussed in chapters 2 and 3, the following all have the achievement of an alternating CV structure as their motivation:

R1   deleting nasals before voiceless stops
R2   deleting voiced stops after nasals
R6   deleting /l/ before consonants
R6B   deleting /t/ after /s/
R7   deleting /s/ preconsonantally
R15   deleting /t/ or /d/ before /r/
R16   deleting post-consonantal sonorants
R21   deleting the second of any remaining consonant clusters
R22   deleting final coronal consonants

Excursus: Cairns' hypothesis

In his article, 'Markedness, neutralisation, and universal redundancy rules' (*Language*, 1969), Cairns suggests that children are born with a set of innate 'neutralization rules' which they gradually 'unlearn' as they master more complex articulations[2] (p. 882) and that moreover, 'there may be a definite order in which the child loses N-rules, because the acquisition of some skills may presuppose the prior acquisition of some others' (*ibid.*), which would result in initial consonant clusters (the only area Cairns deals with) being learnt in a pre-set order. Thus Cairns predicts specifically that CV sequences precede ClV sequences, the next possibility, which in turn precede obstruent clusters. Unfortunately his predictions go no further than this for English as he omits any neutralisation rules for glides (/j/w/) and all his other rules place constraints on voicing combinations, only the simplest of which occur in English. Despite these practical shortcomings, and despite my doubt that it is the child's perceptual skill which needs improving (see the discussion above) it seems useful to bring together all stages of cluster acquisition in A to see what general principles may be inferred (see pp. 53–88, esp. pp. 63ff.). The progression was as follows:

---

[1] Rule R11 is considered under 4.3.4 below, though it clearly belongs partially in this section.

[2] This position is similar to Stampe's (1970).

Stage

1 onwards	CV

9   ClV where C is $\begin{bmatrix} -\text{cor} \\ -\text{cont} \end{bmatrix}$

10   Cl/rV where C is $\begin{bmatrix} -\text{cor} \\ -\text{cont} \end{bmatrix}$

12   Cl/rV where C is [−cont]

13   Cl/rV where if C is [+cont] it must be |f|

22   Cl/rV where if C is [+cont] it must be |f| or |s|, and if |s| then only |r| not |l| follows

23   sl clusters appear

24   sm/sn clusters appear

25   sp/sk clusters appear and all consonants plus |w| appear[1]

26   st clusters appear

29   all consonants plus |j| appear

The most interesting aspects of this ordering are:

(1) The extreme lateness of the glides (especially /j/) as elements of clusters as opposed to liquids.

(2) The heterorganicity of the first clusters:

    (a) At step 9 the elements of the cluster disagree in their values for the features [coronal] and [continuant].

    (b) s+sonorant clusters precede s+obstruent clusters

    (c) sp/sk precedes st.

This latter is surprising in view of the general tendency to consonant harmony elsewhere.[2] The data for one child are clearly inadequate to support any generalisations, and more studies are needed, but on the present evidence there is clearly but little support for Cairns (see below, pp. 200ff.).

4.3.3 Systemic simplification.

The third general function of the realisation rules is to simplify the child's inventory of elements. This is the simplest and most obvious characteristic of child phonology, and the one which most faithfully reflects the traditional view that children master sounds (phonemes or distinctive features) one by one until they

---

[1] In general, clusters containing three elements:

$$\left| s \begin{Bmatrix} p \\ t \\ k \end{Bmatrix} \begin{Bmatrix} l \\ r \\ w \\ j \end{Bmatrix} \right|$$

appeared at the same time as the clusters which constitute them:
|spl| at 25, |skw| at 25, |spj| at 29 etc.

[2] This may imply that consonant harmony should follow cluster reduction in the hierarchy suggested for the functions of the realisation rules below (p. 177) – i.e. harmony applies pre-eminently to a CVCV structure rather than one containing clusters.

finally approximate the adult norm.[1] It is also here that we are most clearly enabled to set up some kind of hierarchy in the inherent difficulty of different sounds by reference to the chronological order in which these occur. Thus children generally seem to master stops first with some variation between the priority of the oral and nasal varieties; with some kind of sonorant ([w/j] or [r/l]) appearing fairly soon thereafter etc.[2] It should be emphasised that the crucial word here is 'mastered'. It quite frequently happens that a particular child's first word or words contain a fricative (A's first word was [u:və] for *hoover*[3]) but this is not the same as using [v] regularly as a term in a phonological system. Accordingly, the sweeping dismissal of any kind of universal hierarchy made by Walburga von Raffler Engel ('A theory of naturalness which posits the appearance of the pertinent stop before that of an affricate in child phonology is sufficiently contradicted by the few cases to the contrary that come readily to mind. My own son's first word was *ciae*', 1971, p. 317) is beside the point, unless it can be demonstrated that the child's phonology made systematic use of [tʃ] before it made systematic use of say [t]. I doubt that this can be shown.[4]

It is often the case in the later stages of the acquisition of the sound system that the simplification is not merely manifest by a reduction of the number of items in the system, such that the child's phonology has a sub-set of the adult system, but merely that the simplification represents a more economic use of the resources controlled by the child. Thus at stage 1 A merely had eight consonantal 'phonemes' at his command – /b d g m n ŋ w l/ – all of which occur in the adult system;[5] but at stage 20 A controlled some nineteen consonants (beside the twenty-four of adult English): |b d g dz p t k ts m n ŋ m̩ n̩ l ɬ w f r h|, of which five – |dz, ts, m̩, n̩, ɬ| – were absent from the adult system (p. 122 above) but which are all plausible in that they utilise combinations of features already mastered (e.g. the voicing contrast has been extended to certain

---

[1] This phenomenon is too well-known and too widespread to need detailed references to the literature.

[2] Data for making universal statements are too scanty to be valid; the details for A are obvious from earlier chapters.

[3] Perhaps the result of imprinting.

[4] Even if it could be shown, I would still wish to retain the generalisation despite the presence of exceptions. Von Raffler Engel's next sentence (*loc. cit.*): 'By definition, general theories are exceptionless' betrays a gross misunderstanding of the nature of scientific theories in general, and linguistic ones in particular.

[5] I am deliberately begging the question of whether A's |b| is the 'same' as ESP /b/ in any useful meaning of the word (see p. 157, n. 1, above).

sonorants). In other words, the simplification of the ESP system of twenty-four consonants to one of nineteen is not merely the result of five holes in the system – it is the result of ten holes and five extra substitutes. This situation can usefully be contrasted with that where the child has nearly mastered the adult system: at 4 years 3 months A had all the items of the adult system except /ʃ, ʒ, θ, ð/ which were replaced by |s|, and |z|, and he had nothing which is not in the adult system (except |sr| clusters reflecting /ʃr/ or /θr/ in ESP). At first sight the difference between a nineteen-term system and a twenty-term system is minimal; but on closer scrutiny is found to be fundamentally different.

Systemic simplification is clearly not restricted to the inventory of distinctive segments set up, but can also apply to their combination and distribution. Enough has already been said about this to make it unnecessary to do more than reiterate the examples of initial |ŋ| (p. 20 above) and the existence of |sr| clusters not found in the adult language.

Of the realisation rules discussed earlier the following all effect simplification of the system in the intended meaning:

R13   deleting /h/
R14   deleting unstressed syllables
R18B, C turning sonorants into non-sonorants or deleting them
R20   merging all labial continuants as |w|
R23   making all coronals anterior; R23A neutralising /d/ and /ð/
R24   making all non-sonorants stops
R25   making all segments voiced
R26   making all non-vowels true consonants
R27   restricting the possible combinations of nasal and consonant clusters
R30   the metathesis rule restricting the possible range of consonant clusters

and presumably R9, R10, and R10A deleting initial /s/, /ʃ/, /j/ in certain environments (p. 67 above).

In fact we shall see below that not all these rules are of the same type (see the discussion on p. 175).

4.3.4 Grammatical simplification. The final general function of the realisation rules is to implement grammatical simplifications. By this is meant simplifications in the child's phonological system which, while perhaps belonging also under one of the headings above, have a clear morphological or syntactic explanation in addition or exclusively. The clearest example of this is provided by R11 and its development (deleting final /z/). This has been exemplified in detail above (pp. 67–70) so I will say no more here except to point out that at least some of the syntactic conditioning seems to be general, in that Klima and Bellugi cite a completely parallel example (1966, pp. 215f.) and draw attention to the detailed discussion in Grégoire (1947, vol. II, *passim*).

A second class of examples is provided by the treatment of (initial) unstressed syllables: where an assumed unique morphological complexity led A to generalise one phonological pattern at the expense of the variety of unstressed syllables found in the adult language.[1] In the early stages A simply omitted unstressed initial syllables (R14, p. 18 above) and then gradually inserted them from about stage 4 onwards (p. 71 above). Then, around stage 26, A generalised the prefixal form /ri(:)/ to most words beginning with the unstressed sequence: (C) $\left\{ \begin{matrix} i \\ ə \end{matrix} \right\}$ (C). Thus he had:

attack	riːˈtæk	(27) cf. earlier tæk
arrange	riˈreɪnz	(26) cf. earlier reɪnz
disturb	riˈstəːv	(27) cf. earlier ḍəːv
exhaust	riˈrɔːst[2]	(26) riˈzɔːst (28)
recorder	riˈkɔːdə	(26)
design	riˈdzaɪn	(27) cf. earlier diˈdaɪn
elastic	riˈlæstik	(27)
enjoy	riˈdzɔi	(27)
escape	riˈskeɪp	(27) cf. earlier ġeɪp, kʰeɪp
giraffe	riˈdzæf[3]	(27) cf. earlier diræf
guitar	riˈtaː	(27)
remember	riːˈmɛmbə	(27) cf. earlier mɛmbə, timɛmbə
addresses	riːˈdrɛsiz	(28)
conductor	riːˈdʌktə	(28)
deserve	riˈzəːv	(28)
digest	riːˈdʒɛst	(28)
adaptor	riːˈdæptə	(28)
infection	riˈfɛksən	(28)

[1] In fact there was considerable inconsistency in A's treatment of words with an unstressed initial syllable. However, the examples given seem sufficiently numerous and regular to warrant discussion.

[2] /z/ regularly became |r| initially at this stage. Most items had |ri-| and |riː| in free variation.

[3] This is probably an example of simple metathesis rather than prefixal generalisation.

estate	riːˈsteɪt	(29)
thermometer	riːˈmɔmitə	(29) cf. earlier ˈmɔmitə
Amita	riˈmiːtə	(29)

For a brief period around stages 28 and 29 he experimented with |in-| instead of |ri-| as the relevant prefix:

| conductor | inˈdʌktə | disgusting | iŋˈgʌstin |
| expensive | inˈspɛnəv | return | inˈtəːn |

before acquiring the correct forms. There were also a few words which, despite conforming to the adult pattern of the words exemplified, were exceptional in *not* having |riː|, viz.:

Veronica	wəˈrɔŋikə	(26)	supposed	əspəuzd	(28)
vanilla	wəˈnilə	(27)	tomato	təˈmaːtəu	(28)
depressed	diˈprɛst	(28)	invited	diˈwaɪtid	(28)
ignition	nisən	(28)			

I have no explanation for these.[1]

That the phonological and morphological characteristics of these items were independently of relevance to A is shown by the differential treatment of the two words 'guitar' and 'sitar' – pronounced in my dialect [giˈta] and [ˈsitaː] with initial and final stress respectively. For A at this stage a final long vowel normally attracted stress (e.g. the pronunciation of his own name as [æˈmaːl] instead of [ˈæmaːl]) so that *sitar* became [siˈtaː] and where, because the stress in the adult form was initial, there was no attempt to replace /si/ by |ri|. With *guitar* however, where there is final stress in the adult form, A had [riˈtaː] making it conform to the majority of other words of this stress pattern.

A further instance of the morphological conditioning of a phonological process is provided by the contrast between:

	gently → dɛŋkli:
and:	slightly → ɬaitli:
cf.	gentle → dɛŋkəl

('slight' did not occur in the data recorded, but would presumably have become: [ɬait]). Here the sequence /tl/ is velarised to |kl| by A (cf. R3) when the /t/ and /l/ are part of the same morpheme, viz. *gentle*; but is retained as |tl| when the /t/ and /l/ are part of different morphemes, viz. *slight* and *-ly*.

[1] Nor for the two words *energy* → [riˈnəːdziː] (29) and *Nigel* (the name of his phantom playmate) → [riːˈnaɪdzəʉ] where there is initial stress in ESP.

A final, marginal, example of the grammatical conditioning of the phonology is provided by the use of irregular strong forms of the type [ræt] for *wrote*, [hud] for *hidden*, etc. Since these are of only peripheral relevance to the development of the phonology in general, I will merely exemplify the various processes here. The usual regularisation was the expected addition to the present tense of a past-tense form |t/d/id|:

> broke → bɹeɪkt
> left → liːvd
> bit → baɪtid etc.

occasionally with a double suffix:

> fixed → fikstid
> closed → kləuzdid etc.

or of an [-ən] for the past participle:

> cut → kʌtən
> bitten → baɪtən
> read → riːdən etc.

occasionally again with a double suffix:

> typed → taɪpənd
> cut → kʌtənd

There were in addition, however, some interesting but unfortunately sparse examples of different regularisations.

e.g. (1)   eaten → ɛtən
>   taken → tukən (earlier [kukən])

where the normal past tense formed the base for the past participle.

To be included here are also such examples as:

> hidden → hudən

where for A the past was regularly |hud| and perhaps:

> driven → druvən

(2) the expected examples of |briŋ| |bræŋ| and |brʌŋ| for *bring*, and |stæŋ| for *stung* – but with the addition of other examples not normally in this paradigm:

e.g.   wrote → ræt (rarely)
>   gave → gæv
>   ate → æt

(3) and lastly a few other apparently random but very consistent examples such as:

> hid → hud (see p. 174 above)
>
> wrote → rut (usually) rit (occasionally)

It should be emphasised that these forms were systemically controlled only from about stage 18. Even very early on (e.g. stage 4 and earlier) there was a phonological contrast between, e.g., *break* → [be:k] and *broke* → [bu:k], but grammatical tense was *not* controlled at this stage, and the form [bu:kənd/bu:gənd] for *broken* at this time represents a phonological generalisation (cf. /n/ → |nd| /——— #) and not a morphologically conditioned one (see p. 97 above). In other words up to stage 18 or so A tended to have all the possible forms of a verb in free variation: e.g. (as late as stage 22 for an extreme example) where [kɔ:t] and [kæs] are in free variation for *catch* in the present tense.

4.3.5 Other functions of the realisation rules? The four tendencies listed and exemplified in the preceding pages give sufficient motivation for the vast majority of the realisation rules – specifically those listed at the end of each subsection. There remain, however, a few rules not justified, and I wish now to look at these to see if they necessitate any further explanatory constructs.[1] The rules in question are (R9, R10, R10A), R24A, R28 and R29. The first three of these are in parentheses as they have been tentatively dealt with under 4.3.3 above (see p. 171). Here it is merely the precise form of the systemic simplification which is in question. That is R9, R10 and R10A act (like R13) by deletion rather than substitution – the only difference between them being that while all occurrences of /h/ are treated in one way, occurrences of /s, ʃ and j/ are treated by more than one method.

Rules R28 and R29 represent generalisations of typical canonical forms – rule R28 (p. 97 above) replaces nasals by clusters of a nasal and its homorganic plosive – the commoner form; and rule R29 (p. 98 above) generalises linking /r/ to non-linking positions. Accordingly it seems reasonable to subsume these rules too under the category of systemic simplification – albeit under an extended definition thereof.

---

[1] It is unfortunate that even the lengthy studies of Leopold and Grégoire are insufficiently documented for it to be possible to establish whether *all* the phenomena discussed there fall under the headings postulated here. It will be clear from the references given earlier that many of them do, but refutation of the claim that these tendencies constitute a sufficient as well as a necessary set of constructs must await further research.

This leaves only rule R24A unaccounted for – a rule which lengthens vowels before voiced consonants (p. 95 above). Although this rule is clearly phonetically well motivated – perhaps universally – it does not fit at all obviously into any of the categories enumerated above. The reason is, I think, clear: namely, rule R24A is an artifact of the method of description in a way that most of the other rules are not. That is, R24A is necessitated by the gradual loss of a realisation rule (R25) which is very highly motivated in terms of systemic simplification; and the only implication of R24A's apparent idiosyncrasy is that, to achieve psychological reality, rule R25 should be complicated instead of rule R24A being interpolated. As, however, the interpolation of R24A is formally simpler I have left it as it stands.

There is also one extremely common type of process in the child's acquisition of phonology which is not obviously covered by the above four tendencies, and which, atypically, did not appear in A's speech – namely reduplication. To the extent that a reduplicated form is a replacement for an adult (non-reduplicated) polysyllable (e.g. [kiki] for *kitchen*), this is clearly but a special case of vowel and consonant harmony (with perhaps cluster simplification as well). However, problems arise when one has reduplicated forms for an adult monosyllable. Even here, I would predict that the former tendencies should account for all possibilities – e.g. *dog* should become: [dɔdɔ]; [gɔgɔ]; [dɔ(d)dɔd]; [gɔ(g)gɔg] etc., but not *[dɔgdɔg];[1] and moreover these should occur only in a child who has *no* CVC patterns at all. Further an adult CV word (e.g. *bee*) should only be reduplicated if *all* items in the child's phonology are CVCV..., an unlikely event: i.e. *bee* should be [biː] or some such, and never [biːbiː].

4.3.6 Formal properties of the realisation rules. One might ask further at this point what the motivation for the four tendencies themselves is. At this degree of abstraction – and only at this degree, I think – does it become meaningful to introduce the old clichés of articulatory simplicity and the principle of least effort. The validity of these concepts is uncontroversial, but I would claim that it is only when viewed within a set of explicit hypotheses of the preceding kind that we have any hope of beginning to understand their precise nature and instantiation. Alternatively one could view the four tendencies listed as a set of con-

---

[1] [dɔgɔ] or [dɔgiː] would be logical possibilities given the tendency to open syllables. (An open [a] would be more likely than [ɔ] but that is not relevant to the point under discussion.)

straints on the realisation rules. That is, only a rule which has the effect of implementing one of these four tendencies can qualify as a realisation rule. Moreover, these four tendencies or 'constraints' appear themselves to be arranged in a hierarchy, such that systemic simplification can only be implemented *after* the child has implemented the tendencies to consonant harmony and cluster reduction. That is, the possibility of simplifying the set of phonological units in his inventory by neutralising the distinction between voiced and voiceless, anterior coronals and non-anterior coronals, etc., is NOT open to the child until the universal trends to vowel and consonant harmony and CVCV... canonical form have been maximised. This in effect explains why the child cannot come up with a system such as that illustrated on p. 162 above, and clearly the hypothesis put forward here postulating a universal hierarchy would be refuted if it could be demonstrated that a child did have a greatly reduced system but one which did not display consonant harmony or cluster reduction first.

At this stage it is interesting to note that the rules which effect systemic simplification are formally differentiable from the others in two ways. First they are context-free rather than context-sensitive, and second they follow all the others in the synchronic ordering of the realisation rules. To be accurate these characterisations apply to the systemic simplification rules *stricto sensu*. That is, of the rules listed in 4.3.3 above the crucial ones are R23–6 and perhaps R13 and R20.[1] Thus we have formal criteria for distinguishing between the different classes of rules and their respective functions: rules effecting harmony and a CVCV canonical form must precede and be more complex than the simple set of neutralisation rules.

In fact even the former classes of rule allow of some formal characterisation: namely, in terms of Kisseberth's notion of 'functional unity'. That is, the sets of rules listed in 4.3.1 and 4.3.2 form what Kisseberth (1971) would call a 'conspiracy': all of them having in common the effecting of one or other unitary phenomenon. I would suggest that the acquisition of phonology is characterised by two 'infantile conspiracies', followed by a set of neutralisation rules (5.3.3 below).

Whether there is any ordering of harmony as opposed to cluster reduction rules in terms of their availability to the child learning his language is not clear; but footnote 2 on p. 169 above may indicate that

---

[1] Note that the motivation for ordering R13 so early is very weak and that R20 has to be ordered only before another inventory simplifying rule R24.

cluster reduction is prior to harmony. Clearly the claim that harmony and cluster reduction rules form conspiracies implies that the members of each cannot all be ordered together in a block; an implication which is borne out by a glance at the table of ordering relations on p. 158, above.

4.4   The evidence for the child having his own system

The preceding discussion gives rise to two further questions:

(i) Is there any evidence that the 'independent system' ascribed to the child has any (psychological) validity of the kind we have seen for the system of adult representation and realisation rules?

(ii) Is there any evidence for a system of representation more abstract than the adult surface forms – i.e. anything comparable to the underlying forms set up for adult English in, for example, Chomsky and Halle, 1968.

4.4.1 Evidence for the child's system being equivalent to his output. Given that we have justification for the validity of the input to the realisation rules – i.e. the adult surface forms – and for at least some aspects of the realisation rules themselves; and given moreover that, by definition, these rules 'predict' all the child's forms,[1] it is necessary to look in the child's 'own system' for formal properties which might explain the data more convincingly than the realisation rules.[2] There is no clear-cut evidence of this kind; but there is perhaps sufficient to make the entire exclusion of the child's own system unwarranted without further studies. Logically, one would look for examples of the validity of the child's system in two places:

(1) In the simplification of the morpheme structure conditions where this is not obviously triggered by completely parallel changes in the realisation rules, or where such rules seem singularly unmotivated. There are three discernible subtypes here:

   (a) The simplification[3] of a single sequential or canonical morpheme
       structure condition.

---

[1] 'Predict' in all cases, 'explain' in at least a few – see the discussion in 4.2 above. I am indebted to T. Moore for bringing the difference between prediction and explanation to my attention.

[2] Clearly the morpheme structure conditions are functions of the realisation rules – a variant containing less information. However as there is an infinite number of such variants possible the actual form of the conditions set up here is not necessarily vacuous.

[3] Or initial simplicity of a condition at its first appearance.

(b) The conflation of two or more morpheme structure conditions as the result of restructuring of the rule system in a direction other than that of the adult system.

(c) The simplification of a segmental morpheme structure condition (i.e. a matrix redundancy rule) leading to pattern congruity of a type not manifest in the adult system.

(2) In simplification of the phonetic rules in a way not paralleled by the adult system.

An example of (1a) might be provided by the appearance of nasal plus consonant clusters discussed on p. 106 above (q.v.), where there seems to be little motivation for the rule R27 (p. 97 above) in terms of the universal tendencies described in 4.3 above, but where the statement of distribution of consonants within A's system is somewhat simpler because of the constraint characterised by morpheme structure condition 13.

Examples of (1b) – the conflation of two or more conditions – did not occur in my analysis of A's development: contrast the lack of converging rules in table 11 (p. 131 above) with the not infrequent conflations of the realisation rules represented in table 4 (p. 102 above). The only apparent candidate, the restructuring of MS17 and MS17A (p. 124 above), was occasioned more by the desire to avoid unduly complex conditions than to capture any greater generality; and in fact, although MS17 and MS17A have lost their separate identities they have been replaced by three rules, not just one.

Examples of (1c) provide perhaps the most convincing evidence for the child's own system. I will look briefly at two cases: the appearance of [ɣ], and the relation of [f] and [w]. Intermittently from stages 4 to 7 there appeared occurrences of a voiced velar fricative [ɣ] as a reflex of an adult coronal continuant velarised by R19 (p. 82 above). Now, the maximally simple operation of R19 itself may be sufficient explanation of the appearance of this non-English sound; but it seems at any rate possible that a contributory cause was the resultant symmetry in the set of underlying segments utilised by A in his phonology. That is, before the advent of [ɣ] we had an asymmetrical eight term system:

|b d g m n ŋ w l|

whereas with the addition of |ɣ| we have a symmetrical three by three system:

|b d g m n ŋ w l ɣ|[1]

---

[1] There are independent reasons for assuming that |w| is a labial (see p. 46 above).

and the concomitant loss of MS10 ([+cont] → [+ant]). A similar argument of simplicity based on pattern congruity obtains in the identification of [f] and [w] first as 'allophones' of a single phoneme in A's system and later as the members of a voiced–voiceless pair; an identification which is clearly impossible in the adult language with a three-way f/v/w contrast (see above, pp. 107–112).[1]

Without more knowledge than we currently possess about low-level phonetic processes and their characterisation in terms of any well-motivated feature system, it is hard to provide examples of (2) above – the simplification or generalisation of phonetic rules. The only example which springs to mind is the apparent generalisation of the feature [distributed] to provide a laminal articulation for alveolars and a bilabial rather than labio-dental articulation for labials (see the examples on p. 109 above), but it is equally likely that this represents random performance variation, rather than any reflection of true competence.

4.4.2 Evidence for the child's system being more abstract than the adult surface system. After this very brief and inconclusive review of putative evidence for the reality of phonological representations and processes peculiar to the child's system, let us turn to the second question broached above – namely, whether there is any evidence for a level of representation more abstract than that of the adult surface forms. The brief answer appears to be 'no'. In general it does not appear to be possible to effect simplifications in the characterisation of A's output by postulating an additional abstract level comparable to that of the lexical entries set up for adult English in, say, Chomsky and Halle, 1968. As, in the early stages, the child has no vowel and consonant alternation of the kind usually used to justify such abstractions,[2] we have to look, for instance, in the distribution of segments within morphemes for evidence of abstraction. One of the best motivated abstractions of this sort in English is that which denies 'phonemic' status to [ŋ], and rather derives

---

[1] Note that the plausibility of these examples loses some of its attractiveness if we reflect on the fact that an analysis predicating the validity of the child's own system as an independent entity has no explanation at all for the free variation of [ɣ] with [g] and of *some* instances of [w] with [f], both of which we explained quite naturally by the realisation rule analysis (see the discussion on p. 135 above).

[2] He probably doesn't in the later stages either. The incidence of weak and strong forms would indicate that particular verbs are entered in the mind with a set of entries – any of which is chosen at random – rather than being derived from some abstract representation (see the discussion of strong forms on p. 175 above). Even taking note of Sampson's critique of the exclusive reliance on alternation as a basis for abstractions (*Language*, 1970) would not materially alter this point.

it from the sequence of /ng/.[1] Amongst other things this derivation accounts for:

(1) the absence of /ŋ/ in initial position
(2) the absence of /ŋ/ from clusters
(3) the parallel absence of final [mb] and [ŋg]
(4) the absence of long vowels before [ŋ] etc.

But in A's speech at stage 4 for instance [ŋ] does occur in initial position:

> neck → ŋɛk

none of the nasals form clusters; [ŋg] does occur (sporadically) in final (and in fact initial position):

> swing → wiŋg
> neck → ŋgɛk

and [ŋ] does occur sporadically after long vowels:

> frying pan → ɸaɪŋ b̥æn

Moreover the irregularities in the distribution of |ŋ| which do exist – e.g. its limitation to syllables ending in a velar (see MS6, p. 42 above) are not explicable in terms of any kind of segmental complexity like that in adult English. Obviously one negative example cannot be taken as conclusive, but I have been unable to find any convincing example of greater abstraction and accordingly assume provisionally that none exists.

In sum I conclude that a good case has been made for the claim that the child's lexical representations are in terms of the adult system, that the realisation rules also have some psychological validity, and that conversely there is very little evidence – if any – to support the alternative hypotheses either that the child has his own system or anything more abstract than the adult system.

4.5 A psychological model of the acquisition of speech

In the foregoing sections of this chapter I have attempted to show that the child's internalised lexical representations are the same as the adult (surface) phonemic form, and that the realisation rules relating these to his own output are independently motivated. Further, I have suggested that no other constructs have any consistent validity for the child: i.e. that the notion of the child's own system is a myth. It remains to incorporate these conclusions into an explicit psychological model –

---

[1] Although, strangely 'ŋ' appears as one of the 'English segments' comparable to such abstractions as Xʷ in Chomsky and Halle, 1968, p. 177.

specifically the logogen model associated with the name of John Morton (see Morton, 1968, 1969, 1970). As a discussion of this model with regard to some of the data of A's language acquisition has appeared elsewhere (Morton and Smith, 1972), it will suffice here to sketch the outlines of the system and briefly exemplify its working by showing how it accounts for the phenomena described in the Introduction. The relevant parts of the model are given in fig. 1 below (reproduced from Morton and Smith, 1972).

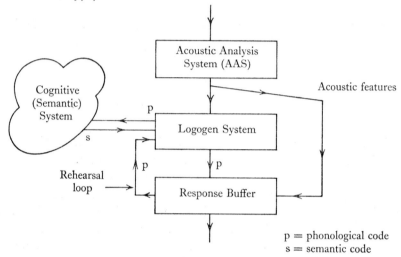

Fig. 1. The logogen model

The central concept in the model is that of 'logogen', a transducer between different kinds of coding which has the function of making words available as responses, and can accept either an articulatory or acoustic input. The words of an individual's vocabulary are each represented by a separate logogen, most probably coded in a phonemic representation,[1] which is linked to the cognitive system on the one hand and

---

[1] Tentative evidence that the logogen code is phonemic rather than phonetic comes from the fact that even segments in absolute exceptions (see 4.1.2.2) usually display the allophonic variants to be expected on general distributional grounds. For instance *knock* at stage 5 following, which should regularly have been [ŋɔk], in fact appeared as [ɡɔk] – |ɡɔɡ|. Interestingly, however, despite its exceptionality, it had the normal allophones [ɡ] and [k] of |ɡ| in initial and final position respectively; indicating that allophonic variants are assigned after the logogen level. Comparable examples could be multiplied considerably. Unfortunately there was so much free variation as well as allophonic variation in A's pronunciation that the evidence is not conclusive. However, the claim of a phonemic coding seems plausible on grounds of general economy as well, and as nothing else depends on this I will continue to make this assumption.

the response buffer on the other. For present purposes I assume that the young child's logogens are stored in terms of the adult phonemic system and that the response buffer consists in part[1] of the set of realisation rules described earlier. Given these two simple postulates, the phenomena described as being in need of explanation in the Introduction are accounted for quite easily. The regularity of the child's acquisition of phonology, the across-the-board nature of his longitudinal development, the many–many relation between the elements of the adult system and the child's system, the appearance of non-English sounds, and the apparent anomalies of 'puzzles' and recidivism are all automatically accounted for if we assume that the realisation rules operate on the adult form of the individual words as the child speaks.

The child's differential understanding of his own deformations (see 4.1.1.1), according as these correspond to an adult surface form or not, is explained by the possibility of taking different paths through the system. In the usual case an acoustic signal comes from the AAS to the logogen system, is paired there with some form of semantic information, and recognised accordingly – e.g. *ship*. In the case where there is no logogen of the required shape available to be paired with the acoustic input – e.g. if the child hears his own form [ki:b] (= adult *squeeze*) – then he will carry the signal through to the response buffer, look up the realisation rules until he can match [ki:b] with /skwi:z/, and then return this articulation code via the rehearsal loop to the logogen system for interpretation.[2] Finally, if the acoustic signal he receives corresponds both to an adult form and a (different) child's form, either of the preceding strategies can be employed, but with obvious preference given to the former. Thus, if he hears [sip], for which a logogen exists as such, the child will at once pair this with the relevant semantic information: viz. 'drink in a certain fashion'. If this interpretation proves wrong, however, as when I rejected his suggestion (see p. 136 above) then he can apply the second strategy, and come up with the meaning 'ship'.[3] Further, in this model, restructuring (see 4.1.1.4) is characterisable as a mis-coding in the logogen system, and accordingly is in terms of adult

---

[1] If we accept the argument of the preceding footnote, it will also contain the phonetic rules, as well as specifications for such features as intonation and other suprasegmentals which are not an integral part of the logogen itself.

[2] The major unsolved problem here lies in the directionality of the realisation rules. As they are formulated here /skwi:z/ could be mapped onto [ki:b] but not vice versa. More research is needed in this area.

[3] For a more detailed account, see Morton and Smith, 1972.

segments;[1] whereas absolute exceptions (see 4.1.2.2) are characterisable as the failure to apply a particular realisation rule, or combination of realisation and phonetic rules.

In sum, a logogen model incorporating a set of realisation rules appears to characterise satisfactorily all the phenomena set up originally for explanation, as well as most other data encountered.

---

[1] With correspondingly greater phonetic plausibility and explanatory power: see the discussion of restructuring referred to. Note also Morton and Smith, 1972, for further suggestions as to the form of the coding of restructured items.

5 Linguistic implications of the child's acquisition of phonology

In the same way that the linguistic change described in historical phonology provides us with 'a window on the form of linguistic competence'[1] so does the linguistic change evidenced in language acquisition provide evidence for the validity or otherwise of the theoretical constructs set up to account for the adult language synchronically. In this chapter I wish to review the implications for phonology in general, and generative phonology in particular, of the foregoing analyses and discussion.

It is not, of course, implied that the facts of one language – or one nascent idiolect – should be definitive for the status of any construct. It is claimed, however, that such facts are theoretically as relevant for the definition of phonological universals as the facts of any other language; and to the extent that they have clear psychological validity, perhaps more relevant.

5.1 Phonological units

5.1.1 Distinctive features versus phonemes. Up to now, it has been assumed without any attempt at justification that the basic unit in terms of which the phonological processes under discussion should be described is the distinctive feature – specifically that variety of the animal dissected in Chomsky and Halle's *The Sound Pattern of English*. It is now time to justify this assumption.

The most compelling argument in favour of distinctive features is the economy and elegance they allow in the formulation of phonological rules. A typical example is provided by rule R19 harmonising certain consonants to the point of articulation of a following velar. The consonants affected are /t d s z ʃ θ tʃ dʒ r l n j/; that is, all and only the ESP consonants which have the feature characterisation [+coronal].[2]

---

[1] Kiparsky, 1968, p. 174.
[2] For examples see above p. 20. There is no occurrence of /ð/ in the relevant environment in English, and none of /ʒ/ in A's vocabulary at a stage when the rule operated.

Without using the feature [coronal] or its equivalent, this set of consonants appears to constitute virtually a random list. Even using the crypto-featural articulatory labels of traditional phonemics – interdental, alveolar, palato-alveolar, palatal – we have a decidedly inelegant and unexpected combination of categories. Yet once we use the feature specification [coronal] it is seen that the class is an entirely natural one, and that the set of consonants in question constitutes the simplest grouping it is possible to characterise.

That this characterisation is not merely a fortunate coincidence is seen by its reappearance at other points in the phonological rules which account for A's output. Thus it is precisely the same set of consonants (actually those listed above plus the two coronals missing there – /ʒ/ and /ð/ – but excluding /n/) which are neutralised as |d| (by rules 23, 24, 25) in the event that they have not been differentiated by earlier rules (see examples on p. 21 above). That is, we now have the natural class $\begin{bmatrix} +\text{coronal} \\ -\text{nasal} \end{bmatrix}$ – i.e. all the coronals which are not also nasal; itself a natural class which recurs in R17 (p. 28 above). Further justification for the feature [coronal] can be seen in the longitudinal development of the same rules (pp. 74 and 81f. above), where the same class is gradually reduced by the exclusion of the glide /j/, of the liquids /l, r/ and of the nasal /n/ – but crucially retaining the otherwise still somewhat heterogeneous elements.

This explanatory power of the use of features (i.e. the prior existence of the feature [coronal] can be viewed as the explanation for why precisely these consonants undergo a particular process) is further illustrated in rules 9 and 10, particularly their conflation at stage 3 (p. 65 above). In this case it will be recalled that the anterior fricative /s/ was deleted before the anterior consonants /n, p/ etc. (labials and alveolars), whereas the non-anterior /ʃ/ (and later /j/) were deleted before the non-anterior consonants /k, g/ (velars). Once again this process appears arbitrary in phonemic terms, but is immediately seen to be plausible in the framework of a set of distinctive features. One could sum up this section by saying simply that the distinctive features are constructs which have psychological validity for the child, and to this extent their status as theoretical primitives is substantiated. Clearly, we cannot prove that the child identifies the set of consonants /t, d/, etc. by reference to the linguist's feature [coronal], but given that he treats these sounds as identical for some purposes (although different for others) the simplest hypothesis is one which equates the linguistic construct and the device isomorphic to it in the child's brain.

A second argument in favour of the use of distinctive features is that they allow the interaction of rules which would otherwise be unrelated. A typical example is provided by rules 19 and 20 (pp. 29 and 30 above). The effect of rule 20 is essentially to convert /f, v/ – i.e. anterior continuants – to |w|. However /f/ and /v/ are not the only segments of the adult phonology which end up as |w| (see such examples as *room* → |wum| etc.; for further examples see p. 20). By letting R19 operate first on all coronals in particular environments – specifically in the present case making them [−coronal] but [+anterior]¹ – and then letting R20 operate on the output of R19, we capture the underlying identity of the process of 'labialisation' in these instances. Other examples can be inferred by the reader on inspection of the derivations given on pp. 31ff. above.

A third argument for distinctive features resides in some exceptional cases of metathesis (pp. 98ff. above). In most examples metathesis operates in terms of entire segments – /dɛsk/ → |dɛks| for instance – but in some cases metathesis operated only on parts of segments:

e.g.   difficult → gipətul (later: gifətəlt)

where we have the regular transposition of the first and third consonants as far as their point of articulation is concerned, but the retention of the voicing sequence of the adult word. That is, we would have expected |kipədul| or |kifədəlt| rather than the actually occurring item. A comparable example, but where point of articulation is preserved and the manner of articulation is (irregularly) changed, is provided by:

Christmas → ġiptit

instead of the expected [ġimtət]. Examples are too few to be more than suggestive, but it would appear that these metatheses can only be satisfactorily explained in terms of the feature composition of the segments involved and not merely in terms of the segments as such.

Having presented evidence for distinctive features it remains to present evidence *against* them. The same arguments which have been used to support distinctive features can normally be turned the other way. Thus,

¹ [+anterior] will be vacuously specified in some cases – e.g. with /s/ – but non-vacuously in, e.g., the case of /ʃ/, /r/ etc.

while economy and elegance in the statement of phonological rules is a prime justification for distinctive features and even makes it appear that they have considerable psychological validity, there are, unfortunately, just as many cases where the use of distinctive features seems to militate against economy. The clearest examples of this are, first, where a single segment is subject to a particular rule and has therefore to be specified by a number of distinctive features; and second where a distinctive feature appears to be characteristic of only one segment. Cases of the first are legion: R7 (p. 25 above) refers only to /s/ and has to mention [coronal, anterior, continuant, strident, and voice]; R9 and R10 refer only to /s/ and /ʃ/ (and perhaps their voiced congeners) and need four distinctive feature specifications each; R11 refers only to /z/ and needs five distinctive feature specifications, etc. A paradigm example is provided by the development of rule R18c, where at stage 12, we have a 'natural' class consisting of /j, z/ (p. 78 above). It is hard to believe that the child is really working in terms of complexes of features rather than unitary (phonemic) segments here. Cases of the second type are provided most obviously by the liquids /l/ and /r/ characterised *inter alia* by the feature [+lateral] and [−lateral] respectively. Although the idiosyncratic behaviour of /l/ in the realisation rules can be formalised quite easily (e.g. rules 3, 4, 6), and there is no *a priori* reason why any distinctive feature should bear other than a minimal functional load[1] (i.e. the natural class [+lateral] in English can never refer to more or less than one item), problems arise in the statement of morpheme structure conditions. Thus, as mentioned on p. 48 above, the formal statement of MS2 'Within a word all consonants must be [ɽ] or none must' is extremely complex; and had the relevant segment been [r] it is virtually impossible. Yet in phonemic terms there is no such problem at all. Again, the child seems to operate with segments rather than features, at least in the statement of such canonical conditions.

The second argument used to support distinctive features is also seen to be somewhat ambivalent on closer inspection. The interaction of realisation rules by virtue of their distinctive feature content is attractive in some ways, but it has two disadvantages. The first of these is that the output of any particular rule may not correspond to any possible combination of features in the language concerned. Thus, for instance, the derivation of *cloth* → [ɡɔk] (p. 34, item xv) goes through a stage repre-

---

[1] Although it is a little disturbing when a feature is needed in *most* languages ([lateral]) but is systematically exploited by only a tiny minority of them.

sentable as [kɔx] – where in fact the feature specification of the final
segment would be

$$\begin{bmatrix} -\text{coronal} \\ -\text{anterior} \\ +\text{continuant} \\ -\text{voice} \end{bmatrix}$$

which is ruled out by MS10 (p. 50 above). Now, it is a truism that the
lines of a derivation – other than the first and the last – have no theoretical status; and accordingly the intermediate stage [kɔx] should occasion
no misgivings. If, however, the attempt is being made to lend support to
distinctive features by reference to their psychological validity and the
psychological validity of the rules of which they form part, as we have
been doing above; then it seems to me that the lack of theoretical status
on any kind of level of these intermediate stages is an argument against
the use of distinctive features. Either we can say that the psychological
validity or reality of the distinctive features and phonological rules is
entirely irrelevant to their theoretical status, and base our definitions of
these constructs on purely linguistic evidence – and thereby put off
indefinitely the prospect of an integrated psycholinguistic model of
competence and performance – or we can admit the relevance of psychological criteria of the type discussed, and admit with them the fact that
the rules as formulated make the wrong predictions in their intermediate
stages. The second drawback is that, if two or more rules are linked in
the way R19 and R20 are, then one would expect the phenomena which
they unite to change diachronically in step – e.g. in the present case that
|w| from /f/ would disappear at much the same time as |w| from /s/. In
fact they changed at quite different stages (roughly 15 and 10 respectively
– see pp. 87 and 85 above).[1] A related disadvantage of the use of
features is that in some instances they lead to highly unnatural derivations from the adult to the child's language: e.g. the change of /r/ from
[+sonorant] to [−sonorant] and back to [+sonorant] on p. 33
above.

The third argument used in favour of distinctive features, metathesis,
in most cases also strongly supports the postulation of psychological
validity for a phoneme-like unit. Although there is by definition no
transposition of a metathetic kind which cannot be characterised in terms

---

[1] Strictly speaking, the absence of parallel change in R19 and R20 is inconclusive.
Only the presence of parallel change would be important here. Accordingly the lack of
simultaneity here is not a very substantial argument.

of distinctive features, it seems significant that the overwhelming majority of examples operate in terms of segments bigger than features (see the examples on pp. 98f. above).

There is a further negative argument against the psychological reality of (some?) distinctive features: namely, the apparent inability of the child (as also the foreign language learner)[1] to form new combinations of features which he has already mastered elsewhere. Thus at the time of writing, A has phonetically perfect [tʃ] and [dʒ], [s] and [z], etc., but is quite incapable of producing [ʃ] or [ʒ]. That is, he can produce fricatives and affricates differentially, and alveolars and palato-alveolars differentially; but is unable to isolate the [− anterior, + high] articulation of [tʃ] without affrication, to produce [ʃ].

On the basis of this discussion it would seem that we have over-whelming evidence in favour of the use of distinctive features, but also strong evidence for the use of a larger unit as well. In fact a larger unit is invariably used in the literature, though with disclaimers such as the following from Chomsky and Halle, 1968: 'alphabetic symbols...are therefore to be regarded as nothing more than convenient *ad hoc* abbre-viations for feature bundles...without systematic import' (p. 64). It seems to me that the convenience is too great and too consistent to be without systematic import, and I would suggest that both features and alphabetic symbols (which in nearly all cases seem to correspond to phonemes) should *both* have a systematic theoretical status. That phono-logical processes should sometimes range over one unit and sometimes over another should occasion no surprise. The interesting problem is to see if the choice of unit is dependent on other formal properties of the relevant rule (e.g. morpheme structure conditions *versus* phonological rules proper).

One could summarise the usual generative phonology position as being that, whatever the psychological etc. validity of the phonemes (see Sapir, 1933) their crucial disadvantage is that they make impossible the statement of some valid generalisation. This argument, however, is valid if and only if one allows no phonological hierarchy – i.e. if the distinctive feature is the *only* unit of representation. Once one allows a hierarchy of units the argument collapses.

It might be mentioned in passing that the behaviour of some entities – e.g. the treatment of /st/ as a unit (see p. 60 etc.) seems to indicate the

---

[1] See the discussion of the filling of *cases vides* in bilingual situations in Weinreich, 1953.

existence of a hierarchy of units along the lines of Fudge, 1969 (p. 268) – i.e. syllable; onset, etc. phoneme; (feature). This leads us directly on to the second point of debate: namely, the status of the syllable, especially in the formulation of morpheme structure conditions.

5.1.2 Syllables versus morphemes. Apart from the use of the feature [syllabic] to characterise vowels, it has been tacitly assumed in the description up to now that phonological rules of all kinds should operate in terms only of distinctive features (and perhaps segments approximating to phonemes), with the additional use of lexically given morpheme boundaries to show the scope of the operation in question. In the present case this has worked generally satisfactorily for the realisation rules and to some extent for the early stages of the morpheme structure conditions. I suspect, however, that in the later stages at least the morpheme structure conditions as such need to be supplemented by syllable structure conditions if we are to capture economically the generalisations present in the data. It should be noted that I am suggesting *supplementing* the morpheme structure conditions – not replacing them. Examples of the sort: 'All consonants within a word must be |l| or none must' (MS2, p. 41 above) clearly have a lexical unit and not a phonological unit as their domain[1] and should be stated accordingly (however difficult that formal statement may be!). There are some cases, however, where the postulation of a *syllable* would simplify the statement of restrictions on the distribution of consonants in words, and would also make the correct claim that such constraints are phonological not lexical. The clearest evidence comes from canonical morpheme structure conditions (especially MS1); in particular where these deal with possible medial consonant clusters. Even at stage 4 (p. 110 above) there is clearly some repetition involved in the statement of MS1''', which could equally well be represented as a syllable structure condition to the effect that all syllables correspond to the pattern (C)V(V)(C). At stage 9, however, when consonant clusters involving an [l] appear, this repetition becomes more obvious (p. 115 above), and is accentuated at each succeeding complication in the statement of clusters – e.g. stage 15 (p. 120), stage 20 (p. 122) and stage 25 (p. 127), where the same change in the possible post-consonantal elements has to be specified twice on each occasion.

---

[1] This is not the same as saying that such words should be characterised by a lexical feature (see p. 48 above).

This uneconomic repetition is perhaps not serious[1] but the situation is worse when we come to other medial combinations; e.g. nasal clusters. In general one can say that nasal clusters are homorganic (although see the discussion of MS1, p. 104), but in examples such as:

camera → ġæmdə	humpty dumpty → ʌmti: dʌmti:
chimney → ḍimni:	twenty → tɛmti: etc.

this generalisation is broken, because the first element of the cluster ends one syllable and the second element begins another syllable.[2] The difficulty with substituting syllable structure conditions for morpheme structure conditions is that precisely the same problem arises – in reverse – with final clusters. In this position (nasal) clusters are homorganic within a morpheme, but are frequently heterorganic within the word because of the morphemic complexity involved; e.g. we have:

-mp -nt -ŋk (as in e.g. *jump, went, gonk*)

but we also have:

-md -ŋd etc. (as in [kʌmd] and [blɔŋd] for *came* and *belonged*)

Because of this ambivalence, and because of the difficulty of finding any workable definition for *syllable*,[3] I have left all conditions stated in terms of morphemes; but the tenor of the preceding sections is that generative phonology should allow some kind of phonological base component (see Sampson, 1970) which will generate the possible set of syllables within a morpheme, further expand these in terms of phonemes, and describe the latter in terms of distinctive features.

5.2   Distinctive features

Assuming the validity of distinctive features – though not the uniqueness of their validity – we can now investigate what evidence is provided by the process of phonological acquisition for the nature of the features

[1] And could be partially avoided by setting up a more complex series of segmental morpheme structure conditions in addition – e.g. merely specifying # [−syll] [−syll] [+syll]... # instead of (C(l))V... but even this sequence would have to be given twice in MS1 as well.

[2] With non-nasal clusters the situation is more complex, although comparable arguments obtain. Thus [kt] clusters occurred far earlier across syllable boundaries (e.g. *doctor* → [ġɔktə]) than they did syllable finally.

[3] Definitions which allow the specification of the number of syllables in any given stretch are easy to produce; and it is number of syllables which naïve speakers are usually able to agree upon. Unfortunately the number of syllables – which can always be simply treated in terms of the distinctive feature [syllabic] – is irrelevant to the present problem, which necessitates the location of syllable boundaries.

necessary in the linguistic description, both in terms of the constitutive members of this set and their individual definitions.[1]

5.2.1 Major class features. Since Jakobson, Fant and Halle, 1951, the basic categorisation of sound segments has been effected by the use of the two features [consonantal] and [vocalic] giving the four-way classification:

True consonants (obstruents)	Vowels	Liquids	Glides
$\begin{bmatrix} +\text{cons} \\ -\text{voc} \end{bmatrix}$	$\begin{bmatrix} -\text{cons} \\ +\text{voc} \end{bmatrix}$	$\begin{bmatrix} +\text{cons} \\ +\text{voc} \end{bmatrix}$	$\begin{bmatrix} -\text{cons} \\ -\text{voc} \end{bmatrix}$

In an afterthought to Chomsky and Halle, 1968 (pp. 353–5), the feature [vocalic] was replaced by a feature [syllabic]. This has two advantages in the present context: (i) it makes it simpler to specify canonical forms of the type seen in MS1 for instance (p. 47 above), as the alternation of consonants and vowels can be characterised in terms of the single feature [syllabic]; and (ii) it avoids the problem of defining [vocalic].[2] There is, however, one major disadvantage, namely the difficulty of characterising the natural class of non-syllabic liquids – specifically [l, r] – without a feature [vocalic] or some *ad hoc* substitute such as [liquid]; and the less serious problem of characterising the natural class of obstruents and glides – the earlier [−vocalic].

The naturalness of the class [l, r] in all varieties of English, and many other languages, is too well known to need elaboration here. It is worth demonstrating, however, that they also constitute a natural class for A, not only where his phonological patterning coincided with that of ESP but also when it diverged from the adult norm. Up to stage 20 [l, r] were definable within A's system as the natural class

$$\begin{bmatrix} +\text{coronal} \\ +\text{continuant} \\ +\text{voice} \end{bmatrix}^3$$

---

[1] It is assumed that there are two basic criteria of relevance for the definition of distinctive features: (i) the existence of clear phonetic correlates, either acoustic or articulatory (or conceivably auditory) and (ii) the regular formation of (natural) classes economically statable in terms of those features. In this discussion I will be dealing mainly with the second category.

[2] Although used to characterise *inter alia* the liquid [l], Chomsky and Halle's definition of [vocalic] (1968, p. 302) should exclude [l] on articulatory grounds. It is significant that *no definition* of [syllabic] is attempted at all!

[3] The presence of [+voice] is already suspicious: it is needed to exclude the voiceless lateral [ɫ] (< ESP /sl/) which does not pattern like its voiced congener; and in the other framework would presumably have been [−voc].

STA

i.e. in terms of features lower in the hierarchy than [consonantal] and [vocalic]; but once other coronal continuants began to appear, specifically [s] and [z] (pp. 124 above), the specification had to change to include [+sonorant], or [−strident], or some other differentiating feature. More significantly, at a stage (12) where A had learnt successfully to distinguish [l] and [r] articulatorily, they still occurred as free variants of adult /j, z/ for him (p. 78 above). That is we found:

> yolk → lo:k *or* ɹo:k
> young → lʌŋ *or* ɹʌŋ
> zebra → li:bɹə *or* ɹi:bɹə

cf.   lady → leɪdi: (*ɹeɪdi:) etc.
> red → ɹɛd (*lɛd) etc.

In other words, we need to refer to the natural class of liquids[1] even where the adult language does not.

Further evidence for the desirability of the feature [vocalic] comes from the differential behaviour of |w| and |l|.[2] At first these were simply characterisable as [+continuant] (or [+sonorant]) and functioned essentially similarly (see p. 41, especially MS3).[3] Then at stage 2 (p. 107 above) |w| began to pattern phonetically with the true consonants (|b d g|) in having a voiceless allophone in final position, while |l| remained unchanged, and at stage 7 (p. 112 above) |w| patterned phonemically like the obstruents in having a voiceless congener |f|, whereas |l| only acquired a voiceless equivalent at stage 15. This necessitated a somewhat arbitrary use of the feature [sonorant] to characterise the class |b d g w| where the earlier characterisation $\begin{bmatrix} -\text{nasal} \\ -\text{vocalic} \end{bmatrix}$ would have been quite adequate and well motivated. Unfortunately, the precise status of [sonorant] is itself ambiguous. It is defined in Chomsky and Halle, 1968, as characterising those 'sounds produced with a vocal tract cavity configuration in which spontaneous voicing is possible' (p. 302), but on phonological grounds it would seem advisable to make this possibility mandatory for a sound to qualify as a sonorant: that is [h, ʔ] and voiceless vowels would be non-sonorant.[4] There seems to be no justification

---

[1] In fact it seems we need to refer to the class $\begin{bmatrix} +\text{voc} \\ +\text{cons} \end{bmatrix}$ − not even just the traditional 'liquid' − because of the need to exclude [ɬ].

[2] For a further example, note the development of R19 (p. 83, esp. n. 1).

[3] |l| was of course quite *sui generis* at this stage (see MS2), but the important point at present is that it also formed a natural class with |w|, as in MS3.

[4] Presumably the glottal stop should be non-sonorant even by Chomsky and Halle's definition, despite its assignment as [+son] (1968, pp. 303, 354).

for lumping [h] together with the nasals, liquids etc., and accordingly I have analysed [h] as being non-sonorant above (e.g. p. 119 above). Essentially what is being suggested here is that the feature [syllabic] be replaced by the original [vocalic], but that *syllables* as (potentially complex) units in a phonological hierarchy be introduced instead. The articulatory or acoustic definition of the feature [vocalic] remains obscure, even though phonologically it is well motivated.

5.2.2 Cavity features: 5.2.2.1 Coronal. The clearest example of the relevance of acquisition for the definition of distinctive features comes with the feature [coronal]. The approximate scope of this feature to cover alveolars, dentals and palato-alveolars is reasonably clear; but the position is not so obvious with the true palatals ([j ɲ c] etc.) which are [−coronal] in Chomsky and Halle, 1968, though they were [−grave] (i.e. treated like all other coronals) in the earlier (Jakobson, Fant and Halle, 1951) system. Once again it would appear that the earlier system was better. Thus, R19 (p. 29 above), which accounts for the initial velar, in:

duck → ġʌk	thank you → ġɛgu:
sing → ġiŋ	snake → ŋe:k etc.

uses the designation [+coronal] to characterise unambiguously all those segments which undergo the rule. At stage 2 there were further examples:

yak → ġɛk
young → ġʌŋ
(yucca → ġʌgə)

which show that /j/ too must be included in the structural description of R19. If we abide by the specification of /j/ in Chomsky and Halle, 1968, as [−coronal], the input to R19 will have to be the disjunction:

$$\left\{ \begin{matrix} [+\text{coronal}] \\ \begin{bmatrix} -\text{consonantal} \\ -\text{syllabic} \\ -\text{anterior} \\ +\text{voice} \end{bmatrix} \end{matrix} \right\}$$

or some such,[1] whereas if we assume /j/ is [+coronal] we simply retain

---

[1] No other [−consonantal] segment is affected:
e.g.   walk → wɔ:k
                                 hang → ɛŋ

the same structural description. Further justification for this categorisation comes from:

(a) The comparable behaviour of /ʃ/ and /j/ with regard to deletion (R10A, p. 66 above) where making /j/ [+coronal] avoids the two unpleasant alternatives of creating a disjunction somewhat more complex than the one above, or of having two (successive) rules with an identical complex environment (p. 67 above).

(b) The behaviour of /j/ before other coronal consonants, a position in which there is normally no assimilation, when it becomes |d| :

shut → d̪ʌt		bite → b̪aɪt
touch → d̪ʌt	cf.	yes → d̪ɛt
wet → wɛt		yawn → d̪ɔːn
cat → ġɛt		yacht → d̪ɔt

(c) The comparable behaviour of /j/ and the coronal liquids /l/ and /r/ as reflected in R18 (pp. 75ff. above).

It would seem then that the definition of [coronal] given in Chomsky and Halle, 1968, should be interpreted to include /j/, an interpretation which is already possible given the vagueness of Chomsky and Halle's definition, and which would also be consistent with their statement (p. 317) that laterals are 'restricted to coronal consonantal sounds'; as the point of articulation of a palatal lateral [ʎ] is far closer to that of [j] than, say, that of [l]. Clearly the facts of this single idiolect are not to be taken as definitive (see the opening paragraph of this chapter) but the phenomenon described is clearly of direct relevance to an ultimate universal definition of the distinctive feature [coronal]. The definition itself will clearly have to await a mass of comparative evidence from the realm of language acquisition and elsewhere. In the present instance, further evidence for the status of [coronal] can be found in Ewe (Smith, 1968), Hungarian (Hall, 1944) and elsewhere.

5.2.2.2 Anterior. In the same way that A's acquisition provides evidence for changing the *interpretation* of the definition of [coronal], rather than changing the definition itself, so also does it provide evidence for modifying the interpretation of [anterior] with regard to the other most common glide /w/. In Chomsky and Halle, 1968, both /j/ and /w/ are classified as $\begin{bmatrix} -\text{coronal} \\ -\text{anterior} \end{bmatrix}$. We have seen that /j/ is [+coronal] (and also [−anterior]); and it would seem that /w/ should be [+anterior] (and also [−coronal]). The evidence for this comes from the mapping characterised by R8 (p. 15 above), from words such as:

> squat → g̣ɔp
> queen → g̣i:m
> twist → tipt etc.

where a post-consonantal /w/ induces a labial consonant after the immediately following vowel. Assuming that this is a further manifestation of consonant harmony (p. 164 above) the simplest way of characterising it is as an assimilation in terms of the features [coronal] and [anterior]; but if /w/ is [−anterior] we have no easy way of explaining the change, particularly as the rule applies to velars as well as alveolars and palato-alveolars:

> quick → kip

Some slight further evidence comes from rule R17 (p. 19 above) which should perhaps have been generalised to labials as well as velars to account for the harmony apparent in:

> whistle → wibu

An alternative possibility would leave /w/ as non-anterior but would utilise a feature [labial], characterising /w/ as well as the bilabials and labio-dentals.[1] There is in fact some indication that such a feature is independently useful. Within the present (*SPE*) system the features [coronal] and [anterior] allow a simple four-way classification of the point of articulation of consonants:

$$\text{dentals and alveolars are:} \begin{bmatrix} +\text{coronal} \\ +\text{anterior} \end{bmatrix}$$

$$\text{labials are:} \begin{bmatrix} -\text{coronal} \\ +\text{anterior} \end{bmatrix}$$

$$\text{palato-alveolars are:} \begin{bmatrix} +\text{coronal} \\ -\text{anterior} \end{bmatrix}$$

$$\text{velars etc. are:} \begin{bmatrix} -\text{coronal} \\ -\text{anterior} \end{bmatrix}$$

With a language where there is only a three-way positional contrast, e.g. *p t k* – i.e. the commonest type, and the one used by A in the early

---

[1] Note that the traditional phonetic description of [w] as a labio-velar allows for an easy statement of this assimilation.

stages – we can characterise the following natural classes with a single feature:

t etc: [+ coronal] p, t etc: [+ anterior]

p, k etc: [− coronal] k etc: [− anterior]

whereas the other two possible combinations – p and $t k$ each require a more complex specification:

$$p \text{ etc:} \begin{bmatrix} -\text{coronal} \\ +\text{anterior} \end{bmatrix}$$

$$t, k \text{ etc:} \begin{bmatrix} \begin{Bmatrix} +\text{coronal} \\ -\text{anterior} \end{Bmatrix} \end{bmatrix}$$

While the complexity of the class consisting of $t k$ etc may be justified, it is not at all obvious that labials should be 'more costly' – i.e. less likely to occur in phonological rules than alveolars or velars, or combinations of alveolars and labials, for instance. Examples of the occurrence of the class $\begin{bmatrix} -\text{coronal} \\ +\text{anterior} \end{bmatrix}$ with various modifications are found in R8 (p. 64 above), and in the development of R24(i) (p. 90 above). The latter accounts for the appearance of the labial fricative [f], and it is noteworthy that there was on no occasion any tendency to generalise the process to the class of anterior consonants as might be expected – i.e. there was no [s] until much later. The (un)natural class $\begin{Bmatrix} +\text{coronal} \\ -\text{anterior} \end{Bmatrix}$ did appear as well (MS3, p. 110 above), but it is possible to reformulate this so that the disjunction disappears (p. 110, n. 3, above). In sum, the evidence is inconclusive; but, if anything, points towards aspects of a Ladefoged-type system as being preferable to the Chomsky and Halle (1968) feature system (see Ladefoged, 1967).

5.2.2.3 **Subsidiary cavity features.** For the remaining cavity features utilised in Chomsky and Halle, 1968, there is little crucial evidence available in the data studied. The features [high], [back] and [low] in their use for the specification of consonantal articulations, are hardly of any relevance at all though there was a faint tendency (see p. 91 above) to use a [+high] articulation instead of a [+delayed release] one for adult affricates: e.g.

jig → ḍig etc.

There was similarly a tendency to 'experiment' with the feature [distributed] (see p. 109 above), as witness the variation between *inter alia* the apical and laminal articulation of coronal consonants, but with no rule applying to a natural class [distributed] at any stage, this experimentation is not of much interest for the features themselves. The need for the feature [lateral] to be used in the morpheme structure conditions before it was necessary for the specification of the systematic phonemes used by A has been discussed already (p. 48) and would indicate that the economy gained by segmental morpheme structure conditions is spurious. Finally, the same section may indicate the need for a further feature [retroflex] for instance, to characterise the non-lateral liquid [r].

5.2.2.4 Other features. Of the other distinctive features used in the analysis, I have already discussed the interaction of [voice] and [length] (p. 135 above), and the possible need for analysing [l] as a non-continuant (see p. 84 above, and Wells, 1971). Beyond this, and the advantage of having some feature which would allow us to capture the similarity of nasals and continuants, since these form a natural class in, e.g., R19(ii) (p. 81), characterisable here only as a disjunction, there seems little which needs to be added to the foregoing.

5.3   Other theoretical constructs

5.3.1 Marking conventions. The use of marking conventions in this study has been mainly conspicuous by its absence, though there are two directions in which they might be of relevance to developmental phonology. First we have the potential corroboration of the form of individual marking conventions by the order of acquisition: e.g. the unmarked obstruent is a plosive rather than a fricative, and plosives occurred regularly in A's speech long before fricatives did. Looking at this from the other point of view we could take the marking convention in question as given and adduce it as an explanation of the sequence of acquisition. Second we have the potential use of the marking conventions in their linking function: that is, we could assume that the realisation rules were like the normal rules of phonology, and that the output of any realisation rule would be further modified by any marking convention whose structural description was met (Chomsky and Halle, 1968, pp. 419ff.) – see, e.g., the discussion of R3 on pp. 23–4 above. In fact, it seems that with the exception of one or two isolated examples of the type cited, marking conventions are completely irrelevant.

A priori, there is no reason to expect that the phenomenon of language acquisition should replicate the phenomena characterised by marking conventions in acquired languages; but it would be nice if they did, and hypotheses such as Cairns' predictions about cluster acquisition set out from the assumption that they will. Unfortunately it appears that they don't – at least not sufficiently regularly to be of great interest. Thus, of the marking conventions in Chomsky and Halle, 1968, ii–iii (p. 404) correctly characterise the typical CVCV...canonical form of children's speech, but say nothing about the unmarked clustering possibilities (with liquids and glides rather than, say, nasals), and nothing about the equally common tendency to some form of vowel and consonant harmony.[1] Moreover, when we look at the consonants we find a virtually random set of correlations. Thus the least marked plosive system is characterised as having bilabial, alveolar and velar elements, but these are voiceless ([p t k]), whereas children generally seem to start with voicing neutralised, but the phonetic manifestation predominantly voiced ([b d g]). The other least marked terms of an elementary consonant system are [n] and [s], whereas it seems normally to be the case that nasals with other points of articulation [m] and [ŋ] appear before the fricatives, and that within the fricatives the more highly marked [f] regularly appears before [s]. Yet in the *SPE* system [m] is as highly marked as [q] – a 'pharyngeal (*sic*) plosive' and [f] as highly marked as [θ]. Examples could be multiplied with reference to the liquids and glides (e.g. there is no difference in markedness between [w] and [j]) but given the inconclusive nature of the data there seems little point in continuing. It does not even look particularly promising to attempt to revise the marking conventions in the light of the evidence from acquisition – at least not until far more data are available – as those cases where the marking conventions make the 'wrong' predictions for acquisition are often precisely those which are best motivated – e.g. the unmarked nature of [s] *vis à vis* [f].

The situation looks a little more hopeful at first sight with the marking conventions used as a linking device. Thus we can satisfactorily explain the common velarisation of alveolars before dark [ł] by having recourse to marking conventions (see above, p. 23). But presumably, if we are going to allow marking conventions to link in with the rules in some instances, we must allow them to link in all cases, and block them where they should not apply. Unfortunately they would need to be blocked, or

---

[1] In the adult language vowel and consonant harmony occur minimally in English, except, of course, in the more sophisticated form of poetical rhyme and assonance.

new conventions would need to be devised[1] in the majority of cases –
making the few occasions when they would be useful unduly expensive.
One example will suffice. Any rule converting a segment to a glide[2] will
also perforce make that segment $\begin{bmatrix} -\text{coronal} \\ -\text{anterior} \end{bmatrix}$ etc. (see *SPE* marking
convention xxxv, p. 407) whereas R18b for instance (p. 29 above) must
convert a coronal sonorant (e.g. /l/) to a non-coronal but [+anterior]
glide.

In general it would seem that the present state of ignorance makes it
impossible to effect any interesting correlation between acquisitional
phenomena and marking conventions, but merely lends support to the
admitted need for some means of characterising symmetric systems and
perhaps phenomena such as consonant and vowel harmony.

5.3.2 Abbreviatory notations.

We have looked at various substantive
universals – namely the distinctive features, their definitions, scope and
interrelationships; and I now wish to look briefly at the evidence for
some formal universals: specifically, the status of the variable α and
curly brackets.

With regard to the α variable (the use of Greek letters as variables
ranging over + and −), there are two cases where their use enables us to
capture clearly and easily the essential nature of the process described;
and a number of other cases where their use seems at best arbitrary, and
at worst misleading.

(i) We have the examples where /s/ and /ʃ/ in initial position were
differentially deleted before a consonant at the end of the same syllable,
and where the longitudinal development of the two rules concerned (R9
and R10) was such that they could be conflated if and only if we utilised
the α notation (p. 66 above) to give us a rule of the form:

$$\begin{bmatrix} +\text{coronal} \\ +\text{continuant} \\ +\text{strident} \\ \alpha\text{anterior} \end{bmatrix} \rightarrow \emptyset /\# \text{-----} [+\text{syll}]\ [\alpha\text{anterior}]$$

That is, the anterior fricative /s/ is deleted before anterior consonants

[1] E.g. a convention to account for the disappearance of the feature [lateral] when a
coronal continuant is made a nasal (see p. 33, Ex. ix, above). At present there is no such
convention, although it seems *prima facie* plausible.

[2] I.e. $\begin{bmatrix} -\text{voc} \\ -\text{cons} \end{bmatrix}$ in the *SPE* system. Although I have not used this formulation, I
assume that comparable marking conventions would apply.

and the non-anterior /ʃ/ is deleted before non-anterior consonants. There seems to be no other explanation available for this than the structural pressure of the rules themselves, assuming the reality of the α variable as a psychological as well as a linguistic entity.

(ii) We have the examples of heterorganic nasal clusters – that is, instead of the expected cluster [mb], A produced clusters with [md] (p. 106 above); i.e. there were three kinds of cluster [nd] [ŋg] and [md], a state of affairs which can be more simply characterised than the expected set [nd, ŋg, mb]. Again, given that A already controlled [b] in other environments, there seems to be no satisfactory explanation of this anomaly besides positing the 'reality' of the α variable.

Unfortunately none of the other uses of α have the explanatory power of these first two. For instance, in the statement of certain morpheme structure conditions we have different features paired by means of the variable, e.g.:

$$\text{MS8}' \quad \begin{bmatrix} \alpha\text{coronal} \\ -\text{anterior} \end{bmatrix} \rightarrow [\alpha\text{continuant}] \text{ (p. 115)}$$

$$\text{MS18}'' \quad \begin{bmatrix} -\text{cons} \\ -\text{syll} \end{bmatrix} \rightarrow [\alpha\text{cor},\ \alpha\text{voice},\ -\text{ant}\ldots] \text{ (p. 126)}$$

but it seems entirely arbitrary that segments should agree in their specification for the features [coronal] and [continuant], and still more so that glides should correlate [coronal] with [voice][1] – especially as there is no diachronic simplification effected by these specifications. Furthermore, the one occasion in the morpheme structure conditions where Greek letter variables seem most needed is the one case where they appear not to work effectively: namely, that characterising words as containing only |l| or no |l| (p. 47 above). Within the realisation rules where we expect greater psychological validity of the rules, the position is no better. Thus, to take one typical example, R19 appears superficially to be a clear example of two rules conflated by means of an α variable; but the rule is optional with one value of α (+) and obligatory with the other (−), and furthermore it soon (stage 3) split into two parts, one for each value of α, which then developed quite independently of each other, assumed different environmental restrictions and finally disappeared at widely differing times (pp. 81ff. above). Clearly the lin-

---

[1] See Smith, 1969, Sampson, 1970, etc. for suggestions about constraining the power of α to link different features.

guistic generalisation captured by the α is not reflecting any comparable generalisation in the child's mind. It could of course be argued that the period of psychological validity of this rule antedated the first stages described here, and that any development away from this earliest stage presupposes a subtler discrimination of the neutralisation forced upon the adult system, a discrimination which is bound to break up some kind of natural class or abbreviatory device.[1] Be that as it may, there is still no *a priori* reason why the disappearance of consonant harmony should not be consistent with the parallel development and simultaneous disappearance of sub-rules abbreviated by any of these notations, and the lack of such parallelism is a strong indication of the lack of psychological reality of the α variable. In sum, the case for α must be assumed 'not proven' though the evidence in favour is certainly strong enough to make rejection of the device premature.

McCawley has suggested[2] that curly brackets are a device for indicating that there is *no* linguistic generalisation available, and that they should accordingly be totally abolished from linguistics. In other words, the use of { } is a sign either that the wrong distinctive features are being used: thus [−syll] captures easily the earlier disjunction of $\left\{\begin{matrix}[+\text{cons}]\\[-\text{voc}]\end{matrix}\right\}$, or that the apparent generalisation captured by the disjunction is spurious or trivial, with one or two marginally more interesting exceptions. This appears to be borne out in general by the numerous occurrences of curly brackets in the present work. For instance, the abbreviation of some four rules affecting non-nasal sonorants by R18 (pp. 29 and 81 above) seems entirely without merit, as also do the disjunctions in R7′ (p. 61), where there appears to be no good reason why non-coronals and sonorants should be linked, or R10A′ (p. 67) where there is a similar spurious combination of non-consonantals and non-sonorants. Examples could be multiplied *ad lib*, but this might indicate merely that the device is too powerful, not that it is totally unnecessary. Accordingly let us look at one or two cases where the generalisation seems more valid. First we have a couple of examples where the same process takes place either before a consonant or a boundary – i.e. $\left\{\begin{matrix}\#\\C\end{matrix}\right\}$ – see e.g. R6 (p. 25), where /l/ is deleted in these two environments; and

---

[1] See p. 29 above, where it is suggested that R19 was originally more general than at stage 1.

[2] In a lecture at University College London (27 November 1969), and in a paper 'On the role of notation in generative phonology.'

MS16A″ (p. 123), where /r/ is excluded from them.[1] This particular combination of environments is very common, but as Halle (1971) has recently pointed out, is usually an indication that 'final word boundary functions on a par with any environment counted to the right of the segment undergoing the rule' (p. 541) and can be captured adequately by the parenthesis notation. Second we have the possible conflation of rules 1 and 2 (p. 23 above) simplifying nasal plus consonant clusters. This seems to be valid at first sight, but the saving effected by the confla-tion – one 'zero' sign (∅) – is hardly very exciting, and more importantly, the apparent justification of the conflation in terms of the functional unity of the rules concerned is doubtful, as such 'conspiracies' represent the one occasion on which overt collapsing of this sort is not necessary (see 5.3.3 below). Lastly, we have a couple of examples which can be interpreted either as support for curly brackets, *or* for a different use of distinctive features. Thus R19(ii) (p. 81) combines $\left\{\begin{array}{l}+\text{nasal}\\+\text{continuant}\end{array}\right\}$ (where the generalisation so laboriously captured would be simply 'continuant' in traditional terms); and we have various cases of a dis-junction which could be avoided if we had a feature [labial] (see above, p. 197).

With all these examples, the crucial point is that there never appears to be any psychological reality to the conflation of such rules by disjunc-tive bracketing. In no case did the sub-parts of rules within curly brackets develop in parallel fashion – by, e.g., the addition of a common environmental restriction, or even by simultaneous disappearance. Ac-cordingly, although negative evidence can never be conclusive, it would seem that McCawley's strictures are justified.

5.3.3 Conspiracies. The last formal consideration to be discussed is another convention for associating, though not conflating, rules: namely Kisseberth's concept of 'functional unity'. Kisseberth has suggested (1971) that rules which have no necessary structural similarity, but which have the same end result – i.e. which are functionally similar – should be evaluated with attention paid to the morpheme structure con-ditions of the language. Where part of a rule replicates (part of) a mor-pheme structure condition, that part should be costless. This notion is

---

[1] The first disjunction in this rule, $\left\{\begin{array}{l}[-\text{cor}]\\[+\text{ant}]\end{array}\right\}$, is probably an indication that we need a special feature for [r], say, [retroflex]; or that we should use negative rather than positive morpheme structure conditions.

clearly relevant here, where there are obvious 'infantile conspiracies' –
i.e. sets of rules – implementing the 'general tendencies' underlying
the realisation rules discussed above (pp. 176ff.), in particular rules
effecting vowel and consonant harmony and rules effecting cluster
simplification.[1] These have been discussed in some detail above and no
more needs to be said here beyond pointing out that in all cases the rules
under discussion would be evaluated more cheaply if they were 'filtered
through' the morpheme structure conditions, and that in all cases it
would be impossible to effect any significant simplification conflating
them. To be more accurate it should perhaps be said that the use of
morpheme structure conditions, *qua* morpheme structure conditions, is
strictly speaking unnecessary for the correct evaluation of these rules,
but that they provide a convenient reference point for recognising the
functional unity of realisation rules. In other words I would not like to
use the superficial utility of morpheme structure conditions as used in
evaluation here, as a justification for the morpheme structure conditions
in general. In the child's acquisition of phonology I still think only the
realisation rules have real validity.

However, it is clear that the notion *conspiracy* gives a formal characterisation of the set of universal tendencies discussed earlier in 4.3.

[1] The rules effecting systemic simplification seem to cluster together and therefore
do not necessarily need the power of a conspiracy to link them. Rules effecting syntactic
simplification are too few to allow of generalisation.

Conclusions

1. By the time he begins to speak, indeed for him to be able to begin to speak, the child's competence insofar as the form of lexical representation is concerned, must be in terms of the adult's surface phonemic system. His performance is then validly characterised as being the result of the application of a set of ordered realisation rules which take the adult form as input and map this onto his output.

2. In general, the child's phonological development is rule-governed and all changes in his output over time are the result of changes in rules applying to phonologically (and grammatically) defined classes. Further, only the *rules* of the child's system can change and not the feature composition of segments which constitute part of his system.

3. The realisation rules correspond to the hypotheses the child makes about the language he is learning, and changes in the realisation rules through time correspond to fresh hypotheses made by him. These hypotheses clearly permit of wide idiosyncratic variation but, equally clearly, are not random. I suggest that they are limited by the set of distinctive features and by pressure from four, hierarchically arranged, universal tendencies. These tendencies or constraints are:

    (i) Vowel and consonant harmonisation.
    (i) Cluster reduction leading to a CVCV...canonical form.
    (iii) Systemic simplification.
    (iv) Grammatical simplification.

That is, one can view these constraints as being part of a universal template which the child has to escape from in order to learn his language. Changes in the realisation rules then represent the idiosyncratically variable attempts of a given child to overcome the universal characteristics of language in his progress towards learning his own specific language. Whether these formal and substantive universals are innate or learned at a very early age seems, at present, not to be an empirical question.

4. The realisation rules mapping the adult forms on to the child's forms, together with the lexical representations of the individual words of his vocabulary, are the only constructs to have any psychological

validity for the child. That is, the child has *no* other system of his own, and the realisation rules are accordingly explanatory and not merely predictive.

5. The child's acquisition of phonology gives us a 'window on to competence', and is therefore of direct relevance for phonological theory. Accordingly, the implications of language acquisition as set out in chapter 5 have a theoretical status at least on a par with those of the phonology of any adult language, if not a higher one. Thus there is evidence suggesting:

(i) The need for a phonological rank-scale of some kind, including not only distinctive features but phonemes (or their equivalent) and syllables.

(ii) The more precise definition of certain distinctive features.

(iii) The dubious status of certain formal universals; e.g. marking conventions and some abbreviatory notations.

(iv) The validity of certain other formal universals: specifically, rule ordering and 'conspiracies'.

Appendixes

Appendix A. Correlation of stages and ages

Stage	From years	From days	To years	To days
1	2	60		
2		115		
3		130		
4	2	134	2	137
5	2	139	2	144
6	2	148	2	152
7	2	156	2	157
8	2	164	2	175
9	2	189	2	196
10	2	198	2	203
11	2	207	2	215
12	2	219	2	227
13	2	233	2	242
14	2	247	2	256
15	2	261	2	271
16	2	275	2	285
17	2	289	2	298
18	2	300	2	312
19	2	317	2	333
20	2	345	2	355
21	2	359	3	10
22	3	22	3	38
23	3	45	3	70
24	3	78	3	96
25	3	104	3	128
26	3	133	3	158
27	3	159	3	206
28	3	208	3	282
29	3	286	3	355

As indicated in the text, odd notes were made both before stage 1 and after stage 29: in the latter case up to about the age of 4 years 4 months.

Appendix B. Assumed feature matrix for the consonants of the adult system serving as input to the realisation rules

	p	b	t	d	k	g	tʃ	dʒ	f	v	θ	ð
consonantal	+	+	+	+	+	+	+	+	+	+	+	+
syllabic	−	−	−	−	−	−	−	−	−	−	−	−
sonorant	−	−	−	−	−	−	−	−	−	−	−	−
coronal	−	−	+	+	−	−	+	+	−	−	+	+
anterior	+	+	+	+	−	−	−	−	+	+	+	+
continuant	−	−	−	−	−	−	−	−	+	+	+	+
nasal	−	−	−	−	−	−	−	−	−	−	−	−
voiced	−	+	−	+	−	+	−	+	−	+	−	+
delayed release	−	−	−	−	−	−	+	+	+	+	+	+
strident	−	−	−	−	−	−	+	+	+	+	−	−
lateral	−	−	−	−	−	−	−	−	−	−	−	−

	s	z	ʃ	ʒ	m	n	ŋ	r	l	w	j	h
consonantal	+	+	+	+	+	+	+	+	+	−	−	−
syllabic	−	−	−	−	−	−	−	−	−	−	−	−
sonorant	−	−	−	−	+	+	+	+	+	+	+	−
coronal	+	+	+	+	−	+	−	+	+	−	+	−
anterior	+	+	−	−	+	+	−	−	+	+	−	−
continuant	+	+	+	+	−	−	−	+	+	+	+	+
nasal	−	−	−	−	+	+	+	−	−	−	−	−
voiced	−	+	−	+	+	+	+	+	+	+	+	−
delayed release	+	+	+	+	−	−	−	−	−	−	−	−
strident	+	+	+	+	−	−	−	−	−	−	−	−
lateral	−	−	−	−	−	−	−	−	+	−	−	−

The cover symbol 'C' is used for the configuration:

$$\begin{bmatrix} +\text{consonantal} \\ -\text{syllabic} \end{bmatrix}$$

The cover symbol 'V' is used for the configuration:

$$\begin{bmatrix} -\text{consonantal} \\ +\text{syllabic} \end{bmatrix}$$

In the realisation rules use is also made of the vowel features:

[high, back, low, round, tense, stress]

Appendix C. Diachronic lexicon

This appendix comprises virtually the entire data on which the preceding study has been directly based; excepting, of course, the syntactic environment of the different items cited. I have excluded only those (many) words which were attested for the first time in the correct adult form, and which were not of direct interest for comparative purposes. Thus *daffodil* was first recorded as ['dæfədil] from stage 16 on, and is accordingly omitted. However, *breeze* which was first recorded as [briːz] from stage 24 is included, because it helps to demonstrate the homonymy of *breathe* and *breeze* at this stage. This implies, of course, that the basis for some omissions and inclusions is partly arbitrary, but it seems essential to be selective in the interests of economy. It is obvious that, even so, the data are not exhaustive of A's vocabulary at any stage, but merely represent what I managed to record.

Items are listed in alphabetical order as follows. The adult orthographic form is given first, and where its pronunciation might not be generally known – as in the case of proper names, for instance – this is followed by a phonemic representation in slashes; e.g. *Saras* /'sʌrəs/. Where the grammatical categorisation of the item is unclear, this is sometimes represented in parentheses after the adult form. In general I have only assigned grammatical categories where there is potential differentiation in the root form of the items concerned, e.g. *stick* (N) as opposed to *stick* (V); but *love*, for instance, is not marked. Morphologically related items are put together; thus for *stuck* look under *stick* (V).

The orthographic entry is then followed by a *phonetic* transcription of A's version of the item, with the number of the stage at which this form first occurred in brackets after it, e.g. '*stick* (V) ġik (4)' means that the verb *stick* first occurred at stage four with the pronunciation [ġik]. If needed, the *phonemic* representation of this form can then be inferred from the description of the diachronic development of the MS conditions in chapter 3. In this particular case, we can see from p. 109 that the phonemic form must be |giġ|.

If the word in question occurred in several forms, these are all entered, separated by oblique strokes, e.g. '*black* ḅæk/blæk (9)' indicates that at stage 9 *black* occurred in two freely variant forms [ḅæk] and [blæk].

When A's form for a word changed diachronically, this is represented by a second line beneath the first, e.g.:

black	ḅæk	(1)
	ḅæk/blæk	(9)
	ḅlæk	(11)
	blæk	(12)

indicates that *black* was first recorded at stage 1 as [ḅæk]; this form persisted until stage 9 when it occurred in free variation with [blæk]; this free variation persisted until stage 11 when the earlier form disappeared, and then at stage 12 the adult form was attained. Clearly not every word was recorded at every stage, and although the implication of the above entry for *black*, namely that [bæk] was the form for all stages from 1 to 8 is probably correct (it was in fact so recorded at stages 1, 5, 7 and 8), in general it cannot be assumed that the stage at which a change is shown was necessarily the first stage at which that change appeared in some other word. Thus the entry for *blow* is:

blow (V) bu: (1)
            blu: (12)

where the post-consonantal [l] is shown as making its first appearance at stage 12, even though we know from other words (e.g. *black*) that A first used [bl] clusters at stage 9. In general I think there are enough examples of every phenomenon recorded not to make this misleading. It merely means that several examples should always be looked at together.

After the stage at which the adult form for a particular word has been mastered no more entries are given, unless the item is exceptional for some reason. Thus *little* which, had it been regular, would have been [likəl], was [litəl] from a much earlier stage than expected; and was in fact finally replaced by [liəl]. The total entry is:

little didi: (1)
          didi:/lidi: (6)
          lidi: (9)
          lidi:/litəl (11)
          lidi:/liti: (13)
          litəl   (14)
          litəl/liəl   (29)

Here the only oddities are the regressive alternation of [lidi:] and [liti:] at stage 13 and the similar alternation of [litəl] and [liəl] at stage 29 – the latter appearing after the word had been correctly pronounced for some fifteen stages.

Occasionally a grammatical specification follows the child's form at a particular stage. This is used only when A's usage was at variance with the adult. Thus *fed-up* has the entry:

fed-up wɛdʌp   (12)
          fɛdʌp   (27) (V)

which indicates that in its early uses *fed-up* behaved as some kind of predicative adjective, i.e. as in adult English, but that at stage 27 it occurred as a verb. In all such cases there is an illustrative example; here, for instance:

[ju: tu: ki:p fɛdin mi: ʌp] – 'You two keep making me fed-up.'

Finally, some entries end with a list of page references, indicating the pages on which they have been discussed. This serves as a word index only; references to individual rules and processes etc. can be found in the index proper. Any item may also have *ad hoc* elaborations or explanations in its entry – e.g. the first entry below – and it should be remembered that items enclosed in parentheses were only obtained by elicitation (see 1.3.1 above).

a   ei (15)
The *a/an* alternation appeared at stage 29.
abbey   æbi: (18)
about   baut (4)
baut (11)
ə'baut (22)
abracadabra   æbrədə'dæbrə (28)
accident   'ækədənt (17)
(*acquittal*   ə'kipəl) (19)
across   ə'klɔt/ə'krɔt (14)
adaptor   ri:'dæptə (28), p. 172
addresses   ri:'drɛsiz (28), p. 172
aeroplane   ɛ:bə?'eⁱn (1)
'ɛəpein/'ɛrəpein/'ɛəplein/
'ɛərəplein (15), pp. 35–6, 99, 101
Afaf/'æfæf/   æʊæf (5)
'æfəf (16)
'æfæf (17)
after   a:ptə (4)
a:ftə (19)

afternoon   a:ptə'nu:n/a:ptə'ɖu:n (7)
a:ptə'nu:n/'a:ptənu:n (12), p. 14
ages   eid^{z}iz (27)
Adrian   e:di: (1)
eidrən/eidərən (17)
air   ɛ: (16)
alligator   'ægəleitə (22), p. 99
alone   ə'lo:n (6)
along   ə'gɔŋ (4)
ə'gɔŋ/ə'wɔŋ/ə'ɣɔŋ (5)
ə'lɔŋ (16)
already   ɔ:'lɛdi: (8)
always   'ɔ:lwe: (9)
'ɔ:lwei (15)
'ɔ:lweiz (28), p. 68
Amahl   'æməl/'æməʉ (4)
'æməl/æ'ma:l (18)
æ'ma:l (22)
'æməl/'æma:l (23)
'æma:l (26), pp. 8, 68, 69–70

It is perhaps worth noting that A stressed his own name correctly earlier in possessive phrases than he did in isolation or in subject position. Thus at stage 20 he had: ['æma:l buk] = 'Amahl's book' but [æ'ma:l/'æməl nəud]='Amahl knows'.

ambulance   ɛbənin(in) (5)
Amita   ri'mi:tə (29), p. 173
Angela   'ændələ (17)
'ændəli:ə (18)
'ænd^{z}ələ (25)
angelica   æn'dɛlikə (15)
angry   ɛɲi: (1)
æŋgi: (2)
æŋgi:/æŋgli:/æŋgʷi: (7)
æŋgi: (8)
æŋgi:/æŋgʷi: (9)
æŋgi: (11)
æŋgi:/æŋgʳi: (12)
æŋgli: (14)
æŋgri: (15), pp. 14, 18, 53, 104, 106, 161
animal   æmələn (25)
æmələn/ænəməl (27). p. 99
ant   ɛt (1)

ant   ænt (27), p. 40
antlers   æŋkləz (28), p. 141
anus   einət (15)
(*anvil*   æmbil) (27), pp. 90, 130
anybody   'ɛni:bɔdi: (11)
anything   'ɛni:ɡiŋ (10)
'ɛni:kiŋ (13)
'ɛni:tʰiŋ (15)
'ɛni:siŋ (22)
'ɛnisiŋ (24) p. 141
apple   ɛbu (1), pp. 15, 24
æpəl (11)
apples   æpəld (18)
æpəlz (24), p. 70
(*apse*   æpt) (14)
arm   a:m (2)
arrange   reinz (23)
reinz/ri'reinz (26), p. 172
ash-tray   'æte: (8)
'æstrei (22)

ask	aːk (2)	*banana*	baːnə (13)
	aːkt (14)		bəˈnaːnə (22), pp. 18, 27–8,
	aːks (21)		34, 45, 161
	aːsk (29), p. 98	*bandage*	ḅændit/ḅæŋgit (4)
asleep	əˈwiːp (8)		ḅæŋgit (5)
	əˈliːp (10)	*bang*	ḅæɲ/ḅæŋ (2)
	əˈɬiːp (18)		ḅaiɲ (7)
(*asp*	æpt) (14), p. 98		ḅæn (12)
(*asthma*	æpmə) (11)		ḅæŋ (16), p. 43
as well	əˈwɛl (17)	*banging*	ḅæɲiŋ (15), pp. 18, 165
ata/aːtə/	aːtəʳ (13), p. 98	*banisters*	ˈḅænitə (13)

This is in fact a Hindi word [aːʈaː] = 'flour'.

			ˈḅænistə (25)
'atishoo'	əˈtisuː/əˈsisuː (22)	*barber*	ˈḅaːbəˈmæn (12)
attack	riˈtæk (27), p. 172	*barrel*	ḅærəl (20)
attacking	tækin (23)	*base*	beit (13)
auntie	aːtiː/aːɖiː (10)	*bash*	ḅæs (27)
	aːntiː (13)	*basket*	ḅaːkit (7)
away	weː/wei (1)		ḅaːkit (15)
	əˈweː/weː (2)	*bath*	ḅaːt (1)
	əˈwei (4), pp. 18, 71, 161		baːt (11)
awkward	ˈɔːkwɔːd (21)		baːtˢ (20)
			baːs (22), pp. 21, 40, 44, 69
baby	ḅeːbiː (1)	*bath-cube*	ġaːpġuːp (8)
	beibi (14)	*bathroom*	baːʂrum (21)
	beibiː/bəibəi (26), p. 44	*bead*	ḅiːt/ḅiːd (1)

This last mispronunciation was a deliberate and common joke on A's part.

		beads	ḅiːd (12)
back	ḅɛk (1)	*bean*	ḅiːn (4)
	bæk (13), p. 41	*beans*	biːnd (19)
backwards	ˈbækvɔːd (19)		biːnẓ (20)
bad	ḅæː (2)		biːnz (23)
	ḅæd (6)	*bear*	ḅɛ (12)
	bæd (19), p. 88		ˈbaːluːbɛə (15)
badly	ḅædi (6)		bɛə (16)
bakewell tart	beikvəl taːt (21)		

[bhaːluː] is the Hindi for 'bear'.

balance	ḅætən (6)	*beard*	ḅiːaːt (2)
	ḅælənt (16)		ḅiːaːd/ḅiːəd (8)
balcony	ˈḅægiː (2)		biːəːd (12)
	ˈḅækiː (4)		biəd (14), p. 40
ball	ḅɔː (1)	*beauty*	ḅuːdi (9)
	ḅɔːl (14), pp. 15, 41, 56, 69	*beautiful*	bruːtifəl (18)
balls	ḅɔːld (19), p. 69		buːtifəl (24), p. 73
balloon	ḅuːn (5)	*because*	inˈkɔːt (9)
	bəˈluːn (22)		inˈkʰɔːt (16)
banana	ḅaːnə (1)		biˈkɔːt (19)
			biˈkɔːt/biˈkɔːʂ (20)

because	bi'kɔːs (21)	*biro*	bæːro (12)
bed	ḅɛt (4)		bæːrəu (19)
	bɛd (14), p. 139		bairəu (23)
bedroom	bɛdrum (24)	*birthday*	bəːsdei (26)
	bɛdrumrum (28)	*biscuit*	ḅigi:/ḅigik (1)
bee	ḅiː (2)		ḅiġiː (2)
bees	ḅiː (14)		ḅikiː (6)
	biːd (17)		ḅiġit (8)
been	ḅiːn (6)		ḅikit (9)
beer	ḅiːa (6)		bikit (14)
beetle	ḅiːgu (1)		biktit (17)
	biːtəl (11), p. 14		biskit (29), pp. 15, 19, 160
behind	aind (7)	*bit* (N)	ḅit (1)
	aind/ḅaind (8)		bit (13), p. 156
	bə'haind (17), p. 28	*bite* (V)	ḅait (2)
being (N)	biːin (15)		ḅaiḍ (8)
bell	ḅɛ (1)		bait (12), p. 196
	ḅɛu (3)	*bit*	baitid (24), p. 174
	ḅɛu/ḅɛl (10)	*biting*	ḅaiḍin (6)
	bɛl (17), pp. 15, 56, 108		ḅaitin (12)
This word appeared as [ḅɛn] before		*bitten*	baitən (19), p. 174
stage 1.		*black*	ḅæk (1)
belong	ḅɔŋ (7)		bæk/ḅlæk (9)
	blɔŋ (11), pp. 18, 28, 161		ḅlæk (11)
belonged	ḅɔŋd (9), p. 192		blæk (12), p. 71
bend	ḅɛnd (5)	*blancmange*	bɔ'tɔm (11)
	bɛnd (11)		blɔ'dɔm/blɔdᶻɔm (27)
bent	bɛnt (11), p. 53		bə'lɔmz (29), pp. 99, 100
best	bɛst/gudist (25)	*blank*	blæŋk (13)
better	ḅɛdə (1)	*blanket*	ḅæŋkiː (6)
	bɛtə (12)		blækit (11)
	mɔː bɛtərə (27), p. 44		blæŋkit (12)
bhindi (okra)	bindiː (23)	*bless you*	blɛtu (20)
bicycle/bike	'ḅaiġuġu/ḅaik (4)		blɛs ruː/blɛs juː (24)
	'ḅaikuku (7)	*blimey*	baimiː/blaimiː/bainiː/
	'ḅaikəsəl (22)		blainiː/bainliː (9)
	'ḅaikisəl (25), p. 99	*blood*	blʌd (11)
big	ḅik (4)	*blow* (V)	ḅuː (1)
	ḅig (11)		bluː (12), p. 40
	big (13)	*blue*	ḅuː (1)
bird	ḅiːbiːp (1)		ḅuː/bluː (9)
	ḅəːḍ (7)		ḅuː/ḅuːl (10)
	ḅəːḍ (10)		bluː (12)
	bəːd (15), pp. 16, 18, 34	*blue-bottle*	'bluːbɔkəl (24)
biro	ḅæo (9)	*blue-ish*	bluːit (14)
	ḅæro (11)	*boat*	buːt (14)

boiler	ḅoijə (5), p. 111	*box*	bɔk (12)
bolt (N)	ḅɔ:t (1), p. 15		bɔk/bɔkt (17)
bonfire	bɔnwææ (12)		bɔkt (19)
book	ḅuk (1)		bɔkt/bɔktˢ (20)
	buk (11), p. 44		bɔkṣ (21)
books	bukt (17)		bɔks (22), pp. 68, 88
	buks (22)	*boxes*	bɔktid (17)
book-case	ḅukke:t (4)	*boxer*	bɔktə (18)
bookmark	ḅukma:k (4)	*boy*	ḅɔi (1)
	bukma:k (14)		ḅɔ:i: (5)
book-shelf	buklɛf (12)		ḅɔi (6)
boot	ḅu:t (4)		bɔi (19), pp. 8, 39, 110
boots	bu:t (19)	*Braj* /brʌdʒ/	blʌd/brʌd/bʌt (11)
	bu:ts (24)		brʌz (23)
border	ḅɔ:də (7)	*brake*	ḅe:k (8)
	bɔ:də (12)		breik (17)
borrow	ḅɔə (9)	*bran*	brænd (14)
	'bɔrəu (20)		bræn (16)
	'bəwəu (23)	*branches*	bra:ntˢiz (25)
Boston	bɔtən (16)	*brandy*	ḅændi: (7)
	bɔstən (24)	*brave*	bleiv (11)
Bosworthick	'bɔtwə:kit (19)	*bread*	ḅɛd (8)
/'bɔswə:ðik/	'Rɔtwə:kis (22), p. 99		bərɛd/bəγɛd (9)
both	ḅu:tḅɔdi: (7)		ḅɛd/ḅrɛd/ḅlɛd (10)
	bu:t (14)		blɛd/brɛd (12)
	bəus (24)		brɛd (13), pp. 72, 139
bother	bɔdə (14)	*break*	ḅe:k (2)
	bɔzə (29)		ḅle:k/ḅre:k (12)
bottle	ḅɔgu (1)		breik (13)
	ḅɔkəl (10)		ble:k/bre:k (14)
	bɔġul (11)		breik (15), p. 175
	bɔkəl (14)	*breaking*	ḅe:ġin (4)
	bɔkəl/bɔtəl (29), pp. 14,	*broke*	ḅu:k (4)
	39, 40, 55, 130, 149, 159		bɹeikt (18)
bottles	bɔkəld (20)		brəuk (23), pp. 174-5
	bɔkəlz (22)	*broken*	ḅugu: (1)
bottom	ḅɔdin (1)		ḅu:gənd/ḅu:kənd (3)
	ḅɔḍəm (2)		ḅu:kənd (5)
	ḅɔtəm (4)		ḅu:kənd/ḅu:kən (6)
	ḅɔdəm/bɔtəm (11)		ḅo:kənd/blo:kənd (9)
	bɔtəm (17), pp. 17, 40, 43,		bru:kənd (14)
	70		bro:k/bro:kən (16)
bow (N)	ḅu:/ḅɛu (8)		brəukən (22), pp. 21, 34,
bowl	bəul (9)		35-6, 44, 97, 163, 175
box	ḅɔk (4)	*break-down*	ḅe:k ḍaun lɔli: (4)
	ḅuk/ḅɔʌt (9)	*lorry*	

breakfast	brɛktit (17)	*bucket*	bʌkit (14)
	brɛkfət (19)	*buckle*	ḅʌgəl (11)
	brɛkfut (20)		bʌkəl (14)
	brɛkfəst (24)	*building* (N)	bildin (18)
breathe	bri:d (19)	*bulb*	bʌbl/bʌəb (17)
	bri:z (23), p. 94		bʌbl (18)
breeze	bri:z (24), p. 94		bʌɣb/bʌlb (22)
brick	brik (16)		bʌlb (23), pp. 57, 98, 100
bricks	brikt (19)	*bullock cart*	ḅuək ġa:t (8)
bridge	ḅit (5)	*bump*	ḅʌp (1), pp. 13, 38
	ḅiḍ (6)	*bumped*	bʌmt/bʌmpt (18)
	brid (18)	*bundle*	ḅʌŋgəl (11)
brief-case	ḅi:k keik (1), pp. 35–6	*burn*	ḅə:n (1)
bring	ḅiŋ (8)		bə:n (14), p. 45
	ḅliŋ (10)	*burnt*	ḅə:nd (4)
	briŋ (16)		bə:nd (15)
bringing	briŋiŋ (17)		bə:nt (26)
brought	ḅiŋd (8)	*burp*	ḅə:p (1), p. 44
	brɔ:t/bɔ:t (23)	*bus*	ḅʌt (1)
	t̠riŋd (27)		bʌt (14), p. 21
	bræŋ [pret] (28)	*bush*	but (16)
	brʌŋ [p.p.] (28), p. 174	*busy*	ḅidi: (4)
broom	ḅu:m (5)		bidi: (14)
	bru:m (13)	(*butler*	bʌklə) (28)
brother	brʌdə (14)	*butter*	bʌtər (14)
	brʌzə (22)		bʌtə (19)
brown	ḅaun (5)	*butterfly*	ḅʌdəwai (1)
	ḅaun/braun/bʷaun/ḅaund		ḅʌdəβai/ḅʌtəwai (5)
	(9)		ḅʌdəwai (7)
	ḅaun/braun/blaun (10)		ḅʌdəvai (9)
	braund (12)		bʌtəflai (17), p. 40
	braun (20), pp. 73, 97	*button*	ḅʌdən/bɔdən (2)
brush (N/V)	ḅʌt (1)		ḅʌdən (8)
	blʌt/brʌt (12)		bʌtən (12)
	brʌt (15)		bʌtun (23)
	brʌts (20)	*buy*	ḅai (5)
	brʌs (23), pp. 18, 21, 39,		bai (14)
	147	*bought*	bɔ:t (11)
brushing (V)	blʌtin (16)	(*bwana*	ġa:mə) (9)
	brʌtin (18)	*bzzzzz*	brrrrd (18)
	brʌsin (26)	Imitation of a bee!	
bubble	ḅʌbu (4)		
	ḅʌbəl (10)	'*c*' *for cat*	ti: wɔ: kæt (12),
	ḅʌbəl (16), p. 100	*cage*	keid (19)
bubbles	ḅʌbəld (19)	*cake*	ġe:k (1)
bucket	ḅʌgit (5)		keik (16)

calendar	ˈġælində (10)
	ˈkælinda: (25)
call	kɔ:l (26)
called	ġɔ:ld (9)
called	kɔ:ld (16), p. 115
Cambridge	keimbriz/keimbrid/
	keimbridᶻ (22)
	keimbriz (26)
camera	ġæmdə (2)
	kæmlə/kæmrə (5)
	kæmlə/kæmdə (6)
	ġæmbə/ġæmlə/ġæmblə (8)
	kæmdə/kæmlə/kæmrə/
	klæmdə/klæmlə/klæmrə
	(10)
	kæmrə (17), pp. 87, 106,
	192
(camphor	ġæpwə) (11)
can (N)	ġæn (9)
	ġæn/kæn (12)
	kæn (14)
cans	kæn (14)
	kænd (17)
can opener	kæn u:pənəʳ (12)
candle	ġæŋgu (7)
	kændəl (29)
candles	kæŋgəlz (27)
can't	ġa:t (11)
	ka:nt (13)
(canvas	kæmbəs) (27)
car	ġa: (2)
	ka: (13)
	ka:ʳ (14)
	ka:ʳ/ka: (15), p. 98
cars	ka:d (14)
	ka:dᶻ/ka:z (21)
	ka:dz (22)
	ka:z (23), p. 93
caravan	ˈġæwəwæn/ġæwəvæn (1)
	ˈġæwəwæn (2), pp. 20, 36,
	38, 45
card	ġa:t (4)
	ġa::d̠ (7)
	ġa:d (12)
	ka:d (13), p. 95
cards	ka:dᶻ/ka:z (21)

cards	ka:dz (22), p. 93
cardboard	ġa:bɔ:d̠ (10)
careful	kɛptu (10)
	ġɛfəl (11)
	kɛ:fəl (13)
carefully	kɛpti: (7)
careful and *carefully* were regularly confused.
careless	kɛ:lit (19)
car-park	ˈġa:ba:k (7)
carpet	ġa:bi: (1)
	ġa:bit (2)
	ġa:pit (12)
	ka:pit (14), p. 21
carrot	ġææt (8)
	ġærət (12)
	kærət (16)
carry	ġæi: (8)
	kæri: (16)
carried	kærid (15)
cart	ġa:t (2)
	ġa:d̠ (7), p. 95
case	keit (17)
in case	in keis (23)
cat	ˈmi:au (1)
	ġæt (2)
	kæt (14), pp. 35, 69, 148,
	196
cats	kæt (14)
	kætˢ (20) pp. 69, 148
catastrophe	ˈġækiwi: (6)
	ˈġægiwi: (8)
catch	ġæt (8)
	kæt (17)
	kæs/kɔ:t (23)
	kæs (25), p. 175
caught	ġɔət (4)
	kætˢt (28)
caterpillar	ġædəpi:ə (7)
cat suit	kæt tu:t (17)
cattle-truck	ˈġægugʌk (4)
cauliflower	ˈkɔi:wæwə (5)
	ˈġɔli:wæwə (8)
ceiling	li:lin/i:lin (6)
	li:lin/d̠i:lin (8)
	ti:lin (14), pp. 18, 165

cement-mixer	'ægəgəg͵migə (4)		*cheque(-book)*	g̣ɛkbuk (4)
Also with the meaning: 'helicopter'.				gɛk (5)
cereals	'si:ri:əlz (24)			g̣ɛk (12)
chain	ḍein (4)			kɛk (13)
	tein (14)			tɛk (15)
	tˢein (20)			sɛk (22)
	tˢein/sein (23)			tˢɛkbuk (27), p. 141
	sein (25)			ḍɛi:/ḍɛli: (5)
	tein/tˢein (27)		*cherry*	tɛri: (15)
	tˢein (28)			tˢɛri: (27)
	tʃein (29), p. 60		*cherries*	tɛrid (18)
chair	ḍɛ (1)			tˢɛrid (20)
	ḍɛ: (4)			
	ḍɛə/tɛˀ (12)		*chest*	ḍɛt (13)
	tɛˀ (13)			tɛst (23), pp. 91, 167
	tˢɛə (21)		*chew*	tu: (15)
	sɛ:/sɛə (22)			tˢu: (27)
	sɛə/tˢɛ:/tˢeijə (27), pp. 3,		*chicken*	g̣ikin (12)
	39, 93, 94, 130, 154			tˢikin/sikin (23)
chalk	g̣ɔ:k (11)			sikin (24)
	g̣ɔ:k/kɔ:k (12)			tʃikin (29)
	tɔ:k (14)		*chicks*	siks (22)
	tɔ:k/trɔ:k (16)		*chief*	ḍi:p (7)
	tˢɔ:k (20)			ti:f (18)
	sɔ:k (25), pp. 60, 91, 141,		*child*	ḍail/ḍaild (9)
	167			ḍaild (10)
chamber	tˢeimbə (23)			saild/taild (22)
change	ḍeind (11)			sæ:ld (25), pp. 91, 167
	teind (18)		*children*	tildən (17)
	seindᶻ (22)			trildrən (26), pp. 91, 167
	seinz (24)		*chimney*	ḍimni: (8)
chapatti	ba:ḍi: (4)			ḍimni:/ḍimmi: (9)
/tʃə'pa:ti:/				timni:/timmi: (13)
Charlie	tˢa:li: (27)			tˢimni: (20)
chase	teis/tˢeis (27)			simni: (24)
cheek	g̣i:k (4)			tˢimni:/tʃimni: (27), p. 192
	ki:k (13)		*chin*	tin (11)
cheeks	si:ks (24), pp. 68, 141			tʰin (18)
cheese	ḍi: (4)			sin (22)
	ḍi:/(ḍi:ḍ) (9)			tˢin (27)
	ti:d (15)		*chip* (V)	tʰip (14)
	tʃi:d (20)		*chipped*	sipt (23)
	si:z (22)		*chisel*	tʰidəl (15)
	si:z/tˢi:z (26)		*chocolate*	g̣ɔgi:/g̣ɔki: (1)
	tˢi:z (27), pp. 68, 94			g̣ɔkḍit (7)
cheetah	tˢi:tə (27)			g̣ɔkit/g̣ɔkḍit (8)
				g̣ɔkit/g̣ɔkḍit/glɔklit (9)

chocolate	gɔklit/glɔklit (11)	*clever*	ġɛvə/ġɛʋə (6)
	kɔklit (14)		ġlɛvə (10)
	tɔklit (15)		klɛvə (19), p. 112
	tɔklit/trɔklit (18)	*climb*	klaim (12)
	trɔklit (19)	*climbed*	klaimd (11)
	tˢɔklit (20)	*clinic*	kliŋeik/(kliŋik/klinik) (13)
	sɔklit (22)	*clip*	ġip/b̬ip (2)
	sɔklit/tˢɔklit/tɔklit (26)		klip (18)
	tʃɔklit (29), pp. 20, 35, 72,	*clippers*	ġlipə (10)
	94, 141	*clock*	ġɔk (5)
choke (N)	ġoːk (4)		ġɔk/kɔk (7)
	koːk/toːk (12)		klɔk/ġlɔk/ɣlɔk (9)
	koːk (13)		klɔk (12)
	toːk (14)	*closing*	kləuzin (24)
	təuk/kəut (17)	*closed*	kləuzdid (27), p. 174
	səuk (22), pp. 96, 140–1	*closer*	kləutə (19)
choose	suːz (24)		kləutˢə (21)
chop (V)	d̬ɔp (10)	*cloth*	ġɔk (1)
	tɔp (14)		ġɔt/ġɔk (4)
	tˢɔp/tʃɔp (27)		klɔt (15)
Christmas	ġiptit (9)		klɔts̬ (21)
	ġiptət (10)		klɔs (27), pp. 18, 19, 34,
	ġiptət/kiptət (12)		39, 45, 69, 75, 148, 163,
	kripməs (21)		188–9
	krisməs (24), pp. 99, 187	*cloths*	klɔtid (18)
Christopher	krispəfə (23)		klɔsiz (23), pp. 69, 148
church	d̬əːt (1)	*clothes*	ġuːd̬ (8)
	tˢəːs (22), p. 21		ġuːd̬/ġluːd (11)
churches	tˢəːtˢiz (27)		ġluːd (12)
chutney	d̬aːd̬in (8), pp. 99, 100		kluːd (13)
cigarette	'tigəɪɛt (19)		kləudz (27)
	'sigəɪɛt (22)		kləuz (28)
circle	ġəːgu (8)	*clothes horse*	'kluːdɔːt (12)
	ġəːkul (10)	*cluster*	ġlʌtə (9)
	təːkəl (14)	*clutch* (N)	klʌt (14)
	səːkəl (23)	*coach*	ġuːk (1), pp. 19, 42, 74
	səːtəl (29), pp. 56, 141	*coat*	ġoːt (2)
circles	səːkəlz (21)		kəut (23)
	səːtəlz (29)	*coati*	kaːpiː (19)
Clapham	klæpən klɔmən (19)	*cobweb*	kɔbwɛp/kɔɸwɛɸ (7)
Common			kʰɔbwɛb/kʰɔβwɛβ (16)
clean	ġiːn (1)	*cobwebs*	kɔbwɛbz̬ (22)
	ġliːn (10)	*cock*	ġɔk (1), p. 41
	kliːn (15), pp. 45, 147, 166	*cock-a-doodle-*	kɔkəduːgəlduː (28)
cleaned	kliːnd (14)	*doo*	
cleaning	kliːnin (15)	*coffee*	ġɔwiː (2)

coffee	kɔwi: (6)	*corner*	ġɔːnə (1)
	ġɔɸiː/ġɔwi: (7)		kɔːnə (18), pp. 19, 38, 42
	ġɔwiː/ġɔvi: (8)		45
	ġɔfi: (10)	*corn-flake*	kɔːn pleik (13)
	kɔfi: (13)	*corridor*	'ġɔiːdɔ: (1)
coins	kɔind (19)		'ġɔi dɔ: (7)
cold	ġuːd̪ (4)		'kɔridɔ:/hɔridɔ: (16),
	ġuːd̪/ġɔːl/ġo: (8)		pp. 19, 40, 104
	kuːld (12)	*cot*	ġɔt (2)
	kəuld (22)		kɔt (15)
collar	ġɔə (4)	*couch*	kaut (13)
	ġɔwə (8), p. 75		kaus (23)
collar-stud	ġɔə d̪ʌd (4)	*cough*	ġɔɸ (2)
colour	ġʌlə (9)		ġɔɸ/kɔf/kɔɸ (6)
	kʌləʳ (13)		kɔɸ (8)
	kʌlə (14)		kɔf (13), pp. 89, 107, 112
coloured	ġʌləd/kʌləd (12)	*coughing*	kɔfin (19)
come	ġʌm (1)	*count* (V)	ġaut (7)
	kʌm (12)		kaunt (19)
come (p.p.)	ġʌmd (8)	*counting*	kauntin (12)
	kʌmd (20)	*cover* (V)	ġʌwə (8)
came	ġʌmd (8)		ġʌβə (11)
	ġeim (10), p. 192	*covered*	kʌvəd (14)
coming	ġʌmin (4)	*cow*	ġau (7)
	kʌmin (13)		kau (11)
come out	ġʌmaut (1)	*crack*	ġlæk (10)
come apart	kʌm tu: paːt/kʌm tu: əpaːt (18)		klæk (14)
			kræk (19)
completely	kliːpli: (27)	*cracked*	krækt/trækt/kækt (13)
concentrating	'kɔntəntreitin (15)	*crane*	ġeːn (5)
conductor	riː'dʌktə (28)		ġlein (10)
	in'dʌktə/(kə'dʌktə) (28), pp. 172–3		krein/klein (14)
		crash	kræs (27)
connector	nɛktə/tə'nɛktə (17)	*crash-helmet*	kræt hɛlmɛt (17)
	tə'nɛktə (18)	*cream*	ġiːm (1), pp. 38, 40, 45
cook	kuk (23)	*crib*	ġib̪ (1)
cooked	ġukt (7)		ġlib (10)
cooking	kukin (26)		ġlib/ġib (11)
cool	ġuː/(ġuːl) (8)		krib (15), pp. 38, 45
	kuːl (16)	*crisp*	kript (18)
cooler	ġuːlə (8)	*crocodile*	ġɔgidaju/ġɔgidæjə (2)
Copydex	ġɔbiːġɛk (9)		ġɔgudæjə (5)
	d̪ɔpiːgɛk (10)		ġɔgədæːə (8), p. 111
	kɔpiːdɛks (29), pp. 99, 100	*crocus*	kroːkət (16)
At stage 29 this occurred with the meaning		*cross*	ġɔt (10)
'index' (finger).			ġlɔt/klɔt (11)

ross	ġlɔt/ġrɔt/krɔt (12)	*cute*	ġu:t (9)
	klɔt (14)		ku:t (22), p. 73
	krɔt (15)		
	krɔs (24)	*Daddy*	ḍɛdi: (1)
rown	ġaun (5)		dædi: (13), pp. 9, 10, 21,
	ġlaun (10)		38, 68, 70
	kraund (12)	*daisy*	deidᶻi: (20)
	kraun (16)	*daisies*	deiziz (22)
rumb	ġʌm (1)	*damage*	dæmid (20)
	kʌm/klʌm (9)	*damp*	ḍæp (8)
	krʌm (13), pp. 18, 71	*dance*	da:ns/dãs (22)
rumbs	krʌmd (17)	*dancing*	da:tin (13)
rumbs	krʌmz (28)	*dandelion*	'dændi:læ:n (20)
rust	ġʌt/ġʷʌt (8)		'dændi:lain (22)
	krʌt (19)	*Daniel*	'dæni:l/dæ'ni:l (13)
ry	ġai (2)		'dæni:l (19)
ried	kraid (24)	*dark*	ġa:k (1)
rying	ġaiin (1), p. 17		da:k (14), pp. 20, 141, 163
ube	ġu:p (4), p. 73	*darling*	da:lin (22)
ubes	ku:bd (20)	*day*	dei (19)
ucumber	'ku:kʌmbə (20)	*days*	deid (18)
uddle	kʌdəl (18)	*dead*	ḍɛt (2)
	kʌgəl (25)		dɛd (24)
cudgel	kʌdᶻəl) (23), p. 14		dɛd (V) (20)
uff	kʌf (14)	e.g. [dædi: dɛd it] = 'Daddy killed it.'	
uff-link	ġʌpwin (4)	*deer*	ḍiə (9)
unning	kʌnin (17)	*delicate*	dɛkələt/dɛləkət (15)
upboard	ġʌbə (1)		dɛkələt (16), p. 99
	ġʌbəḍ (6)	(*delve*	dɛlv (19)
	ġʌbəd (12)		dɛvl) (20), p. 98
	kʰʌbəd/kˣʌbəd (13)	*den*	ḍɛn (12)
	kʌbəd (14), pp. 21, 45, 91,		dɛn (24)
	118	*dent*	ḍɛnt (12)
urtain	ġə:ġən (1)	*depressed*	di'prɛst (28), p. 173
	ġə:dən (2), pp. 38, 42,	*deserve*	ri'zə:v (28), p. 172
	74-5	*design*	di'dain (11)
urtains	kə:tənz (27)		ri'dzain (27), p. 172
ushion	ġutən (4)	*desk*	ġɛk (5)
	kutən (14)		gɛk (12)
	kusən (24)		gɛk/dɛk (13)
ut	ġʌt (2)		dɛk (14)
	kʌt (13)		dɛk/dɛkt (18)
ut (p.p.)	kʌtən (15)		dɛkt/dɛktˢ (20)
	kʌtən/kʌtənd (18), p. 174		dɛks (21)
utting	ġʌdin (5)		dɛsk (27), pp. 98, 141, 187
	kʌtin (14), p. 68	(*dew*	d,u:) (24)

Dhanbad   'ḍʌnba:ḍ   (8)
/dʌn'ba:d/
(Hindi:
[dhənbad])

diaper   ḍæpə   (4)
ḍæ:ḅə   (8)
ḍæpə   (18)

diary   ḍʌ:i: (4)
dæ:i:/dæri: (13)
dæ:ri: (19), p. 110

different   ḍipi: (4)
ḍipti:/ḍipi: (9)
dipi: (12)
difrənt   (18)
diflənt   (20)

difficult   ġiptu/ġiptul   (13)
gipətul   (16)
gifətəlt   (20)
gifətəlt/gipətəlt   (22)
difkəlt   (26)
difikəlt   (27), pp. 99, 100,
101, 151, 187

digest (V)   ri:'dʒɛst   (28), p. 172

ding-dong   ġiŋġɔŋ   (1)

dinner   ḍinə   (7)
ḍinə   (12)
ḍinə/ḍinəʳ   (18)

dipping   ḍipin   (19)

dirty   ḍi:di:/ḍidi: (2)
ḍi:di: (6)
də:ti: (13)

disgusting   iŋ'gʌstin/dəs'gʌstin   (28),
p. 173

dish   ḍit/ḍixt   (7)
ḍit   (8)
dit   (11)

distance   ḍitən   (7)
distəns   (24), p. 151

disturb   ḍə:v   (9)
ḍə:β   (11)
tʰə:v   (14)
ri'stə:v   (26), p. 172

disturbs   ri'stə:vz   (27)

do   ḍu: (4)
ḍu:/tu:/ḍu: (12)
du: (13)

does   dʌd   (19)
dʌz   (21)

doesn't   dʌdṇt/dəunt   (19)

dock   ġɔk   (10)

doctor   ġɔgə/ġɔktə   (2)
ġɔktə   (5)
ġɔktə/ḍɔktə   (11)
dɔktə   (14), pp. 85, 87, 88
105, 140–1, 192

dog(gie)   wowo   (1)
ġɔgi:/ġɔġ   (2)
ġɔg   (10)
dɔg/gɔg/dɔk   (13)
dɔg   (14), pp. 35, 69, 85,
141

Donald   dɔnəld   (27)

donkey   ġɔki: (5)
ġɔġi: (7)
dɔŋki: (15)

door   ḍɔ: (1)
dɔ:/dɔ:r   (16)
dɔ:r   (17)
dɔ: (19), p. 3

doors   dɔ:d   (19)

Doris   ḍɔit   (10)

Dorothy   'dɔrəsi: (22)

Dougal   ġu:gu   (2)

down   ḍaun   (8)
daun   (12), p. 39

downstairs   daun'tʰɛˀ/daun'tʰɛˀd   (16)
daun'tɛ:d   (17)

draught   wa:ft/wa:pt   (3)
ḍa:pt   (7)
ḍa:pt/dəra:fpt/dʳa:pt/
ġla:pt   (11), pp. 71, 89,
90, 108

draw   ḍɔ: (9)
dɔ:/tɔ: (10)
drɔ: (14)

drawn   dɔ:n/drɔ:n   (13)

drawer   dɔ: (4)
drɔ: (11), pp. 71, 74, 167

dressed   drɛt   (17)

dressing-gown   drɛtin ga:m   (17)
drɛsin ga:m/gaun   (22)

Drew   du:/dru: (14)

drill	ḍttu (2)	*dumper*	dʌḅtə/dʌp:ə (10)
	dril (15)	(*dwarf*	wɔ:f) (17)
drink	ġik (1)	(*dwell*	ḍɛl) (11), p. 64
	ġriŋk (12)		
	diŋk/gliŋk/griŋk/giŋk/gik	*each*	i:t (9)
	(13)	*eagle*	i:gəl (15)
	driŋk (15), pp. 13, 20, 21,	*ear*	i:ə (4)
	74, 85, 141		i:ə^r (12)
drank	driŋt/driŋkt (19)		iə (23), pp. 40, 97
drunk	driŋt (13)	*ears*	iəd (17)
	drʌŋk (19), p. 141		iəẓ (21)
drinking	driŋkin (13), p. 141		iəz (22)
dripping (N)	ḍipən (12)	*earth*	ə:t (15)
drive	ḍaiɣ (7)		ə:s (22)
	daiv (12)	*Easter*	i:stə (24)
	draiv (13)		i:stə/ri:stə (29)
	draiv/draiβ (15), p. 74	*easy*	i:di: (20)
drove	ḍo:v (9)	(more) *easily*	i:dəri:ə (19)
driven	druvən (28), p. 174	*eat*	i:t (6)
driver	ḍaivə/ḍaiwə (2)	*eaten*	ɛtən (13)
	ḍaiβə (6)		i:tən (18)
	ḍaivə/ḍaiβə (8)		i:tən/ætən (28), p. 174
	draivə^r (12), pp. 97, 112	*eating*	i:din (7)
driving	waibin (1)		i:tin (14)
	ḍaivin (7)	*ate*	æt (28)
	d^raivin (10)	*edge*	ɛd (18)
	draivin (17), 17, 18, 20,	*egg*	ɛk (2)
	32–3, 74, 167		ɛgi: (7)
drop	ḍop (8)		ɛg (13)
dropping	dropin (15)	*eggs*	ɛgz (24)
dropped	dropt (16)	*egg-shell*	'ɛglɛf (11)
drops	drops (22)	*egg-whisk*	'eg‚wiktə (16)
drum	ḍʌm (1)	*either*	aidə (19)
	drʌm (15)	*elastic*	ri:'læstik (27), p. 172
	drʌm/dʌm (16)	*Elastoplast*	'la:təḅla:t (12)
	drʌm (18), pp. 20, 45		'la:təpla:t (17)
drunken	gʌkən (11)	*elbow*	ɛbu: (1)
dry	ḍai (1)		ɛbo:/ɛubo:/a:mbo: (3)
	drai (17)		ɛubo: (4)
	d^wai (23)		ɛbo:/ɛubo: (5), pp. 15, 56
duck	ġʌk (1)	*Eleanor*	'ɛli:ən (23)
	gʌk/dʌk (13)	*elephant*	'ɛbininin (2)
	dʌk (14), pp. 41, 43, 140–		'ɛpinin (4)
	1, 195		'ɛbənin/'ɛbəninin (5)
ducks	dʌks (27)		'ɛpininin (10)
dumper	ḍʌpə (7)		'ɛpinin/'ɛfələnt (17)

elephant	'εpinin/'εfələnt/'εləfənt (18)	*eye*	ai (1), p. 17
	'εləfənt (19)	*eyes*	aiz (25), p. 68
	'εli:fənt (26), pp. 99, 101	*eyebrow*	'aibau (4)
		eyelash	'ailæt (8)

At stage 5 this was homophonous with 'ambulance'.

		face	we:t (4)
(*elf*	εf) (11), p. 57		(fe:t) (6)
else	εlt (10)		weit/feit (10)
	εlt\u02e2 (20)		weit/we:t (12)
	εls (22)		feit/ɸeit (16)
emergency	mə:dənri: (22)		feit (17)
empty	εbi: (1)		feiṇ (21)
	ʌpti: (8)	*fact*	wæt (10)
	εmpti: (20)		wækt (12)
	εmti: (23)	*fairy*	wεi:/wεri: (11)

The form [εbi:] had the meaning: 'cup', pp. 13, 21, 34, 166

		fall	wɔ: (7)
energy	ri'nə:dzi: (29), p. 173		wɔ:/wɔ:l (9)
engine	εndin (14)		wɔ:l (12)
English	iŋglis (23)		fɔ:l (15)
enjoy	ri:'dzɔi (27), p. 172	*fallen*	wɔ:lən (10)
enough	nʌp/i'nʌp (2)		fɔ:lən (18)
	i'nʌp (4)	*fell*	fεl (23)
	ə'nʌp (8)	*fall over*	wɔ:l u:və (12)
	ə'nʌf (13)	*fan*	wæn/βæn (8)
	i'nʌf (21), p. 71		fæn (16), p. 86
envelope	εmbə?o:p (9)	*fang*	wæŋ/wæŋk (5)
	εmbələ?o:p (11)	*far*	wa: (9)
	εmbəlo:p (12), p. 90	*fast*	wa:t/fa:t (15)
envelopes	εmbələups (22)		fa:t (16)
equal	i:kəl (12)		fa:ṣ (21)
escape	ġe:p (1)	*fat*	wæt (7)
	kʰeip (17)	*father*	wa:də (9)
	ri'skeip (27), pp. 15, 18, 161, 172		wa:də/fa:də (10)
			wa:də (11)
estate	ri:'steit (29), pp. 130, 173		fa:zə (24)
evening	i:vin (21)		fa:d\u1d58ə (27)
	i:vnin (24)	*favourite*	βe:βit/we:vit (5)
everybody	ḅɔdi: (2)		we:vit (6)
	'εβi:ḅɔdi: (8)		we:βit/ʋe:ʋit (7)
everything	'εvi:ġiŋ (12)		we:βit (8)
	'εvri:tʰiŋ (16)		we:vit (9)
excluder	ġu:də/igu:də/ġlu:də/ iglu:də (11)		γle:vlit (12)
			freivrit (20)
exhaust (N)	ri:'rɔ:st (26), p. 172	*feather*	tεdə (19)
expensive	in'spεnəv (28), p. 173		tεdə/t\u02e2εdə (20)
			tsεdə (21), pp. 2, 147

fed-up	wɛdʌp (12)		The distinction between 'finish' and
	fɛd ʌp (V) (27)		'finished' was frequently unclear.

fed-up	wɛdʌp (12)
	fɛd ʌp (V) (27)

See the introductory remarks to this appendix, p. 211.

feed	fi:d (16)		*fire*	wæ: (1)
feet	wi:t (1)			wæə/βæə (5)
	fi:t (15)			wæə (7)
	fi:t/futs (24), pp. 2, 3, 17,			fæ:ʳ (15)
	20, 39			fæ: (18), pp. 2, 3, 20, 39
felt (N)	wɛlt (9)		*fire-guard*	'fæ:ga:d (16)
	fɛlt (21), pp. 57, 115		*first*	wə:t (11)
fetch	wɛt (4)			fə:t (14)
(*fetlock*	wɛtlɔk/witlɔk) (12)			fə:st (24)
few	wu: (13)		*fish*	wit (7)
	fu: (20)			fit/ɣit (15)
	fju: (29), p. 73			fit (16), pp. 59, 87, 145–6
fiddle	figəl (17)		*fishes*	witit (13)
Fido	faido:/ɸaido:/paido: (15)			fitid (17)
field	wi:ld (13)			fisidᶻ/fiṣiz (21)
fighting	waitin (10)		*fit*	wit (12)
film	flim (17), pp. 98, 100			ɸit (14)
find	waind (6)		*five*	waiv (11)
	waind/faind/βaind (8)			faiv (15)
	waind (11)		*fix*	fikt (20)
	waind/faind/ɣaind (15)		*fixed*	fikstid (28), p. 174
	faind (18), pp. 59, 69, 86		*flag*	wæġ (8)
find out	faind aut (17)			ɣlæġ (9)
found	waund (9)			ɸlæg (15)
	faund (16)			flæg/ɣlæg (16), pp. 86, 147
	faindid (27)		*flames*	fleimd (17)
finger	wiŋə (1)		*flapjack*	læpgæk (10)
	wiŋgə (2)			læpdæk (14)
	wiŋgə/wiŋgəʳ/ɣiŋgə (12)			læpdæk/ɬæpdæk (15)
	wiŋgə/fiŋgə (14)			ɬæpdæk (16)
	fiŋgə (16), pp. 2, 3, 14, 20,			flæpdzæk/flæpzæk (24)
	45, 83, 87, 97			flæpdᶻæk (27), pp. 141,
finish	witi: (4)			147
	widi:/widin (7)		*flesh*	ɣlɛt (12)
	witi: (8)		*flex*	wɛpt (4)
	witi:/winit (14)			ɣlɛk (13)
	witi:/fiti:/finti (15)		*floor*	wɔ: (4)
	fiti:/ɸiti: (16)			wɔ:/wlɔ: (11)
	fiti: (17)			ɣlɔ: (13)
	fidi:/fidit/finit (18)			ɣlɔ:/βlɔ: (15)
	fidi: (19)			ɣlɔ:/flɔ: (20)
	finist (24), p. 99			flɔ: (22), pp. 71, 87, 147,
				166
			florin	wɔlin (12)

flow	flu: (17)	*Foster*	wɔtə/fɔtə (14)
flower	wæwə (1)		fɔtə/fɔt:ə/fɔtsə (22)
	læwə (9)		fɔstə (26), p. 87
	læwə/ɬæwə (15)	*four*	wɔ: (6)
	ɬæwə (16)		fɔ:/ɣɔ: (11)
	flauə (24), pp. 18, 20, 43, 147		fɔ: (15)
			fɔ:r (18)
flowers	ɬæwəd (19)		fɔ: (24)
	ɬæwəz (21)	*fox*	wɔg̈ (7)
	ɬæwəz/flæwəz (23)		wɔkt (11)
	flauəz (24)		ʋɔk (12)
flower-pot	læwə pɔt/ɬæwə pɔt (15)		wɔk (14)
	ɬæwə pɔt (16)		fɔkt (16)
fly	wai/βʷai (4)		fɔk (17)
	wai (7)	*France*	fra:nt (19)
	ʋai/vai/lai/wai/vlai/ʋlai/ɣlai (9)	*freeze*	wi:d (10), p. 69
	ɣlai (12)	*fridge*	ɣrid (17)
	flai (17), pp. 86, 147		friz (22)
fog	wɔg̈ (5)	*friend*	wɛn/wɛnd (2)
folk	wo:k (11)		wɛnd (5)
follow	wɔwu: (1), pp. 19, 43, 45		ɣrɛnd (16)
food	wu:d (5)		frɛnd (25), pp. 54, 97, 147
	wu:d (14)		
	fu:d (15)	*friends*	frɛnz/frɛndz (24)
foot	wut (1)	*friendly*	wɛndi: (8)
	fut/ɸut (15)	*frightened*	waitənd (4)
	fut (19), pp. 17, 39, 59, 87, 107, 145–6		waidənd (8)
See also 'feet' above.		*frog*	wɔg̈ (7)
footprint	wutplit (10)		flɔg/wɔg/wlɔg/βʳɔg (11)
	wutplit/wutprit (12), p. 139		ɣrɔg (13)
for	wɔ: (12)		ɣlɔg (14)
	wɔ:/wɔ:r (15)		frɔg (15), pp. 71, 86, 87, 144
	fɔ: (16)	*from*	blɔm (11)
forehead /fɔrid/	wɔ:it (4)		fɔm (18)
			frɔm (26)
	fɔrid (18), p. 75	*front*	wʌt (8)
fork	wɔ:k (1)		ɣrʌnt (13)
	wɔ:k/fɔ:k (15)		frʌnt (20)
	fɔ:k (18), pp. 2, 3, 45, 59, 143	*frost*	frɔt/wrɔt (11), p. 87
		froth	wɔt/wɔf/wrɔf (10)
forsythia	fɔ:'taitəri:ə (18)		frɔtˢ/frɔʂ (20)
Foster	wɔt:ə (8)		frɔs (22), pp. 73, 116
	wɔtə (13)	*fru-grain*	'wu:ge:n (8)
		fruit	wu:d (6)
			wu:t/ɣlu:t (11)

fruit	wuːt (14), p. 86	*got*	ġɔt (4)
frying-pan	ɸaiŋ ḅæn (4), p. 181		gɔt (15)
full	wu (8)	*ghost*	ġoːt (11)
	wul/vul/ful (13)	*giant*	dæːnt (19)
funnel	fʌnəl (28)		dzaiᵊnt (28)
funny	wʌniː (2)	*Gilbert*	ġiːbət (5)
	wʌniː/ɣʌniː (14)		ġilbət/ġilblət (10), pp. 56,
	fʌniː (20), p. 87		72
further	fəːʋə (16)	*gin*	ḍin (4)
	fəːzə (27)		tin (11)
fuse	fuːd (20)		din (18)
	fuːẓ (21)	*ginger*	ḍində (8)
			dᶻindᶻə (27)
(*gag*	dæg/gæg) (13)	*giraffe*	diˈræf (13)
gaining	ġeinin (10)		riˈdzæf/dz,iˈræf (27),
galloping	gæpəlin (19), p. 99		pp. 99, 100, 172
game	ġeim (10)	*giraffes*	diˈræfs (23)
games	geimz (21)	*girl*	ġol (5)
Ganesh	ġəˈneːt/ġəˈneːʃt (5), p. 111		ġəːu (7)
/gəˈneiʃ/			gəːl (13), p. 57
garage	ġæəḍ (9)	(*girth*	ġəːt) (12)
/ˈgæraːʒ/	ġæit (11)	*give*	ġiβ (4)
	gærət (14)		ġiβ/ġiv (5)
	gærət/gæraːt (16)		ġiv (12)
	gærət (19)		giv (21)
	gæraːtˢ (21)	*given*	givən (14)
	gærəs (22)	*gave*	gæv (24)
	gærəs/gærəts/gæraːts (23)		givd (26), p. 174
	gærəs (27), pp. 3, 21, 76	*glass*	ġlaːt (10)
garbage	ġaːbit (2)		glaːt (14)
	gaːbid (15)	*glasses*	ġaːgiː (1)
	gaːbit (21)		glaːtit (11)
	gaːbiz (22)		glaːtid (17)
garden	ġaːdən (4)		glaːsiz (27), pp. 17, 19,
	gaːdən (17)		45, 74–5
gate	ġeːt (7)	*Gloucester*	ġɔdə (8)
gathering	gædərin (17)		glɔtə (14)
Gauguin	ġogɛ̃ (10)	*glove*	glʌv (14)
gentle	dɛŋkəl (16), p. 173	*glue*	ġuː/ġuːl (9)
gently	dɛŋkliː (17)		gluː (11), p. 72
	dɛŋkliː/dᶻɛŋkliː (20)	*go*	gəu (19)
	dzɛŋkliː (28), pp. 60, 173	*goes*	gəud (19), p. 27
get	ġɛt (2)	*going*	ġuːin (2)
	gɛt (15)		goːin (15), pp. 68, 70
getting	ġɛḍin (4)	*gone*	ġɔn (2)
	gɛtin (18)		gɔn (11)

went	wɛt (8), p. 192	*guava*	ġa:və/ġa:wə (2)
God	ġɔt (2)	*guitar*	riˈta: (27), pp. 172–3
	ġɔd̦ (8)	(*gulping*	gɔfin) (17)
	gɔd (13)	*gut*	ġʌt (10)
gollywog	ˈgɔli:wɔg (15)		
gollywogs	ˈgɔli:wɔgd (19)	'*h*'	eit/eitç (19)
gonk	ġɔk (4)	*hair*	ɛ (1)
	(ġɔŋk) (10)		ɛᵊ (10)
	ġɔŋk (12), p. 192		hɛᵊ (14)
good	ġug (1)		hɛ: (17), pp. 18, 40
	ġud̦ (8)	*hair-cream*	ˈɛ:ġi:m (7)
	gud (18), pp. 19, 38, 42	*half*	a:f (6)
goose	gu:t (16)		ha:f (15)
	gu:ts/gu:s (22)	*halves*	ha:fs (26)
	gu:s (23)	*hallelujah*	ˈhæpi:ˈlu:lə (27)
gown	ga:m (16)	*ham*	æm (7)
	ga:m/gaun (17)	*hammer*	ɛmə (1)
gracious	geitət/greitət (11)		æmə/hæmə (15), p. 18
grandmother	ˈgændmʌdə/ˈglændmʌdə	*hand*	ɛn (1)
	(10)		ænd (2)
Grandpa	b̦ʌbʌ (2), pp. 29, 35–6		hænd (14)
Granna	læla: (1), pp. 35–6, 41		hænd/ænd (15)
/ˈgræna:/			hænd (16), pp. 14, 18, 70,
Granny	ġlæni: (10)		97, 106
grape	ġeip (1)	*hand-brake*	ændbreik/ændbleik (13)
	ġe:p (2)		hændbreik (16)
	gʳeip/gleip (10)	*handkerchief*	ˈæŋki:wi:f (12)
grass	ġla:t (10)		ˈhæŋkəsi:f (22)
	ġa:t (11)		ˈhæŋkətˢi:f (23)
	gra:t (16)	*handle*	ɛŋu (1)
	gra:s (22)		æŋgu (2)
grater	gleitə/gleitə (9), p. 72		æŋgu/æŋgul (9)
great	ġe:t (4)		æŋgəl (12)
Greco	ġlɛko:/ġɛkəl (10), p. 99		æŋgəl/hæŋgəl (15)
greedy	ġi:di: (1), pp. 19, 35, 42,		hæŋgəl (26)
	45		hændəl (29), pp. 14, 32,
green	ġi:n (2)		54, 56, 57, 106
	kli:n/kˣi:n/tli:n (9)	*happy*	æbi: (8)
	gri:n (14), p. 72		hæpi: (16)
grey	ġe: (4)	*hard*	a:t (1)
grip	ġip (7)		a:d̦ (2)
groin	grɔin (13)		ha:d (17), pp. 38, 39
ground	ġaund/glaund (10), pp.		From stage 21 this word also had the
	73, 139		meaning 'loud'.
guard	ġa:d (11)	*hardly*	ha:dli: (15)
	ga:d (15)	*harness*	a:nit (11)

harness	haːnit (19)	*hey-diddle-diddle*	'eigigəl (11)
have	æv/æβ (4)	*hide*	aiḍ (5)
	æv (9)		haid (16)
	hæv (18), pp. 110, 112	*hiding*	aidin (7)
having	ævin (8)		haidin (21)
	hævin (17)	*hid*	haidid/hud/hid (25),
had	hæd (16)		p. 175
has	hæd (19)	*hidden*	hudən (21)
have to	hæftuː/hæptuː (18)		hud/hudən (27)
	hæftuː (28)		haidid/hudən (28), p. 174
hat	æt (5)	*hide and seek*	'haid ən tiːk (16)
	æt/hæt (14)	*hill*	hil (16)
	hæt (17), p. 70	*hills*	hild (19)
haystack	'eiġæk (8)	*hinge*	hinz (24)
	'eitʰæk (15)		hindᶻ (27)
head	ɛḍ (1)	*hippopotamus*	hi'pɔtəməs (22)
	ɛd (11)		hipə'pɔtəməs (27)
	hɛd (17), pp. 18, 21	*hold*	uːḍ (5)
head-ache	'ɛdeːk/'ɛgeːk (4)		uːld (9)
	'hɛdeik (16)		həuld (19), pp. 56–7, 69
healthy	hɛltiː (17)	*holding*	uːdin (7)
heart	aːt (14)	*hole*	uuː (4)
hearth	aːt (11)		uː (6)
heater	iːdə (4)		oᵘ (8)
heavy	æviː/æwiː (2)		oːl (9)
	hɛʋi (16)		uːl (12)
	hɛʋi (22)		oːl/uːl/huːl (15)
hedge-hog	'ɛdɔġ (2)		hoːl (16)
Helen	hɛlun/hɛlin (23)		həul (19), p. 57
helicopter	'æġəġəġə (4)	*home*	uːm (1)
	'hɛlikɔktə (19), p. 164		oːm (4)
hello	ɛluː (1)		həum (17)
	hɛləu (16), pp. 19, 27, 38,	*honey*	ʌniː (10)
	41		hʌniː (16)
helmet	ɛlmɛt (12)	*(hoof*	uːf/ʌf) (12)
help	ɛp (4)	*hook*	uk (10)
	hɛp (17)	*Hoover*	uːʋə (11)
	hɛp/hɛlp (18)		uːʋə/huːʋə (15), p. 170
helping	ɛpin/ɛplin (13)	This word was in fact recorded earlier – as	
	hɛpin (18), pp. 98, 100	A's first word.	
helped	hɛlpt (28)	*horn*	ɔːn (7)
hen	ɛn (7)	*Horner*	ɔːnə (15)
here	ḍiə (11)	*horror*	ɔə/ɔwə (4)
	tiə (13)	*horse*	iːɔ (2)
	tiə/hiə (19)		ɔːḍiː/iːɔ (8)
	hiə (23)		ɔːt (12)

horse hɔːt (14)
         hɔːs (23)
horses ɔːdid̦ (9)
          ɔːtit (14)
          hɔːtid (19), pp. 64, 148
Until stage 8 horses and donkeys were
semantically non-distinct.
hospital hɔspikəl/hɔtpikəl (22)
            hɔspikəl (23)
hot ɔt (1)
       hɔt (19)
house aut (1)
         aut/haut (15)
         haut (16)
         haus (21)
houses hauşiẓ (21)
          hausiz (22), p. 130
how au (4)
       hau/ə (19)
huge uːd/huːd (14)
        uːd (16)
        huːdz, (28)
        huːdʒ (29), p. 70
human-being huːmən/hjuːmən biːin (29)
humpty- ʌptiː dʌptiː (8)
   dumpty ʌmtiː dʌmtiː (12), p. 192
hungry ʌŋgʷiː (7)
          ʌŋgiː (9)
hurry hʌwiː (24)
hurt əːt (1)
        həːt (16), p. 18
hurting əːdin (4)
(*husband* ʌptəm/ʌptəmb) (14),
        p. 98
hydraulic lift ˈai ˈdɔli: ˈlipt (11)

ice ait (5)
       aitˢ (20)
       ais (22)
icicle ˈaikitəl/ˈaitikəl/ˈaikikəl
         (16), pp. 99, 101, 151
icing aitin (16)
ignition nisən (28), p. 173
imaginary mædərin (20)
             mædᶻərin (21)
             mæzənriː (24)

important pɔːtənt (17)
             ʌmˈpɔːtənt (18)
index ˈindɛktˢ (20)
India ˈindiːaː/indiːja: (8)
infection riˈfɛksən (28), p. 172
ingenious inˈdiːnit (10)
ink iŋk (12)
inside inˈdaid̦ (2)
         indaid (11)
         intaid (14)
         intˢaid (20)
         inṣaid (21)
         insaid (23), p. 106
instead of stɛd əv (28)
invited diˈwaitid (28), p. 173
iris æːrit (15)
iron æːn/ain (7)
       æːn (17)
ironing-board ainin b̦ɔːd̦/aindin b̦ɔːd̦ (7),
       p. 97
itself itˈlɛf (15)
         itˈɬɛf (23)
         itˈslɛf (24)

Jack dæk/dræk (15)
        dzæk/dʒæk (26)
        dzæk (28), p. 91
jacket ġækit (8)
          dækit (16)
          drækit (19)
(*Jacques* zæk) (29), p. 94
jam d̦ɛm (1)
       dæm (14)
       dræm (18)
       dzæm (22), p. 93
jammed dæmd/dᶻæmd (20), p. 60
Jane dzein (26)
jar daːʳ (12)
       dlaː (15)
       dzaː (22), pp. 93, 97
jars dzaːz (27)
jeep d̦iːp (8)
       dziːp (24)
jelly d̦ɛiː/d̦ɛliː (5)
        d̦ɛiː (6)
        dɛliː (14)

jelly	dᶻɛli: (27), p. 91	*jumping*	dʌpin/(dʌmpin) (5)
jellies	dɛlid (23)		dʌbin (6)
Jemima	di'maimə (16)		dzʌmpin (24), p. 111
Jenny	dɛni:/dzɛni: (25)	*jumped*	dʌpt (5)
jibber-jabber-	dᶻibə dᶻæbə dᶻu: (27)		dʌpt/dʌmpt (13)
joo			dʌmpt (17)
jig	d,ig (14), pp. 91, 141, 198	*junket*	drʌŋkit (19)
jig-saw	dig sɔ: (23)	*just*	dʌt (2)
Jill	dil/d,il (15)		dʌt (12)
	dil/dril (16), p. 91		dʌs/dʌst (22)
Jim	dim (16)		dʌst (25)
jingle	dziŋgəl/dʒiŋgəl (26)		
job	dɔb (20)	*keep*	ġi:p (2)
jog	ġɔk (4)		ki:p (15)
	ġɔg (10)	*keeping*	kʰi:pin (13)
	dɔg/drɔg (15)	*kennel*	kɛŋəl (27), p. 149
	dᶻɔg (23)	*kettle*	ġɛgu (7)
jogging	dɔgin (17)		kɛkəl (17)
	dzɔgin (25)	*key*	ġi: (1)
John	dɔn (1)		ki: (22)
	dɔn (14)	*kick*	kik (17)
	drɔn (15)	*kicking*	ġikin (10)
	dɔn/drɔn/rɔn (18)	*kind* (N)	ġaind (9)
	drɔn (19)		kaind (17)
	dzɔn (24), pp. 3, 21, 45	*kinds*	kaindz (26)
join	drɔin (14), pp. 91, 167	*king*	kiŋ (9)
joke	ġo:k (9)	*kiss*	ġik (1)
	ġo:k (12)		ġit (7)
	ġo:k (13)		kit (13), pp. 17, 91, 21,
	do:k (16), pp. 96, 141		74, 163
jolly	dɔli: (18)	*kissing*	ġitin (12)
	dzɔli: (23)		kitin (16)
Jonathan	dɔnəsən/dzɔnəsən (26)		kisin (21)
	dzɔnəsən (28)	*kissed*	kistid (27)
Joseph	dᶻəusif (27)	*kitchen*	ġigən (1)
journal	dzə:ŋəl (28)		ġitin (4)
jug	ġʌk (7)		ġitən/ġitin/kitin (12)
	dʌg (14), pp. 43, 141		kitən (13)
jugs	dᶻʌgz (27)		kitˢin (20)
juice	du:t (1)		kisin (22)
	du:t (12)		kitˢin (27), pp. 19, 43, 75
	dᶻu:tˢ/du:ṣ/dᶻu:s (21)	*knee*	ni: (1)
	dzu:s/dʒu:s (26), p. 95	*knees*	ni:d (18)
jump	dʌp (5)	*knife*	maip (1)
	dʌmp (13)		maip/(naip) (3)
	dzʌmp (26), pp. 10, 192		maip (5)

knife	maip/naip (8)	*larks*	la:kt/ġa:kt (7)
	maif/naif (9)	*Larry*	læli: (27), p. 75
	naif (11), pp. 20, 21, 32,	*lash*	ḍæt (1)
	42, 45, 82, 84, 163		læt (11)
knives	naift (19)	*last*	ḍa:t/la:t (5)
	naifs (29)		la:t (10)
knob	mɔḅ (2)	*later*	ḍe:də (1)
	mɔḅ/nɔḅ (6)	*later on*	leitə ɔn (16)
	nɔb (11), p. 83		leitərɔn (18)
knock	ġɔk (5)	*laugh*	la:f (28)
	ġɔk/ŋɔk (6)	*laughed*	wa:pt (8)
	ġɔk/nɔk (7)		la:pt (11)
	lɔk (8)	*laughing*	la:fin (18)
	lɔk/ŋɔk (12)	*lavatory*	wæwi: (5)
	lɔk/nɔk (13)		wæwi:/wæβi: (6)
	nɔk (19), p. 182		wæwiti: (8)
knot	nɔt (6)		lævətri: (23)
know	no: (8)	*lawn-mower*	mɔ:mə (1)
	nəu (23)		'lɔ:n mo:wə/'nɔ:nmo:wə
knows	nəud (19)		(8)
kudu	ġu:du: (7)		'lɔ:n mu:ə (16), pp. 35–6,
			45
label	we:bu (4)	*Lawrence*	'lɔləns (24)
	leibəl (12), p. 109	*lazy*	ḍeⁱdi: (1)
laces	leitid (16)		le:di: (4), pp. 17, 149
ladder	ḍɛdə (1)	*leaf*	li:f (15)
	lædə (5)	*leaves*	(li:vd) (19)
	lædəʳ (12)		li:fs (23)
	lædə/lædəʳ (18)	*leaking*	li:kin (10)
ladle	leigu/leigul (13)	*leash*	li:ɫ (11)
	leigəl (15)	*leather*	lɛvə/lɛv̰ə (15)
lady	ḍeⁱdi: (1)		lɛvə/lɛdə (16)
	ḍe:di:/le:di: (2)		lɛdə (19)
	le:di: (4)	*leave*	li:v (14)
	le:di:/ḍe:di: (6)	*left* (past)	li:vd (18)
	le:di: (7)		li:vd/lɛft (19), p. 174
	leidi: (12), pp. 3, 76, 88,	*left* (Adj)	wɛpt (3)
	105, 152, 194		lɛpt (10)
ladybird	'ḍeidi:bə:t (1)		lɛft (17)
	'leidi:bə:d (17)		lɛpt (18)
lamb	læm (13)		lɛft (19), pp. 89, 90,
lamp	wæp (5)		122
landing	lændin (15)	*leg*	ġɛk (1)
Lapland	'æplæn/æplænd/læplæn/		ġɛġ (2)
	læplænd (9)		ɣɛġ/lɛġ (8)
large	la:d (16)		lɛg (11), p. 20

legs   lɛgd (19)
                lɛgẕ (21)
                lɛgz (24)

Lego   ġɛgu: (1)
                ġɛgo:/jɛgo/ʎɛgo/ɣɛgo (4)
                ġɛgo:/lɛgo: (5)
                lɛgo:/łɛgo:/ɣɛgo: (8)
                lɛgo: (12)
                lɛgəu (23), pp. 82, 109,
                  153

Leicester lɛtə (17)

lemonade lɛmə'neid/ɛmən'eild (19)

lesson   lɛtən (17)

lessons   lɛtənd (17)

let   lɛt (5)

let's   lɛt (13)
                lɛts (26)

letter   ḍɛdə (1)
                ḍɛtə (2)
                lɛdə (4)
                lædə (5)
                lɛdə (7)
                lɛtə (14)

lever   wi:wə (8)
                li:və (15)

library   'læ:bəri: (23)

lick   ġik (4)
                ġik/lik (7)
                ʎik (8)
                lik (15), p. 82

licking   likin (17)

licked   likt (18)

lid   lid (12)

lie (down) ḍai daun (1)
                lai ḍaun (5)
                lai daun (11)

life   laif/laiɸ (11)
                laif (13)

lift   wipt (6)
                lipt (9)
                lipt/lift (20), pp. 68, 83,
                  84, 112, 153

lifting   lipin/liptin (6)
                lipin (9), pp. 83, 88, 112,
                  167

light   ḍait (1)

light   lait (4), pp. 2, 4, 5, 19, 39,
                41, 110, 135, 152–3

like   ġaik (1)
                ġaik/ɣaik/jaik (4)
                ġaik/laik (5)
                laik (7)
                laik/ɣaik (8)
                laik (10), pp. 2, 29, 32, 41,
                82, 105, 108, 153

linguist ġimdit (4)
                ġiŋgit (10)

lion   læ:n (7)
                læ:n/lain/læ³n (12)
                læ:n (13)
                læ:n/lain (23)
                laiən (28)

lip   lip (9)

lips   lipt (18), pp. 68, 70, 84

listen   lidən (6)
                litən (10)

little   ḍidi: (1)
                ḍidi:/lidi: (6)
                lidi: (9)
                lidi:/litəl (11)
                lidi:/liti: (13)
                litəl (14)
                litəl/liəl (29), pp. 35–6,
                125, 151–2, 163

loaf   lu:f (9), p. 84

lock   ġɔk (1)

lock   lɔk (15), p. 21

log   lɔg (10)

lolly(pop) ɔli: (1)
                lɔli:bɔp (6), pp. 35–6, 41

long (Adj) ġɔŋ (2)
                ġɔŋ/lɔŋ (4)
                łɔŋ (8)
                lɔŋ (11), pp. 82, 109

longing lɔŋiŋ (10), p. 18

look   ġuk (2)
                ġuk/ɣuk (4)
                ġuk/luk (5)
                ɣuk/luk/lɣuk (7)
                łuk/ʎɣk (8)
                luk (9), pp. 82, 90, 108

loose   lu:t (19)

loose	lu:s (21)	*Mac Fisheries*	'mæk'fisəriz (23)
lorry	lɔli: (1)	*machine*	mə'ti:n (13)
	lɔri: (28), pp. 2, 19, 33,	*mad*	mæd (8)
	36, 38, 41 ,45, 75, 129,	*magic*	mæzik (25)
	137, 152		mæzik/mædzik (26)
lorries	lɔlid (18)		mædzik (28)
	lɔriz (28)	*magnet*	mæŋgit (10)
lose	lu:d (10), p. 69		mægnit (17), pp. 99, 100
lost	lɔt (10)	*make*	meik/me:k (4)
	lɔst (22)		meik (10)
lot	lɔt (12)	*makes*	meikt (18)
lots	lɔt (8)	*making*	meikin (16)
	lɔt/lɔs (21)	*made*	meid (11)
	lɔts (23)		meikən (23)
lotion	ḍu:dən (1)	*malt*	mɔ:lt (12)
	lo:dənd (8)	*man*	mæn/mɛn (1)
loud-speaker	laud ḅi:kə (11)		mæn (10), p. 39
	laud spi:kə (28)	*men*	mæn/mɛn (1)
louse	laut (11)		mɛn (10), p. 39
lout	laut (4)	*manage*	mæniz (27)
love	wʌḅ (8)	*Manchuria*	mæn'tˢuəri:ə (26)
	lʌv (12)	*mango*	mæŋgo: (2)
loving	lʌvin (16)	*mantelpiece*	'mæŋku ḅi:t/mæŋkəl ḅi:t
lovely	wʌwi: (8)		(11), p. 53
	lʌvi: (12)	*marble*	ma:bəl (11)
	lʌvli: (27)	*marbles*	ma:bəldᶻ (20)
Lucinda	'ḍu:dənində (4)	*marigolds*	'mæri:gəulz (23)
	'ḍu:dənində/'lu:tənində	*mark*	ma:k (2)
	(6)	*Marks and*	ma:ks ən pɛnsiv (23)
	lu:'tində/lu:'tindəʳ (12)	*Spencer*	
	lu:'tində (13)	*mash*	mæt (11)
	lu:'tˢində (17)	*mashed*	mæt (16)
	lu:'sində (21), p. 97	*mass*	mæt (11)
luck	lʌk (12), p. 43	*master*	ma:tə (11)
lunch	ḍʌt (4)		ma:ṣtə (21)
	lʌt (6)	*mat*	mæt (13)
	lʌnt (13)	*mats*	mæts/mæs (22)
	lʌntˢ/lʌntʃ (20)	*match*	mæt (4)
	lʌntˢ (21)		mæs (24)
	lʌns (22)	*matches*	mætit (12)
	lʌntˢ (27), p. 153		mætˢiz (27)
lungs	lʌŋ (10)	*maybe*	me:bi: (6)
	lʌmd (20)	*maze*	meid (11)
	lʌmz/lʌŋz (21)	*meant*	mɛt (12), pp. 14, 22, 134,
	lʌmz (22)		166
	lʌŋz (26)	*measure*	mɛzə (22)

meat	mi:t (4)	*mixer*	migə (1)
medal	mɛgəl/mɛdəl (14)		miktə (15), pp. 21, 45, 88
medicine	mɛdin (2)	*mixing-bowl*	miktin/miksin bəul (20)
	mɛdətən (19)	(*montbretia*	'mɔm‚bri:tə) (15)
	mɛditˢin (20)	*money*	mʌni: (2)
medium-size	mi:dəm tʰaid (14)	*monkey*	mʌgi:/mʌg̈i: (6)
	mi:d‚əm saiz (27)		mʌgi: (7)
melt	mɛlt (16)		mʌŋki: (12)
melted	mɛᵘdiḍ (8)	*monkeys*	mʌŋkid (16)
melting	mɛltin (22)	*monkier*	mʌŋki:ə (23)
mend	mɛn (1)	With the meaning: 'more similar to a	
	mɛnd (5), pp. 14, 22, 45,	monkey'.	
	134, 166	*monster*	mɔntə (13)
mendable	mɛndəbəl/mɛlbədən (24),	*moon*	mu:/mu:n (1)
	pp. 99, 100		mu:n (2), pp. 21, 42
metal	mɛg̈u (4)	*more*	mɔ: (1)
	mɛkəl (14)		mɔ:r (17)
	mɛtəl (29)		mɔ: (20), pp. 38, 39, 98
meter	mi:də (8)	*morning*	'mɔ:niŋ‚daim (8)
Michelle	mi'ḍɛl (10)		'mɔ:nin (16), p. 70
/mi'ʃɛl/		*this morning*	ə'm̥ɔ:nin (18)
microphone	'maikrəfrəun (20)	*mother*	mʌzə (22)
middle	migu (8)	*motor*	mu:də (4)
	migəl (11)	*motor-bike*	'mu:gəga:baik (2)
Mike	maik (1)		'mu:təbaik (16), p. 83
milk	mik (1)	*motor-car*	'mu:gəga: (1)
	milk/mlik (10)		'mu:kəka: (12)
	milk (11), pp. 15, 33, 41,		'mu:təka:/'mo:kəka: (13)
	45, 98, 100, 166		'mu:təka: (14)
milk-shake	milk tˢeik/treik (20)		'mo:təka:r (16)
mind	maind (7)		'məutəka: (17), pp. 20,
minute	minit (4)		41, 83
mirror	mi:jə (8)	*mouse*	maut (7)
	mi:jə/mi:ə (11)		mautˢ (20)
	mirə (12), p. 76		mauṣ (21)
mischief	'mistˢi:f (27)		maus (22)
miserable	'mizbərəl (23), p. 99	*mice*	mait (1)
misery	'midəri: (20)		mausiz (24)
missing	mitin (19)		maisiz (28), pp. 3, 15, 17,
Mister	mitə (17)		45, 137
	mistə (23)	At stage 28 the singular form was [mais].	
mix	mik (19)	*mouth*	maut (2)
	mikt (20)		mautˢ (20)
mixing	mikin/miktin (18)		mauṣ (21)
mixed up	migdʌp (5)		maus (22), p. 137
	miktʌp (16)	*move*	mu:/mu:ɸ (5)

move	mu: (6)	*nanga*	nʌŋgə (24), p. 42
	mu:ɣ/mu:d (12)		Hindi: [nəŋgə] = 'naked'.
	mu:ʊ (17)	*napkin*	æpkin (25)
	mu:v (26)	*nasty*	na:ti: (12)
moved	mu:d (15)	*naughty*	nɔ:di: (1)
moving	mu:ʊin (16)		nɔ:ti: (14), p. 45
	mu:vin (22)	*neck*	ŋɛk/ŋgɛk (4)
Mrs	mitit (20)		nɛk (5)
much	mʌt (4)		ŋɛk/ɣɛk (8)
	mʌtˢ (21)		ŋɛk (10)
	mʌs (24)		nɛk (13), pp. 4, 41, 83,
	mʌs/mʌtˢ (27)		97, 157, 181
	mʌtˢ (28)	*necklace*	ġɛgit (2)
	mʌtʃ (29)		nɛkit (5), p. 85
mucus	mu:kəs (27)	*need*	ni:ḍ (7)
mud	mʌḍ (5)		ni:d (12)
	mʌd (10)	*needle*	ni:gu (7)
muddle	mʌgəl (11), p. 159		ni:gəl (15), p. 113
Mummy	mʌmi: (2)	*Neil*	ni:u (4)
mumps	mʌmt/mʌmp (18)	*never*	nɛvə (8)
muscle	mʌtu (11), pp. 96, 159	*new*	nu: (1)
mushroom	mʌʂrum/mʌtrum (18)		nu:/nju: (24)
	mʌsrum (23)		nu: (25)
music	mu:gi: (2)		nju: (29), pp. 18, 63, 71,
	mu:gi:/mu:dik (15)		73, 157, 161
	mu:gi: (16)	*news*	nu: (14)
	mu:zik (27), p. 99		nu:d/nu:dᶻ (20)
must	mʌs (23)	*next*	ŋɛkt (5), p. 83
mustn't	mʌdəd (11)	*nibbling*	nibəlin (20)
	mʌtənt (14)	*nice*	nait (1)
(*mutt*	mʌd/mʌt) (10)		naitˢ/naiṣ (21)
muzzle	mʌdil/mʌdu (11)		nais (22), pp. 15, 42, 45
	mʌdəl (13), p. 96	*nicer*	naisə (26)
mynah	'mainə bə:di: (19)	*nicely*	naitli: (19)
myself	mai'ɬɛf (19)	*Nigel*	ri:'naidzəl (29), p. 173
	mai'ɬɛf/mai'lɛf (20)	*night*	nait (5), p. 19
	mai'ɬɛf/mai'slɛf (23)	*nineteen*	'naiti:n (15)
	mai'slɛf (24)	*ninety-one*	'nænti: wʌn (15)
	mai'sɛlf (27)		'nãiti: wʌn (16)
		nip	nip (11)
nail	neil (12)	*nipple*	mibu (1)
nails	neilz (24)		mipu (3)
nail-brush	neil brʌt (19)		miḅu (8)
nail-clippers	neil ġlipə (10)		nipəl (11), pp. 15, 20, 42,
	neil klipə (17)		45, 82
nanga /nʌŋgə/	ŋʌŋgə (2)	*noddle*	nɔgu/nɔgul/ŋɔgu (11)

noddle	nɔgəl (13), pp. 24, 150	*off*	ɔf (16)
noise	nɔi: (4)	*often*	ɔfən (26)
	nɔ:i: (5)	*oil*	oij/oijə (2)
	nɔi:/nɔid (14)		oijə (6)
	nɔid (15)		ɔ:l (18)
	nɔiz (21)	*oily*	ɔ:li: (23)
noisy	nɔ:ni: (1)	*old*	u:ld (14)
	nɔidi: (17), pp. 15, 39, 42,		əuld (23)
	45, 164	*on*	ɔn (1)
nonsense	nɔntənt (18)	*once*	wʌt (11)
north	nɔ:t (9)	*one*	wʌn (1)
Norwich	lɔlit (8)		wʌn/vʌn (18)
nose	nu: (1)		wʌn (19), pp. 45, 68,
	nu:/nu:d (14)		145–6
	nu: (15)	*ones*	wʌnd (19)
	no:d (16)	*onion*	ʌnrən/ʌni:ən (19), p. 73
	nəuz (21), pp. 17, 38, 68,	*only*	u:li: (6)
	69, 110		o:li: (9)
nose-thumper	nəud tʰʌmpə (19)		əunli: (21), p. 10
nostril	nɔtil (11)	*open*	ubu: (1)
nothing	nʌtin (11)		o:pən/u:pən (5)
	nʌsin (22), p. 18		u:b̩ən (7)
now	nau (1)		u:pən (14)
	nɛu/nau (13)		u:pən/əupən (17)
	nau (14)		əupən (18), pp. 21, 35
nozzle	nɔdəl (11), p. 150	*opened*	o:b̩ənd̩ (9)
number	nʌmdə (2)		əupənd (17)
	nʌmbə (9)	*orange*	ɔin (2)
	nʌmbər (13), pp. 53, 105,		ɔind (7)
	106		ɔrind (19)
numbers	nʌmbəd̩ᶻ (20)		ɔind̩ᶻ (21)
nurse	nə:s (22)		ɔr,inz (24), pp. 53, 110
nursery	'nə:təri: (15)	*ordinary*	(ɔ:dənri:) (14)
nut	nʌt (1)		ɔ:dəri: (17)
nutmeg	nʌpmɛg (18)		ɔ:dənri: (19)
nuzzling	'nʌdəlin (20)	*other*	ʌdə (1)
			ʌdə/ʌd̩ᶻə/ʌzə (21)
oak-tree	nu:k tri: (24)		ʌdə/ʌzə (22)
oats	o:t (16)		ʌzə (24), p. 21
	əus (22)	*otherwise*	ʌdəwai (9)
obey	ri:'bei (27)		ʌdəwaid (19)
octopus	'ɔktəpət (12)	*our*	wi: (15)
	'ɔktəpəs (25)	*out*	aut (1)
off	ɔf (3)	*outside*	autd̩ait (1)
	ɔɸ (5)		autd̩aid̩ (7)
	ɔf/ɔɸ (8)		autd̩aid̩ (12)

outside	auttʰaid (13)	*passing*	ba:din (7)
	auttˢaid (21)	*passer*	pa:sə (24)
	autsaid (22)	*patchwork*	ˈpæswə:k (24)
owl	au (7)	*paw*	bɔ: (7)
	aul (12)	*pea*	bi: (4)
owls	aul (16)		pʰi: (14), p. 69
own	u:n (12)	*peas*	pʰi:d (14)
	əun (18)		pi:z (23), p. 69
		peach	pi:tˢ/pi:s (21)
paddling pool	pægəlin pu:l (23)		pi:s (23)
page	beid (10)	*peaches*	pi:tˢid/pi:tˢiz (21)
	peid (17)	*pear*	bɛ (2)
	peidᶻ (20)	*pears*	pɛəz (23)
	peiz (26)	*pedal*	begu (1)
pages	be:did (9), p. 68		begəl (11)
pain	be:n (6)		pɛgəl (14), pp. 14, 54, 149
paint	pʰeint (14)		begin (4)
paint brush	peint brʌs (23)	*pedalling*	pɛgəlin (17)
panda	bændə (11)	*peel*	bi:u (7)
panther	bændə (7)		pʰi:l (13), p. 118
	bædə/(bændə) (11), p. 53	*peep*	bi:p (2)
pants	bæt (7)	*peg*	bɛk (1)
paper	be:bə (2)		bɛġ (4)
	beibə (11)	*pen*	ben (1)
	pe:pə (12)		pʰɛn (13), pp. 36, 69
	pʰeipə/pʰeipər/pʰeibər (13)	*pens*	pʰɛn (14), p. 69
	pʰeipə (14)	*pencil*	bɛtəl/bɛdu (5)
paper-bag	be:bəbæġ (4)		bɛtu (9)
parcel	pa:təl (19)		bɛtu/bɛtul/pɛtəl (10)
	pa:səl (24)		bɛdəl (11)
parcels	pa:səlz (22)		bɛntil/pɛntəl (12)
pardon	ba:dən/pa:dən/bʌ:dən (12)		pɛntəl (13)
	pa:dən (13)		pɛnṣəl (21)
park	ba:k (1)		pɛnsəl (22), pp. 53, 56
	pa:k (15)	*pencils*	pɛnᵗsəlẓ (21)
parsley	pa:tli: (15)	*penguin*	wiŋgin (7)
	pa:təli: (19)	*penis*	binin (1)
parsnip	ba:pmip (4)		bitin (4)
	ba:pmip/ba:pnip (7)		pinit (5)
	ba:pmip (8)		pi:nit (6)
	pʰa:pnip (16)		bi:nit/bi:nət/bi:nʌt (11)
part	ba:t (5)		pʰi:nit (13)
	ba:t/pa:t (12)		pi:nət (17)
	pa:t (20)		pi:nis (22)
party	ba:ti: (10)		pi:nəs (25), pp. 15, 99, 100
pass	pa:tˢ (20)	*pen-knife*	bɛnmaip (4)

pen-knife	pɛnnaif (13)	*pinching*	pintˢin (27)
pepper	bɛbə (8)	*pink*	bik (7)
perhaps	præps (28)		biġ (11)
person	pə:tən (17)		biŋk/piŋk (12)
petal	pɛkəl (22)		pʰiŋk (13), p. 95
petrol	pɛtrəl (18)	*pip*	bip (1)
	pɛtˢrəl (21)		pip (16)
phone	wo:n (8)	*pipe*	baip (10)
phone-call	wu:n kɔ:/wu: kɔ:n (7)	*pistol*	pitəl (14), pp. 24, 55, 149,
piano	'pʰæno:/'ᵖæno: (15)		160, 167
	'pʰænəu (18), pp. 73, 166	*pitch fork*	pit fɔ:k (17)
pickle(s)	pikəl (23)	*pith*	pitˢ/pit/piθ (19)
	pikləz (25)	*plastic*	'blætit (11)
	pitəl (29)		plæktit (16)
picture	bikḍə (2)		pla:tik (18)
	biktə (4)		plækit (19), p. 99
	piktə (15)	*plasticine*	'pla:ti:n (14)
	piktə/piktˢə (27), p. 88		'pla:təli:n (18)
pictures	piksəz (22)		'pla:stəsi:n (24)
	piktəz/piktˢəz (23)	*plate*	be:t (2)
	piksəz/piktˢəz (26)	*play*	bei (1)
pie	bai (7)		be: (2)
	pʰai (18)		bei/plei (9)
piece	pʰi:t (14)		bei/blei/bəlei (10)
	pi:s (24)		blei (11)
pieces	bi:dit (8)		plei (13), pp. 18, 161, 166
	pʰi:tid (16)	*playing*	be:in (6)
	pi:siz (21)	*playground*	bɛiġaun/bɛiġaund (4)
pig	bik (2)		be:gaund/be:gʳaund (5)
	biġ (4)	*playschool*	'pleikʰu:l (14)
	bigi: (8)		'pʰeikʰu:l (15)
	big (11)		'pleisku:l (25)
	big/pig (12)	*please*	bi: (1)
	pig (13), p. 95		bi:/bi:d (9)
pillow	bilo (11)		pli:/bli: (10)
	pʰilo (14)		pli: (11)
	piləu (16), p. 76		pli:/pli:d (14)
pilot-light	baijət lait/bailət lait (5)		pli:d (15)
	baijə/baijət/bailə (6)		pli:dᶻ/pli:z (20)
	bailə lait/bailət lait (7),		pli:z (22), pp. 17, 34, 68
	p. 111	*pleased*	bi:d (2)
pin	bin (2)		pli:d (12)
	pin (13), p. 58		pli:dᶻ (19)
pins	pind (19)		pli:zd (23)
	pinz (24)	*pliers*	baiə (2)
pinch	pins (25)		bæə (5)

pliers	plæ: (15)	*powder*	b̥audə (4)
	plæ:d (20)	*precious*	b̥ɛtət (6)
plug	b̥lʌg (12)	*press*	b̥rɛt (12)
	plʌg (15)		prɛt (18)
plugs	plʌgz (21)		prɛs (23)
plum	plʌm/b̥lʌm (15)	*pretending*	pi'tɛndin/pri'tɛndin (26)
	plʌm (22)	*pretty*	b̥idi:/b̥ʷidi: (9)
pocket	b̥ɔkit (5)		pr̥iti: (16)
	pɔkit (21)		priti: (19)
point	pɔint (11)	*prick*	b̥rik/pr̥ik (16)
poke	pʰu:k (14)	*probably*	pɔbli:/plɔbli: (11)
poked	pʰu:kt (14)		pɔbəli: (15)
police	b̥i:t/b̥ʷi:t/b̥u:i:t (6)		prɔbəli: (24), p. 96
	b̥i:t/bui:t (9)	*projector*	b̥ə'gɛktə (12)
polish	pɔlit (12)	*properly*	b̥lɔpli: (11)
	pɔlis (22)		plɔpli: (12)
polythene	'pɔləti:n (17)		prɔpəli: (16)
poodle	pu:gəl (16)		pɔpəli: (17)
poor	b̥u (2)		prɔpəli: (21), p. 96
	pur/puər/pʉə (19)	*pudding*	b̥udin (11), pp. 18, 96
	pʉə (23), p. 40	*puddle*	b̥ʌgu (8)
position	pə'zisən (27)		pʌgəl (14)
	pə'dʒisən (29)		pʌdəl (29), pp. 4, 14, 55,
post	b̥u:t (11)		149, 154
	pu:t (13)	*pull*	b̥u (4)
	pəut (17)		pul (17)
	pəus (21)	*puller*	pulə (15)
postman	pəusmən (22)	*pulling*	b̥uin (8)
	pəustmən (24)	*pullover*	pul'ovəʳ (13)
post-office	pu:t ɔfit (18)		pul'əuwə/pul'əuβə (20)
	pəust ɔfis (23)	*purple*	b̥ə:bu (4)
(postal	pʰo:təl) (14)		b̥ə:b̥əl (11)
potato	b̥eito (5)		pə:pəl (14)
	b̥e:to (7)	*purse*	b̥ə:t (5)
	b̥eito/d̥eito (11)		pʰə:t (14)
	peito (16)	*push*	b̥ut (5)
	pʰeitəu (17), p. 28		put (15)
potato-masher	peitəu mæʂə (20)		pus (21)
pouffe	b̥u:p (4)	*pussy-cat*	pudi: kæt (12)
	b̥u:f/b̥u:ɸ (10)		pʰuti: kʰæt (14)
	pu:f (11)		putˢi: kæt (21)
	pu:f/b̥u:f (12)		pusi: kæt (22)
	pu:f/pu:ɸ (14)	*put*	b̥ut (4)
	pu:f (20)		b̥ut/put (6)
pour	b̥ɔ: (2)		put (14)
poured	pɔ:d (23)		puʔ (29)

put (p.p.)	putən (20)	*rain*	rein (18), pp. 3, 39, 77
putting	b̩utin (5)	*raining*	le:nin (5)
	b̩udin (8)		re:nin/le:nin/d̩e:nin (8)
	b̩utin (11)		reinin (12), p. 77
	putin (13), p. 96	*rake*	leik/ʁeik/ɣeik (9)
puzzle	pʌdəl (11)		reik (14), p. 84
	pʌzəl (27), pp. 4, 14, 55,	*ram*	wæm (2)
	149, 159	*ramp*	wæp (4)
pyjamas	d̩a:mə (8)	*rascal*	ra:kəl (18)
	pə'da:məd (17)	*rash*	ræʂ/ræt (11)
	da:mə/da:məd (18), p. 28		ræt (12)
python	paifən/(paisən) (29)	*rat*	d̩æt/ræt (2)
			læt/d̩æt/Ræt/ʁæt (7)
'Q-tip'	'ku:tip (25)		ræt (13), pp. 76, 88
quack(-quack)	kæp(-kæp) (21)	*rattle*	ræku (12)
quarry	kʰɔfəri:/kʰɔɣəri: (14),		rækəl (28)
	p. 64	*raw*	d̩ɔ:/lɔ: (7)
quarter	kɔ:pə (23)		rɔ: (13), p. 98
queen	ġi:m (8)	*ray*	d̩e:/re: (2), pp. 76, 88
	ki:m/(ki:n) (10)	*razor*	reidə (15)
	kʰi:m (14)		reidəʳ (19)
	kwi:n (25), pp. 16, 65, 73,	*razor-blade*	'le:dəbe:d̩ (8)
	164, 166, 197	*reach*	ri:t (11)
quick	ġip/(ġik) (11)		ri:t/d̩i:t (12)
	kip/klip (12)		ri:t (13)
	kʰip (14)		ri:s (24)
	kwik (25), pp. 10, 64, 65,	*read*	li:d̩ (7)
	73, 137, 197		ri:d (19)
quickly	kipli: (23)	*reading*	ri:din (20)
quicker	kwikə/mɔ: kwikə (25)	*read* (past)	ri:did (25)
quiet	kʰæ:p (17)	*read* (p.p.)	ri:dən (28), p. 174
	kwæ:t (26)	*ready*	lɛdi: (8)
quietly	kwæ:tli: (25)		rɛdi: (19)
quite	kaip (9)	*real*	li:u/li:uɫ (8)
	kwait (25), pp. 26, 64, 71		li:l (9)
			ri:l (20)
rabbit	wæbit (6)	*realise*	liəlaid/riəlaid (15), p. 75
	ræbit (12)	*really*	li:li: (10)
racing-car	'reitin(ka:r) (16)		li:li:/ri:li: (11)
	'reitin ka: (18)		li:li: (15)
racquet	Rækit (11)		ri:li: (18), p. 75
radio	'le:di:do: (4), pp. 75, 77	*record*	'ġɛkɔ:d̩ (4)
rain	d̩ein (1)		'ġɛkɔ:d̩/lɛkɔ:d̩/jɛkɔ:d̩ (6)
	le:n (5)		'lɛkɔ:d (8)
	rein (11)		'rɛkɔ:d (15), p. 82
	rein/lein (14)	*red*	d̩ɛt (1)

red	rɛd/lɛd (4)	*ring*	riŋ (11), pp. 20, 39, 90
	lɛd (7)	*ringing*	ġiŋiŋ (3)
	rɛd/lɛd/dɛd (8)		riŋiŋ (10)
	rɛd/lɛd/wɛd (9)		riŋiŋ/riŋin (18)
	rɛd (10), pp. 77, 88, 114,	*(risk*	rikt) (14), p. 98
	194	*rivet*	rivit (13)
reindeer	'reindiə/leindiə (9)	*road*	lo:d (5)
	'reindiə (19)		rəud (17)
reins	rein (12)	*Robbie*	wɔbi: (1), p. 30
remember	mɛmbə (11)	*robin*	rɔbin (20)
	mɛmbər (12)	*rock*	ġɔk (2)
	mɛmbə (13)	*roll*	rəul (17)
	ti'mɛmbə (17)	*rolling*	lolin/rolin/ʒolin (7)
	ri:'mɛmbə (27), pp. 97,		lolin/rolin (17)
	172	*roller*	lo:l (14)
reply	pə'lai (17)	*rolling-pin*	ro:lin pin (18)
rest	lɛt/dɛt (7)	*roof*	wu:p (7)
	rɛt (14)		wu:p/ru:p (9)
	rɛt/rɛts (19)		ru:p/ru:f (11)
	rɛts (20)		ru:f (14), p. 84
return	tə:n (19)	*room*	wum (1)
	in'tə:n (29), p. 173		wum/rum (11)
rhinoceros	hai'nɔrətət (19)		rum (12)
	hai'nɔsərəs (21), p. 99		ju:m (23)
rhinoceroses	hai'nɔsərəsəz (27)		rum (24), pp. 20, 30, 45,
rhyme	raim (11)		84, 86, 187
Ribena	l̩ai'bi:nə/rai'bi:nə/	*rose* (N)	rəuz (25)
	ḍai'bi:nə (4)	*roses*	ro:did (15)
	'rai'bi:nə (13)	*(rosette*	ro'dɛt) (12)
	rai'bi:nə (24), p. 77	*rough*	wʌf (7)
rice	rait/rais (12)	*round*	ḍaun (1)
Richard	ritsəd (27)		raun/laund (4)
ride	laiḍ (7)		laun/laund (6)
	raid (24)		laund (7)
riding	raidin/laidin/ḍaidin (7)		raund (10), pp. 14, 77
rider	laidə (5)	*row* /rəu/	ro: (4)
	laidə/raidə (12)		rəu (23), p. 77
	raidər (13)	*rub*	wʌp (4)
right	lait/rait/jait (8)		rʌb/lʌb (14)
	rait/lait (15)	*rubbing*	wʌbin (4)
	rait (21), pp. 77, 135		rʌbin (11)
ring	ġiŋ (1)	*rubber*	ḅʌbə (1)
	liŋ/ġiŋ/ʁiŋ (6)		wʌbə (4)
	liŋ/ɣiŋ/ʁiŋ (7)		rʌbə (12), p. 20
	łiŋ (8)	*rubber-band*	ḅʌbə'bæn (1)
	riŋ/rin (10)		wʌbə'bæn/wʌbə'bænd (5

rubber-band	wʌbə'bænd (6)	*sandalwood*	æŋgəlwud (10)
	rʌbə'bæn/dʌbə'bæn (10)		ġæŋgəlwud (11)
	rʌbə'bænd (11), pp. 30,		sæŋgəlwud (24)
	86	*sandwich*	dæmdit (10)
rubbish	rʌbit/rʌbitˢ/rʌbiṣ (19)		tæmbit/tæmwit (17)
rug	ġʌk (2)		tæmdit (18)
	lʌġ (8)		tæmbid (19)
	rʌg (10), p. 43		tˢæmbit (20)
ruler	lu:lə (11)		sæmbiz (24)
run	dʌn (2)		sæmbiz/sæmwiz (26)
	rʌn/lʌn (6)	*sandwiches*	tæmwidid/sæmwidid (20)
	lʌn (8)		sæmbədziz (28)
	rʌn (18)	*sap*	wæp (4)
running	dʌnin (1)	*Saras* /sʌrəs/	dʌrət/dʌət (11), p. 70
	rʌnin (10), pp. 43, 45,	*sari*	ta:ri: (19)
	165		tˢa:ri:/sa:ri: (20)
Russell	rʌṣəl (20)	*sash*	dæt (8)
			ræt (13)
'*s*'	ɛtˢ (20)	(*satchel*	ɫætəl (15)
saddle	lægu/lægul (12)		sætˢəl) (23), pp. 14, 149
safe	deif (10)	*sauce*	dɔ:d (2)
	tʰeif (14)		dɔ:t (4)
safely	teifli: (19)		tʰɔ:t (14)
sailor	leilə (10)		tɔ:t/tˢɔ:tˢ/ṣɔ:tˢ (20)
	leilə/deilə (12)		ṣɔ:ṣ (21)
	tʰeilə (13)	*saucepan*	dɔ:pən (10)
St Paulin	sæm 'pɔ:lə (27)		tɔ:pən/tˢɔ:pən/ṣɔ:pən (20)
/sɛ̃'pɔ:lɛ̃/			sɔ:pən (21)
salad	dæləd (11)	*saucer*	tʰɔ:tə (15)
(*saliva*	ləv'laivə/lə'laivə (15)	*sausage*	dɔdid (5)
	ɫə'laivə/ɫə'ɫaivə) (16), p. 99		lɔdid/dɔdid (6)
salt	dɔ:t (8)		lɔdit (8)
	lɔlt/dɔlt (13)		dɔdid (11)
	tɔlt (16)		tʰɔtid (13)
	ṣɔ:lt (21)		tʰɔdid (14)
(*salver*	ɫævlə) (17)		tʰɔtid (16), pp. 80, 153
same	we:m (4)	*sausages*	tɔtədid (19)
	we:m/de:m/le:m (9)		ṣɔsidᶻid (20)
	deim (10)		sɔsəzəz (23)
	tʰeim (13)	*savages*	sæbə dziz (28)
	tˢeim (20), pp. 60, 84,	*save*	dei:v (10)
	145–6, 153	*say*	de: (6)
sandal	tæŋgəl (19)		tˢei (13)
	sæŋgəl (29)		tʰei (15)
sandals	sæŋgəlz (23)		tˢei (20)
sandalwood	ġæŋgəlwud/læŋgəlwud/		tˢei/sei (21)

say	sei (23), pp. 10, 60, 68, 92, 93, 118, 141–2, 154	*screw-driver*	'kru:draivə (15)
		scribble	skribəl (27)
says	tʰei (19)	*sea*	ti: (16)
	tˢei (20)	*seal*	ti:l (16)
	seiz (22)	*seals*	ti:l (16)
saying	teiin (18)	*sea-lion*	'ti:læ:n (19)
said	ḍeiḍ (11)	*sea-side*	'tˢi:said/'si:said (22)
	tʰeid (14)	*seat*	i:t (1)
	seid (22)		ḍi:t (12)
scales	ġeil (12)		tʰi:t (15)
	kʰeil (14)		si:t (27), p. 16
	keild (19)	*see*	ḍi: (2)
	keilz (22)		li: (5)
scarf	ġa:f (11)		ḍi: (11)
scent	ḍɛt (2)		tʰi:/tˢi: (13)
	sɛnt (24)		tʰi: (14)
school	ġu: (7)		ᵗsi:/si: (21)
	ku:l (12)		si: (22), pp. 80, 91, 118, 153
scissors	ḍidə (1)		
	lidə (6)	*saw*	ɔ:/ḍɔ: (9)
	ḍidə (8)		tʰɔ: (14)
	tidə/tʰidəʳ (13)		sɔ: (27)
	tʰidə (14)		sɔ:/sɔ:n (28)
	tʰidəd (19)	*seed*	ti:d (19)
	tˢidᶻədᶻ (20)	*seek*	ġi:k/ɣi:k/i:k (7)
	sizəz (22), pp. 3, 16, 17, 45, 69, 94		tʰi:k (16)
		see-saw	¹tʰi:tʰɔ: (15)
scramble	kæmbəl (16)	*seize*	ḍi:d (10)
scrambled	kæmbəld (14)		ti:d (15), p. 69
scrape	kreip (20), p. 61	*self*	wɛp (8)
scraped	kreipt (20)		lɛp/lɛf (10)
scratch	ġæt/gʳæt (9)		lɛf (13)
	kræt (16)		ɬɛf (16)
	kræs (22)		ɬɛf/slɛf (23), pp. 57, 98, 100
	skræs/skwæs (25), p. 94		
scream	ġi:m (1)	*selfish*	lɛfit (11), p. 98
	kli:m (13)	*sell*	tʰɛl (13)
	kri:m (18), p. 15	*Sellotape*	'ḍɛi:ḍe:p (4)
screaming	ġi:min (6)		'ḍɛli:ḍeip (12)
	kri:min (15)		'tɛli:teip (13), p. 75
screen	ġi:n (8)	*send*	tˢɛnd (21)
screw	ġu: (1)	*sensibly*	'tɛntəlbli: (18)
	ku: (9)	*separate*	preit/pə'reit (24)
	kru: (13)	*separating*	preitin (20)
	skru: (26), p. 39	*seven*	tʰɛvən (19)
screw-driver	'ġu:daibə/'ġu:daivə (2)	*several*	sɛvrəl (29)

sew	tu: (14)	*sharpener*	ḍa:pənə (10)
shack	γæk (4), pp. 66, 90, 108		tʰa:pənə (14)
'shhhh'	ssss (25)		tˢa:pənə (21)
shade	le:t (5), pp. 80, 153		sa:pənə (24)
shading	seidin (23)	*shave*	we:v (4)
shadow	ḍædo (2)		weiv/ḍeiv (10)
	lædo/ḍædo/jædo (5)		ḍeiv (11), p. 85
	ḍædo (11)	*shaver*	tʰeivə (15)
	sædəu (24), p. 80	*shaving*	we:vin (8), p. 84
shake	ġeik (12)	*shaving-cream*	seivin [kri:m] (22)
	tʰeik (19)	*sheath*	tʰi:t (18)
	tˢeik/treik (20)		si:tˢ (21)
	seik (23), p. 60		si:s (28)
shook	teikt (19)	*sheep*	wi:p (4)
shaker	seikə (29)		ḍi:p (11)
shall	tæl (20)		ti:p (13)
	ṣæl (21)		si:p (24)
	sæl (22), p. 93	*shelf*	wɛp (5)
should	tud (19)		lɛf (10)
	sud (27)		ɬɛf (16)
shallow	lælo (12)		ɬɛf/tlɛf (18)
shame	ḍeim (11)		slɛf/ṣɛlf (23)
shampoo	'wæpu: (7)		slɛf (24), pp. 57, 86, 98,
	'ḍæpu: (10)		100
	'ḍæ'pu: (11)	*shelves*	ɬɛft (19)
	'tˢæmpu: (20)	*shell*	lɛɬ (8)
	'sæmpu: (24), p. 85		ḍɛl (10)
shape	ḍeip (11)		tɛl (13)
	teip (13)	*shepherd*	wɛpəd (9), p. 84
shapes	seips (24)	*sherry*	ḍɛi: (7)
share	lɛə (6)		tɛri: (12)
	tɛə (16)		tˢɛri: (27)
	sɛ: (24)	*Sheryl*	sɛrəl (27)
sharp	a:p (1)	*shilling*	liliŋ/liŋiŋ (11)
	wa:p (3)		liliŋ/liŋiŋ/ġiŋiŋ (12)
	wa:p/ḍa:p (10)		liŋiŋ/giŋliŋ (13)
	ḍa:p (11)		liŋiŋ/tʰiŋiŋ (14)
	ḍa:p/ta:p (12)		tʰiŋiŋ (16)
	tʰa:p (13)	*shin*	tin (18)
	sa:p (24), pp. 16, 26, 65,		sin/tˢin (27), p. 94
	82, 84, 85	*shining*	ḍainin (11)
sharpen	wa:pən (9)	*shiny*	tʰaini: (14)
	ḍa:pən (12)		saini: (26)
	tʰa:pən (15)	*ship*	wip (4)
sharpening	tʰa:pənin (14)		ḍip (10)
sharpener	wa:pənə (9)		tip (14)

ship	sip (22), pp. 136–7, 183	*shower*	ḍauə (11)
shirt	ḍəːt (1)		tauə (14)
	təːt (12)	*Shredded*	trɛdiːwiːt (16)
	səːt (24), pp. 3, 5, 17, 45,	*Wheat*	
	136	*Shreddies*	ḍɛdiː (11)
shoe	ḍuː (1)		srɛdiz (23), pp. 61, 124,
	ḍuː/tuː (12)		130
	tuː (13)	*shriek*	triːk (15)
	tuː/truː (19)	*shrieking*	ʁiːkin/ǧiːkin (9)
	tˢuː/suː/ʃuː (21)	*shut*	ḍʌt (2)
	s̩uː (22)		lʌt/ḍʌt (6)
	suː (26)		lʌt (8)
	suː/sjuː (29), pp. 17, 136		ḍʌt (12)
shoes	tuːd (16)		tʌt (16)
	s̩uːz (22)		tˢʌt (20)
	suːz (23)		sʌt (22), pp. 60, 93, 94,
shoot	s̩uːt (21)		153, 196
shooter	suːtə (23)	*shy*	ḍai (2)
(= 'gun')		*sick*	tʰik (14)
shop	wɔp (4)		tˢik (20)
	ḍɔp (10)		tˢik/sik (23)
	ḍɔp/tɔp (12)		sik (24), p. 141
	tʰɔp (13)	*side*	ḍait (1)
	tʰɔp/trɔp (19)		ḍaiḍ (2)
	t,ɔp/trɔp (20)		lait/ḍaiḍ (7)
	s̩ɔp (21)		ḍaid (10)
	sɔp (22), p. 45		taid (18), pp. 4, 5, 153
shopping	wɔbin (1)		liv (10)
	tɔpin (16)	*(sieve*	div) (11)
	sɔpin (27), pp. 16, 20	*sign*	lain (8)
shorter	tʰɔːtə (16)		ḍain/ain (9)
shoulder	ḍuːdə (1)	*sill*	til (13)
	ḍuːldə (5)		ɬiv (22)
	tʰoːldə (14)	*silly*	ḍiliː/liliː (4)
	sɔuldə (21), pp. 17, 56,		ḍiliː (12)
	80, 111		tiliː (13)
shout	laut (6)		siliː (21), pp. 75, 80, 152
shouting	ḍaudin (2)	*silver*	wivə (6)
	ḍaudin/lautin (7)		livlə (11)
show	ḍoː (4)		(ɬilvə) (16)
	toː (12)		ɬivlə (17)
	tʰuː (14)		ɬivlə/tivlə/tilvə (18)
	təu (20)		silvlə/sivlə (23)
	səu (24)		silvə (26), pp. 57, 98
showing	təuin/tuːin (19)	*Silvester*	tilˈvɛtːə (17)
shower	wæwə/læwə (8)	*Simon*	taimən (17)

Simon	saimən (24), p. 146
simple	timpəl (17)
sing	ġiŋ (12)
	tiŋ (16)
	tˢiŋ/siŋ/tiŋ (20)
	ṣiŋ (21)
	siŋ (23), pp. 16, 93, 147, 195
sang	tˢiŋd (20)
singing	ġiŋiŋ (1)
	ġiŋiŋ/iŋiŋ/ɣiŋiŋ (7)
	ġiŋgiŋ/ġiŋgin (8)
	ġiŋgiŋ/ġiŋiŋ (10)
	tiŋiŋ (14)
	siŋiŋ/siŋin (26)
	siŋin (29), pp. 18, 20, 38, 43, 45, 97, 141, 165
sink	tʰiŋk (14)
	tˢiŋk/siŋk (20), p. 141
sip	wip (4)
	ḍip (10)
	tˢip (20), pp. 56, 145, 183
siren	tʰæ:rən (16)
	tˢæ:rən/sæ:rən (21)
sister	ḍitə (7)
	sistə (22)
sit	lit (7)
	lit/ḍit/it/wit (8)
	ḍit (9)
	tit (15)
	ṣit (21)
	sit (23), pp. 141–2
sitting	ḍiḍin (2)
	tʰitin (15)
	tʰitiŋ (16)
	tʰitin (20)
	sitin (22)
sat	læt/ḍæt (8)
	læt (9)
	ḍæt (11)
	tæt (13)
	tʰæt (14)
sitar	si'ta: (27), p. 173
sitting-room	ḍiḍiŋ rum (8)
	ḍitin rum (11)
	tʰitin rum (14)
sitting-room	ṣiṣin rum (21)
	sitin rum (22)
six	ġikt (9)
	tikt (15)
	tikt/tik (16)
	siks (24), p. 68
size	taid (14)
	saiz (26)
skin	ġin (1), pp. 15, 19, 38, 42, 160
skip	ġip (5)
skipping	kipin (13)
skipping-rope	skipin rəup (25), p. 62
sky	ġai (1)
	kʰai (14)
sledge	lɛd (9)
	lɛd (11)
	ɬɛd (19)
sleep	wi:p (2)
	li:p (11)
	ɬi:p (15)
	sli:p (25), pp. 58, 86, 147
sleeping	li:pin (11)
	ɬi:pin (16)
	sli:pin (26)
sleeping-bag	li:pin bæg (12)
sleepy	sli:pi: (23)
sleeve	wi:v/wi:β (4)
	ḍi:v/li:v (11)
	li:v (13)
	ɬi:v (15)
	ɬi:b (16)
	ɬi:v (17)
sleeves	ɬi:vd (18), p. 70
slicer	laitə (14)
	ɬaisə/slaisə (23), p. 62
slices	laiḍit (9), p. 68
slide	lait (6)
	laid (11)
	ɬaid (15)
	slaid (24), pp. 58, 147
slightly	laidi: (9)
	ɬaitli: (17), p. 173
slip	wip/lip (7)
	ḍip (11), pp. 83, 166
slipping	slipin (24)

slipper	ḅibə (1)	*smiling*	m̥æ:lin (23)
	lipə (10)	*Smith*	mit (1)
	lipə/dipə/dipələ (11)		mit/m̥it (15)
	lipə/libə/lipəʳ (12)		m̥it (16)
	ɬipə (15)		m̥its (21)
	ɬipə/slipə (23), pp. 30, 35,		m̥is (23)
	62, 85, 86, 97, 124,		smis (25), pp. 4, 15, 58,
	139]		62, 69, 160
slippers	ɬipə (17)	*smoke*	mu:k (12)
	ɬipəd (20)		m̥o:k (15)
	ɬipəz (21)		m̥əuk/məuk/s:m̥əuk (23)
	slipəz (24), p. 99		sməuk (25), pp. 59, 62
(*slough*	lʌf) (11)	*smooth*	mu:d (10)
slow-coach	ˈsləukəus (26)		m̥u:z (24)
slowly	ḍo:di:/ḍu:di: (5)	*smoothly*	m̥u:zli: (24)
	tlo:li:/tro:li: (16)	*Smyrna*	mə:nə (10)
	tlo:li: (19)	*snack*	n̥æk (23)
	ɬəuli:/sləuli: (23), p. 62	(*snaffle*	næɸəl) (12)
slug	lʌg (10)	*snail*	n̥eil (15)
	ɬʌg (15)		n̥eil/s:n̥eil (23)
	ɬʌg/slʌg (23), pp. 4, 58,		sneil (25), pp. 59, 62
	139	*snake*	ŋeˡk (1)
smack	m̥æk (16), p. 61		neik (14)
smacked	m̥ækt (20)		n̥eik (15), pp. 4, 20, 31,
smacking	mækin (12)		38, 41, 42, 45, 195
small	mɔ: (5)	*snap*	snæp (25), p. 62
	mɔ:l/m̥ɔ:l (17)	*snapdragon*	ˈn̥æp drægən (23)
	m̥ɔ:l (21)	*sneeze*	n̥i:d (15), pp. 4, 59
	smɔ:l (25)	*sneezed*	ni:d (11)
smaller	m̥ɔ:lə (16)		n̥i:zd (23)
smart	m̥a:t (19)	*sneezing*	ni:din (13)
Smartie	səˈma:ti: (25)		n̥i:zin (24)
smash	m̥æt (16)	*sniff*	nif (11)
smell	mɛn (1)	*sniffing*	snifin (28)
	mɛu (4)	*snow*	nu: (14)
	mɛu/mɛl (8)		n̥o: (15)
	mɛl (14)		n̥əu (21)
	m̥ɛl (16)	*snow-plough*	ˈn̥o:plau (16)
	smɛl (26), pp. 15, 33, 62,	*so*	təu (17)
	164		səu (21)
smells (V)	m̥ɛl (17)	*soap*	u:p (1)
	m̥ɛld (19)		ḍo:p (10)
	m̥ɛlz (22)		ḍo:p/ḍu:p/o:p (11)
smelling	m̥ɛlin (19)		ḍo:p/to:p (12)
smile	maiu (8)		tʰu:p (14)
smiling	mæ:in/maiuin (8)		təup (19)

soap	tˢəup (20), pp. 16, 39, 65, 66, 145	*something*	(tʌmpin) (17)
			fʌmpin/wʌmpin (18)
sober	lo:bə (10)		fʌmpin (19)
	lo:bə/blo:bə (12)		fʌmpin/sʌmpin (25)
sock	ġɔk (1)		sʌmpin (26), pp. 18, 53,
	ġɔk/łɔk (8)		130, 145–6
	ġɔk (10)	*sometimes*	'wʌmḑaim (11)
	kʰɔk/tʰɔk (13)		'fʌmtaimd (20)
	tʰɔk (14)		'sʌmtaimz (27), pp. 145–6
	tɔk/tˢɔk (20)	*somewhere*	'wʌmwɛ: (13)
	ṣɔk (22), pp. 3, 16, 21, 29, 65, 85, 141, 143, 153		'fʌmwɛ: (16)
			'sʌmweijə (27), pp. 145–6
socks	ġɔk (11)	*Sona*	ḑu:nə (3)
	tʰɔkt (17)		ḑu:nə/u:nə/lu:nə (5)
	tˢɔktˢ (20)		ḑo:nə/lo:nə (6)
sofa	ḑofər (12)		ḑo:nə (10)
soft	wɔpt (3)		tʰəunə (19)
	ḑɔp/ḑɔf/ḑɔft/ḑɔpt/wɔpt (10)		tˢəunə (20)
			səunə (22), pp. 80, 153
	ḑɔpt (11)	*song*	tɔŋ (16)
	tɔpt (13)		tˢɔŋ (20)
	tsɔft (21)	*soon*	ḑu:n (1)
	sɔft (24), pp. 66, 82, 88, 93, 147		tʰu:n (13), pp. 16, 152
		soot	tʰut (15)
softer	ṣɔftə (21), p. 93	*sorry*	lɔli: (4)
softly	sɔftli: (23)		ḑɔi: (10)
sole (of a shoe)	tu:l wɔ: tu: (12)		ḑɔri: (11)
			tɔri: (13)
solid	tʰɔlid (16)		sɔri: (22), pp. 75, 80
(solvent	tɔləmpt) (15), pp. 99, 100	*sort*	tʰɔ:t (13)
		soup	u:p (1)
some	wʌm (9)		ḑo:p (10)
	wʌm/ḑʌm (11)		ḑo:p/to:p (12)
	wʌm (12)		tʰu:p (13)
	wʌm/(tʌm) (14)		təup (19)
	wʌm (15)		su:p (23), pp. 16, 26, 39, 145
	wʌm/fʌm (16)		
	fʌm (17), pp. 84, 145–6	*sour*	tauə (13)
somebody	'wʌmbɔdi: (7)		sauə (22)
	'fʌmbɔdi: (22), pp. 145–6	*sow* /səu/	ḑo: (11)
someone	'sʌmwʌn (27)	*spade*	ḅeⁱd (5)
something	wʌpin (9)		pʰeid (14)
	wʌpin/wʌmpin (11)	*spanner*	ḅænə (1)
	wʌpin (12)		pʰænə (13), p. 61
	wʌmpin (14)	*spare*	pʰɛ: (18)
	wʌpin/fʌmpin (16)		spɛ: (28)

spare-wheel	'ḅɛːˈwiːɫ (14)	*squash*	kɔp (22)
special	pɛtəl (15)	*squat*	ġɔḅ (9)
	spɛsəl (27)		ġɔp/kɔp (12)
spice	pais (25)		kɔp (13), pp. 16, 164, 197
spider	ḅaidə (2)	*squats*	kʰɔpt (18)
	pʰaidəʳ (13)		kɔps (23)
	paidə (15)	*squatting*	ġɔpin (2)
	spaidə (27)		kʰɔpin (18), p. 70
spiders	paidəz (23)	*squawk*	kɔːp (22)
spikes	paikid/paikt (19)	*squeak*	kiːp (15)
spill	ḅiu (5)		kiːk (16), p. 64
	pil (22)	*squeaks*	kiːpt (19)
	pil/spil (25), pp. 56, 62	*squeaking*	kiːpin (23)
spin	pʰin (13), p. 58	*squeaker*	kiːpə (19)
spinach	piniz (23)	*squeaky*	kiːpiː (18)
	spinidz (29)		skwiːkiː (26)
spindle	spiŋgəl (27)	*squeegee*	kiːbiː (20)
spiral	pʰæːrəl (15)	*squeeze*	ġiːḅ (9)
spit	ḅit (4)		ġiːb (10)
	pit (16)		kiːb/kiːv (12)
	spit (27), p. 156		kʰiːb (16)
spitting	ḅidin (4)		kwiːz/skwiːz (25)
(*spittle*	pikəl) (14), p. 55		skwiːz (26), pp. 16, 65,
splash	ḅlæt (11)		136, 183
	plæt (15)	*squeezed*	kʰiːbd (14)
spoil	pɔil/spɔil (25)	*squeezing*	kiːbin (16)
sponge	pʌnd (11)	*squirrel*	ġibəl/ġivəl (12)
	pʌndᶻ (20)		(kʷirəl/kᵝirəl) (24)
	pʌndᶻ (21)	*stain*	ḍein (12)
	pʌndᶻ/pʌnz (22)	*stains*	seinz (24)
	pʌnz (23)	*stairs*	ḍɛə/tɛə (12)
	spʌndz (28)	*stalk*	ġɔːk (1)
spoon	ḅuːn (1)		tʰɔːk (16)
	ḅuːn/puːn (11)	*stamp*	ḍæp (1)
	pʰuːn (15), p. 15		tʰæmp (13)
sport	ḅɔːt (1)		sæmp (22)
spots	pɔᵗs (21)		sæmp/tˢæmp/tæmp (24),
	spɔts (25), p. 69		pp. 13, 20, 32, 45, 82, 94
spread	prɛd (19)	*stamps*	tæmt/tæmpt (17)
spreading	prɛdin (20)		tʰæmpt (18)
spreader	prɛdə (18)	*stand*	ḍænd (5)
spring	ḅiŋ (4)		tʰænd (16)
	ḅliŋ (12)		tˢænd (21)
square	kʰɛə (11)		tˢænd/sænd (22)
	skweijə (27), p. 130		sænd (23)
squash	kɔf (13)	*standing*	ḍændin/ḍænin (6)

standing	tˢændin (21)
star	ḍa: (2)
	tʰa:/tʰa:r (15)
	tsa:/s̜a: (21), p. 93
stars	ta:rd (19)
	sa:z (22)
	sta:z (27)
starling	sa:lin (23)
start	ta:t/tˢa:t (20)
	sa:t (23)
	sta:t (26), pp. 60, 136
station	tʰeitən (15)
	seisən (22)
	seitˢən (23)
	steisən (27), p. 94
stay	ḍe: (2)
	ḍei (11)
	tʰei (13)
	tˢei (21)
	sei (22)
	stei (26), p. 93
steady	tʰɛdi: (18)
	sɛdi: (24)
steadier	mɔ: sɛdi:ə (25)
steam	ti:m (14)
	si:m/sti:m (25)
steam-roller	tʰi:m lo:lə/ro:lə (15)
steering	ḍi:rin/ḍi:din (12)
steering-wheel	ḍi:in wi:u (8)
	tʰi:lin wi:ł (14)
	si:rin/siərin wi:l (22)
step	ḍɛp (7)
	sɛp (24)
steps	stɛps (26)
stepped	ḍɛpt (8)
stew	tru: (19)
	s:tu: (25)
	stu:/tsu: (26)
	st,u: (28), p. 73
stick (N)	ġik (4)
stick (V)	ġik (5)
	tʰik (14)
	sik/sʌk (22)
	sik/tˢik (23)
	stik (27), p. 141
sticking	tʰikin (18)

sticking	tˢikin/sikin (22)
stuck	ġʌk (1)
	sʌk/tˢikt (21)
	sikt (22)
	sʌk (23), pp. 20, 43
sticky	ġigi: (1)
	ġiki: (7)
	ġigi: (8)
	tʰiki: (14)
	tiki:/tˢiki: (20)
	stiki: (27), p. 60
stiff	ḍif (2)
	ḍip (8)
	tif (18)
	sif (24), pp. 89, 107
still	tʰil (13)
	tˢil (21)
	sil (22)
	stil (27)
sting	stin (28)
stung	ġʌn (8)
	stæn (28), p. 174
stir	tˢə: (21)
stirring	tə:rin (20)
	sə:rin (25)
(stirrup	ḍiəp) (12)
stitches	sisiz/sitˢiz (23)
stone	ḍu:n (4)
	səun (22)
stones	təund (19)
	səunz (23)
stop	bɔp/ḍɔp (1)
	ḍɔp (4)
	tʰɔp (13)
	tˢɔp/sɔp (20)
	sɔp (21)
	stɔp (26), pp. 20, 42, 166, 167
stopped	ḍɔpt (7)
	tʰɔpt (16)
	sɔpt (22)
story	ḍɔ:i: (10)
	tʰɔ:ri: (13)
	tˢɔ:ri: (21)
	stɔ:ri: (28)
stories	sɔ:riz/tɔ:riz (24)

stove	ḍuːv (10)	*study*	tʌdiː/tˢʌdiː (20)
	tˢəuv/səub (22)		ṣʌdiː (21)
	səuv (24)		sʌdiː (22)
	stəuv (29)		stʌdiː (26), p. 60
straight	treit (16)	*stuff*	ḍʌp (4)
	seit (22)	*submarine*	'tʌbməriːn (19)
strainer	treinə (15)		'ṣʌbməriːn (20)
strange	ḍreind (17)	*such*	ḍʌt (11)
strap	sræp/(træp) (24)		sʌs (26)
straw	trɔː/tɔː (15)	*suck*	tʰʌk (15)
	trɔː/srɔː (22)	*suede*	weid (10)
	srɔː (23)		feid (15)
strawberry	tɔːbriː (15)	*sugar*	ugə (3)
	tˢɔːbəri (21)		ġugə (11)
	sɔːbriː/srɔːbriː (22)		ugə/ġugəʳ (12)
	srɔbɪː (24)		kugə/tugə (13)
	strɔːbriː/strɔːbəri (26),		tʰugə (14)
	pp. 61, 63		tˢugə/sugə/ṣugə/tʳugə (20)
strike	ġaik (4)		tˢugə/sugə (21)
string	giŋ (11)		sugə (22)
	triŋ (17)		sugə/sjugə (29), pp. 16,
	trɪŋ/sriŋ (22)		26, 34, 65, 66, 141
	sriŋ/sːtiŋ (25)	*sugar-puffs*	'ugəpʌp (8)
strings	striŋz (27)		'tˢugəpʌft (20)
stroke	ġɔːk (1)	*suit*	tʰuːt (15)
	ġroːk (12)		suːt (24)
	ġroːk/ġruːk (13), p. 141		sjuːt (29), pp. 59, 63
	troːk (15)	*sultana*	tˢul'taːnə/sul'taːnə (21)
stroking	troːkin (15)	*summer*	tʌmə (11)
stroller	ḍoːlə/ḍoːldə (8)		tˢʌmə (20)
	səulə (21)		sʌmə (23), p. 146
	səulə/srəulə (22)	*sun*	ʌn/dʌn/lʌn (5)
	srəulə (23), p. 61		ḍʌn/lʌn (7)
strong	glɔŋ (11)		ḍʌn/lʌn/ʌn/rʌn (9)
	trɔŋ (13)		tʌn (13), pp. 3, 16, 34, 65,
	tʰɔŋ/trɔŋ (14)		80, 145
	trɔŋ (15)	*sunny*	tˢʌniː (20)
	ṣɔŋ (21)	*sun-room*	'rʌn rum (9)
	tˢrɔŋ/trɔŋ/srɔŋ (22)		'rʌn rum/ḍʌn rum (10)
	srɔŋ (23)		'ʌn rum/ʌn lum (11)
	trɔŋ/strɔŋ (26), pp. 61,		'rʌn rum (12)
	141		'rʌn rum/tʰʌn rum (14)
stronger	srɔŋə (24)		'tʰʌn rum (16)
(studs	tˢʌdz) (24)		'sʌn rum (22)
students	suːdənts/tˢuːdənts (24)	*sunshine*	'ḍʌn ḍain/ʌn ḍain (1)
study	tʌdiː (15)		'tʰʌn tʰain (14)

supposed	pʰoːd (13)
	ə'spəuzd (28), pp. 99, 100, 173
swallow	fɔləu (23)
swan	fɔm/fɔn (15)
sweat	vɛt (10)
sweep	wiːp (5)
	fiːp/swiːp (25)
sweeping	w̥iːpin (15), pp. 59, 62
sweet(ie)	wiːd̥iː (2)
	wiːt (6)
	v̥iːt/w̥iːt (15)
	w̥iːt/f̥iːt (16)
	f̥iːt (17)
	fiːt/swiːt (25), pp. 16, 59, 62, 107
sweeties	fiːtid (17)
	fiːtiz (21)
swim	fim (15)
swimming	wimin (14)
	fimin (16)
swimming-pool	swimin/sfimin puːl (25), p. 62
swing	wiŋ (1)
	wiŋg (4)
	wiŋ (5)
	wiŋg/wiŋ (11)
	fiŋ (23)
	swiŋ (25), pp. 15, 45, 147, 181
swinging	fiŋiŋ (24)
Swiss roll	wit roːl/(kip/lif roːl) (12)
switch	wit (1)
	fit/w̥it (15)
	f̥it (16)
	fit/fitˢ (20)
	fis (25)
	swis (26), pp. 59, 166
swollen	tʰəulən (18)
sword	tʰɔːd (17)
	tˢɔːd/sɔːd (21)
swords	tʰɔːdid (17)
symbol	wimbu (8)
	wimbəl (11), p. 146
symphony	tʰimpəni:/tʰipəni: (15)
	simpəni: (29)

syrup	d̥irəp (12)
	tirəp (19)
	sirəp (22)
tab	d̥æb̥ (10)
table	b̥eːbu (1)
	d̥eːbu (2)
	d̥eibəl (10)
	teibəl (13), pp. 15, 20, 38, 42, 82
tail	d̥eu (7)
	teil (12)
take	ġeːk (2)
	ġeik (10)
	kʰeik/tʰeik (13)
	kʰeik (14)
	teik (23), pp. 68, 85, 140–1, 144
taking	ġeⁱkin (1)
	ġeːgin (4), pp. 17, 43, 144, 165
took	teikt (26)
taken	kʰukən (18)
	tukən (23), pp. 144, 174
talk	ġɔːk (4)
	tʰɔːk (16)
talkative	tɔːkiː (28)
talking	ġɔːkin (6)
	tɔːkin (28)
tap	d̥æp (5)
tape-measure	tʰeip mɛd̥ə (15)
	teip mɛzə (27)
tassle	tʰætəl (14)
taste	d̥eːt (5)
	teist (26)
taxi	ġægi: (1)
	tʰækti: (15)
	tʰækti:/tʰæki: (18)
	tæki: kaːr (19), pp. 20, 21, 88, 166
tea	ti: (5)
	d̥i: (7)
	tʰi: (13)
tea-bag	'd̥i:ġʌb̥b̥æġ (4), p. 83
tea-cloth	'ti:klɔs (22)
tea-cup	'd̥i:kəp (4)

tea-cup	'tʰi:kʌp (16), p. 83	*thank-you*	ġæku:/ḍæku:
tea-leaves	'ḍi:wi:f/'ḍi:wi:p/ḍi:wi:ɸ (4)		ġæku: (11)
tea-pot	'ḍi:pɔt (7)		tʰæŋku: (14)
	'ti:pɔt (20)		ṣæŋku: (20)
teach	tʰi:t (14)		sæŋku: (22)
teacher	ti:sə (26)		sæŋks (24), pp. 13, 141,
tear/tɛə/	tɛ:r(it) (17)		153, 195
	tɛ: (27)	*that*	ḍæt (4)
tearing	tɛ:rin (17)		dæt (13)
tears	tɛ:z (21)		dæt/zæt (24)
teddy	ḍɛdi: (1)		dæt (25), pp. 79, 125
	tɛdi: (12), pp. 21, 38	*that's*	dæs (24)
teeth	ḍi:t (1)	*thatch*	tæt (12)
	tʰi:t (15)	*themselves*	dei:ˡ‡ɛf (18)
	ti:s/ti:tˢ/ti:θ (23)	*then*	dɛn (18)
	ti:s/ti:siz (26)		(vɛn) (29)
	ti:s (27), p. 3	*there*	ḍɛ (1)
telephone	'ḍɛwi:bu:/ḍɛwi:bu:n (1)		ḍɛ/dɛ (12)
	'ḍɛi:bo:n (2)		dɛ (14)
	'ḍɛi:ḅu:n (8)		dɛ:/zɛ: (22)
	'tʰɛli:bu:n (15)		dɛ: (23)
	'tɛli:fəun (23), pp. 9, 19,		deijə (27), pp. 3, 79, 130
	21, 35–6, 40, 75	*there's*	dɛ: (16)
television	'ḍɛi:widən (9)		dɛriz (26)
	'ḍɛli:widən (11)	*thermometer*	ˡmɔmitə (24)
	'tɛli:widən (12)		ri:ˡmɔmitə (29), pp. 130,
	'tɛli:wizən (27), p. 76		173
tell	ḍɛl/ḍɛu (9)	*these*	ḍi:d (9)
	ḍɛl (12)		di:d/di:t (13)
	tɛl (13)		di:d (14)

This word was used consistently with
the meaning of 'ask'. For A [a:sk]usually
meant 'ask for'.

			di:z (22), p. 68
ten	ḍɛn (12)	*they*	dei (18)
tennis	tɛnis (22)	*thick*	ġik (5)
tent	ḍɛt (1)		ʑik (8)
	ḍɛnt (11), pp. 13, 22		ġik (12)
testicle	tɛkətəl (19)		tʰik (17)
	tɛstəkəl (27), pp. 99, 101,		tˢik (20)
	151	*thickie*	sik (23)
than	dæn/dən/zən (24)	*thigh*	siki: (23)
(thane	sein) (29)		ḍai (11)
thank you	ġɛġu: (1)		tai (12)
	ġæku: (4)	*thimble*	wimbu (8)
	ġæku:/læku:/læŋku: (7)		ḍimbəl (11)
	ġæku: (8)	*thin*	win (8)
			ḍin (10)
			tin (12)

thin	sin (27), p. 94
thing	ġiŋ (9)
	giŋ/kiŋ (13)
	tʰiŋ (15)
	tˢiŋ (20)
	tˢiŋ/ṣiŋ (21)
	siŋ (22), pp. 60, 93, 141
things	tʰiŋd (19)
	tˢiŋẓ (21)
	siŋz (22)
	siŋz/tˢiŋz (23)
	siŋz (24)
think	ġik (5)
	ġik/ġiŋk (12)
	giŋk/kiŋk/tʰiŋk (13)
	tʰiŋk (14)
	ṣiŋk (21)
	siŋk (26), pp. 53, 94, 141
thinking	ġigin (5)
	ġiġin/ɣikin (7)
	tʰiŋkin (16)
	ṣiŋkin (21), p. 90
thought	ḍɔ:t (11)
	tɔ:t (20)
	sɔ:t (23), p. 92
thirsty	ḍə:ḍi: (2)
	tə:ti: (12)
this	ḍit (11)
	dit (13)
	dit/ditˢ (20)
	dis (21), p. 92
thistle	fisəl (27)
	fisəl/(sisəl) (29)
(thong	sɔŋ) (29)
thorn	fɔ:n/(sɔ:n) (29)
those	ḍo:ḍ (9)
	do:ḍ/du:ḍ (12)
	do:ḍ (13)
	dəud (19)
	dəudᶻ (20)
	dəuz/do:ẓ (21)
	dəuz (22), pp. 68, 92
thread	lɛd (11)
	rɛd (14)
	trɛd (15)
	ṣrɛd (22)
thread	srɛd (24), pp. 61, 124
three	li:/ḷi: (7)
	ḍi: (8)
	ti:/tri: (11)
	tri: (12)
	ti:/tri: (16)
	tri: (18)
	ṣri: (20)
	ṣi: (21)
	ṣri: (23)
	sri: (24), pp. 61, 74, 123
throat	trəut (19)
throttle	srɔkəl (29)
through	ḍu: (12)
	tru: (16)
	sru: (24), p. 74
throw	ḍu: (4)
	ḍo: (8)
	ḍu: (12)
	to: (14)
	trəu (19)
	səu/srəu (22)
	ṣrəu (23)
	srəu (25), p. 61
threw	ḍu: (7)
	tru: (17)
throwings	srəuinz (24)
thrush	srʌs (29), p. 130
thumb	wʌm (4)
	ḍʌm (10)
	ḍʌm/tʌm (11)
	tʰʌm (13)
	tˢʌm (20)
	sʌm (23), pp. 60, 83, 84, 92
thump	wʌp (6)
	ḍʌp (11)
	tʰʌmp (13)
	tˢʌmp (21)
	sʌmp (24)
thumping	tʰʌmpin (18)
	sʌmpin (23)
thumper	tʰʌmpə (19)
thunder	fʌndə/sʌndə (23)
thunderstorm	sʌndətˢɔ:m (22)
(tiara	ḍi:a:ə/ḍi:a:wə) (5)

ticket	tʰikit (17)	*tomato*	'maːdo/dəˈmaːdo (2)
tickets	tikis (22)		'maːdo (4)
tickle	ġigu (1)		'maːto (14)
	ġikəl (11)		'maːto/pəˈmaːto (17)
	kikəl (12)		'maːtəu (20)
	kʰikəl/tʰikəl (14)		təˈmaːtəu (28), pp. 28, 173
	tʰikəl (15), pp. 15, 141	*tomorrow*	tuːˈmɔrəu (21)
tickling	tikəlin (21)		təˈmɔwəu (23)
tiddly-pom	didəli: pɔm (11)	*tongue*	ġʌŋ (1)
tiddly-winks	tigəli: wiŋks (23)		tʌŋ (13), pp. 45, 141
tie	dai (1)	*too*	duː (11)
	dʌiː (4)	*toothbrush*	'tiːtbrʌt/tuːtbrʌt (12)
	dai (12)	*top*	dɔp (7)
	tai (19), pp. 110, 148		tʰɔp (14)
tiger	ġaigə (1)	*Topstreet*	dɔptiːt vei (10)
	ġaigə/kaigə (12)	*Way*	
	tʰaigə (15)	*torch*	dɔːt (8)
tigers	taigəd (19)		tʰɔːt (13)
tight	dait (6)		tɔːtˢ (27), p. 148
	tait (21)	*torn*	dɔːn (7)
tighter	tʰaitə (18)		tʰɔːn (14)
tightly	taitli: (28)	*tortoise*	tɔːsəs (22)
tika /tiːkə/	diːkə/ġiːkə (4)	*touch*	dʌt (2)
(= 'caste-	ġiːġə (8), p. 83		dʌt/tʌt (12)
mark')			tʰʌt (14)
tile	dail (11)		tʌs (27), p. 196
time	daim (5)	*touched*	tʌt (12)
	tʰaim (13)	*tough*	tʌf (13)
tiny	daini: (4)	*towel*	dau: (7)
	taini: (12)		tæwəl (22)
	tʰaini: (14)		tauəl (23)
tipper-lorry	'tʰipələri:/'tʰipələli: (14)	*tower*	dæwə (4)
tired	tʰæːd (13)		dauə (7)
tiring	tæːrin (24)		tʰæwə/tʰæwər (18)
toast	təutˢ (20)	*town*	daun (10)
	təust (22)	*toy*	dɔi (2)
today	tuːˈdei (20)		dɔi: (8)
	təˈdei (23)		tʰoi: (14)
toe	duː (11)	*toys*	tʰɔid (18)
	duː/tuː (12)		tɔiz (21)
	toː (13)	*trafficator*	'ġæwidiːleːtə/ġædiweːtə
	təu (17), pp. 154		(8), p. 99
toes	tʰəud (17)	*train*	deːn (4)
together	əˈgɛdə (9)		tʳein (14)
	tuːˈgɛzə (23)		trein (15)
	təˈgɛzə (27)	*tramp*	træmp/tlæmp (17)

tray	ḍei (11)		*tummy*	ḍʌmi: (6)
	trei (12), p. 74			tʰʌmi: (14)
tread	trɛd (16)		*tummy-button*	ḍʌmi: bʌdən (4)
tree	ḍi: (10)			tʰʌmi: bʌtən (14)
	ḍi:/ti: (11)		*tuna*	tju:nə fis (29)
	tri: (15), pp. 61, 160		*tune*	tʰu:n (14)
triangle	'tʰaiæŋgəl (14)			tˢu:n (24)
	'traiɔŋæŋgəl (17)			su:n/tu:n (26)
	'traiɔŋæŋgu (18)			tju:n (29), p. 63
tripped	ḍipt (11)		*tunes*	tʰu:nd (18), p. 70
troddler	lɔlə (1)		*tunnel*	tʌnəl (28)
	ġɔgə (2)		*turn*	də:n (1)
	ġɔgə/glɔglə (10)			tʰə:n (13)
	gɔglə/glɔglə (11)		*turtle*	tʰə:kəl (15)
	tʰɔglə (15)		*tusk*	ġʌk (2)
	trɔglə (16)		*twelve*	tɛlv (24)
	trɔglə/srɔglə/sɔglə (22),		*twenty*	ḍɛpti: (10)
	pp. 18, 41, 74, 85			tʰɛmti: (14)
trolly	lɔli: (1)			tɛmpi:/tɛmti: (23), pp.
	ḍɔli: (12), pp. 18, 36, 74			119, 192
trousers	ḍaudə (11)		*twice*	(ḍaif) (9)
	traudəd (19)			(ḍaip) (10)
	trauzə (22), p. 61			taip (22)
trowel	ḍau (1), p. 15			taif (24)
truck	ġʌk (1)			twais (25), pp. 16, 64, 65
	ġlʌk (10)			73, 164, 166
	trʌk (18), pp. 38, 43, 72,		*twig*	tʰig (17)
	74, 85			tib/tig (23)
Trugel	'tru:drɛl (29), pp. 91, 129		*(twill*	ḍil) (11), p. 64
trunk	ġʌk (9), p. 71		*(twinge*	ḍind) (11)
truth	tru:t (15)		*twirly*	tə:li: (23)
try	ḍai (2)		*twist*	(ḍit) (11)
	trai (15)			tʰip (13)
trying	ḍaiin (7)			tʰipt (14), p. 197
	train (20)		*twisted*	ḍiptid (10)
	traiin (28)		*(twit*	ḍip (9)
tube	ḍu:ḅ (12)			twit) (24)
	tju:b (29)		*two*	ḍu: (5)
tuck	ġʌk (8)			ḍu:/ḍu:/tu: (12)
	kʌk (12)			tʰu: (14), p. 69
	tʰʌk (14), p. 141		*typed* (p.p.)	taipənd (28), p. 174
Tuesday	tˢu:zdi:/su:zdi: (24)			
tulip	tʰu:lip (16), p. 73		'*u*'	ḍu: (5)
tulips	tu:lipt (19)			lu:/ru: (13)
tumble drier	ḍʌmbəl ḍæ: (12)		*umbrella*	ʌm'bɛjə (8)
	tʰʌmbəl dræ: (16)		*uncle*	ʌgu (1)

uncle	ʌgəl (11)	*vanilla*	wə'nilə (27), p. 173
	ʌŋkəl (23), pp. 13, 15	*veal*	viːl (17)
under	ʌndə (11)	*vein*	veːn (7)
underneath	ʌndə'niːt (6)	*ventilator*	'wɛntileitə/vɛntileitə (16)
	ʌndə'niːs (22)	*Veronica*	wə'rɔɲikə/wə'rɔɲikə (26),
understand	ʌndə'tænd (16)		p. 173
	ʌndə'sænd (24)	*very*	vɛi: (4)
undo	'ʌndu: (12)		vɛri:/vɛli: (14)
unhappy	'ʌn'hæpi: (24)		vɛri: (15)
unicorn	'ɖuːnikɔːn/juːnikɔːn (10)		vɛri:/wɛri: (19)
	'luːnikɔːn/nuːnikɔːn (12)		vɛri: (20)
	'ruːnikɔːn (13)		vɛri:/ʋɛri: (24)
	'ruːnikɔːn/luːnikɔːn (16)		vɛri: (26), pp. 75, 119,
	'ruːnikɔːn (19), p. 78		130, 151
unscrew	ʌn'kru: (20)	*vest*	wɛt (11)
up	ʌp (1)		vɛtˢ (20)
further up	ʌpə (21)		vɛst (24)
upstairs	ʌp'tɛə (13)		wɛst (27)
	ʌp'tsɛːz/ʌp'sɛːd (21)		wɛst/vɛst (29), p. 130
	ʌp'sɛəz (22)	*vet*	vɛt (15)
urinate	wiːwi: (1), p. 35		βɛt (18)
use (V)	ɖuːɖ (8)		wɛt (24)
	luːd/ɖuːd (12)		wɛt/(vɛt) (29)
	ruːd (17), pp. 78, 79	*(vexed*	wɛkt/vɛkt) (11), p. 87
using	luːdin/'duːdin (9)	*vice*	wais (27)
	duːdin/juːdin (12)	*vim*	wim (24)
	ruːdin (18), p. 78	*vinegar*	vinəgə/viɲəgə/wiɲəgə (17)
used	ɖuːd (7)	*violet*	vælit/læwit (15), pp. 99,
	ɖuːd (14), p. 95		100
used to	tuːt (14)	*violin*	wæː'lin/wai'lin (7)
	tʰuːtə (15)	*visitor*	wizitə/bizitə (26)
	tuːtu: (20)		wizitə (27)
	tsuːtə (23)	*voice*	wɔit/vɔit (16)
	suːstə (27)	*vulture*	wʌlʔtsə (28)
useful	juːsfəl (24)		
usually	luːli: (8)	*'w'*	'dʌbəlu: (14)
	ruːdəli: (18)	*wafer*	weifə (19)
	juːzəli: (24)	*wait*	weːt (4)
			weit/veit (19)
valve	wælβ (24)		weit/βeit (20)
van	væn/wæn (4)	*waiting*	weitin (20)
	βæn (7)	*wake-up*	weːk ʌp (8)
	wæn (12)		weik (14)
	væn/wæn (19)	*walk*	wɔːk (4), pp. 41, 95
	βæn (20)	*walking*	wɔːgin (7)
	wæn (26)		wɔːkin/wɔːkiŋ (12)

walking stick	wɔ:kin tʰik (16)
wall	wɔ: (4)
	wɔ:l (9)
walls	wɔ:ld (19), p. 69
wallet	wɔlit (8)
want	wɔt (2)
	wɔt/wɔnt (12)
	wɔnt (13)
wants	wɔnts (23)
wanted	wɔntid (18)
ward-robe	'wɔ:do: (8)
warm	wɔ:m (4)
warmer	wɔ:mə (8)
warmth	wɔ:mf (29)
was	wɔḏ (10)
	wɔḏ/wɔd (12)
	wɔd (14)
	wɔdᶻ (21), p. 69
wash	wɔt (1)
	wɔtˢ (20)
	wɔs (24), pp. 3, 45
washing	wɔtin (12)
wash up	wɔs ʌp (21)
washing-	'wɔtin mə'tin (11)
machine	'wɔsin mə'si:n (23)
wasp	wɔsp (23)
wasps	wɔsps/wɔsts (23)
	wɔsps (24)
waste-paper	'weit peipə (17)
watch	wɔt (1)
	wɔtˢ (20)
	wɔs (23)
	wɔtˢ (27)
water	wɔ:ḏə (2)
	wɔ:tə (10)
waving	we:vin (7)
wax	wæks (23)
way	we: (5)
	wei (13)
wear	wɛ: (6)
wears	wɛəz (23)
weasel	wi:dəl (14)
	wi:dᶻəl (21)
weather	wɛzə (26)
weeds	wi:dz (23)
week	wi:k (12)

weeny	wi:ni: (8)
Weetabix	'wi:təbiks̩ (21)
	'wi:təbiks (22)
well	wɛu (8)
	wɛl (16)
wet	wɛt (1)
	ʋɛt (24)
	wɛt (25), pp. 145, 196
what	wɔt (7)
	wɔʔ/wɔt (23)
	wɔt (24), p. 9
wheel	wi: (1)
	wi:/wi:u (6)
	wi:u (8)
	wi:l (12), pp. 15, 57
wheel-barrow	'wi:bæwu: (1)
	'wi:lbæə/wi:lbæwə (2)
	'wi:bæu (6)
	'wi:bæo/wi:ubæo (7)
	'wi:lbærəu (18), pp. 45, 57
when	wɛn (4)
	wɛn/vɛn (19)
	wɛn (20)
where	wɛ (4)
whether	wɛzə (V) (28)

As in: [aim wɛzərin pi:pəl wɛ: dɛ: bɛst
klɔuz ət həum] = 'I'm wondering
whether people wear their best clothes
at home.'

which	wit (11)
	witˢ (14)
	wit (17)
	witˢ (21)
	wis (23)
	wits (28)
while	wæu (8)
	wail/wæ:l (12)
	wæ:l (14)
whine	wain (10)
whining	wainin (15)
whisker	witkə (7)
	wiktə (14), pp. 99, 113, 114
whistle	wibu/wipu (1)
	witəl (13)

whistle	wisəl/ʋisəl (24), pp. 3, 14, 19, 46, 149, 197	*wolf* (*wolves*	wuf/wulf (27), p. 99 wuvl) (17)
whistling	witəlin (14)	*won't*	wont/ʔont (12)
white	wait (4)		wu:nt/nɔt wil (13)
	wait/vait (9)		wu:nt (14)
	wait (12)		wəunt (17)
	wait/ʋait (14)	*wood*	wud (12)
	wait (15)	*wooden*	wudən (4)
	ʋait (19)	*work* (V)	wə:k (4)
	wait (22)		wə:k/və:k (19)
who	hu: (16)		wə:k (22)
why	wai (11)	*works*	wə:kt (18)
wife	vaif (20)		wə:ks (21)
	waif (27)	*working*	wə:gin (1)
(*wig*	wiġ) (2)		wə:kin (5)
will	wil (12)		wə:gin (7)
wind (N)	wind (7)		wə:kin (11), pp. 17, 39, 45, 165
winding	waindin (12)		
window	winu: (1)	*workbench*	'wə:kbɛntˢ (20)
	windo: (8)	*workroom*	'wə:kwum (1)
	windu: (19)	*world*	ʋə:ld (18)
	windəu (21), pp. 3, 14, 38, 42, 45	*worm*	wə:m (15)
windows	windəud/windᶻəudᶻ (20)	*worms*	wə:md (18), p. 70
window-sill	windo: lil/windo: lif (13)	*worse*	wə:t (12)
	windo: ɫil/windo: ɫiv (16)	(*wrath*	ra:s) (29)
	windəu ɫiv (22)	*wren*	rɛn (7)
windscreen wiper	kri:n waipə (13)	*wriggling*	rigəlin (28)
		wrist	rit/ḍit (7)
winkle	wintəl (29)	*write*	ḍait (1)
wipe	waip (2)		dʷait (3)
wiped (p.p.)	waipənd (17)		ḍait/lait (4)
wire	wæ/wæᵊ (8)		lait (6)
with	wid (12)		lait/ḍait/rait (9)
	wiz (22)		rait (10)
	wiz/wid (23)		rait/lait (12)
	wiz (24), p. 59		rait (13), pp. 19, 21, 77
without	aut (12)	*writing*	raitin (13)
	wid'aut (16)		waitin (23)
	wid'aut/wiz'aut (23), p. 28		raitin (24)
wobbly	wɔbli:/wɔgli: (18)	*wrote*	rut (21)
	wɔbəli: (19)		ræt/raitid (26)
wobbling	wɔbəlin (21)		rut/ɾaitid (27)
wolf	wuf (17)		rit/ræt (28), p. 175
	wuf/wufl (18)	*written*	litən (8)
	wuf/vuf (22)		litən/ritən (10)
			ritən (13)

written	ræʔən (29)	*yesterday*	lɛɖədei (8)
wrong	wˠɔŋ (4)		ɖɛɖədei (9)
	lɔŋ (8)		rɛtədei (17)
	rɔŋ (15)		jɛstədei (22)
			rɛstədei (23), pp. 77, 79
yacht	(ɖɔt) (2)	*yet*	ɖɛt (7)
	(jɔt) (11)		jɛt/dɛt/ɖɛt/lɛt (14)
	rɔt (12), pp. 66, 76, 78, 196		jɛt/rɛt (15)
			rɛt (17)
yak	ġæk (2)		rɛt/jɛt (24)
	jæk (5), pp. 66, 195		rɛt (26), pp. 78, 79, 89
yam	ræm (14)	*yoghourt*	u:gə (2)
Yamuna	rɛmnə (23)		o:ġə (5)
/jemnə/			o:ġət (8)
yawn	ɖɔ:n (2), pp. 76, 196		lo:gət (11)
yawning	ɖɔ:nin (6)		lɔgət (12)
	jɔ:nin (13)		ɔgət (13)
year	riə (27)		jɔgət (15)
yell	rɛl (16)		o:kə/lo:kə/jɔkʰət (16)
yelling	lɛlin (27), p. 75		ro:gət/o:gət (17)
yellow	lɛlu: (1)		rɔgət (18)
	lɛlo (2)		rɔgət/jɔgət (26), pp. 66, 67, 78, 79, 88
	lɛlo/ʎɛlo (6)		
	lɛlo (7)	*(yogi*	ġo:gi:/ʔo:gi:) (2)
	lɛlo/jɛlo/d,ɛlo (13)	*yolk*	u:k (2)
	lɛlo (14)		ġo:k/jo:k (4)
	lɛlu: (17)		lo:k/jo:k/o:k (10)
	lɛləu/rɛləu (23)		lo:k/jo:k (11)
	jɛləu (29), pp. 19, 75, 137		lo:k/ro:k (12)
yes	ɖɛt (1)		ro:k/ɖo:k (14)
	ɖɛt/jɛt (8)		ro:k/lo:k (15)
	ɖɛt/ʤɛt (12)		ro:k (17)
	rɛt (14)		rəuk (20)
	jɛt (15)		rəuk/jəuk (29), pp. 66, 67, 78, 82, 109, 194
	jɛt/ɖɛt (16)		
	jɛt/rɛt (17)	*York*	rɔ:k (15)
	rɛt (19)	*you*	ɖu: (3)
	rɛt/rɛtˢ (20)		ru: (12)
	rɛtˢ/jɛtˢ/r,ɛs (21)		ru:/ju: (18)
	rɛs/jɛs (22)		ru:/ju:/ɽu: (24)
	rɛs (23)		ru:/ju: (25)
	rɛs/ɽɛs (24)		ru:/ju:/ɽu: (27)
	rɛs (26)		ju: (29), pp. 78, 79
	rɛs/ɽɛs/jɛs (27), pp. 3, 19, 21, 78, 79, 196	*your*	ɖɔ: (7)
yesterday	ɖɛɖədei/jɛɖədei (5)		rɔ: (18)
			rɔ:/jɔ: (27), p. 78

yours	ḍɔːd (11)	*zebra*	riːbrə/dᶻiːbrə (18)
	rɔːd (20)		riːbrə (19), pp. 17, 20, 45,
	rɔːdᶻ/rɔːz (21)		78, 79, 194
yourself	jɔːˈɬɛf (23)	(*zinc*	ġik) (4), pp. 9, 11
	jɔːˈslɛf (26)	*zip*	wip (5)
yourselves	jɔːˈslɛfs (26)		ḍip (10)
	jɔːˈsɛlfs (27)		ḍip/rip/zip (11)
young	ġʌŋ (2)		ḍip/ ⊕ip (12)
	ġʌŋ/jʌŋ/ɣʌŋ (4)		ḍip/rip/ ⊕ip (17)
	ġʌŋ/jʌŋ/ʎʌŋ/ŋʌŋ (7)		rip (18)
	lʌŋ/rʌŋ (12)		rip/zip (22)
	rʌŋ (13), pp. 66, 76, 78,		zip (27), pp. 78, 79
	82, 88, 90, 108, 194, 195	*Zoë*	zəui: (23)
younger	rʌŋgə (28)	*zoo*	ḍu: (4)
yo-yo	loro/roro/ʔoro (12), p. 78		dᶻu: (13)
(*yucca*	ġʌġə) (2), pp. 66, 195		ru:/ ⊕u: (17)
			ru: (18)
'z'	rɛd (19), p. 92		ru:/dru: (19)
zebra	wiːbə (1)		ʐu: (21)
	liːbrə/riːbrə/riːbə (12)		zu: (22), pp. 3, 21, 79, 92,
	diːbrə (13)		149
	tiːbəʳ (15)	*zoos*	ru:d (17), p. 79
	diːbrə/ ⊕iːbrə (17)	*zoom*	ru:m (17), p. 79

References

Albright, R. W. and J. B. Albright (1956). 'The phonology of a two-year-old child', *Word* **12**, 382–90.

Anderson, S. (1970). 'On Grassmann's Law in Sanskrit', *Linguistic Inquiry* **1**, 387–96.

Apronti, E. (1971). 'The language of a two-year-old Dangme', *Proceedings of the 8th West African Languages Congress, Abidjan (1969)*.

Bailey, C.-J. (1970). 'Towards specifying constraints on phonological metathesis', *Linguistic Inquiry* **1**, 347–9.

Bar-Adon, A. (1971). 'Primary syntactic structures in Hebrew child language.' In A. Bar-Adon and W. Leopold (eds.), *Child Language: A Book of Readings*, Prentice-Hall.

Bloch, B. (1941). 'Phonemic overlapping', *American Speech* **16**, 278–84. Reprinted in M. Joos (ed.), *Readings in Linguistics*, 1957, pp. 93–6.

Cairns, C. (1969). 'Markedness, neutralisation, and universal redundancy rules', *Language* **45**, 863–85.

Chao, Y.-R. (1951). 'The Cantian idiolect: an analysis of the Chinese spoken by a twenty-eight-months-old child', *University of California Publications in Semitic Philology* **11**, 27–44. Reprinted in A. Bar-Adon and W. Leopold (eds.), *Child Language: A Book of Readings*, Prentice-Hall, 1971.

Chomsky, N. (1964). 'The logical basis of linguistic theory', *Proceedings of the IXth International Congress of Linguists*, pp. 914–1008, Mouton.

(1965). *Aspects of the Theory of Syntax*, M.I.T. Press.

(1967). 'Some general properties of phonological rules', *Language* **43**, 102–28.

Chomsky, N. and M. Halle (1968). *The Sound Pattern of English*, Harper and Row.

Fry, D. B. (1966). 'The development of the phonological system in the normal and the deaf child'. In F. Smith and G. Miller (eds.), *The Genesis of Language*, M.I.T. Press.

Fudge, E. (1969). 'Syllables', *Journal of Linguistics* **5**, 253–86.

Grégoire, A. (1937, 1947). *L'apprentissage du langage*, 2 vols. Bibliothèque de la Faculté de Philosophie et Lettres de l'Université de Liège, Fasc. 73, 106.

Hall, R. (1944). *Hungarian Grammar*, Language Monograph 21.

Halle, M. (1971). 'Word boundaries as environments in rules', *Linguistic Inquiry* **2**, 540–1.

Jakobson, R. (1941). *Kindersprache, Aphasie und allgemeine Lautgesetze*, Uppsala.

(1949). 'Les lois phoniques du langage enfantin et leur place dans la phonologie générale.' Supplement to: N. Trubetskoi (translated by Cantineau), *Principes de Phonologie*, Paris.

Jakobson, R., Fant, G. and M. Halle (1951). *Preliminaries to Speech Analysis*, M.I.T. Press.

King, R. (1969). *Historical Linguistics and Generative Grammar*, Prentice-Hall.

Kiparsky, P. (1968). 'Linguistic universals and linguistic change'. In Bach, E. and R. Harms (eds.), *Universals in Linguistic Theory*, Holt.

Kisseberth, C. (1971). 'On the functional unity of phonological rules', *Linguistic Inquiry* 1, 291–306.

Unpublished. 'The Tunica stress conspiracy'.

Klima, E. and U. Bellugi (1966). 'Syntactic regularities in the speech of children'. In J. Lyons and R .Wales (eds.), *Psycholinguistics Papers*, Edinburgh University Press.

Kornfeld, J. (1971). 'What initial clusters tell us about a child's speech code', *Massachusetts Institute of Technology Research Laboratory of Electronics Quarterly Progress Report* 101, pp. 218–21.

Ladefoged, P. (1967). *Linguistic Phonetics*, Working Papers in Phonetics 6. U.C.L.A.

Leopold, W. (1939, 1947, 1949, 1949). *Speech Development of a Bilingual Child*, 4 vols., Northwestern University Humanities Series, vols 6, 11, 18 and 19.

Lewis, M. M. (1936). *Infant speech*, London.

Lightner, T. (1965). 'On the description of vowel and consonant harmony', *Word* 21, 244–50.

McCawley, J. Unpublished. 'On the role of notation in generative phonology'.

Menyuk, P. (1971). *The Acquisition and Development of Language*, Prentice-Hall.

Morton, J. (1968). 'Consideration of grammar and computation in language behaviour.' In J. Catford (ed.), *Studies in Language and Language Behaviour*, Progress Report VI, Ann Arbor.

(1969). 'Interaction of information in word recognition', *Psychological Review* 76, 165–78.

(1970). 'A functional model for memory.' In D. Norman (ed.), *Models for Human Memory*, Academic Press.

Morton, J. and N. Smith (1972). 'Some ideas concerning the acquisition of phonology', *Proceedings of the Colloque International du CNRS – Current Problems in Psycholinguistics*.

Moskowitz, A. (1970). 'The two-year-old stage in the acquisition of English phonology', *Language* 46, 426–41.

Olmsted, D. (1966). 'A theory of the child's learning of phonology', *Language* 42, 531–5.

Raffler Engel, W. von (1971). 'Theoretical phonology and first language acquisition', *Folia Linguistica* 4, 316–29.

Raven, J. (1938). *Raven's Progressive Matrices*, H. K. Lewis, London.

Sampson, G. (1970). 'On the need for a phonological base', *Language* 46, 586–626.

Sapir, E. (1933). 'The psychological reality of phonemes.' Reprinted in D. Mandelbaum (ed.), *Selected Writings of Edward Sapir*, pp. 46–60. U.C.L.A.

Smith, N. (1968). 'Tone in Ewe', *Massachusetts Institute of Technology Research Laboratory of Electronics Quarterly Progress Report* 88, pp. 290–304.

(1969). Review of: Schane, S. *French Phonology and Morphology* in *Language* 45, pp. 398–407.

(1970). 'The acquisition of phonology.' Mimeographed.

(1970–1). 'Bedik and binarity', *African Language Review* 9, pp. 90–8.

(1971). 'Puggles and lellow lollies', *Listener*, vol. 86, No. 2227, pp. 759–60.

Stampe, D. n.d. [1970/71]. 'The acquisition of phonetic representation.' Unpublished.

Stanford Binet Intelligence Scale, Form L-M Revision (1960). Terman and Merrill, Windsor.

Stanley, R. (1967). 'Redundancy rules in phonology', *Language* 43, 393–436.

Trim, J. (1961). 'English Standard Pronunciation', *English Language Teaching* 26.

Twaddell, W. (1935). *On Defining the Phoneme*, Language Monograph 16.

Velten, H. V. (1943). 'The growth of phonemic and lexical patterns in infant language', *Language* 19, 281–92.

Waterson, N. (1970). 'Some speech forms of an English child: a phonological study', *Transactions of the Philological Society*.

(1971a). 'Child phonology: a prosodic view', *Journal of Linguistics* 7, 179–211.

(1971b). 'Some views on speech perception', *Journal of the International Phonetic Association* 1, 81–96.

Watt, W. C. (1970). 'On two hypotheses concerning psycholinguistics.' In J. Hayes (ed.), *Cognition and the Development of Language*, Wiley, New York.

Weinreich, U. (1953). *Languages in Contact*, Mouton, The Hague.

Wells, J. C. (1971). 'A Scots diphthong and the feature "continuant"', *Journal of the International Phonetic Association* 1, 29–32.

Woolley, D. (1968). 'Some observations on stridency in English.' In C.-J. Bailey, B. J. Darden and A. Davison (eds.), *Papers from the Fourth Regional Meeting of the Chicago Linguistic Society*, pp. 141–5.

Index

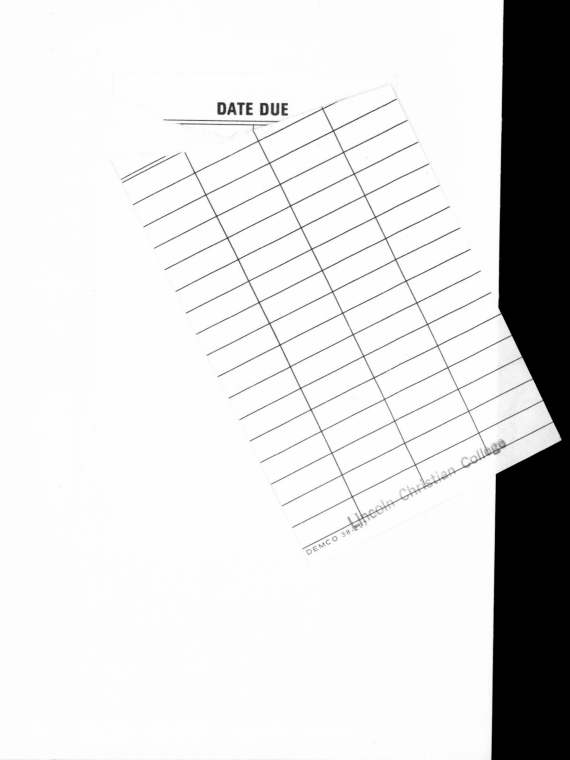

DATE DUE

Lincoln Christian College

DEMCO 38-297